# Learning XML

# Other XML resources from O'Reilly

**Related titles**

| | |
|---|---|
| XML in a Nutshell | Programming Web Services with XML-RPC |
| XML Pocket Reference | |
| XSLT | XPath and XPointer |
| XSLT Cookbook | XSL-FO |
| XML Schema | Perl and XML |
| Web Services Essentials | Python and XML |
| SVG Essentials | Java and XML |
| Programming Web Services with SOAP | Java and XML Data Binding |
| | Java and XSLT |

**XML Books Resource Center**

*xml.oreilly.com* is a complete catalog of O'Reilly's books on XML and related technologies, including sample chapters and code examples.

*XML.com* helps you discover XML and learn how this Internet technology can solve real-world problems in information management and electronic commerce.

**Conferences**

O'Reilly & Associates brings diverse innovators together to nurture the ideas that spark revolutionary industries. We specialize in documenting the latest tools and systems, translating the innovator's knowledge into useful skills for those in the trenches. Visit *conferences.oreilly.com* for our upcoming events.

Safari Bookshelf (*safari.oreilly.com*) is the premier online reference library for programmers and IT professionals. Conduct searches across more than 1,000 books. Subscribers can zero in on answers to time-critical questions in a matter of seconds. Read the books on your Bookshelf from cover to cover or simply flip to the page you need. Try it today with a free trial.

SECOND EDITION

# Learning XML

*Erik T. Ray*

**O'REILLY**®

Beijing · Cambridge · Farnham · Köln · Paris · Sebastopol · Taipei · Tokyo

**Learning XML, Second Edition**
by Erik T. Ray

Copyright © 2003, 2001 O'Reilly Media, Inc. All rights reserved.
Printed in the United States of America.

Published by O'Reilly Media, Inc., 1005 Gravenstein Highway North, Sebastopol, CA 95472.

O'Reilly Media, Inc. books may be purchased for educational, business, or sales promotional use. On-line editions are also available for most titles (*safari.oreilly.com*). For more information, contact our corporate/institutional sales department: (800) 998-9938 or *corporate@oreilly.com*.

| | |
|---|---|
| **Editor:** | Simon St.Laurent |
| **Production Editor:** | Philip Dangler |
| **Cover Designer:** | Ellie Volckhausen |
| **Interior Designer:** | David Futato |

**Printing History:**

| | |
|---|---|
| January 2001: | First Edition. |
| September 2003: | Second Edition. |

Nutshell Handbook, the Nutshell Handbook logo, and the O'Reilly logo are registered trademarks of O'Reilly Media, Inc. *Learning XML, Second Edition*, the image of a hatching chick, and related trade dress are trademarks of O'Reilly Media, Inc. Many of the designations used by manufacturers and sellers to distinguish their products are claimed as trademarks. Where those designations appear in this book, and O'Reilly Media, Inc. was aware of a trademark claim, the designations have been printed in caps or initial caps.

While every precaution has been taken in the preparation of this book, the publisher and author assume no responsibility for errors or omissions, or for damages resulting from the use of the information contained herein.

 This book uses RepKover™, a durable and flexible lay-flat binding.

ISBN-10: 0-596-00420-6
ISBN-13: 978-0-596-00420-0
[M]                                                                    [10/06]

# Table of Contents

# Foreword

In 1976, two landers named Viking set down on Mars and turned their dish-shaped antennae toward earth. A few hours later, delighted scientists and engineers received the first pictures from the surface of another planet. Over the next few years, the Viking mission continued to collect thousands of images, instrument readings, and engineering data—enough to keep researchers busy for decades and making it one of the most successful science projects in history.

Of critical importance were the results of experiments designed to detect signs of life in the Martian soil. At the time, most researchers considered the readings conclusive evidence against the prospect of living organisms on Mars. A few, however, held that the readings could be interpreted in a more positive light. In the late 1990's, when researchers claimed to have found tiny fossils in a piece of Martian rock from Antarctica, they felt it was time to revisit the Viking experiment and asked NASA to republish the results.

NASA staff retrieved the microfilm from storage and found it to be largely intact and readable. They then began scanning the data, intending to publish it on CD-ROM. This seemed like a simple task at first—all they had to do was sort out the desired experiment data from the other information sent back from the space probes. But therein lay the problem: how could they extract specific pieces from a huge stream of munged information? All of the telemetry from the landers came in a single stream and was stored the same way. The soil sampling readings were a tiny fraction of information among countless megabytes of diagnostics, engineering data, and other stuff. It was like finding the proverbial needle in a haystack.

To comb through all this data and extract the particular information of interest would have been immensely expensive and time-consuming. It would require detailed knowledge of the probe's data communication specifications which were buried in documents that were tucked away in storage or perhaps only lived in the heads of a few engineers, long since retired. Someone might have to write software to split the mess into parallel streams of data from different instruments. All the information was there. It was just nearly useless without a lot of work to decipher it.

Luckily, none of this ever had to happen. Someone with a good deal of practical sense got in touch with the principal investigator of the soil sampling experiment. He happened to have a yellowing copy of the computer printout with analysis and digested results, ready for researchers to use. NASA only had to scan this information in and republish it as it was, without the dreaded interpretation of aging microfilm.

This story demonstrates that data is only as good as the way it's packaged. Information is a valuable asset, but its value depends on its longevity, flexibility, and accessibility. Can you get to your data easily? Is it clearly labeled? Can you repackage it in any form you need? Can you provide it to others without a hassle? These are the questions that the Extensible Markup Language (XML) was designed to answer.

# Preface

Since its introduction in the late 90s, Extensible Markup Language (XML) has unleashed a torrent of new acronyms, standards, and rules that have left some in the Internet community wondering whether it is all really necessary. After all, HTML has been around for years and has fostered the creation of an entirely new economy and culture, so why change a good thing? XML isn't here to replace what's already on the Web, but to create a more solid and flexible foundation. It's an unprecedented effort by a consortium of organizations and companies to create an information framework for the 21st century that HTML only hinted at.

To understand the magnitude of this effort, we need to clear away some myths. First, in spite of its name, XML is not a markup language; rather, it's a toolkit for creating, shaping, and using markup languages. This fact also takes care of the second misconception, that XML will replace HTML. Actually, HTML is taking advantage of XML by becoming a cleaner version of itself, called XHTML. And that's just the beginning. XML will make it possible to create hundreds of new markup languages to cover every application and document type.

The standards process will figure prominently in the growth of this information revolution. XML itself is an attempt to rein in the uncontrolled development of competing technologies and proprietary languages that threatens to splinter the Web. XML creates a playground where structured information can play nicely with applications, maximizing accessibility without sacrificing richness of expression.

XML's enthusiastic acceptance by the Internet community has opened the door for many sister standards. XML's new playmates include stylesheets for display and transformation, strong methods for linking resources, tools for data manipulation and querying, error checking and structure enforcement tools, and a plethora of development environments. As a result of these new applications, XML is assured a long and fruitful career as the structured information toolkit of choice.

Of course, XML is still young, and many of its siblings aren't quite out of the playpen yet. Many XML specifications are mere speculation about how best to solve problems. Nevertheless, it's always good to get into the game as early as possible rather than be taken by surprise later. If you're at all involved in information management or web development, then you need to know about XML.

This book is intended to give you a birds-eye view of the XML landscape that is now taking shape. To get the most out of this book, you should have some familiarity with structured markup, such as HTML or TeX, and with World Wide Web concepts such as hypertext linking and data representation. You don't need to be a developer to understand XML concepts, however. We'll concentrate on the theory and practice of document authoring without going into much detail about writing applications or acquiring software tools. The intricacies of programming for XML are left to other books, while the rapid changes in the industry ensure that we could never hope to keep up with the latest XML software. Nevertheless, the information presented here will give you a decent starting point for jumping in any direction you want to go with XML.

# What's Inside

The book is organized into the following chapters:

Chapter 1, *Introduction*, is an overview of XML and some of its common uses. It's a springboard to the rest of the book, introducing the main concepts that will be explained in detail in following chapters.

Chapter 2, *Markup and Core Concepts*, describes the basic syntax of XML, laying the foundation for understanding XML applications and technologies.

Chapter 3, *Modeling Information*, delves into the concepts of data modeling, showing how to encode information with XML from simple software preferences to complex narrative documents.

Chapter 4, *Quality Control with Schemas*, shows how to use DTDs and various types of schemas to describe your document structures and validate documents against those descriptions.

Chapter 5, *Presentation Part I: CSS*, explores Cascading Style Sheets (CSS), a technology for presenting your XML documents in web browsers.

Chapter 6, *XPath and XPointer*, explains XPath, a vocabulary for addressing parts of XML documents that is useful both for transformations and programming, as well as its extensions into XPointer.

Chapter 7, *Transformation with XSLT*, applies XPath, demonstrating how to use Extensible Stylesheet Language Transformations (XSLT) to transform XML documents into other XML documents.

Chapter 8, *Presentation Part II: XSL-FO*, describes and demonstrates the use of Extensible Stylesheet Language Formatting Objects (XSL-FO) to create print representations of XML documents.

Chapter 9, *Internationalization*, examines internationalization issues with XML, including character encoding issues, language specification, and the use of MIME media type identifiers.

Chapter 10, *Programming*, describes various approaches to processing XML documents and creating programs around XML.

Appendix A, *Resources*, lists resources which may be useful in your further exploration of XML.

Appendix B, *A Taxonomy of Standards*, provides a list of the many standards at the heart of XML.

## Style Conventions

Items appearing in this book are sometimes given a special appearance to set them apart from the regular text. Here's how they look:

*Italic*
> Used for commands, email addresses, URIs, filenames, emphasized text, first references to terms, and citations of books and articles.

Constant width
> Used for literals, constant values, code listings, and XML markup.

*Constant width italic*
> Used for replaceable parameter and variable names.

**Constant width bold**
> Used to highlight the portion of a code listing being discussed.

## Examples

The examples from this book are freely downloadable from the book's web site at *http://www.oreilly.com/catalog/learnxml2*.

## Comments and Questions

We have tested and verified the information in this book to the best of our ability, but you may find that features have changed (or even that we have made mistakes!). Please let us know about any errors you find, as well as your suggestions for future editions, by writing to:

> O'Reilly & Associates, Inc.
> 1005 Gravenstein Highway North
> Sebastopol, CA 95472
> (800) 998-9938 (in the United States or Canada)
> (707) 829-0515 (international or local)
> (707) 829-0104 (fax)

We have a web page for this book, where we list errata, examples, or any additional information. You can access this page at:

*http://www.oreilly.com/catalog/learnxml2*

To comment or ask technical questions about this book, send email to:

*bookquestions@oreilly.com*

You can sign up for one or more of our mailing lists at:

*http://elists.oreilly.com*

For more information about our books, conferences, software, Resource Centers, and the O'Reilly Network, see our web site at:

*http://www.oreilly.com*

You may also write to the author directly at *etr@ravelgrane.com*.

## Acknowledgments

I wish to thank my reviewers, Jeni Tennison, Mike Fitzgerald, and Jeff Maggard, for their excellent advice and enthusiasm. Thanks to the open source community for making software development as fun as it is useful. And thanks to my friends and family for putting up with all this geeky stuff when I really should have been out working on my tan.

# CHAPTER 1
# Introduction

Anywhere there is information, you'll find XML, or at least hear it scratching at the door. XML has grown into a huge topic, inspiring many technologies and branching into new areas. So priority number one is to get a broad view, and ask the big questions, so that you can find your way through the dense jungle of standards and concepts.

A few questions come to mind. What is XML? We will attack this from different angles. It's more than the next generation of HTML. It's a general-purpose information storage system. It's a markup language toolkit. It's an open standard. It's a collection of standards. It's a lot of things, as you'll see.

Where did XML come from? It's good to have a historical perspective. You'll see how XML evolved out of earlier efforts like SGML, HTML, and the earliest presentational markup.

What can I do with XML? A practical question, again with several answers: you can store and retrieve data, ensure document integrity, format documents, and support many cultural localizations. And what can't I do with XML? You need to know about the limitations, as it may not be a good fit with your problem.

How do I get started? Without any hesitation, I hope. I'll describe the tools you need to get going with XML and test the examples in this book. From authoring, validating, checking well-formedness, transforming, formatting, and writing programs, you'll have a lot to play with.

So now let us dive into the big questions. By the end of this chapter, you should know enough to decide where to go from here. Future chapters will describe topics in more detail, such as core markup, quality control, style and presentation, programming interfaces, and internationalization.

# What Is XML?

XML is a lot like the ubiquitous plastic containers of Tupperware®. There is really no better way to keep your food fresh than with those colorful, airtight little boxes. They come in different sizes and shapes so you can choose the one that fits best. They lock tight so you know nothing is leaking out and germs can't get in. You can tell items apart based on the container's color, or even scribble on it with magic marker. They're stackable and can be nested in larger containers (in case you want to take them with you on a picnic). Now, if you think of information as a precious commodity like food, then you can see the need for a containment system like Tupperware®.

## An Information Container

XML contains, shapes, labels, structures, and protects information. It does this with symbols embedded in the text, called *markup*. Markup enhances the meaning of information in certain ways, identifying the parts and how they relate to each other. For example, when you read a newspaper, you can tell articles apart by their spacing and position on the page and the use of different fonts for titles and headings. Markup works in a similar way, except that instead of spaces and lines, it uses symbols.

Markup is important to electronic documents because they are processed by computer programs. If a document has no labels or boundaries, then a program will not know how to distinguish a piece of text from any other piece. Essentially, the program would have to work with the entire document as a unit, severely limiting the interesting things you can do with the content. A newspaper with no space between articles and only one text style would be a huge, uninteresting blob of text. You could probably figure out where one article ends and another starts, but it would be a lot of work. A computer program wouldn't be able to do even that, since it lacks all but the most rudimentary pattern-matching skills.

XML's markup divides a document into separate information containers called *elements*. Like Tupperware® containers, they seal up the data completely, label it, and provide a convenient package for computer processing. Like boxes, elements nest inside other elements. One big element may contain a whole bunch of elements, which in turn contain other elements, and so on down to the data. This creates an unambiguous hierarchical structure that preserves all kinds of ancillary information: sequence, ownership, position, description, association. An XML *document* consists of one outermost element that contains all the other elements, plus some optional administrative information at the top.

Example 1-1 is a typical XML document containing a short telegram. Take a moment to dissect it with your eyes and then we'll walk through it together.

*Example 1-1. An XML document*

```
<?xml version="1.0"?>
<!DOCTYPE telegram SYSTEM "/xml-resources/dtds/telegram.dtd">
<telegram pri="important">
  <to>Sarah Bellum</to>
  <from>Colonel Timeslip</from>
  <subject>Robot-sitting instructions</subject>
  <graphic fileref="figs/me.eps"/>
  <message>Thanks for watching my robot pal
    <name>Zonky</name> while I'm away.
    He needs to be recharged <emphasis>twice a
    day</emphasis> and if he starts to get cranky,
    give him a quart of oil. I'll be back soon,
    after I've tracked down that evil
    mastermind <villain>Dr. Indigo Riceway</villain>.
  </message>
</telegram>
```

Can you tell the difference between the markup and the data? The markup symbols are delineated by angle brackets (<>). <to> and </villain> are two such symbols, called *tags*. The data, or *content*, fills the space between these tags. As you get used to looking at XML, you'll use the tags as signposts to navigate visually through documents.

At the top of the document is the XML declaration, <?xml version="1.0"?>. This helps an XML-processing program identify the version of XML, and what kind of character encoding it has, helping the XML processor to get started on the document. It is optional, but a good thing to include in a document.

After that comes the document type declaration, containing a reference to a grammar-describing document, located on the system in the file */xml-resources/dtds/telegram.dtd*. This is known as a document type definition (DTD). <!DOCTYPE...> is one example of a type of markup called a *declaration*. Declarations are used to constrain grammar and declare pieces of text or resources to be included in the document. This line isn't required unless you want a parser to validate your document's structure against a set of rules you provide in the DTD.

Next, we see the <telegram> tag. This is the start of an element. We say that the element's name or type (not to be confused with a data type) is "telegram," or you could just call it a "telegram element." The end of the element is at the bottom and is represented by the tag </telegram> (note the slash at the beginning). This element contains all of the contents of the document. No wonder, then, that we call it the *document element*. (It is also sometimes called the *root element*.) Inside, you'll see more elements with start tags and end tags following a similar pattern.

There is one exception here, the empty tag <graphic.../>, which represents an empty element. Rather than containing data, this element references some other information that should be used in its place, in this case a graphic to be displayed. Empty elements do not mark boundaries around text and other elements the way container elements do, but they still may convey positional information. For example, you might place the graphic inside a mixed-content element, such as the message element in the example, to place the graphic at that position in the text.

Every element that contains data has to have both a start tag and an end tag or the empty form used for graphic. (It's okay to use a start tag immediately followed by an end tag for an empty element; the empty tag is effectively an abbreviation of that.) The names in start and end tags have to match exactly, even down to the case of the letters. XML is very picky about details like this. This pickiness ensures that the structure is unambiguous and the data is airtight. If start tags or end tags were optional, the computer (or even a human reader) wouldn't know where one element ended and another began, causing problems with parsing.

From this example, you can see a pattern: some tags function as bookends, marking the beginning and ending of regions, while others mark a place in the text. Even the simple document here contains quite a lot of information:

*Boundaries*
> A piece of text starts in one place and ends in another. The tags <telegram> and </telegram> define the start and end of a collection of text and markup.

*Roles*
> What is a region of text doing in the document? Here, the tags <name> and </name> give an obvious purpose to the content of the element: a name, as opposed to any other kind of inline text such as a date or emphasis.

*Positions*
> Elements preserve the order of their contents, which is especially important in prose documents like this.

*Containment*
> The nesting of elements is taken into account by XML-processing software, which may treat content differently depending on where it appears. For example, a title might have a different font size depending on whether it's the title of a newspaper or an article.

*Relationships*
> A piece of text can be linked to a resource somewhere else. For instance, the tag <graphic.../> creates a relationship (link) between the XML fragment and a file named *me.eps*. The intent is to import the graphic data from the file and display it in this fragment.

An important XML term to understand is *document*. When you hear that word, you probably think of a sequence of words partitioned into paragraphs, sections, and chapters, comprising a human-readable record such as a book, article, or essay. But in XML, a document is even more general: it's the basic unit of XML information, composed of elements and other markup in an orderly package. It can contain text such as a story or article, but it doesn't have to. Instead, it might consist of a database of numbers, or some abstract structure representing a molecule or equation. In fact, one of the most promising applications of XML is as a format for application-to-application data exchange. Keep in mind that an XML document can have a much wider definition than what you might think of as a traditional document. The following are short examples of documents.

The Mathematics Markup Language (MathML) encodes equations. A well-known equation among physicists is Newton's Law of Gravitation: $F = GMm / r^2$. The document in Example 1-2 represents that equation.

*Example 1-2. A MathML document*

```
<?xml version="1.0"?>
<math xmlns="http://www.w3.org/1998/Math/MathML">
  <mi>F</mi>
  <mo>=</mo>
  <mi>G</mi>
  <mo>&InvisibleTimes;</mo>
  <mfrac>
    <mrow>
      <mi>M</mi>
      <mo>&InvisibleTimes;</mo>
      <mi>m</mi>
    </mrow>
    <apply>
      <power/>
      <ci>r</ci>
      <cn>2</cn>
    </apply>
  </mfrac>
</math>
```

While one application might use this input to display the equation, another might use it to solve the equation with a series of values. That's a sign of XML's power.

You can also store graphics in XML documents. The Scalable Vector Graphics (SVG) language is used to draw resizable line art. The document in Example 1-3 defines a picture with three shapes (a rectangle, a circle, and a polygon).

*Example 1-3. An SVG document*

```
<?xml version="1.0" standalone="no"?>
<!DOCTYPE svg
    PUBLIC "-//W3C//DTD SVG 20001102//EN"
    "http://www.w3.org/TR/2000/CR-SVG-20001102/DTD/svg-20001102.dtd">
<svg>
  <desc>Three shapes</desc>
  <rect fill="green" x="1cm" y="1cm" width="3cm" height="3cm"/>
  <circle fill="red" cx="3cm" cy="2cm" r="4cm"/>
  <polygon fill="blue" points="110,160 50,300 180,290"/>
</svg>
```

It's also worth noting that a document is not necessarily the same as a file. A *file* is a package of data treated as a contiguous unit by the computer's operating system. This is called a *physical* structure. An XML document can exist in one file or in many files, some of which may be on another system. It may not be in a file at all, but generated in a stream from a program. XML uses special markup to integrate the contents of different files to create a single entity, which we describe as a *logical* structure. By keeping a document independent of the restrictions of a file, XML facilitates a linked web of document parts which can reside anywhere.

That's XML markup in a nutshell. The whole of the next chapter is devoted to this topic. There, we'll go into deeper detail about the picky rules and describe some new components you haven't seen yet. You'll then be able to tear apart any XML document and know what all the pieces are for, and put together documents of your own.

## A Markup Language Toolkit

Strictly speaking, XML is not a markup language. A language has a fixed vocabulary and grammar, but XML doesn't actually define any elements. Instead, it lays down a foundation of syntactic constraints on which you can build your own language. So a more apt description might be to call XML a markup language toolkit. When you need a markup language, you can build one quickly using XML's rules, and you'll be comfortable knowing that it will automatically be compatible with all the generic XML tools out there.

The telegram in Example 1-1 is marked up in a language I invented for fun. I chose a bunch of element names that I thought were important to represent a typical telegram, and a couple that were gratuitously silly, like villain. This is okay, because the language is for my use and I can do whatever I want with it. Perhaps I have something in mind for the villain element, like printing it in a different color to stand out. The point is that XML gives me the ability to tailor a markup language any way I want, which is a very powerful feature.

### Well-formedness

Because XML doesn't have a predetermined vocabulary, it's possible to invent a markup language as you go along. Perhaps in a future telegram I want to identify a new kind of thing with an element I've never used before. Say I wrote to a friend inviting her to a party, and I enclosed the date in an element called, appropriately, date. Free-form XML, as I like to call it, is perfectly legal as long as it's well-formed. In other words, as long as you spell tags correctly, use both start tags and end tags, and obey all the other minimal rules, it's good XML.

Documents that follow the syntax rules of XML are *well-formed* XML documents. This piece of text would fail the test on three counts:

```
<equation<a < b<equation>
```

Can you find all the problems? First, the start tag is spelled incorrectly, because it has two left brackets instead of a left and a right. Second, there is a left bracket in the content of the element, which is illegal. Third, the end tag of the element is missing a slash. This is not well-formed XML. Any program that parses it should stop at the first error and refuse to have anything more to do with it.

Well-formedness is XML's "purity test." What does this get us? Compatibility. It allows you to write a program or a library of routines that know nothing about the incoming data except that it will be well-formed XML. An XML editor could be used to edit any XML document, a browser to view any document, and so on. Programs are more robust and less complex when the data is more consistent.

## Validity

Some programs are not so general-purpose, however. They may perform complex operations on highly specific data. In this case, you may need to concretize your markup language so that a user doesn't slip in an unexpected element type and confuse the program. What you need is a formal *document model*. A document model is the blueprint for an *instance* of a markup language. It gives you an even stricter test than well-formedness, so you can say that Document X is not just well-formed XML, but it's also an instance of the Mathematics Markup Language, for example.

When a document instance matches a document model, we say that it is *valid*. You may hear it phrased as, "this is valid XHTML" or "valid SVG." The markup languages (e.g., XHTML and SVG) are *applications* of XML. Today, there are hundreds of XML applications for encoding everything from plays to chemical formulae. If you're in the market for a markup language, chances are you'll find one that meets your needs. If not, you can always make your own. That's the power of XML.

There are several ways to define a markup language formally. The two most common are document type definitions (DTDs) and schemas. Each has its strong points and weak points.

## Document type definitions (DTDs)

DTDs are built into the XML 1.0 specification. They are usually separate documents that your document can refer to, although parts of DTDs can also reside inside your document. A DTD is a collection of rules, or *declarations*, describing elements and other markup objects. An element declaration adds a new element type to the vocabulary and defines its *content model*, what the element can contain and in which order. Any element type not declared in the DTD is illegal. Any element containing something not declared in the DTD is also illegal. The DTD doesn't restrict what kind of data can go inside elements, which is the primary flaw of this kind of document model.

### Schemas

Schemas are a later invention, offering more flexibility and a way to specify patterns for data, which is absent from DTDs. For example, in a schema you could declare an element called date and then require that it contains a legal date in the format YYYY-MM-DD. With DTDs the best you could do is say whether the element can contain characters or elements. Unfortunately, there is a lot of controversy around schemas because different groups have put forth competing proposals. Perhaps there will always be different types of schemas, which is fine with me.

# An Open Standard

As Andrew Tanenbaum, a famous networking researcher, once said, "The wonderful thing about standards is that there are so many of them." We've all felt a little bewildered by all the new standards that support the information infrastructure. But the truth is, standards work, and without them the world would be a much more confusing place. From Eli Whitney's interchangeable gun parts to standard railroad gauges, the industrial revolution couldn't have happened without them.

The best kind of standard is one that is open. An open standard is not owned by any single company or individual. It is designed and maintained based on input from the community to fit real needs, not to satisfy a marketing agenda. Therefore, it isn't subject to change without notice, nor is it tied to the fortune of a company that could disappear in the next market downturn. There are no licensing fees, nondisclosure agreements, partnerships, or intellectual property disputes. It's free, public, and completely transparent.

The Internet was largely built upon open standards. IP, TCP, ASCII, email, HTML, Telnet, FTP—they are all open, even if they were funded by private and government organizations. Developers like open standards because they can have a say in how they are designed. They are free to use what works for them, rather than be tied to a proprietary package. And history shows that they work remarkably well.

XML is an open standard. It was designed by a group of companies, organizations, and individuals called the World Wide Web Consortium (W3C). The current recommendation was published in 1998, with a second edition published in 2000, although a new version (1.1, which modifies the list of allowable characters) is currently in the draft stage. The specification is free to the public, on the web at *http://www.w3.org/TR/REC-xml*. As a recommendation, it isn't strictly binding. There is no certification process, but developers are motivated to comply as closely as possible to attract customers and community approval.

In one sense, a loosely binding recommendation is useful, in that standards enforcement takes time and resources that no one in the consortium wants to spend. It also allows developers to create their own extensions, or to make partially working implementations that do a pretty good job. The downside, however, is that there's no guarantee anyone will do a really good job. For example, the Cascading Style Sheets standard has languished for years because browser manufacturers couldn't be bothered to fully implement it. Nevertheless, the standards process is generally a democratic and public-focused process, which is a Good Thing.

## A Constellation of Standards

Many people agree that spending money is generally more fun than saving it. Sure, you can get a little thrill looking at your bank statement and seeing the dividend from the 3% interest on your savings account, but it isn't as exciting as buying a new plasma screen television. So it is with XML. It contains information like a safe holds money, but the real fun comes from using that information. Whether you're publishing an XHTML document to the Web or generating an image from SVG, the results are much more gratifying than staring at markup.

XML's extended family provides many ways to squeeze usefulness out of XML documents. They are extensions and applications of XML that build bridges to other formats or make it easier to work with data. All the names and acronyms may be a little overwhelming at first, but it's worth getting to know this growing family.

Let's look at these categories in more detail.

*Core syntax*
> These are the minimal standards required to understand XML. They include the core recommendation and its extension, Namespaces in XML. The latter piece allows you to classify markup in different groups. One use of this is to combine markup from different XML applications in the same document. The core syntax of XML will be covered thoroughly in Chapter 2.

*Human documents*
> This category has markup languages for documents you'll actually read, as opposed to raw data. XHTML, the XML-friendly upgrade to the Hypertext Markup Language, is used to encode web pages. DocBook is for technical manuals which are heavy in technical terms and complex structures like tables, lists, and sidebars. The Wireless Markup Language (WML) is somewhat like XHTML but specializes in packaging documents for tiny screens on cellular phones. We will discuss this narrative style of document in Chapter 3.

*Modeling*
> In this group are all the technologies developed to create models of documents that formalize a markup language and can be used to test document instances against standard grammars. These include DTDs (part of the core XML 1.0 recommendation), the W3C's XML Schema, RELAX NG, and Schematron, all of which will be covered in Chapter 4.

# The W3C and the Standards Process

The W3C has taken on the role of the unofficial smithy of the Web. Founded in 1994 by a number of organizations and companies around the world with a vested interest in the Web, their long-term goal is to research and foster accessible and superior web technology with responsible application. They help to banish the chaos of competing, half-baked technologies by issuing technical documents and recommendations to software vendors and end users alike.

Every recommendation that goes up on the W3C's web site must endure a long, tortuous process of proposals and revisions before it's finally ratified by the organization's Advisory Committee. A recommendation begins as a project, or *activity*, when somebody sends the W3C Director a formal proposal called a *briefing package*. If approved, the activity gets its own working group with a charter to start development work. The group quickly nails down details such as filling leadership positions, creating the meeting schedule, and setting up necessary mailing lists and web pages.

At regular intervals, the group issues reports of its progress, posted to a publicly accessible web page. Such a *working draft* does not necessarily represent a finished work or consensus among the members, but is rather a progress report on the project. People in the community are welcome to review it and make comments. Developers start to implement parts of the proposed technology to test it out, finding problems in the process. Software vendors press for more features. All this feedback is important to ensure work is going in the right direction and nothing important has been left out particularly when the *last call working draft* is out.

The draft then becomes a *candidate recommendation*. At this stage, the working group members are satisfied that the ideas are essentially sound and no major changes will be needed. Experts will continue to weigh in with their insights, mostly addressing details and small mistakes. The deadline for comments finally arrives and the working group goes back to work, making revisions and changes.

Satisfied that the group has something valuable to contribute to the world, the Director takes the candidate recommendation and blesses it into a *proposed recommendation*. It must then survive the scrutiny of the Advisory Committee and perhaps be revised a little more before it finally graduates into a recommendation.

The whole process can take years to complete, and until the final recommendation is released, you shouldn't accept anything as gospel. Everything can change overnight as the next draft is posted, and many a developer has been burned by implementing the sketchy details in a working draft, only to find that the actual recommendation is a completely different beast. If you're an end user, you should also be careful. You may believe that the feature you need is coming, only to find it was cut from the feature list at the last minute.

It's a good idea to visit the W3C's web site (*http://www.w3.org*) every now and then. You'll find news and information about evolving standards, links to tutorials, and pointers to software tools. It's listed, along with some other favorite resources, in Appendix B.

*Locating and linking*

Data is only as useful as it is easy to access it. That's why there is a slew of protocols available for getting to data deep inside documents. XPath provides a language for specifying the path to a piece of data. XPointer and XLink use these paths to create a link from one document to another. XInclude imports files into a document. The XML Query Language (XQuery), still in drafts, creates an XML interface for non-XML data sources, essentially turning databases into XML documents. We will explore XPath and XPointer in Chapter 6.

*Presentation*

XML isn't very pretty to look at directly. If you want to make it presentable, you need to use a stylesheet. The two most popular are Cascading Style Sheets (CSS) and the Extensible Style Language (XSL). The former is very simple and fine for most online documents. The latter is highly detailed and better for print-quality documents. CSS is the topic of Chapter 5. We will take two chapters to talk about XSL: Chapter 7 and Chapter 8.

*Media*

Not all data is meant to be read. The Scalable Vector Graphics language (SVG) creates images and animations. The Synchronized Multimedia Integration Language (SMIL) scripts graphic, sound, and text events in a timeline-based multimedia presentation. VoiceML describes how to turn text into speech and script interactions with humans.

*Science*

Scientific applications have been early adopters of XML. The Chemical Markup Language (CML) represents molecules in XML, while MathML builds equations. Software turns instances of these markup languages into the nicely rendered visual representations that scientists are accustomed to viewing.

*Resource description*

With so many documents now online, we need ways to sort through them all to find just the information we need. Resource description is a way of summarizing and showing relationships between documents. The Resource Description Framework (RDF) is a language for describing resources.

*Communication*

XML is an excellent way for different systems to communicate with each other. Interhost system calls are being standardized through applications like XML-RPC, SOAP, WSDL, and UDDI. XML Signatures ensures security in identification by encoding unique, verifiable signatures for documents of any kind. SyncML is a way to transfer data from a personal computer to a smaller device like a cellular phone, giving you a fast and dependable way to update address lists and calendars.

*Transformation*

Converting between one format and another is a necessary fact of life. If you've ever had to import a document from one software application into another, you know that it can sometimes be a messy task. Extensible Style Language Transformations (XSLT) can automate the task for you. It turns one form of XML into another in a process called *transformation*. It is essentially a programming language, but optimized for traversing and building XML trees. Transformation is the topic of Chapter 7.

*Development*

When all else fails, you can always fall back on programming. Most programming languages have support for parsing and navigating XML. They frequently make use of two standard interfaces. The Simple API for XML (SAX) is very popular for its simplicity and efficiency. The Document Object Model (DOM) outlines an interface for moving around an object tree of a document for more complex processing. Programming with XML will be the last topic visited in this book, in Chapter 10.

This list demonstrates that XML has worked well as a basis for information exchange and application in a variety of fields.

# Where Did XML Come From?

XML is the result of a long evolution of data packaging reaching back to the days of punched cards. It is useful to trace this path to see what mistakes and discoveries influenced the design decisions.

## History

Early electronic formats were more concerned with describing how things should look (presentation) than with document structure and meaning. troff and T<sub>E</sub>X, two early formatting languages, did a fantastic job of formatting printed documents, but lacked any sense of structure. Consequently, documents were limited to being viewed on screen or printed as hard copies. You couldn't easily write programs to search for and siphon out information, cross-reference information electronically, or repurpose documents for different applications.

*Generic coding*, which uses descriptive tags rather than formatting codes, eventually solved this problem. The first organization to seriously explore this idea was the Graphic Communications Association (GCA). In the late 1960s, the GenCode project developed ways to encode different document types with generic tags and to assemble documents from multiple pieces.

The next major advance was Generalized Markup Language (GML), a project by IBM. GML's designers, Charles Goldfarb, Edward Mosher, and Raymond Lorie,[*] intended it as a solution to the problem of encoding documents for use with multiple information subsystems. Documents coded in this markup language could be edited, formatted, and searched by different programs because of its content-based tags. IBM, a huge publisher of technical manuals, has made extensive use of GML, proving the viability of generic coding.

Inspired by the success of GML, the American National Standards Institute (ANSI) Committee on Information Processing assembled a team, with Goldfarb as project leader, to develop a standard text-description language based upon GML. The GCA GenCode committee contributed their expertise as well. Throughout the late 1970s and early 1980s, the team published working drafts and eventually created a candidate for an industry standard (GCA 101-1983) called the Standard Generalized Markup Language (SGML). This was quickly adopted by both the U.S. Department of Defense and the U.S. Internal Revenue Service.

In the years that followed, SGML really began to take off. The International SGML Users' Group started meeting in the United Kingdom in 1985. Together with the GCA, they spread the gospel of SGML around Europe and North America. Extending SGML into broader realms, the Electronic Manuscript Project of the Association of American Publishers (AAP) fostered the use of SGML to encode general-purpose documents such as books and journals. The U.S. Department of Defense developed applications for SGML in its Computer-Aided Acquisition and Logistic Support (CALS) group, including a popular table formatting document type called CALS Tables. And then, capping off this successful start, the International Standards Organization (ISO) ratified a standard for SGML (ISO 8879:1986).

SGML was designed to be a flexible and all-encompassing coding scheme. Like XML, it is basically a toolkit for developing specialized markup languages. But SGML is much bigger than XML, with a more flexible syntax and lots of esoteric parameters. It's so flexible that software built to process it is complex and generally expensive, and its usefulness is limited to large organizations that can afford both the software and the cost of maintaining SGML environments.

The public revolution in generic coding came about in the early 1990s, when Hypertext Markup Language (HTML) was developed by Tim Berners-Lee and Anders Berglund, employees of the European particle physics lab CERN. CERN had been involved in the SGML effort since the early 1980s, when Berglund developed a publishing system to test SGML. Berners-Lee and Berglund created an SGML document type for hypertext documents that was compact and efficient. It was easy to write

---

[*] Cute fact: the acronym GML also happens to be the initials of the three inventors.

software for this markup language, and even easier to encode documents. HTML escaped from the lab and went on to take over the world.

However, HTML was in some ways a step backward. To achieve the simplicity necessary to be truly useful, some principles of generic coding had to be sacrificed. For example, one document type was used for all purposes, forcing people to overload tags rather than define specific-purpose tags. Second, many of the tags are purely presentational. The simplistic structure made it hard to tell where one section began and another ended. Many HTML-encoded documents today are so reliant on pure formatting that they can't be easily repurposed. Nevertheless, HTML was a brilliant step for the Web and a giant leap for markup languages, because it got the world interested in electronic documentation and linking.

To return to the ideals of generic coding, some people tried to adapt SGML for the Web—or rather, to adapt the Web to SGML. This proved too difficult. SGML was too big to squeeze into a little web browser. A smaller language that still retained the generality of SGML was required, and thus was born the Extensible Markup Language (XML).

## The Goals of XML

Dissatisfied with the existing formats, a group of companies and organizations began work in the mid-1990s at the World Wide Web Consortium (W3C) on a markup language that combined the flexibility of SGML with the simplicity of HTML. Their philosophy in creating XML is embodied by several important tenets:

*Form should follow function*
> In other words, markup languages need to fit their data snugly. Rather than invent a single, generic language to cover all document types (badly), let there be many languages, each specific to its data. Users can choose element names and decide how they should be arranged in a document. The result will better labeling of data, richer formatting possibilities, and enhanced searching capability.

*A document should be unambiguous*
> A document should be marked up in such a way that there is only one way to interpret the names, order, and hierarchy of the elements. Consider this example from old-style HTML:

```
<html>
  <body>
    <p>Here is a paragraph.
    <p>And here is another.
  </body>
</html>
```

> Before XML, this was acceptable markup. Every browser knows that the beginning of a <p> signals the end of an open p element preceding it as well as the

beginning of a new p element. This prior knowledge about a markup language is something we don't have in XML, where the number of possible elements is infinite. Therefore, it's an ambiguous situation. Look at this example; does the first element contain the other, or are they adjacent?

```
<flooby>an element
<flooby>another element
```

You can't possibly know, and neither can an XML parser. It could guess, but it might guess incorrectly. That's why XML rules about syntax are so strict. It reduces errors by making it more obvious when a document has mis-coded markup. It also reduces the complexity of software, since programs won't have to make an educated guess or try to fix syntax mistakes to recover. It may make it harder to write XML, since the user has to pay attention to details, but this is a small price to pay for robust performance.

*Separate markup from presentation*

For your document to have maximum flexibility for output format, you should strive to keep the style information out of the document and stored externally. Documents that rely on stylistic markup are difficult to repurpose or convert into new forms. For example, imagine a document that contains foreign phrases that are marked up to be italic, and emphatic phrases marked up the same way, like this:

```
<example>Goethe once said, <i>Lieben ist wie
Sauerkraut</i>. I <i>really</i> agree with that
statement.</example>
```

Now, if you wanted to make all emphatic phrases bold but leave foreign phrases italic, you'd have to manually change all the <i> tags that represent emphatic text. A better idea is to tag things based on their meaning, like this:

```
<example>Goethe once said, <foreignphrase>Lieben
ist wie Sauerkraut</foreignphrase>. I <emphasis>really</emphasis>
agree with that statement.</example>
```

Instead of being incorporated in the tag, the style information is defined in another place, a document called a *stylesheet*. Stylesheets map appearance settings to elements, acting as look-up tables for a formatting program. They make things much easier for you. You can tinker with the presentation in one place rather than doing a global search and replace operation in the XML. If you don't like one stylesheet, you can swap it for another. And you can use the same stylesheet for multiple documents.

Keeping style out of the document enhances your presentation possibilities, since you are not tied to a single style vocabulary. Because you can apply any number of stylesheets to your document, you can create different versions on the fly. The same document can be viewed on a desktop computer, printed, viewed on a handheld device, or even read aloud by a speech synthesizer, and you never have to touch the original document source—simply apply a different stylesheet. (It is of course possible to create presentation vocabularies in XML—XSL-FO is an excellent example. In XSL-FO's case, however, its creators expect developers to create XSL-FO through XSLT stylesheets, not directly.)

*Keep it simple*

For XML to gain widespread acceptance, it had to be simple. People don't want to learn a complicated system just to author a document. XML 1.0 is intuitive, easy to read, and elegant. It allows you to devise your own markup language that conforms to some logical rules. It's a narrow subset of SGML, throwing out a lot of stuff that most people don't need.

Simplicity also benefits application development. If it's easy to write programs that process XML files, there will be more and cheaper programs available to the public. XML's rules are strict, but they make the burden of parsing and processing files more predictable and therefore much easier.

*It should enforce maximum error checking*

Some markup languages are so lenient about syntax that errors go undiscovered. When errors build up in a file, it no longer behaves the way you want it to: its appearance in a browser is unpredictable, information may be lost, and programs may act strangely and possibly crash when trying to open the file.

The XML specification says that a file is not well-formed unless it meets a set of minimum syntax requirements. Your XML parser is a faithful guard dog, keeping out errors that will affect your document. It checks the spelling of element names, makes sure the boundaries are airtight, tells you when an object is out of place, and reports broken links. You may carp about the strictness, and perhaps struggle to bring your document up to standard, but it will be worth it when you're done. The document's durability and usefulness will be assured.

*It should be culture-agnostic*

There's no good reason to confine markup in a narrow cultural space such as the Latin alphabet and English language. And yet, earlier markup languages do just that. Irked by this limitation, XML's designers selected Unicode as the character set, opening it up to thousands of letters, ideographs, and symbols.

# What Can I Do with XML?

Let me tackle that question by sorting the kinds of problems for which you would use XML.

## Store and Retrieve Data

Just about every software application needs to store some data. There are look-up tables, work files, preference settings, and so on. XML makes it very easy to do this. Say, for example, you've created a calendar program and you need a way to store holidays. You could hardcode them, of course, but that's kind of a hassle since you'd have to recompile the program if you need to add to the list. So you decide to save this data in a separate file using XML. Example 1-4 shows how it might look.

*Example 1-4. Calendar data file*

```
<caldata>
  <holiday type="international">
    <name>New Year's Day</name>
    <date><month>January</month><day>1</day></date>
  </holiday>
  <holiday type="personal">
    <name>Erik's birthday</name>
    <date><month>April</month><day>23</day></date>
  </holiday>
  <holiday type="national">
    <name>Independence Day</name>
    <date><month>July</month><day>4</day></date>
  </holiday>
  <holiday type="religious">
    <name>Christmas</name>
    <date><month>December</month><day>25</day></date>
  </holiday>
</caldata>
```

Now all your program needs to do is read in the XML file and convert the markup into some convenient data structure using an *XML parser*. This software component reads and digests XML into a more usable form. There are lots of libraries that will do this, as well as standalone programs. Outputting XML is just as easy as reading it. Again, there are modules and libraries people have written that you can incorporate in any program.

XML is a very good choice for storing data in many cases. It's easy to parse and write, and it's open for users to edit themselves. Parsers have mechanisms to verify syntax and completeness, so you can protect your program from corrupted data. XML works best for small data files or for data that is not meant to be searched randomly. A novel is a good example of a document that is not randomly accessed (unless you are one of those people who peek at the ending of a novel before finishing), whereas a telephone directory *is* randomly accessed and therefore may not be the best choice to put in a single, enormous XML document.

If you want to store huge amounts of data and need to retrieve it quickly, you probably don't want to use XML. It's a sequential storage medium, meaning that any search would have to go through most of the document. A database program like Oracle or MySQL would scale much better, caching frequently used data and using a hash table to zero in on records with lightning speed.

## Format Documents

I mentioned before that a large class of XML documents are narrative, meaning they are for human consumption. But we don't expect people to actually read text with XML markup. Rather, the XML must be processed to put the data in a presentable form. XML has a number of strategies and tools for turning the unappealing mishmash of marked-up plain text into eye-pleasing views suitable for web pages, magazines, or whatever you like.

Most XML markup languages focus on the task of how to organize information semantically. That is, they describe the data for what it is, not in terms of how it should look. Example 1-2 encodes a mathematical equation, but it does not look like something you'd write on a blackboard or see in a textbook. How you get from the raw data to the finished product is called *formatting*.

### CSS

There are a number of different strategies for formatting. The simplest is to apply a Cascading Style Sheet (CSS) to it. This is a separate document (not itself XML) that contains mappings from element names to presentation details (font style, color, margins, and so on). A formatting XML processor such as a web browser, reads the XML data file and the stylesheet, then produces a formatted page by applying the stylesheet's instructions to each element. Example 1-5 shows a typical example of a CSS stylesheet.

*Example 1-5. A CSS stylesheet*

```
telegram {
  display: block;
  background-color: tan;
  color: black;
  font-family: monospace;
  padding: 1em;
}
message {
  display: block;
  margin: .5em;
  padding: .5em;
  border: thin solid brown;
  background-color: wheat;
  whitespace: normal;
}
to:before {
  display: block;
  color: black;
  content: "To: ";
}
from:before {
  display: block;
  color: black;
```

*Example 1-5. A CSS stylesheet (continued)*

```
  content: "From: ";
}
subject:before {
  color: black;
  content: "Subject: ";
}
to, from, subject {
  display: block;
  color: blue;
  font-size: large;
}
emphasis {
  font-style: italic;
}
name {
  font-weight: bold;
}
villain {
  color: red;
  font-weight: bold;
}
```

To apply this stylesheet, you need to add a special instruction to the source document. It looks like this:

```
<?xml-stylesheet type="text/css" href="ex2_memo.css"?>
```

This is a *processing instruction*, not an element. It will be ignored by any XML processing software that doesn't handle CSS stylesheets.

To see the result, you can open the document in a web browser that accepts XML and can format with CSS. Figure 1-1 shows a screenshot of how it looks in Safari version 1.0 for Mac OS X.

CSS is limited to cases where the output text will be in the same order as the input data. It would not be so useful if you wanted to show only an excerpt of the data, or if you wanted it to appear in a different order from the data. For example, suppose you collected a lot of phone numbers in an XML file and then wanted to generate a telephone directory from that. With CSS, there is no way to sort the listings in alphabetical order, so you'd have to do the sorting in the XML file first.

### Transformation to presentational formats

A more powerful technique is to transform the XML. *Transformation* is a process that breaks apart an XML document and builds a new one. The new document may or may not use the same markup language (in fact, XML is only one option; you can transform XML into any kind of text). With transformation, you can sort elements, throw out parts you don't want, and even generate new data such as headers and footers for pages. Transformation in XML is typically done with the language XSLT,

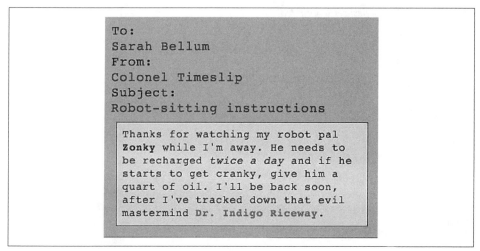

*Figure 1-1. Screenshot of a CSS-formatted document*

essentially a programming language optimized for transforming XML. It requires a transformation instruction which happens to be called a stylesheet (not to be confused with a CSS stylesheet). The process looks like the diagram in Figure 1-2.

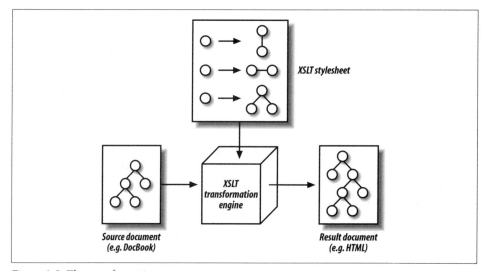

*Figure 1-2. The transformation process*

A popular use of transformations is to change a non-presentation XML data file into a format that combines data with presentational information. Typically, this format will throw away semantic information in favor of device-specific and highly presentational descriptions. For example, elements that distinguish between filenames and emphasized text would be replaced with tags that turn on italic formatting. Once you lose the semantic information, it is much harder to transform the document back to the original data-specific format. That is okay, because what we get from presentational formats is the ability to render a pleasing view on screen or printed page.

There are many presentational formats. Public domain varieties include the venerable troff, which dates back to the first Unix system, and T$_E$X, which is still popular in universities. Adobe's PostScript and PDF and Microsoft's Rich Text Format (RTF) are also good candidates for presentational formats. There are even some XML formats that can be included in this domain. XHTML is rather generic and presentational for narrative documents. SVG, a graphics description language, is another format you could transform to from a more semantic language.

Example 1-6 shows an XSLT stylesheet that changes any `telegram` document into HTML. Notice that XSLT is itself an XML application, using namespaces (an XML syntax for grouping elements by adding a name prefix) to distinguish between XSLT commands and the markup to be output. For every element type in the source document's markup language, there is a corresponding rule in the stylesheet describing how to handle it. I don't expect you to understand this code right now. There is a whole chapter on XSLT (Chapter 7) after which it will make more sense to you.

*Example 1-6. An XSLT script for telegram documents*

```
<xsl:transform
  xmlns:xsl="http://www.w3.org/1999/XSL/Transform"
  version="1.0">

<xsl:template match="telegram">
  <html>
    <head><title>telegram</title></head>
    <body>
      <div style="background-color: wheat; padding=1em; ">
        <h1>telegram</h1>
        <xsl:apply-templates/>
      </div>
    </body>
  </html>
</xsl:template>

<xsl:template match="from">
  <h2><xsl:text>from: </xsl:text><xsl:apply-templates/></h2>
</xsl:template>

<xsl:template match="to">
  <h2><xsl:text>to: </xsl:text><xsl:apply-templates/></h2>
</xsl:template>

<xsl:template match="subject">
  <h2><xsl:text>subj: </xsl:text><xsl:apply-templates/></h2>
</xsl:template>

<xsl:template match="message">
```

*Example 1-6. An XSLT script for telegram documents (continued)*

```
    <blockquote>
      <font style="font-family: monospace">
        <xsl:apply-templates/>
      </font>
    </blockquote>
</xsl:template>

<xsl:template match="emphasis">
  <i><xsl:apply-templates/></i>
</xsl:template>

<xsl:template match="name">
  <font color="blue"><xsl:apply-templates/></font>
</xsl:template>

<xsl:template match="villain">
  <font color="red"><xsl:apply-templates/></font>
</xsl:template>

<xsl:template match="graphic">
  <img width="100">
    <xsl:attribute name="src">
      <xsl:value-of select="@fileref"/>
    </xsl:attribute>
  </img>
</xsl:template>

</xsl:transform>
```

When applied against the document in Example 1-1, this script produces the following HTML. Figure 1-3 shows how it looks in a browser.

```
    <html>
    <head>
    <meta content="text/html; charset=UTF-8" http-equiv="Content-Type">
    <title>telegram</title>
    </head>
    <body><div style="background-color: wheat; padding=1em; ">
    <h1>telegram</h1>
      <h2>to: Sarah Bellum</h2>
      <h2>from: Colonel Timeslip</h2>
      <h2>subj: Robot-sitting instructions</h2>
      <blockquote><font style="font-family: monospace">Thanks for watching
    my robot pal
        <font color="blue">Zonky</font> while I'm away.
        He needs to be recharged <i>twice a
        day</i> and if he starts to get cranky,
        give him a quart of oil. I'll be back soon,
        after I've tracked down that evil
        mastermind <font color="red">Dr. Indigo Riceway</font>.
      </font></blockquote>
    </div></body>
    </html>
```

# telegram

**to: Sarah Bellum**

**from: Colonel Timeslip**

**subj: Robot-sitting instructions**

```
Thanks for watching my robot pal Zonky
while I'm away. He needs to be recharged
twice a day and if he starts to get
cranky, give him a quart of oil. I'll be
back soon, after I've tracked down that
evil mastermind Dr. Indigo Riceway.
```

*Figure 1-3. Transformation result*

### Transformation and formatting objects

Transforming XML into HTML is fine for online viewing. It is not so good for print media, however. HTML was never designed to handle the complex formatting of printed documents, with headers and footers, multiple columns, and page breaks. For that, you would want to transform into a richer format such as PDF. A direct transformation into PDF is not so easy to do, however. It requires extensive knowledge of the PDF specification which is huge and difficult, and much of the content is compressed.

A better solution is to transform your XML into an intermediate format, one that is generic and easy for humans to understand. This is XSL-FO, the style language for formatting objects. A *formatting object* is an abstract representation for a portion of a formatted page. You use XSLT to map elements to formatting objects, and an XSL formatter turns the formatting objects into pages, paragraphs, graphics, and other presentational components. The process is illustrated in Figure 1-4.

The source document on the left is first transformed, using an XSLT stylesheet and XSLT processor, into a formatting object tree using XSLT. This intermediate file is then fed into the XSL formatter which processes it into a presentational format, such as PDF. The beauty of this system is that it is modular. You can use any compliant XSLT processor and XSL formatter. You don't need to know anything about the

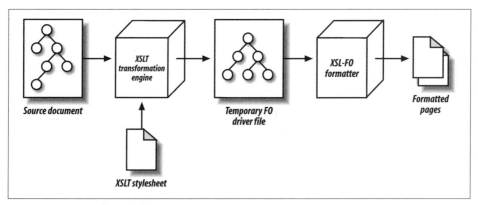

*Figure 1-4. How XSL works*

presentational format because XSL is so generic, describing layout and style attributes in the most declarative form. I will describe XSL in more detail in Chapter 8.

### Programming solutions

Finally, if stylesheets do not fit the bill, which may be the case if your source data is just too raw for direct transformation, then you may find a programming solution to be to your liking. Although XSLT has much to offer in transformation, it tends to be rather weak in some areas, such as processing character data. I often find that, despite my best efforts to stay inside the XSLT paradigm, I sometimes have to resort to writing a program that preprocesses my XML data before a transformation. Or I may have to write a program that does the whole processing from source to presentational format. That option is always available, and we will see it in detail in Chapter 10.

## Ensure Data Integrity

Trust is important for data—trust that it hasn't been corrupted, truncated, mistyped or left incomplete. Broken documents can confuse software, format as gibberish, and result in erroneous calculations. Documents submitted for publishing need to be complete and use only the markup that you specify. Transmitting and converting documents always entails risk that some information may be lost.

XML gives you the ability to guarantee a minimal level of trust in data. There are several mechanisms. First, there is well-formedness. Every XML parser is required to report syntax errors in markup. Missing tags, malformed tags, illegal characters, and other problems should be immediately reported to you. Consider this simple document with a few errors in it:

```
<announcement<
  <TEXT>Hello, world! I'm using XML & it's a lot of fun.</Text>
</anouncement>
```

---

When I run an XML well-formedness checker on it, here is what I get:

```
> xwf t.xml
t.xml:2: error: xmlParseEntityRef: no name
  <TEXT>Hello, world! I'm using XML & it's a lot of fun.</Text>
                                        ^

t.xml:2: error: Opening and ending tag mismatch: TEXT and Text
  <TEXT>Hello, world! I'm using XML & it's a lot of fun.</Text>
                                                            ^

t.xml:3: error: Opening and ending tag mismatch: announcement and
anouncement
</anouncement>
           ^
```

It caught two mismatched tags and an illegal character. And not only did it tell me what was wrong, it showed me where the errors were, so I can go back and correct them more easily. Checking if a document is well-formed can pick up a lot of problems:

- Mismatched tags, a common occurrence if you are typing in the XML by hand. The start and end tags have to match exactly in case and spelling.

- Truncated documents, which would be missing at least part of the outermost document (both start and end tags must be present).

- Illegal characters, including reserved markup delimiters like <, >, and &. There is a special syntax for complex or reserved characters which looks like &lt; for <. If any part of that is missing, the parser will get suspicious. Parsers should also warn you if characters in a particular encoding are not correctly formed, which may indicate that the document was altered in a recent transmission. For example, transferring a file through FTP as ASCII text can sometimes strip out the high bit characters.

The well-formedness check has its limits. The parser doesn't know if you are using the right elements in the right places. For example, you might have an XHTML document with a p element inside the head, which is illegal. To catch this kind of problem, you need to test if the document is a valid instance of XHTML. The tool for this is a *validating parser*.

A validating parser works by comparing a document against a set of rules called a *document model*. One kind of document model is a *document type definition* (DTD). It declares all the elements that are allowed in a document and describes in detail what kind of elements they can contain. Example 1-7 is a small DTD for telegrams.

*Example 1-7. A telegram DTD*

```
<!ELEMENT telegram (from,to,subject,graphic?,message)>
<!ATTLIST telegram pri CDATA #IMPLIED>
<!ELEMENT from (#PCDATA)>
<!ELEMENT to (#PCDATA)>
<!ELEMENT subject (#PCDATA)>
<!ELEMENT graphic EMPTY>
```

*Example 1-7. A telegram DTD (continued)*

```
<!ATTLIST graphic fileref CDATA #REQUIRED>
<!ELEMENT message (#PCDATA|emphasis|name|villain)*>
<!ELEMENT emphasis (#PCDATA)>
<!ELEMENT name (#PCDATA)>
```

Before submitting the telegram document to a parser, I need to add this line to the top:

```
<!DOCTYPE telegram SYSTEM "/location/of/dtd">
```

Where "/location..." is the path to the DTD file on my system. Now I can run a validating parser on the telegram document. Here's the output I get:

```
> xval ex1_memo.xml
ex1_memo.xml:13: validity error: No declaration for element villain
    mastermind <villain>Dr. Indigo Riceway</villain>.
                                                      ^
ex1_memo.xml:15: validity error: Element telegram content doesn't
follow the DTD
</telegram>
        ^
```

Oops! I forgot to declare the villain element, so I'm not allowed to use it in a telegram. No problem; it's easy to add new elements. This shows how you can detect problems with structure and grammar in a document.

The most important benefit to using a DTD is that it allows you to enforce and formalize a markup language. You can make your DTD public by posting it on the web, which is what organizations like the W3C do. For instance, you can look at the DTD for "strict" XHTML version 1.0 at *http://www.w3.org/TR/xhtml1/DTD/xhtml1-strict.dtd*. It's a compact and portable specification, though a little dense to read.

One limitation of DTDs is that they don't do much checking of text content. You can declare an element to contain text (called PCDATA in XML), or not, and that's as far as you can go. You could not check whether an element that should be filled out is empty, or if it follows the wrong pattern. Say, for example, I wanted to make sure that the to element in the telegram isn't empty, so I have at least someone to give it to. With a DTD, there is no way to test that.

An alternative document modeling scheme provides the solution. XML Schemas provide much more detailed control over a document, including the ability to compare text with a pattern you define. Example 1-8 shows a schema that will test a telegram for completely filled-out elements.

*Example 1-8. A schema for telegrams*

```
<xs:schema xmlns:xs="http://www.w3.org/2001/XMLSchema">

  <xs:element name="telegram" type="telegramtype" />

  <xs:complexType name="telegramtype">
```

*Example 1-8. A schema for telegrams (continued)*

```
    <xs:sequence>
      <xs:element name="to" type="texttype" />
      <xs:element name="from" type="texttype" />
      <xs:element name="subject" type="texttype" />
      <xs:element name="graphic" type="graphictype" />
      <xs:element name="message" type="messagetype" />
    </xs:sequence>
    <xs:attribute name="pri" type="xs:token" />
  </xs:complexType>

  <xs:simpleType name="texttype">
    <xs:restriction base="xs:string">
      <xs:minLength value="1" />
    </xs:restriction>
  </xs:simpleType>

  <xs:complexType name="graphictype">
    <xs:attribute name="fileref" type="xs:anyURI" use="required" />
  </xs:complexType>

  <xs:complexType name="messagetype" mixed="true">
    <xs:choice minOccurs="0" maxOccurs="unbounded">
      <xs:element name="emphasis" type="xs:string" />
      <xs:element name="name" type="xs:string" />
      <xs:element name="villain" type="xs:string" />
    </xs:choice>
  </xs:complexType>

</xs:schema>
```

So there are several levels of quality assurance available in XML. You can rest assured that your data is in a good state if you've validated it.

## Support Multiple Languages

XML wants to be useful to the widest possible community. Things that have limited other markup languages from worldwide acceptance have been reworked. The character set, for starters, is Unicode, which supports hundreds of scripts: Latin, Nordic, Arabic, Cyrillic, Hebrew, Chinese, Mongolian, and many more. It also has ample supplies of literary and scientific symbols. You'd be hard-pressed to think of something you can't express in XML. To be flexible, XML also supports many character encodings.

The difference between a character set and a character encoding can be a little confusing. A *character set* is a collection of symbols, or *glyphs*. For example, ASCII is a set of 127 simple Roman letters, numerals, symbols, and a few device codes. A *character encoding* is a scheme for representing the characters numerically. All text is just a string of numbers that tell a program what symbols to render on screen. An encoding may be as simple as mapping each byte to a unique glyph. Sometimes the number of characters is so large that a different scheme is required.

For example, UTF-8 is an encoding for the Unicode character set. It uses an ingenious algorithm to represent the most common characters in one byte, some less common ones in two bytes, rarer ones in three bytes, and so on. This makes the vast majority of files in existence already compatible with UTF-8, and it makes most UTF-8 documents compatible with most older, 1-byte character processing software.

There are many other encodings, such as UTF-16 and ISO-8859-1. You can specify the character encoding you want to use in the XML prologue like this:

```
<?xml version="1.0" encoding="iso-8859-1"?>
```

This goes at the very top of an XML document so it can prepare the XML parser for the text to follow. The encoding parameter and, in fact, the whole prologue, is optional. Without an explicit encoding parameter, the XML processor will assume you want UTF-8 or UTF-16, depending on the first few bytes of the file.

It is inconvenient to insert exotic characters from a common terminal. XML provides a shorthand, called *character entity references*. If you want a letter "c" with a cedilla (ç), you can express it numerically like this: &#224; (decimal) or &#xe7; (hexadecimal), both of which use the position of the character in Unicode as an identifier.

Often, there may be one or more translations of a document. You can keep them all together using XML's built-in support for language qualifiers. In this piece of XML, two versions of the same text are kept together for convenience, differentiated by labels:

```
<para xml:lang="en">There is an answer.</para>
<para xml:lang="de">Es gibt ein Antwort.</para>
```

This same system can even be used with dialects within a language. In this case, both are English, but from different locales:

```
<para xml:lang="en-US">Consult the program.</para>
<para xml:lang="en-GB">Consult the programme.</para>
```

# How Do I Get Started?

By now you are chomping at the bit, eager to gallop into XML coding of your own. Let's take a look at how to set up your own XML authoring and processing environment.

## Authoring Documents

The most important item in your XML toolbox is the XML editor. This program lets you read and compose XML, and often comes with services to prevent mistakes and clarify the view of your document. There is a wide spectrum of quality and expense in editors, which makes choosing one that's right for you a little tricky. In this section, I'll take you on a tour of different kinds.

Even the lowliest plain-text editor is sufficient to work with XML. You can use TextEdit on the Mac, NotePad or WordPad on Windows, or vi on Unix. The only limitation is whether it supports the character set used by the document. In most cases, it will be UTF-8. Some of these text editors support an XML "mode" which can highlight markup and assist in inserting tags. Some popular free editors include vim, elvis, and, my personal favorite, emacs.

*emacs* is a powerful text editor with macros and scripted functions. Lennart Stafflin has written an XML plug-in for it called psgml, available at *http://www.lysator.liu.se/~lenst/*. It adds menus and commands for inserting tags and showing information about a DTD. It even comes with an XML parser that can detect structural mistakes while you're editing a document. Using psgml and a feature called "font-lock," you can set up *xemacs*, an X Window version of *emacs*, to highlight markup in color. Figure 1-5 is a snapshot of *xemacs* with an XML document open.

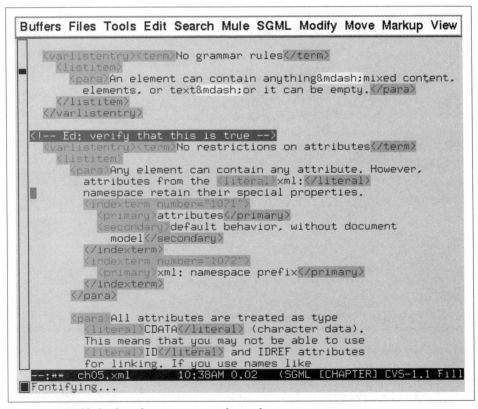

*Figure 1-5. Highlighted markup in xemacs with psgml*

Morphon Technologies' XMLEditor is a fine example of a graphical user interface. As you can see in Figure 1-6, the window sports several panes. On the left is an outline view of the book, in which you can quickly zoom in on a particular element, open it, collapse it, and move it around. On the right is a view of the text without markup. And below these panes is an attribute editing pane. The layout is easy to customize and easy to use. Note the formatting in the text view, achieved by applying a CSS stylesheet to the document. Morphon's editor sells for $150 and you can download a 30-day demo at *http://www.morphon.com*. It's written in Java, so it supports all computer platforms.

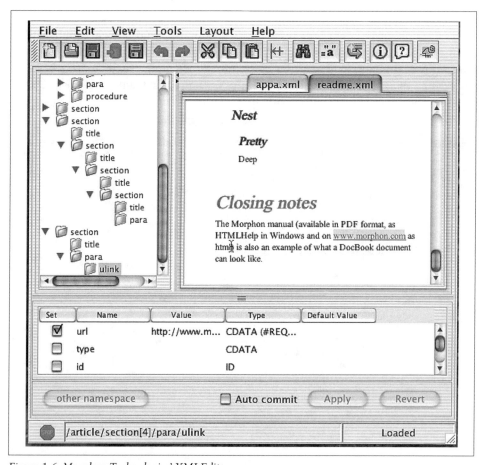

*Figure 1-6. Morphon Technologies' XMLEditor*

Arbortext's Epic Editor is a very polished editor that can be integrated with digital asset management systems and high-end compositing systems. A screenshot is shown in Figure 1-7. Like Morphon's editor, it uses CSS to format the text displayed. There are add-ons to extend functionality such as multiple author collaboration, importing from and exporting to Microsoft Word, formatting for print using a highly detailed stylesheet language called FOSI, and a powerful scripting language. The quality of output using FOSI is good enough for printing books, and you can view how it will look on screen. At around $700 a license, you pay more, but you get your money's worth with Epic.

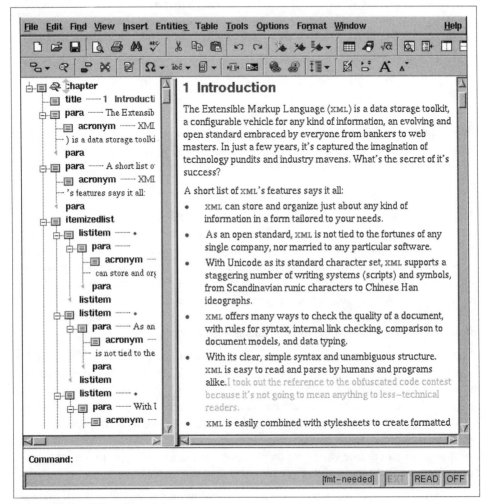

*Figure 1-7. Epic Editor from Arbortext*

These are just a few of the many XML editors available. Table 1-1 lists a few more, along with their features and prices.

Table 1-1. Comparison of XML editor features

| editor | tag highlighting | structure checking | validity checking | element menus | macros | unicode support | outline view | formatted display | cost |
|---|---|---|---|---|---|---|---|---|---|
| Adobe FrameMaker 7.0 | yes | yes | yes | yes | yes | no | yes | yes | $800 Mac and Windows, $1300 Unix |
| Arbortext Adept | yes | yes | yes | yes | yes | yes | yes | yes | $700 |
| Corel XMetal | yes | yes | yes | yes | yes | yes | yes | yes | $500 |
| emacs/psgml | yes | yes | yes | yes | yes | no | no | no | free |
| Morphon XMLEditor | yes | yes | yes | yes | yes | no | yes | yes | $150 |
| XML Spy | yes | yes | yes | yes | | | | yes | $200 |

The features of structure and validity checking can be taken too far. All XML editors will warn you when there are structural errors or improper element placement (validity errors). A few, like Corel's XMetal, prevent you from even *temporarily* making the document invalid. A user who is cutting and pasting sections around may temporarily have to break the validity rules. The editor rejects this, forcing the user to stop and figure out what is going wrong. It's rather awkward to have your creativity interrupted that way. When choosing an editor, you'll have to weigh the benefits of enforced structure against the interruptions in the creative process.

A high-quality XML authoring environment is configurable. If you have designed a document type, you should be able to customize the editor to enforce the structure, check validity, and present a selection of valid elements to choose from. You should be able to create macros to automate frequent editing steps and map keys on the keyboard to these macros. The interface should be ergonomic and convenient, providing keyboard shortcuts instead of many mouse clicks for every task. The authoring tool should let you define your own display properties, whether you prefer large type with colors or small type with tags displayed.

Configurability is sometimes at odds with another important feature: ease of maintenance. Having an editor that formats content nicely (for example, making titles large and bold) means that someone must write and maintain a stylesheet. Some editors have a reasonably good stylesheet-editing interface that lets you play around with element styles almost as easily as creating a template in a word processor. Structure enforcement can be another headache, since you may have to create a document type definition (DTD) from scratch. Like a stylesheet, the DTD tells the editor how to handle elements and whether they are allowed in various contexts. You may decide that the extra work is worth it if it saves error-checking and complaints from users down the line.

Editors often come with interfaces for specific types of markup. XML Spy includes many such extensions. It will allow you to create and position graphics, write XSLT stylesheets, create electronic forms, create tables in a special table builder, and create XML Schema. Tables, found in XML applications like HTML and DocBook, are complex structures, and believe me when I tell you they are not fun to work with in markup. To have a specialized table editor is a godsend.

Another nicety many editors provide is automatic conversion to terminal formats. FrameMaker, Epic, and others, can all generate PDF from XML. This high-quality formatting is difficult to achieve, however, and you will spend a lot of time tweaking difficult stylesheets to get just the appearance you're looking for. There is a lot of variation among editors in how this is achieved. XML Spy uses XSLT, while Epic uses FOSI, and FrameMaker uses its own proprietary mapping tables. Generating HTML is generally a lot easier than PDF due to the lower standards for documents viewed on computer displays, so you will see more editors that can convert to HTML than to PDF.

Database integration is another feature to consider. In an environment where data comes from many sources, such as multiple authors in collaboration, or records from databases, an editor that can communicate with a database can be a big deal. Databases can be used as a repository for documents, giving the ability to log changes, mark ownership, and store older versions. Databases are also used to store raw data, such as personnel records and inventory, and you may need to import that information into a document, such as a catalog. Editors like Epic and XML Spy support database input and collaboration. They can update documents in many places when data sources have changed, and they can branch document source text into multiple simultaneous versions. There are many exciting possibilities.

Which editor you use will depend a lot on your budget. You can spend nothing and get a very decent editor like emacs. It doesn't have much of a graphical interface, and there is a learning curve, but it's worked quite well for me. Or, for just a couple hundred dollars, you can get a nice editor with a GUI and parsing ability like Morphon XMLEdit. You probably wouldn't need to spend more unless you're in a corporate environment where the needs for high-quality formatting and collaboration justify the cost and maintenance requirements. Then you might buy into a suite of high-end editing systems like Epic or FrameMaker. With XML, there is no shortage of choices.

## Viewing Documents

If the ultimate purpose of your XML is to give someone something to look at, then you may be interested in checking out some document viewers. You've already seen examples of editors displaying XML documents. You can display XML in web browsers too. Of course, all web browsers support XHTML. But Internet Explorer can handle any well-formed XML.

Since version 5.0 on Macintosh and 5.1 on Windows, Internet Explorer has had the ability to read and display XML. It has a built-in validating XML parser. If you specify a DTD in the document, IE will check it for validity. If there are errors, it will tell you so and highlight the affected areas. Viewing a document in IE looks like Figure 1-8.

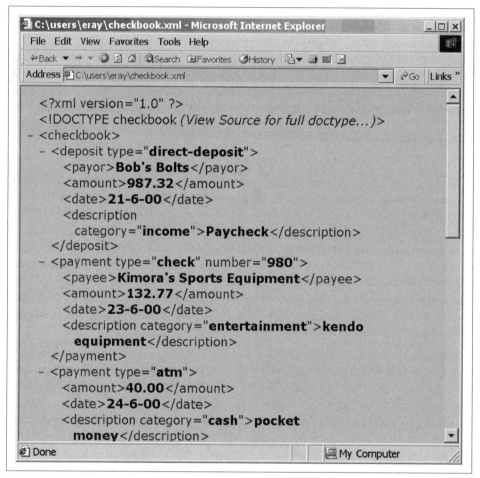

*Figure 1-8. Internet Explorer's XML outline view*

You may have noticed that the outline view in IE looks a lot like the outline view in Morphon XMLEdit. It works the same way. The whole document is the root of a tree, with branches for elements. Click on one of the minus icons and it will collapse the element, hiding all of its contents. The icon will become a plus symbol which you can click on to open up the element again. It's a very useful tool for navigating a document quickly.

For displaying formatted documents on computer monitors, the best technology is CSS. CSS has a rich set of style attributes for setting colors, typefaces, rules, and margins. How much of the CSS standard is implemented, however, varies considerably across browsers. There are three separate recommendations, with the first being quite widely implemented, the second and more advanced less so, and the third rarely.

IE also contains an XSLT transformation engine. This gives yet another way to format an XML document. The XSLT script pointed to by your document transforms it into XHTML which IE already knows how to display. So you have two ways inside IE to generate decent presentation, making it an invaluable development tool. Since not all browsers implement CSS and XSLT for XML documents, it's risky to serve XML documents and expect end user clients to format them correctly. This may change soon, as more browsers catch up to IE, but at the moment it's safer to do the transformation on the server side and just serve HTML.

There are a bunch of browsers capable of working with XML in full or limited fashion. The following list describes a few of the more popular and interesting ones. Some technologies, like DOM and CSS, are broken up into three levels representing the relative sophistication of features. Most browsers completely implement the first level of CSS (CSS1), a few CSS2, and hardly any completely support the third tier of CSS.

*Amaya*
> Amaya is a project by the W3C to demonstrate technologies working together. It's both a browser and an editor with built-in XML parsing and validating. It supports XHTML 1.1, CSS1 and parts of CSS2, MathML, and much of SVG. It is not able to format other kinds of XML, however.

*Konquerer*
> Available for flavors of Unix, this browser has lovely HTML formatting, but only limited support for XML. Its standards set includes HTML 4, most of CSS1 and part of CSS2, DOM1, DOM2, and part of DOM3.

*Microsoft Internet Explorer*
> Microsoft has tried very hard to play ball with the open standards community and it shows with this browser. XML parsing is excellent, along with strong support for DTDs, XSLT, CSS1, SVG (with plug-in), and DOM.
>
> Strangely, Internet Explorer is split into two completely different code bases, with versions for Windows and Macintosh independent from each other. This has led to wacky situations such as the Mac version being for a time more advanced than its Windows cousin. The best versions (and perhaps last) available are 6.0 on Windows and 5.1 for Macintosh.

*Mozilla 1.4*

Mozilla is an open source project to develop an excellent free browser that supports all the major standards. At Mozilla's heart is a rendering engine, code-named Gecko, that parses markup and churns out formatted pages. It's also the foundation for Netscape Navigator and IBM's Web Browser for OS/2.

How is it for compliance? Mozilla fully supports XML using James Clark's Expat parser, a free and high-quality tool. Other standards it implements include HTML 4, XHTML, CSS1, CSS2, SVG (with plug-in), XSLT, XLink, XPath, MathML (with plug-in), RDF, and Unicode. Some standards are only partially supported, such as XBase, XLink, and CSS3. For more information about XML in Mozilla, go to the Web at *http://mozilla.org/newlayout/xml*.

*Netscape Navigator*

As of version 6, Navigator has been based on the Mozilla browsers internal workings. Therefore, it supports all the same standards.

*Opera*

Opera is a fast and efficient browser whose lead designer was one of the codevelopers of CSS1. Standard support varies with platform, the Windows version being strongest. It implements XML parsing, CSS up to level 2, WAP and WML (media for wireless devices such as cell phones), and Unicode. An exciting new joint venture with IBM has formed recently to develop a multimodal browser that will handle speech as well as keyboard/mouse control. Opera's weakest point is DOM, with only limited support.

*X-Smiles*

This fascinating tool describes itself as "an open XML browser for exotic devices." It supports some standards no other browsers have touched yet, including SMIL, XForms, X3D (three-dimensional graphics) and XML Signature. Using a Java-based plug-in, it can parse XML and do transformations with XSLT.

You can see browsers vary considerably in their support for standards. CSS implementation is particularly spotty, as shown in Eric Meyer's Master Compatibility Chart at *http://www.webreview.com/style/css1/charts/mastergrid.shtml*. People aren't taking the situation lying down, however. The Web Standards Project (*http://www.web-standards.org/* monitors browser vendors and advocates greater compliance with standards.

Things get really interesting when you mix together different XML applications in one document. Example 1-9 is a document that combines three applications in one: XHTML which forms the shell and handles basic text processing, SVG for a vector graphic, and MathML to include an equation at the end. Figure 1-9 shows how it looks in the Amaya browser.

*Example 1-9. A document composed of XHTML, SVG, and MathML*

```
<?xml version="1.0"?>
<html xmlns="http://www.w3.org/1999/xhtml">
  <head>
    <title>T E L E G R A M</title>
    <!-- CSS stylesheet -->
    <style>
body       { background-color: tan; font-family: sans-serif; }
.telegram { border: thick solid wheat; }
.message  { color: maroon; }
.head     { color: blue; }
.name     { font-weight: bold; color: green; }
.villain  { font-weight: bold; color: red; }
    </style>
  </head>
  <body>
    <div class="telegram">
      <h1>Telegram</h1>
      <h2><span class="head">To:</span> Sarah Bellum</h2>
      <h2><span class="head">From:</span> Colonel Timeslip</h2>
      <h2><span class="head">Subj:</span> Robot-sitting instructions</h2>

      <!-- SVG Picture of Zonky -->
      <svg xmlns="http://www.w3.org/2000/svg" width="100" height="100">
        <rect x="5" y="5" width="90" height="95" fill="none"
          stroke="black" stroke-width="1"/>
        <rect x="25" y="75" width="50" height="25" fill="gray"
          stroke="black" stroke-width="2"/>
        <rect x="30" y="70" width="40" height="30" fill="blue"
          stroke="black" stroke-width="2"/>
        <circle cx="50" cy="50" r="20" fill="blue" stroke="black"
          stroke-width="2"/>
        <circle cx="43" cy="50" r="5" fill="yellow" stroke="brown"/>
        <circle cx="57" cy="50" r="5" fill="yellow" stroke="brown"/>
        <text x="25%" y="25%" fill="purple" font-size="18pt"
          font-weight="bold" font-style="italic">Zonky</text>
        <text x="40" y="85" fill="white" font-family="sans-serif">Z-1</text>
      </svg>

      <!-- Message -->
      <div class="message">
        <p>Thanks for watching my robot pal
          <span class="name">Zonky</span> while I'm away.
          He needs to be recharged <em>twice a
          day</em> and if he starts to get cranky,
          give him a quart of oil. I'll be back soon,
          after I've tracked down that evil
          mastermind <span class="villain">Dr. Indigo
          Riceway</span>.</p>

        <p>P.S. Your homework for this week is to prove
          Newton's theory of gravitation:
```

*Example 1-9. A document composed of XHTML, SVG, and MathML (continued)*

```
            <!-- MathML Equation -->
            <math xmlns="http://www.w3.org/1998/Math/MathML">
              <mrow>
                <mi>F</mi>
                <mo>=</mo>
                <mi>G</mi>
                <mo>&InvisibleTimes;</mo>
                <mfrac>
                  <mrow>
                    <mi>M</mi>
                    <mo>&InvisibleTimes;</mo>
                    <mi>m</mi>
                  </mrow>
                  <mrow>
                    <msup>
                      <mi>r</mi>
                      <mn>2</mn>
                    </msup>
                  </mrow>
                </mfrac>
              </mrow>
            </math>
          </p>
        </div>
      </div>
    </body>
</html>
```

## Parsing

If you're going to be using XML from error-prone sources such as human authors, you will probably want to have a parser (preferably with good error reporting) in your XML toolkit. XML's strict rules protect programs from unpredictable input that can cause them to crash or produce strange results. So you need to make sure that your data is clean and syntactically correct. Before I talk about these tools, let me first explain how parsing works. With a little theoretical grounding, you'll be in good shape for understanding the need for parsers and knowing how to use them.

Every program that works with XML first has to parse it. *Parsing* is a process where XML text is collected and broken down into separate, manageable parts. As Figure 1-10 shows, there are several levels. At the lowest level are characters in the input stream. Certain characters are special, like <, >, and &. They tell the parser when it is reading a tag, character data, or some other markup symbol.

The next level of parsing occurs when the tags and symbols have been identified and now affect the internal checking mechanisms of the parser. The well-formedness rules now direct the parser in how to handle tokens. For example, an element start tag tells the parser to store the name of the element in a memory structure called a

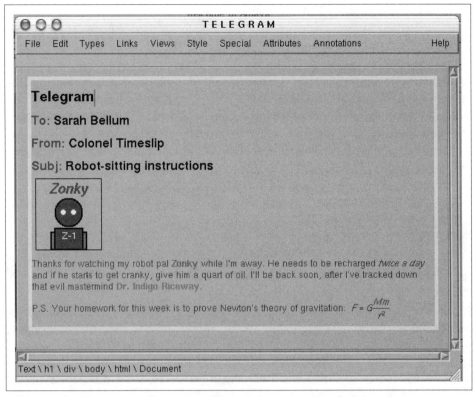

Figure 1-9. Amaya showing a document with XHTML, SVG, and MathML

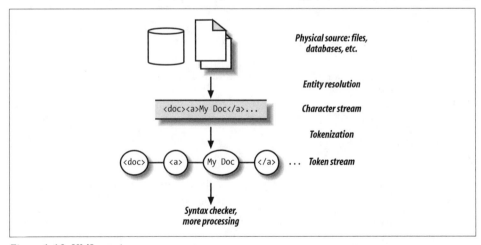

Figure 1-10. XML parsing

stack. When an element end tag comes along, it's checked against the name in the stack. If they match, the element is popped out of the stack and parsing resumes. Otherwise, something must have gone wrong, and the parser needs to report the error.

One kind of symbol, called an *entity reference*, is a placeholder for content from another source. It may be a single character, or it could be a huge file. The parser looks up the source and pops it into the document for parsing. If there are entity references inside that new piece of content, they have to be resolved too. XML can come from many sources, including files, databases, program output, and places online.

Above this level is the structure checking, also called *validation*. This is optional, and not all parsers can do it, but it is a very useful capability. Say, for example, you are writing a book in XML and you want to make sure that every section has a title. If the DTD requires a title element at the beginning of the section element, then the parser will expect to find it in the document. If a `<section>` start tag is followed by something other than a `<title>` start tag, the parser knows something is wrong and will report it.

Parsers are often used in conjunction with some other processing, feeding a stream of tokens and representative data objects to be further manipulated. At the moment, however, we're interested in parsing tools that check syntax in a document. Instead of passing on digested XML to another program, standalone parsers, also called well-formedness checkers, tell you when markup is good or bad, and usually give you hints about what went wrong. Let's look at an example. In Example 1-10 I've written a test document with a bunch of syntax errors, guaranteed to annoy any XML parser.

*Example 1-10. A document that is not well-formed XML*

```
<!-- This document is not well-formed and will invoke an error
     condition from an XML parser. -->
<testdoc>
  <e1>overlapping <e2> elements </e1> here </e2>
  <e3>missing end tag
  <e4>illegal character (<) </e4>
</testdoc>
```

Any parser worth its salt should complain noisily about the errors in this example. You should expect to see a stream of error messages something like this:

```
$ xwf ex4_noparse.xml

ex4_noparse.xml:5: error: Opening and ending tag mismatch: e2 and e1
    <e1>overlapping <e2> elements </e1> here </e2>
                                      ^
ex4_noparse.xml:5: error: Opening and ending tag mismatch: e1 and e2
    <e1>overlapping <e2> elements </e1> here </e2>
                                               ^
```

```
ex4_noparse.xml:7: error: xmlParseStartTag: invalid element name
  <e4>illegal character (<) </e4>
                         ^
ex4_noparse.xml:8: error: Opening and ending tag mismatch: e3 and
testdoc
</testdoc>
         ^
```

The tool helpfully points out all the places where it thinks the XML is broken and needs to be fixed, along with a short message indicating what's wrong. "Ending tag mismatch," for example, means that the end tag in question doesn't match the most recently found element start tag, which is a violation. Many parsing tools will also validate if you supply a DTD for them to check against.

Where can you get a tool like this? The easiest way is to get an XML-aware web browser and open up an XML file with it. It will point out well-formedness errors for you (though often just one at a time) and can also validate against a DTD. Figure 1-11 shows the result of trying to load a badly formed XML document in Mozilla.

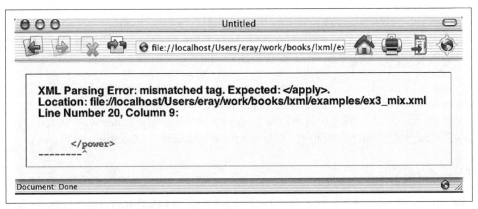

*Figure 1-11. Browser showing XML syntax error*

If you prefer a command-line tool, like I do, you can find one online. James Clark's nsgmls at *http://www.jclark.com/sp/*, originally written for SGML, has served me well for many years.

If you are a developer, it is not hard to use XML parsers in your code. Example 1-11 is a Perl script that uses the XML::LibXML module to create a handy command-line validation tool.

*Example 1-11. A validating parser in Perl*

```perl
#!/usr/bin/perl
use XML::LibXML;                  # import parser library
my $parser = new XML::LibXML;     # create a parser object
$parser->validation(1);           # turn on validation
```

*Example 1-11. A validating parser in Perl (continued)*

```
$parser->load_ext_dtd(1);                      # read the external DTD
my $doc = $parser->parse_file( shift @ARGV );  # parse the file
if( $@ ) {                                      # test for errors
    print STDERR "PARSE ERRORS\n", $@;
} else {
    print "The document '$file' is valid.\n";
}
```

XML::LibXML is an interface to a C library called libxml2, where the real parsing work is done. There are XML libraries for Java, C, Python, and almost any other programming language you can think of.

The parser in the this example goes beyond just well-formedness checking. It's called a *validating parser* because it checks the grammar (types and order of elements) of the document to make sure it is a valid instance of a document type. For example, I could have it check a document to make sure it conforms to the DTD for XHTML 1.0. To do this, I need to place a line in the XML document that looks like this:

```
<!DOCTYPE html PUBLIC "..." "...">
```

This tells the parser that it needs to find a DTD, read its declarations, and then be mindful of element types and usage as it parses the document. The location of the DTD is specified in two ways. The first is the *public identifier*, inside the first set of quotes above. This is like saying, "go and read the Magna Carta," which is an unambiguous command, but still requires you to hunt around for a copy of it. In this case, the parser has to look up the actual location in a concordance called a *catalog*. Your program has to tell the parser where to find a catalog. The other way to specify a DTD is to give a *system identifier*. This is a plain ordinary URL or filesystem path.

## Transformation

The act of changing XML from one form to another is called transformation. This is a very powerful technique, employed in such processes as print formatting and conversion to HTML. Although most often used to add presentation to a document, it can be used to alter a document for special purposes. For example, you can use a transformation to generate a table of contents, construct an excerpt, or tabulate a column of numbers.

Transformation requires two things: the source document and a transformation stylesheet. The stylesheet is a recipe for how to "cook" the XML and arrive at a desired result. The oven in this metaphor is a transformation program that reads the stylesheet and input document and outputs a result document. Several languages have been developed for transformations. The Document Style Semantics and Specification Language (DSSSL) uses the programming language Lisp to describe transformations functionally. However, because DSSSL is rather complex and difficult to work with, a simpler language emerged: the very popular XSLT.

XSLT didn't start off as a general-purpose transformation language. A few years ago, there was a project in the W3C, led by James Clark, to develop a high-quality style description language. The Extensible Style Language (XSL) quickly evolved into two components. The first, XSLT, concentrated on transforming any XML instance into a presentational format. The other component of XSL, XSL-FO (the FO stands for Formatting Objects), describes that format.

It soon became obvious that XSLT was useful in a wider context than just formatting documents. It can be used to turn an XML document into just about any form you can imagine. The language is generic, using rules and templates to describe what to output for various element types. Mr. Clark has expressed surprise that XSLT is being used in so many other applications, but it is testament to the excellent design of this standard that it has worked so well.

XSLT is an application of XML. This means you can easily write XSLT in any non-validating XML editor. You cannot validate XSLT because there is no DTD for it. An XSLT script contains many elements that you define yourself, and DTDs do not provide that kind of flexibility. However, you could use an XML Schema. I usually just check well-formedness and rely on the XSLT processor to tell me when it thinks the grammar is wrong.

An *XSLT processor* is a program that takes an XML document and an XSLT stylesheet as input and outputs a transformed document. Thanks to the enthusiasm for XSLT, there are many implementations available. Microsoft's MSXML system is probably the most commonly used. Saxon (*http://saxon.sourceforge.net/*) is the most compliant and advanced. Others include Apache's Xalan (*http://xml.apache.org/xalan-j/index.html*) and GNOME's libxslt (*http://www.xmlsoft.org/XSLT.html*).

Besides using a programming library or command-line tool, you could also use a web browser for its built-in XSLT transformer. Simply add a line like this to the XML document to tell the browser to transform it:

```
<?xml-stylesheet type="text/xsl" href="/path/to/stylesheet"?>
```

Replace */path/to/stylesheet* with a URL for the actual location of the XSLT stylesheet. This method is frequently used to transform more complex XML languages into simpler, presentational HTML.

## Formatting for Print

Technology pundits have been predicting for a long time the coming of the paperless office. All data would be stored on computer, read on monitors and passed around through the network. But the truth is, people use paper now more than ever. For reading a long document, there is still no substitute for paper. Therefore, XML has had to embrace print.

Formatting for print begins with a transformation. Your XML document, which is marked up for describing structure and information, says nothing about the appearance. It needs to be converted into a presentational format that describes how things should look: typefaces, colors, positions on the page, and so on. There are many such formats, like TeX, PostScript and PDF. The trick is how to get from your XML to one of these formats.

You could, theoretically, write a transformation stylesheet to mutate your XML into PostScript, but this will give you nightmares and a head full of gray hairs. PostScript is UGLY. So are most other presentational formats like troff, RTF, and MIF. The fact that they are text (not binary) doesn't make them much easier to understand. Any transformation stylesheet you write will require such intimate knowledge of byzantine rules and obscure syntactic conventions that it will quickly lead to madness. Believe me, I've done it.

Fortunately, somebody has had the brilliant idea to develop a formatting language based on plain English, using XML for its structural markup. XSL-FO, the cousin of XSLT, uses the same terminology as CSS to describe typefaces, inline styles, blocks, margins, and all the concepts you need to create a nice-looking page. You can look at an XSL-FO document and easily see the details for how it will be rendered. You can edit it directly and it won't blow up in your face. Best of all, it works wonderfully with XSLT.

In the XSL process (see Figure 1-4), you give the XSLT transformer a stylesheet and an input document. It spits out an XSL-FO document that contains the data plus style information. A formatter takes the XSL-FO instance and renders that into a terminal format like PDF which you can print or view on a computer screen. Although you could edit the XSL-FO directly, it's unlikely you would want to do that. Much better would be to edit the original XML source or the XSLT stylesheet and treat the XSL-FO as a temporary intermediate file. In fact, some implementations won't even output the XSL-FO unless you request it.

My favorite XSL-FO formatter is called FOP (Formatting Object Processor) and it's a project of the prodigious Apache XML Project (*http://xml.apache.org/fop/*). FOP is written in Java and comes bundled with a Java-based parser (Xerces) and a Java-based XSLT transformer (Xalan). The whole thing runs as a pipeline, very smooth and clean.

As an example, I wrote the XSLT script in Example 1-12. Unlike Example 1-6, which transforms its source into HTML, this transforms into XSL-FO. Notice the use of *namespace qualifiers* (the element name parts to the left of colons) to distinguish between XSLT instructions and XSL-FO style directives. The elements that start with xsl: are XSLT commands and elements that start with fo: are formatting object tags.

*Example 1-12. An XSLT stylesheet for telegram bound for FO*

```
<?xml version="1.0" encoding="utf-8"?>
<xsl:stylesheet version="1.0"
                xmlns:xsl="http://www.w3.org/1999/XSL/Transform"
                xmlns:fo="http://www.w3.org/1999/XSL/Format">

  <xsl:template match="/">
    <fo:root>
      <fo:layout-master-set>
        <fo:simple-page-master master-name="only">
          <fo:region-body region-name="xsl-region-body"
                          margin="1.0in"
                          padding="10pt"/>
          <fo:region-before region-name="xsl-region-before"
                          extent="1.0in"
                          display-align="before"/>
          <fo:region-after region-name="xsl-region-after"
                          extent="1.0in"
                          display-align="after"/>
        </fo:simple-page-master>
      </fo:layout-master-set>
      <fo:page-sequence master-reference="only">
        <fo:flow flow-name="xsl-region-body">
          <xsl:apply-templates/>
        </fo:flow>
      </fo:page-sequence>
    </fo:root>
  </xsl:template>

  <xsl:template match="telegram">
    <fo:block font-size="18pt"
              font-family="monospace"
              line-height="24pt"
              space-after.optimum="15pt"
              background-color="blue"
              color="white"
              text-align="center"
              padding-top="0pt">
      <xsl:text>TELEGRAM</xsl:text>
    </fo:block>
    <xsl:apply-templates/>
  </xsl:template>

  <xsl:template match="to">
    <fo:block font-family="sans-serif" font-size="14pt">
      <xsl:text>To: </xsl:text>
      <xsl:apply-templates/>
    </fo:block>
  </xsl:template>

  <xsl:template match="from">
    <fo:block font-family="sans-serif" font-size="14pt">
      <xsl:text>From: </xsl:text>
```

*Example 1-12. An XSLT stylesheet for telegram bound for FO (continued)*

```
      <xsl:apply-templates/>
    </fo:block>
  </xsl:template>

  <xsl:template match="subject">
    <fo:block font-family="sans-serif" font-size="14pt">
      <xsl:text>Subj: </xsl:text>
      <xsl:apply-templates/>
    </fo:block>
  </xsl:template>

  <xsl:template match="message">
    <fo:block font-family="monospace"
              font-size="10pt"
              text-align="justify">
      <xsl:apply-templates/>
    </fo:block>
  </xsl:template>

  <xsl:template match="emphasis">
    <fo:inline font-style="italic">
      <xsl:apply-templates/>
    </fo:inline>
  </xsl:template>

  <xsl:template match="name">
    <fo:inline color="green">
      <xsl:apply-templates/>
    </fo:inline>
  </xsl:template>

  <xsl:template match="villain">
    <fo:inline color="red">
      <xsl:apply-templates/>
    </fo:inline>
  </xsl:template>

</xsl:stylesheet>
```

After running the telegram example through FOP with this stylesheet, Figure 1-12 is the result. FOP outputs PDF by default, but other formats will be available soon. There is work right now to add MIF and PostScript as formats.

## Programming

When all else fails, you can write a program.

Parsers are the front line for any program that works with XML. There are several strategies available, depending on how you want to use the XML. The "push" technique, where data drives your program, is like a one-way tape drive. The parser reads

```
                            TELEGRAM

To: Sarah Bellum
From: Colonel Timeslip
Subj: Robot-sitting instructions
Thanks for watching my robot pal Zonky while I'm away. He needs to be
recharged twice a day and if he starts to get cranky, give him a quart
of oil. I'll be back soon, after I've tracked down that evil mastermind
Dr. Indigo Riceway.
```

*Figure 1-12. A PDF document generated by FOP*

the XML and calls on your program to handle each new item in the stream, hence the name *stream processing*. Though fast and efficient, stream processing is limited by the fact that the parser can't stop and go back to retrieve information from earlier in the stream. If you need to access information out of order, you have to save it in memory.

The "pull" technique allows the program to access parts of the document in any order. The parser typically reads in a document and stores it in a data structure. The structure resembles a tree, with the outermost element as the root, and its contents branching out to the innermost text which are like leaves. *Tree processing*, as we call it, gives you a long-lasting representation of the document's data and markup. It requires more memory and computation, but is often the most convenient way to accomplish a task.

Developers have come up with standard programming interfaces for each of these techniques. The Simple API for XML (SAX) specifies how a parser should interact with a program for stream processing. This allows programs to use interchangeable modules, greatly enhancing flexibility. It's possible to write *drivers*, programs that simulate parsers but get their input data from databases or non-XML formats, and know that any SAX-enabled program will be able to handle it. This is illustrated in Figure 1-13.

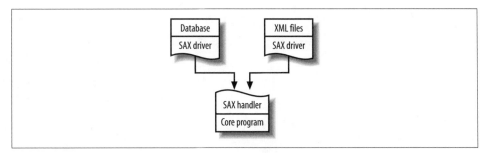

*Figure 1-13. SAX makes programs modular and interchangeable*

What SAX does for stream processing, the Document Object Model (DOM) does for tree processing. It describes a wide variety of accessor methods for objects containing parts of an XML document. With DOM, you can crawl over all the elements in a document in any order, rearrange them, add or subtract parts, and extract any data you want. Many web browsers have built-in support for DOM, allowing you to select and repackage information from a server using Java or JavaScript.

SOAP is a way for browsers to trade complex data packages with servers. Unlike HTML, which marks up data based on appearance, it describes its contents as data objects with types, names, and values, which is much more handy for computer processing.

Extracting data from deep inside a document is a common task for developers. DOM and SAX are often too complex for a simple query like this. XPath is a shorthand for locating a point inside an XML document. It is used in XPointers and also in places like XSLT and some DOM implementations to provide a quick way to move around a document. XPointer extends XPath to create a way to specify the location of a document anywhere on the Internet, extending the notion of URLs you know from the a element in HTML.

# CHAPTER 2

# Markup and Core Concepts

There's a *Far Side* cartoon by Gary Larson about an unusual chicken ranch. Instead of strutting around, pecking at seed, the chickens are all lying on the ground or draped over fences as if they were made of rubber. You see, it was a *boneless* chicken ranch.

Just as skeletons give us vertebrates shape and structure, markup does the same for text. Take out the markup and you have a mess of character data without any form. It would be very difficult to write a computer program that did anything useful with that content. Software relies on markup to label and delineate pieces of data, the way suitcases make it easy for you to carry clothes with you on a trip.

This chapter focuses on the details of XML markup. Here I will describe the fundamental building blocks of all XML-derived languages: elements, attributes, entities, processing instructions, and more. And I'll show you how they all fit together to make a well-formed XML document. Mastering these concepts is essential to understanding every other topic in the book, so read this chapter carefully.

All of the markup rules for XML are laid out in the W3C's technical recommendation for XML version 1.0 (*http://www.w3.org/TR/2000/REC-xml-20001006*). This is the second edition of the original which first appeared in 1998. You may also find Tim Bray's annotated, interactive version useful. Go and check it out at *http://www.xml.com/axml/testaxml.htm*.

## Tags

If XML markup is a structural skeleton for a document, then tags are the bones. They mark the boundaries of elements, allow insertion of comments and special instructions, and declare settings for the parsing environment. A parser, the front line of any program that processes XML, relies on tags to help it break down documents into discrete XML objects. There are a handful of different XML object types, listed in Table 2-1.

Table 2-1. Types of tags in XML

| Object | Purpose | Example |
|---|---|---|
| empty element | Represent information at a specific point in the document. | \<xref linkend="abc"/> |
| container element | Group together elements and character data. | \<p>This is a paragraph.\</p> |
| declaration | Add a new parameter, entity, or grammar definition to the parsing environment. | \<!ENTITY author "Erik Ray"> |
| processing instruction | Feed a special instruction to a particular type of software. | \<?print-formatter force-linebreak?> |
| comment | Insert an annotation that will be ignored by the XML processor. | \<!-- here's where I left off --> |
| CDATA section | Create a section of character data that should not be parsed, preserving any special characters inside it. | \<![CDATA[Ampersands galore! &&&&&]]> |
| entity reference | Command the parser to insert some text stored elsewhere. | &company-name; |

Elements are the most common XML object type. They break up the document into smaller and smaller cells, nesting inside one another like boxes. Figure 2-1 shows the document in Chapter 1 partitioned into separate elements. Each of these pieces has its own properties and role in a document, so we want to divide them up for separate processing.

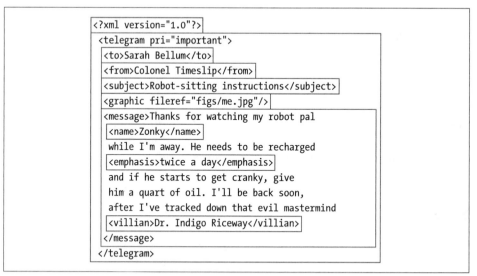

Figure 2-1. Telegram with element boundaries visible

Inside element start tags, you sometimes will see some extra characters next to the element name in the form of *name*="*value*". These are *attributes*. They associate information with an element that may be inappropriate to include as character data. In the telegram example earlier, look for an attribute in the start tag of the telegram element.

*Declarations* are never seen inside elements, but may appear at the top of the document or in an external document type definition file. They are important in setting parameters for the parsing session. They define rules for validation or declare special entities to stand in for text.

The next three objects are used to alter parser behavior while it's going over the document. *Processing instructions* are software-specific directives embedded in the markup for convenience (e.g., storing page numbers for a particular formatter). *Comments* are regions of text that the parser should strip out before processing, as they only have meaning to the author. *CDATA sections* are special regions in which the parser should temporarily suspend its tag recognition.

Rounding out the list are *entity references*, commands that tell the parser to insert predefined pieces of text in the markup. These objects don't follow the pattern of other tags in their appearance. Instead of angle brackets for delimiters, they use the ampersand and semicolon.

In upcoming sections, I'll explain each of these objects in more detail.

# Documents

An XML document is a special construct designed to archive data in a way that is most convenient for parsers. It has nothing to do with our traditional concept of documents, like the Magna Carta or *Time* magazine, although those texts could be stored as XML documents. It simply is a way of describing a piece of XML as being whole and intact for parsing.

It's important to think of the document as a *logical* entity rather than a *physical* one. In other words, don't assume that a document will be contained within a single file on a computer. Quite often, a document may be spread out across many files, and some of these may live on different systems. All that is required is that the XML parser reading the document has the ability to assemble the pieces into a coherent whole. Later, we will talk about mechanisms used in XML for linking discrete physical entities into a complete logical unit.

As Figure 2-2 shows, an XML document has two parts. First is the *document prolog*, a special section containing metadata. The second is an element called the *document element*, also called the *root element* for reasons you will understand when we talk about trees. The root element contains all the other elements and content in the document.

The prolog is optional. If you leave it out, the parser will fall back on its default settings. For example, it automatically selects the character encoding UTF-8 (or

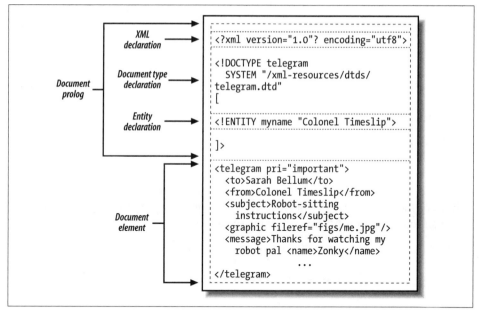

*Figure 2-2. Parts of an XML document*

UTF-16, if detected) unless something else is specified. The root element is required, because a document without data is just not a document.[*]

## The Document Prolog

Being a flexible markup language toolkit, XML lets you use different character encodings, define your own grammars, and store parts of the document in many places. An XML parser needs to know about these particulars before it can start its work. You communicate these options to the parser through a construct called the document prolog.

The document prolog (if you use one) comes at the top of the document, before the root element. There are two parts (both optional): an XML declaration and a document type declaration.[†] The first sets parameters for basic XML parsing while the second is for more advanced settings. The XML declaration, if used, has to be the first line in the document. Example 2-1 shows a document containing a full prolog.

---

[*] Interestingly, there is no rule that says the root element has to contain anything. This leads to the amusing fact that the following smiley of a perplexed, bearded dunce is a well-formed document: <:-/>. It's an empty element whose name is ":-".

[†] Don't confuse *document type declaration* with *document type definition*, a completely different beast. To keep the two terms distinct, I will always refer to the latter one with the acronym "DTD."

*Example 2-1. A document with a full prolog*

```
<?xml version="1.0" standalone="no"?>       The XML declaration
<!DOCTYPE                                    Beginning of the DOCTYPE declaration
  reminder                                   Root element name
  SYSTEM "/home/eray/reminder.dtd"           DTD identifier
  [                                          Internal subset start delimiter
    <!ENTITY smile "<graphic file="smile.eps"/>">  Entity declaration
  ]>                                         Internal subset end delimiter
<reminder>                                   Start of document element
  &smile;                                    Reference to the entity declared above
  <msg>Smile! It can always get worse.</msg>
</reminder>                                  End of document element
```

## The XML Declaration

The XML declaration is a small collection of details that prepare an XML processor for working with a document. It is optional, but when used it must always appear in the first line. Figure 2-3 shows the form it takes. It starts with the delimiter <?xml (1), contains a number of parameters (2), and ends with the delimiter ?> (3).

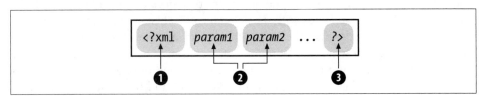

*Figure 2-3. Form of the XML declaration*

Each parameter consists of a name, an equals sign (=), and a quoted value. The version parameter must appear if the other parameters are used:

version

> Declares the version of XML used. At the moment, only version 1.0 is officially recognized, but version 1.1 may be available soon.

encoding

> Defines the character encoding used in the document. If undefined, the default encoding UTF-8 (or UTF-16, if the document begins with the xFEFF Byte Order Mark) will be used, which works fine for most documents used in English-speaking countries. Character encodings are explained in Chapter 9.

standalone

> Informs the parser whether there are any declarations outside of the document. As I explain in the next section, declarations are constructs that contribute information to the parser for assembling and validating a document. The default value is "no"; setting it to "yes" tells the processor there are no external declarations required for parsing the document. It does not, as the name may seem to imply, mean that no other resources need to be loaded. There could well be parts of the document in other files.

Parameter names and values are case-sensitive. The names are always lowercase. Order is important; the version must come before the encoding which must precede the standalone parameter. Either single or double quotes may be used. Here are some examples of XML declarations:

```
<?xml?>
<?xml version="1.0"?>
<?xml version='1.0' encoding='US-ASCII' standalone='yes'?>
<?xml version = '1.0' encoding= 'iso-8859-1' standalone ="no"?>
```

## The Document Type Declaration

There are two reasons why you would want to use a document type declaration. The first is to define entities or default attribute values. The second is to support validation, a special mode of parsing that checks grammar and vocabulary of markup. A validating parser needs to read a list of declarations for element rules before it can begin to parse. In both cases, you need to make declarations available, and the place to do that is in the document type declaration section.

Figure 2-4 shows the basic form of the document type declaration. It begins with the delimiter <!DOCTYPE (1) and ends with the delimiter > (7). Inside, the first part is an element name (2), which identifies the type of the document element. Next is an optional identifier for the document type definition (3), which may be a path to a file on the system, a URL to a file on the Internet, or some other kind of unique name meaningful to the parser. The last part, enclosed in brackets (4 and 6), is an optional list of entity declarations (5) called the *internal subset*. It complements the external document type definition which is called the *external subset*. Together, the internal and external subsets form a collection of declarations necessary for parsing and validation.

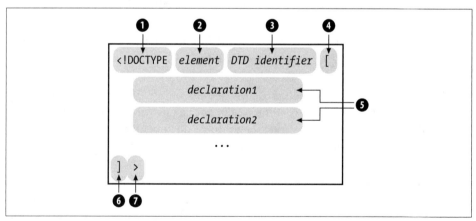

*Figure 2-4. Form of the document type declaration*

### System and public identifiers

The DTD identifier supports two methods of identification: system-specific and public. A *system identifier* takes the form shown in Figure 2-5, the keyword SYSTEM (1) followed by a physical address (3) such as a filesystem path or URI, in quotes (2).

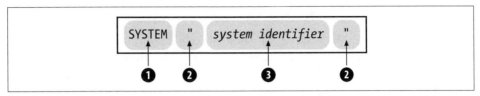

*Figure 2-5. Form of the system identifier*

Here is an example with a system identifier. It points to a file called *simple.dtd* in the local filesystem.

```
<!DOCTYPE doc
    SYSTEM "/usr/local/xml/dtds/simple.dtd">
```

An alternative scheme to system identifiers is the *public identifier*. Unlike a system path or URI that can change anytime an administrator feels like moving things around, a public identifier is never supposed to change, just as a person may move from one city to another, but her social security number remains the same. The problem is that so far, not many parsers know what to do with public identifiers, and there is no single official registry mapping them to physical locations. For that reason, public identifiers are not considered reliable on their own, and must include an emergency backup system identifier.

Figure 2-6 shows the form of a public identifier. It starts with the keyword PUBLIC (1), and follows with a character string (3) in quotes (2), and the backup system identifier (4), also in quotes (2).

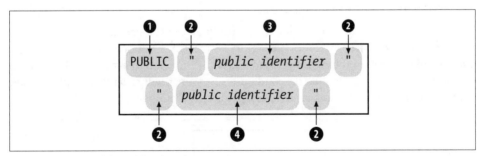

*Figure 2-6. Form of the public identifier*

Here is an example with a public identifier:

```
<!DOCTYPE html
    PUBLIC "-//W3C//DTD HTML 3.2//EN"
    "http://www.w3.org/TR/HTML/html.dtd">
```

## Declarations

Declarations are pieces of information needed to assemble and validate the document. The XML parser first reads declarations from the external subset (given by the system or public identifier), then reads declarations from the internal subset (the portion in square brackets) in the order they appear. In this chapter, I will only talk about what goes in the internal subset, leaving the external subset for Chapter 3.

There are several kinds of declarations. Some have to do with validation, describing what an element may or may not contain (again, I will go over these in Chapter 3). Another kind is the *entity declaration*, which creates a named piece of XML that can be inserted anywhere in the document.

The form of an entity declaration is shown in Figure 2-7. It begins with the delimiter <!ENTITY (1), is followed by a name (2), then a value or identifier (3), and the closing delimiter > (4).

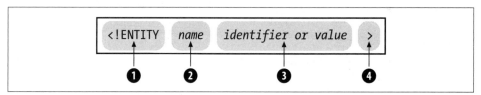

*Figure 2-7. Form of an entity declaration*

The value or identifier portion may be a system identifier or public identifier, using the same forms shown in Figure 2-5 and Figure 2-6. This associates a name with a piece of XML in a file outside of the document. That segment of XML becomes an *entity*, which is a component of the document that the parser will insert before parsing. For example, this entity declaration creates an entity named chap2 out of the file *ch02.xml*:

    <!ENTITY chap2 SYSTEM "ch02.xml">

You can insert this entity in the document using an *entity reference* which takes the form in Figure 2-8. It consists of the entity name (2), bounded on the left by an ampersand (1), and on the right by a semicolon (3). You can insert it anywhere in the document element or one of its descendants. The parser will replace it with its value, taken from the external resource, before parsing the document.

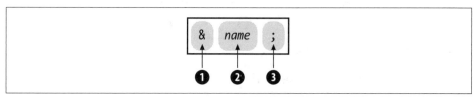

*Figure 2-8. Form of an entity reference*

In this example, the entity reference is inserted in the XML inside a book element:

```
<book><title>My Exciting Book</title>
&chap2;
</book>
```

Alternatively, an entity declaration may specify an explicit value instead of a system or public identifier. This takes the form of a quoted string. The string can be mixed content (any combination of elements and character data). For example, this declaration creates an entity called `jobtitle` and assigns it the text `<jobtitle>Herder of Cats</jobtitle>`:

```
<!ENTITY jobtitle "<jobtitle>Herder of Cats</jobtitle>">
```

We're really just scratching the surface of entities. I'll cover entities in much greater depth later in the chapter.

# Elements

Elements are the building blocks of XML, dividing a document into a hierarchy of regions, each serving a specific purpose. Some elements are containers, holding text or elements. Others are empty, marking a place for some special processing such as importing a media object. In this section, I'll describe the rules for how to construct elements.

## Syntax

Figure 2-9 shows the syntax for a container element. It begins with a start tag consisting of an angle bracket (1) followed by a name (2). The start tag may contain some attributes (3) separated by whitespace, and it ends with a closing angle bracket (4). After the start tag is the element's content and then an end tag. The end tag consists of an opening angle bracket and a slash (5), the element's name again (2), and a closing bracket (4). The name in the end tag must match the one in the start tag exactly.

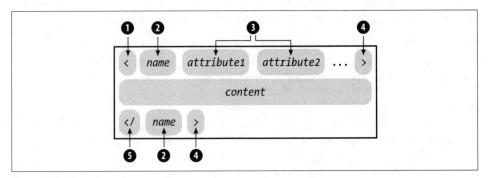

*Figure 2-9. Container element syntax*

An empty element is very similar, as seen in Figure 2-10. It starts with an angle bracket delimiter (1), and contains a name (2) and a number of attributes (3). It is closed with a slash and a closing angle bracket (4). It has no content, so there is no need for an end tag.

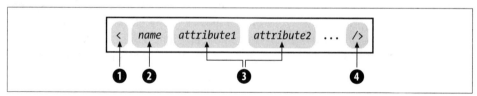

*Figure 2-10. Empty element syntax*

An attribute defines a property of the element. It associates a name with a value, which is a string of character data. The syntax, shown in Figure 2-11 is a name (1), followed by an equals sign (2), and a string (4) inside quotes (3). Two kinds of quotes are allowed: double (") and single ('). Quote characters around an attribute value must match.

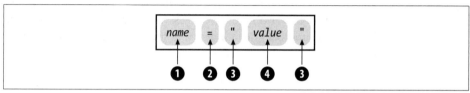

*Figure 2-11. Form of an attribute*

Element naming must follow the rules of *XML names*, a generic term in the XML specification that also applies to names of attributes and some other kinds of markup. An XML name can contain any alphanumeric characters (a–z, A–Z, and 0–9), accented characters like ç, or characters from non-Latin scripts like Greek, Arabic, or Katakana. The only punctuation allowed in names are the hyphen (-), underscore (_) and period (.). The colon (:) is reserved for another purpose, which I will explain later. Names can only start with a letter, ideograph, or underscore. Names are case-sensitive, so Para, para, and pArA are three different elements.

The following elements are well-formed:

```
<to-do>Clean fish tank</to-do>
<street_address>1420 Sesame Street</street_address>
<MP3.name>Where my doggies at?</MP3.name>
<α3/>
<_-_>goofy, but legal</_-_>
```

These element names are not:

```
<-item>Bathe the badger</-item>
<2nd-phone-number>785-555-1001</2nd-phone-number>
<notes+comments>Huh?</notes+commments>
```

Technically, there is no limit to the length of an XML name. Practically speaking, anything over 50 characters is probably too long.

Inserting whitespace characters (tab, newline, and space) inside the tag is fine, as long as they aren't between the opening angle bracket and the element name. These characters are used to separate attributes. They are also often used to make tags more readable. In the following example, all of the whitespace characters are allowed:

```
<boat
  type="trireme"
><crewmember   class="rower">Dronicus Laborius</crewmember   >
```

There are a few important rules about the tags of container elements. The names in the start and end tags must be identical. An end tag has to come after (never before) the start tag. And both tags have to reside within the same parent element. Violating the last rule is an error called *overlapping*. It's an ambiguous situation where each element seems to contain the other, as you can see here:

```
<a>Don't <b>do</a> this!</b>
```

These untangled elements are okay:

```
<a>No problem</a><b>here</b>
```

Container elements may contain elements or character data or both. Content with both characters and elements is called *mixed content*. For example, here is an element with mixed content:

```
<para>I like to ride my motorcycle
<emphasis>really</emphasis> fast.</para>
```

## Attributes

In the element start tag you can add more information about the element in the form of attributes. An *attribute* is a name-value pair. You can use it to add a unique label to an element, place it in a category, add a Boolean flag, or otherwise associate some short string of data. In Chapter 1, I used an attribute in the telegram element to set a priority level.

One reason to use attributes is if you want to distinguish between elements of the same name. You don't always want to create a new element for every situation, so an attribute can add a little more granularity in differentiating between elements. In narrative applications like DocBook or HTML, it's common to see attributes like class and role used for this purpose. For example:

```
<message class="tip">When making crop circles,
push down <emphasis>gently</emphasis> on the stalks to
avoid breaking them.</message>

<message class="warning">Farmers don't like finding people in
their fields at night, so be <emphasis role="bold">very
quiet</emphasis> when making crop circles.</message>
```

The class attribute might be used by a stylesheet to specify a special typeface or color. It might format the `<message class="warning">` with a thick border and an icon containing an exclamation point, while the `<message class="tip">` gets an icon of a light bulb and a thin border. The emphasis elements are distinguished in whether they have an attribute at all. The second does, and its purpose is to override the default style, whatever that may be.

Another way an attribute can distinguish an element is with a *unique identifier*, a string of characters that is unique to one particular element in the document. No other element may have the same identifier. This gives you a way to select that one element for special treatment, for cross referencing, excerpting, and so on.

For example, suppose you have a catalog with hundreds of product descriptions. Each description is inside a product element. You want to create an index of products, with one line per product. How do you refer to a particular product among hundreds? The answer is to give each a uniquely identifying label:

```
<product id="display-15-inch-apple">
  ...
</product>
<product id="display-15-inch-sony">
  ...
</product>
<product id="display-15-inch-ibm">
  ...
</product>
```

There is no limit to how many attributes an element can have, as long as no two attributes have the same name. Here's an example of an element start tag with three attributes:

```
<kiosk music="bagpipes" color="red" id="page-81527">
```

This example is not allowed:

```
<!-- Wrong -->
<team person="sue" person="joe" person="jane">
```

To get around this limitation, you could use one attribute to hold all the values:

```
<team persons="sue joe jane">
```

You could also use attributes with different names:

```
<team person1="sue" person2="joe" person3="jane">
```

Or use elements instead:

```
<team>
  <person>sue</person>
  <person>joe</person>
  <person>jane</person>
</team>
```

In a DTD, attributes can be declared to be of certain types. An attribute can have an enumerated value, meaning that the value must be one of a predefined set. Or it may have a type that registers it as a unique identifier (no other element can have the same value). It may be an identifier reference type, requiring that another element somewhere has an identifier attribute that matches. A validating parser will check all of these attribute types and report deviations from the DTD. I'll have more to say about declaring attribute types in Chapter 4.

 Some attribute names are reserved in XML. Typically, they start with the prefix "xml," such as xmlns. To avoid a conflict, choose names that don't start with those letters.

## Namespaces

Namespaces are a mechanism by which element and attribute names can be assigned to groups. They are most often used when combining different vocabularies in the same document, as I did in Chapter 1. Look at that example, and you'll see attributes in some elements like this one:

```
<math xmlns="http://www.w3.org/1998/Math/MathML">
```

Example 2-2 is another case. The part-catalog element contains two namespaces which are declared by the attributes xmlns:nw and xmlns. The elements inside part-catalog and their attributes belong to one or the other namespace. Those in the first namespace can be identified by the prefix nw:.

*Example 2-2. Document with two namespaces*

```
<part-catalog
  xmlns:nw="http://www.nutware.com/"
  xmlns="http://www.bobco.com/"
>
  <nw:entry nw:number="1327">
    <nw:description>torque-balancing hexnut</nw:description>
  </nw:entry>
  <part id="555">
    <name>type 4 wingnut</name>
  </part>
</part-catalog>
```

The attributes of part-catalog are called *namespace declarations*. The general form of a namespace declaration is illustrated in Figure 2-12. It starts with the keyword xmlns: (1) is followed by a *namespace prefix* (2), an equals sign (3), and a *namespace identifier* (5) in quotes (4).

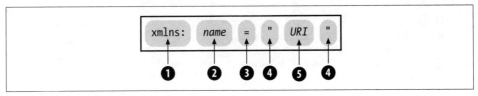

*Figure 2-12. Namespace declaration syntax*

Avoid using xml as a namespace prefix, as it is used in reserved attributes like xml:space.

In a special form of the declaration, the colon and namespace prefix are left out, creating an implicit (unnamed) namespace. The second namespace declared in the example above is an implicit namespace. part-catalog and any of its descendants without the namespace prefix nw: belong to the implicit namespace.

 Namespace identifiers are, by convention, assigned to the URL subset of URIs, not the more abstract URNs. This is not a requirement, however. The XML processor doesn't actually look up any information located at that site. The site may not even exist. So why use a URL?

The namespace has to be assigned some kind of unique identifier. URLs are unique. They often contain information about the company or organization. So it makes a good candidate.

Still, many have made the point that URLs are not really *meant* to be used as identifiers. Resources are moved around often, and URLs change. But since no one has found a better method yet, it looks like namespace assignments to URLs is here to stay.

To include an element or attribute in a namespace other than the implicit namespace, you must use the form in Figure 2-13. This is called a *fully qualified name*. To the left of the colon (2) is the namespace prefix (1), and to the right is the *local name* (3).

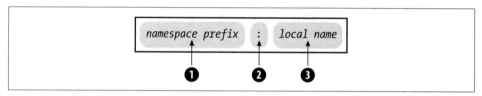

Figure 2-13. Fully qualified name

Namespaces only affect a limited area in the document. The element containing the declaration and all of its descendants are in the scope of the namespace. The element's siblings and ancestors are not. It is also possible to override a namespace by creating another one inside it with the same name. In the following example, there are two namespaces named flavor, yet the chocolate-shell element is in a different namespace from the element chewy-center. The element flavor:walnut is in the latter namespace.

```
<flavor:chocolate-shell
  xmlns:flavor="http://www.deliciouscandy.com/chocolate/">
  <flavor:chewy-center
    xmlns:flavor="http://www.deliciouscandy.com/caramel/">
    <flavor:walnut/>
  </flavor:chewy-center>
</flavor:chocolate-shell>
```

How an XML processor reacts when entering a new namespace depends on the application. For a web document, it may trigger a shift in processing from one kind (e.g., normal web text) to another (e.g., math formulae). Or, as in the case of XSLT, it may use namespaces to sort instructions from data where the former is kind of like a meta-markup.

Namespaces are a wonderful addition to XML, but because they were added after the XML specification, they've created a rather tricky problem. Namespaces do not get along with DTDs. If you want to test the validity of a document that uses non-implicit namespaces, chances are the test will fail. This is because there is no way to write a DTD to allow a document to use namespaces. DTDs want to constrain a document to a fixed set of elements, but namespaces open up documents to an unlimited number of elements. The only way to reconcile the two would be to declare every fully qualified name in the DTD which would not be practical. Until a future version of XML fixes this incompatibility, you will just have to give up validating documents that use multiple namespaces.

## Whitespace

You'll notice in my examples, I like to indent elements to clarify the structure of the document. Spaces, tabs, and newlines (collectively called *whitespace* characters) are often used to make a document more readable to the human eye. Take out this visual padding and your eyes will get tired very quickly. So why not add some spaces here and there where it will help?

One important issue is how whitespace should be treated by XML software. At the parser level, whitespace is always passed along with all the other character data to the application level of the program. However, some programs may then *normalize the space*. This process strips out whitespace in element-only content, and in the beginning and end of mixed content. It also collapses a sequence of whitespace characters into a single space.

If you want to prevent a program from removing any whitespace characters from an element, you can give it a hint in the form of the xml:space attribute. If you set this attribute to preserve, XML processing software is supposed to honor the request by leaving all whitespace characters intact.

Consider this XML-encoded haiku:

```
<poem xml:space="preserve">
A wind shakes the trees,
          An empty sound of sadness.
  The file      is not      here.
</poem>
```

I took some poetic license by putting a bunch of spaces in there. (Hey, it's art!) So how do I keep the XML processor from throwing out the extra space in its normalization process? I gave the poem element an attribute named xml:space, and set its value to preserve. In Chapter 4, I'll show you how to make this the standard behavior for an element, by making the attribute implicit in the element declaration.

 It is not necessary to declare a namespace for xml:space. This attribute is built into the XML specification and all XML processors should recognize it.

Some parsers, given a DTD for a document, will make reasonably smart guesses about which elements should preserve whitespace and which should not. Elements that are declared in a DTD to allow mixed content should preserve whitespace, since it may be part of the content. Elements not declared to allow text should have whitespace dropped, since any space in there is only to clarify the markup. However, you can't always rely on a parser to act correctly, so using the xml:space attribute is the safest option.

## Trees

Elements can be represented graphically as upside-down, tree-like structures. The outermost element, like the trunk of a tree, branches out into smaller elements which in turn branch into other elements until the very innermost content—empty elements and character data—is reached. You can think of the character data as leaves of the tree. Figure 2-14 shows the telegram document drawn as a tree.

Since every XML document has only one possible tree, the diagram acts like a fingerprint, uniquely identifying the document. It's this unambiguous structure that makes XML so useful in containing data. The arboreal metaphor is also useful in thinking about how you would "move" through a document. Documents are parsed from beginning to end, naturally, which happens to correspond to a means of traversing a tree called *depth-first searching*. You start at the root, then move down the first branch to an element, take the first branch from there, and so on to the leaves. Then you backtrack to the last fork and take the next branch, as shown in Figure 2-15.

Let me give you some terminology about XML trees. Every point in a tree—be it an element, text, or something else—is called a *node*. This borrows from graph theory in mathematics, where a tree is a particular type of graph (directed, non-cyclic). Any branch of the tree can be snapped off and thought of as a tree too, just as you can plant the branch of a willow tree to make a new willow tree.* Branches of trees are often called *subtrees* or just trees. Collections of trees are appropriately called *groves*.

An XML tree or subtree (or subsubtree, or subsubsubtree…) must adhere to the rules of well-formedness. In other words, any branch you pluck out of a document could be run through an XML parser, which wouldn't know or care that it wasn't a

---

* Which is why you should never make fenceposts out of willow wood.

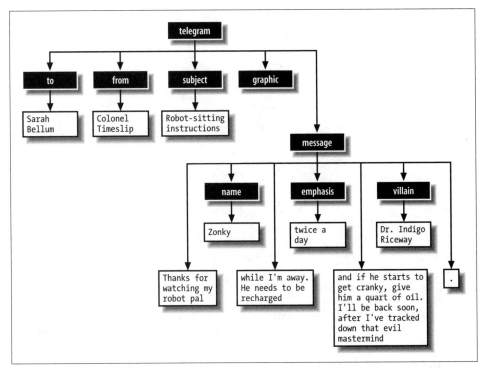

*Figure 2-14. A document tree*

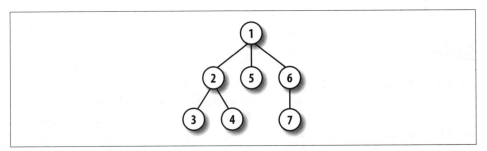

*Figure 2-15. Depth-first search*

complete document. But a grove (group of adjacent trees) is not well-formed XML. In order to be well-formed, all of the elements must be contained inside just one, the document element.

To describe elements in relation to one another, we use genealogical terms. Imagine that elements are like single-celled organisms, reproducing asexually. You can think of an element as the parent of the nodes it contains, known as its children. So the root of any tree is the progenitor of a whole family with numerous descendants. Likewise, a node may have ancestors and siblings. Siblings to the left (appearing earlier in the document) are *preceding siblings* while those to the right are *following siblings*. These relationships are illustrated in Figure 2-16.

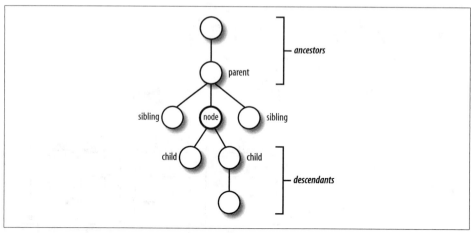

*Figure 2-16. Genealogical concepts*

The tree model of XML is also important because it represents the way XML is usually stored in computer memory. Each element and region of text is packaged in a cell with pointers to children and parents, and has an object-oriented interface with which to manipulate data. This system is convenient for developers because actions, like moving document parts around and searching for text, are easier and more efficient when separated into tree structures.

# Entities

Entities are placeholders in XML. You declare an entity in the document prolog or in a DTD, and you can refer to it many times in the document. Different types of entities have different uses. You can substitute characters that are difficult or impossible to type with character entities. You can pull in content that lives outside of your document with external entities. And rather than type the same thing over and over again, such as boilerplate text, you can instead define your own general entities.

Figure 2-17 shows the different kinds of entities and their roles. In the family tree of entity types, the two major branches are *parameter* entities and *general* entities. *Parameter entities* are used only in DTDs, so I'll talk about them later, in Chapter 4. This section will focus on the other type, general entities.

An entity consists of a name and a value. When an XML parser begins to process a document, it first reads a series of *declarations*, some of which define entities by associating a name with a value. The value is anything from a single character to a file of XML markup. As the parser scans the XML document, it encounters *entity references*, which are special markers derived from entity names. For each entity

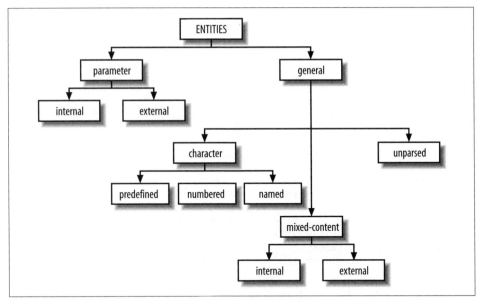

*Figure 2-17. Entity types*

reference, the parser consults a table in memory for something with which to replace the marker. It replaces the entity reference with the appropriate replacement text or markup, then resumes parsing just before that point, so the new text is parsed too. Any entity references inside the replacement text are also replaced; this process repeats as many times as necessary.

Recall from "The Document Type Declaration" earlier in this chapter that an entity reference consists of an ampersand (&), the entity name, and a semicolon (;). The following is an example of a document that declares three general entities and references them in the text:

```
<?xml version="1.0"?>
<!DOCTYPE message SYSTEM "/xmlstuff/dtds/message.dtd"
[
  <!ENTITY client "Mr. Rufus Xavier Sasperilla">
  <!ENTITY agent "Ms. Sally Tashuns">
  <!ENTITY phone "<number>617-555-1299</number>">
]>
<message>
<opening>Dear &client;</opening>
<body>We have an exciting opportunity for you! A set of
ocean-front cliff dwellings in Pi&#241;ata, Mexico, have been
renovated as time-share vacation homes. They're going fast! To
reserve a place for your holiday, call &agent; at &phone;.
Hurry, &client;. Time is running out!</body>
</message>
```

The entities &client;, &agent;, and &phone; are declared in the internal subset of this document (discussed in "The Document Type Declaration") and referenced in the

`<message>` element. A fourth entity, `&#241;`, is a numbered character entity that represents the character ñ. This entity is referenced but not declared; no declaration is necessary because numbered character entities are implicitly defined in XML as references to characters in the current character set. (For more information about character sets, see Chapter 9.) The XML parser simply replaces the entity with the correct character.

The previous example looks like this with all the entities resolved:

```
<?xml version="1.0"?>
<!DOCTYPE message SYSTEM "/xmlstuff/dtds/message.dtd">
<message>
<opening>Dear Mr. Rufus Xavier Sasperilla</opening>
<body>We have an exciting opportunity for you! A set of
ocean-front cliff dwellings in Piñata, Mexico, have been
renovated as time-share vacation homes. They're going fast! To
reserve a place for your holiday, call Ms. Sally Tashuns at
<number>617-555-1299</number>.
Hurry, Mr. Rufus Xavier Sasperilla. Time is running out!</body>
</message>
```

All entities (besides predefined ones, which I'll describe in a moment) must be declared before they are used in a document. Two acceptable places to declare them are in the internal subset, which is ideal for local entities, and in an external DTD, which is more suitable for entities shared between documents. If the parser runs across an entity reference that hasn't been declared, either implicitly (a predefined entity) or explicitly, it can't insert replacement text in the document because it doesn't know what to replace the entity with. This error prevents the document from being well-formed.

## Character Entities

Entities that contain a single character are called, naturally enough, *character entities*. These fall into a few groups:

*Predefined character entities*

Some characters cannot be used in the text of an XML document because they conflict with the special markup delimiters. For example, angle brackets (<>) are used to delimit element tags. The XML specification provides the following *predefined character entities*, so you can express these characters safely.

| Entity | Value |
|--------|-------|
| amp | & |
| apos | ' |
| gt | > |
| lt | < |
| quot | " |

*Numeric references*

XML supports Unicode, a huge character set with tens of thousands of different symbols, letters, and ideograms. You should be able to use any Unicode character in your document. It isn't easy, however, to enter a nonstandard character from a keyboard with less than 100 keys, or to represent one in a text-only editor display. One solution is to use a *numbered character reference* which refers to the character by its number in the Unicode character set.

The number in the entity name can be expressed in decimal or hexadecimal format. Figure 2-18 shows the form of a numeric character entity reference with a decimal number, consisting of the delimiter &# (1), the number (2), and a semicolon (3).

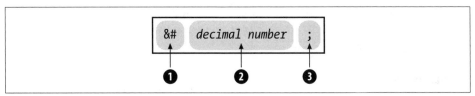

*Figure 2-18. Numeric character reference (decimal)*

Figure 2-19 shows another form using a hexadecimal number. The difference is that the start delimiter includes the letter "x."

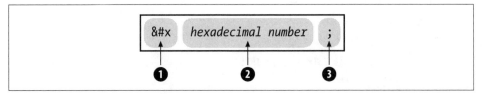

*Figure 2-19. Numeric character entity reference (hexadecimal)*

For example, a lowercase c with a cedilla (ç) is the 231st Unicode character. It can be represented in decimal as &#231; or in hexadecimal as &#xe7;. Note that the hexadecimal version is distinguished with an x as the prefix to the number. Valid characters are #x9, #xA, #xD, #x20 through #xD7FF, #xE000 through #xFFFD, and #x10000 through #x10FFFF. Since not all hexadecimal numbers map to valid characters, this is not a continuous range. I will discuss character sets and encodings in more detail in Chapter 9.

*Named character entities*

The problem with numbered character references is that they're hard to remember: you need to consult a table every time you want to use a special character. An easier way to remember them is to use mnemonic entity names. These *named character entities* use easy-to-remember names like &THORN;, which stands for the Icelandic capital thorn character (Þ).

Unlike the predefined and numeric character entities, you do have to declare named character entities. In fact, they are technically no different from other general entities. Nevertheless, it's useful to make the distinction, because large groups of such entities have been declared in DTD modules that you can use in your document. An example is ISO-8879, a standardized set of named character entities including Latin, Greek, Nordic, and Cyrillic scripts, math symbols, and various other useful characters found in European documents.

## Mixed-Content Entities

Entity values aren't limited to a single character, of course. The more general *mixed-content entities* have values of unlimited length and can include markup as well as text. These entities fall into two categories: internal and external. For *internal entities*, the replacement text is defined in the entity declaration; for *external entities*, it is located in another file.

### Internal entities

Internal mixed-content entities are most often used to stand in for oft-repeated phrases, names, and boilerplate text. Not only is an entity reference easier to type than a long piece of text, but it also improves accuracy and maintainability, since you only have to change an entity once for the effect to appear everywhere. The following example proves this point:

```
<?xml version="1.0"?>
<!DOCTYPE press-release SYSTEM "http://www.dtdland.org/dtds/reports.dtd"
[
  <!ENTITY bobco "Bob's Bolt Bazaar, Inc.">
]>
<press-release>
<title>&bobco; Earnings Report for Q3</title>
<par>The earnings report for &bobco; in fiscal
quarter Q3 is generally good. Sales of &bobco; bolts increased 35%
over this time a year ago.</par>
<par>&bobco; has been supplying high-quality bolts to contractors
for over a century, and &bobco; is recognized as a leader in the
construction-grade metal fastener industry.</par>
</press-release>
```

The entity &bobco; appears in the document five times. If you want to change something about the company name, you only have to enter the change in one place. For example, to make the name appear inside a companyname element, simply edit the entity declaration:

```
<!ENTITY bobco
  "<companyname>Bob's Bolt Bazaar, Inc.</companyname>">
```

When you include markup in entity declarations, be sure not to use the predefined character entities (e.g., &lt; and &gt;) to escape the markup. The parser knows to read the markup as an entity value because the value is quoted inside the entity declaration. Exceptions to this are the quote-character entity &quot; and the single-quote character entity &apos;. If they would conflict with the entity declaration's value delimiters, then use the predefined entities, e.g., if your value is in double quotes and you want it to contain a double quote.

Entities can contain entity references, as long as the entities being referenced have been declared previously. Be careful not to include references to the entity being declared, or you'll create a circular pattern that may get the parser stuck in a loop. Some parsers will catch the circular reference, but it is an error.

### External entities

Sometimes you may need to create an entity for such a large amount of mixed content that it is impractical to fit it all inside the entity declaration. In this case, you should use an *external entity*, an entity whose replacement text exists in another file. External entities are useful for importing content that is shared by many documents, or that changes too frequently to be stored inside the document. They also make it possible to split a large, monolithic document into smaller pieces that can be edited in tandem and that take up less space in network transfers.

External entities effectively break a document into multiple physical parts. However, all that matters to the XML processor is that the parts assemble into a perfect whole. That is, all the parts in their different locations must still conform to the well-formedness rules. The XML parser stitches up all the pieces into one logical document; with the correct markup, the physical divisions should be irrelevant to the meaning of the document.

External entities are a linking mechanism. They connect parts of a document that may exist on other systems, far across the Internet. The difference from traditional XML links (XLinks) is that for external entities the XML processor must insert the replacement text at the time of parsing.

External entities must always be declared so the parser knows where to find the replacement text. In the following example, a document declares the three external entities &part1;, &part2;, and &part3; to hold its content:

```
<?xml version="1.0"?>
<!DOCTYPE doc SYSTEM "http://www.dtds-r-us.com/generic.dtd"
[
  <!ENTITY part1 SYSTEM "p1.xml">
  <!ENTITY part2 SYSTEM "p2.xml">
  <!ENTITY part3 SYSTEM "p3.xml">
]>
<longdoc>
  &part1;
  &part2;
  &part3;
</longdoc>
```

As shown in Figure 2-20, the file at the top of the pyramid, which we might call the "master file," contains the document declarations and external entity references. The other files are subdocuments—they contain XML, but are not documents in their own right. You could not legally insert document prologs in them. Each may contain more than one XML tree. Though you can't validate them individually (you can only validate a complete document), any errors in a subdocument will affect the whole. External entities don't shield you from parse errors.

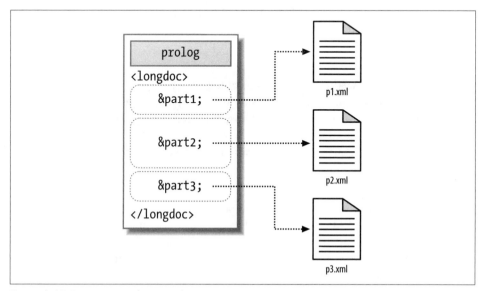

*Figure 2-20. Document with external entities*

 Whenever possible, make each subdocument contain at most one XML tree. While you can't validate a subdocument on its own, you can usually perform a well-formedness check if it has no more than one tree. The parser will think it's looking at a lone document without a prolog. This makes it a lot easier to manage a large document, especially if you have different people working on it at the same time. (This gets tricky if your subdocument uses entities defined in the main document, however.)

The syntax just shown for declaring an external entity uses the keyword SYSTEM followed by a quoted string containing a filename. This string is called a *system identifier* and is used to identify a resource by location. The quoted string is actually a URL, so you can include files from anywhere on the Internet. For example:

```
<!ENTITY catalog SYSTEM "http://www.bobsbolts.com/catalog.xml">
```

The system identifier suffers from the same drawback as all URLs: if the referenced item is moved, the link breaks. To avoid that problem, you can use a public identifier in the entity declaration. In theory, a public identifier will endure any location shuffling and still fetch the correct resource. For example:

```
<!ENTITY faraway PUBLIC "-//BOB//FILE Catalog//EN"
    "http://www.bobsbolts.com/catalog.xml">
```

Of course, for this to work, the XML processor has to know how to use public identifiers, and it must be able to find a catalog that maps them to actual locations. In addition, there's no guarantee that the catalog is up to date. A lot can go wrong. Perhaps for this reason, the public identifier must be accompanied by a system identifier (here, `"http://www.bobsbolts.com/catalog.xml"`). If the XML processor for some reason can't handle the public identifier, it falls back on the system identifier. Most web browsers in use today can't deal with public identifiers, so including a backup is a good idea.

 The W3C has been working on an alternative to external parsed entities, called XInclude. For details, see *http://www.w3.org/TR/xinclude/*.

## Unparsed Entities

The last kind of entity discussed in this chapter is the *unparsed entity*. This kind of entity holds content that should not be parsed because it contains something other than text or XML and would likely confuse the parser. The only place from which unparsed entities can be referred to is in an attribute value. They are used to import graphics, sound files, and other noncharacter data.

The declaration for an unparsed entity looks similar to that of an external entity, with some additional information at the end. For example:

```
<!DOCTYPE doc [
  <!ENTITY mypic SYSTEM "photos/erik.gif" NDATA GIF>
]>
<doc>
  <para>Here's a picture of me:</para>
  <graphic src="&mypic;" />
</doc>
```

This declaration differs from an external entity declaration in that there is an `NDATA` keyword following the system path information. This keyword tells the parser that the entity's content is in a special format, or *notation*, other than the usual parsed mixed content. The `NDATA` keyword is followed by a *notation identifier* that specifies the data format. In this case, the entity is a graphic file encoded in the GIF format, so the word `GIF` is appropriate.

# Miscellaneous Markup

Rounding out the list of markup objects are comments, processing instructions, and CDATA sections. They all have one thing in common: they shield content from the parser in some fashion. Comments keep text from ever getting to the parser. CDATA sections turn off the tag resolution, and processing instructions target specific processors.

## Comments

Comments are notes in the document that are not interpreted by the XML processor. If you're working with other people on the same files, these messages can be invaluable. They can be used to identify the purpose of files and sections to help navigate a cluttered document, or simply to communicate with each other.

Figure 2-21 shows the form of a comment. It starts with the delimiter <!-- (1) and ends with the delimiter --> (3). Between these delimiters goes the comment text (2) which can be just about any kind of text you want, including spaces, newlines, and markup. The only string not allowed inside a comment is two or more dashes in succession, since the parser would interpret that string as the end of the comment.

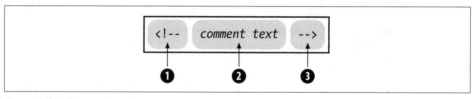

*Figure 2-21. Comment syntax*

Comments can go anywhere in your document except before the XML declaration and inside tags. The XML processor removes them completely before parsing begins. So this piece of XML:

```
<p>The quick brown fox jumped<!-- test -->over the lazy dog.
The quick brown <!-- test --> fox jumped over the lazy dog. The<!--

test

-->quick brown fox
jumped over the lazy dog.</p>
```

will look like this to the parser:

```
<p>The quick brown fox jumpedover the lazy dog.
The quick brown  fox jumped over the lazy dog. Thequick brown fox
jumped over the lazy dog.</p>
```

Since comments can contain markup, they can be used to "turn off" parts of a document. This is valuable when you want to remove a section temporarily, keeping it in the file for later use. In this example, a region of code is commented out:

```
<p>Our store is located at:</p>
<!--
<address>59 Sunspot Avenue</address>
-->
<address>210 Blather Street</address>
```

When using this technique, be careful not to comment out any comments, i.e., don't put comments inside comments. Since they contain double dashes in their delimiters, the parser will complain when it gets to the inner comment.

## CDATA Sections

If you mark up characters frequently in your text, you may find it tedious to use the predefined entities &lt;, &gt;, and &amp;. They require typing and are generally hard to read in the markup. There's another way to include lots of forbidden characters, however: the CDATA section.

CDATA is an acronym for "character data," which just means "not markup." Essentially, you're telling the parser that this section of the document contains no markup and should be treated as regular text. The only thing that cannot go inside a CDATA section is the ending delimiter (]]>).

A CDATA section begins with the nine-character delimiter <![CDATA[ (1), and it ends with the delimiter ]]> (3). The content of the section (2) may contain markup characters (<, >, and &), but they are ignored by the XML processor (see Figure 2-22).

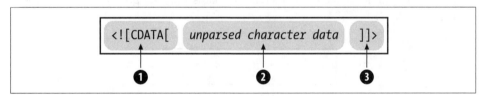

*Figure 2-22. CDATA section syntax*

Here's an example of a CDATA section in action:

```
<para>Then you can say "<![CDATA[if (&x < &y)]]>" and be done
with it.</para>
```

This is effectively the same as:

```
<para>Then you can say "if (&amp;x &lt; &amp;y)" and be done
with it.</para>
```

CDATA sections are convenient for large swaths of text that contains a lot of forbidden characters. However, the very thing that makes them useful can also be a problem. You will not be able to use any elements or attributes inside the marked region. If that's a problem for you, then you would probably be better off using character entity references or entities.

 You can't nest CDATA sections, because the closing ]]> of the nested CDATA section will be treated as the end of the first CDATA section. Because of its role in CDATA sections, you also can't use an unescaped ]]> *anywhere* in XML document text.

## Processing Instructions

Presentational information should be kept out of a document whenever possible. Still, there may be times when you don't have any other option, for example, if you need to store page numbers in the document to facilitate generation of an index. This information applies only to a specific XML processor and may be irrelevant or misleading to others. The prescription for this kind of information is a *processing instruction*. It is a container for data that is targeted toward a specific XML processor.

Processing instructions (PIs) contain two pieces of information: a target keyword and some data. The parser passes processing instructions up to the next level of processing. If the processing instruction handler recognizes the target keyword, it may choose to use the data; otherwise, the data is discarded. How the data will help processing is up to the developer.

A PI (shown in Figure 2-23) starts with a two-character delimiter <? (1), followed by a *target* (2), an optional string of characters (3) that is the data portion of the PI, and a closing delimiter ?> (4).

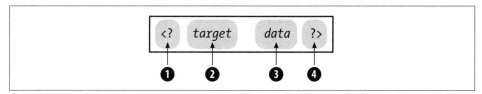

*Figure 2-23. Processing instruction syntax*

"Funny," you say, "PIs look a lot like the XML declaration." You're right: the XML declaration can be thought of as a processing instruction for all XML processors* that broadcast general information about the document, though the specification defines it as a different thing.

---

\* This syntactic trick allows XML documents to be processed by older SGML systems; they simply treat the XML declaration as another processing instruction, ignoring it since it obviously isn't meant for them.

The target is a keyword that an XML processor uses to determine whether the data is meant for it or not. The keyword doesn't necessarily mean anything, such as the name of the software that will use it. More than one program can use a PI, and a single program can accept multiple PIs. It's sort of like posting a message on a wall saying, "The party has moved to the green house," and people interested in the party will follow the instructions, while those who aren't interested won't.

The PI can contain any data except the combination ?>, which would be interpreted as the closing delimiter. Here are some examples of valid PIs:

```
<?flubber pg=9 recto?>
<?thingie?>
<?xyz stop: the presses?>
```

If there is no data string, the target keyword itself can function as the data. A forced line break is a good example. Imagine that there is a long section heading that extends off the page. Rather than relying on an automatic formatter to break the title just anywhere, we want to force it to break in a specific place.

Here is what a forced line break would look like:

```
<title>The Confabulation of Branklefitzers <?lb?>in a Portlebunky
Frammins <?lb?>Without Denaculization of <?lb?>Crunky Grabblefooties
</title>
```

Now you know all the ins and outs of markup. You can read and understand any XML document as if you were a living XML parser. But it still may not be clear to you *why* things are marked up as they are, or *how* to mark up a bunch of data. In the next chapter, I'll cover these issues as we look at the fascinating topic of data modeling.

# CHAPTER 3
# Modeling Information

Designing a markup language is a task similar to designing a building. First, you have to ask some questions: Who am I building it for? How will it be constructed? How will it be used? Do I give it many small rooms or a few large ones? Will the rooms be generic and interchangeable or specialized? Is there a role for the building, like storage, office space, or factory work? It takes a lot of planning to do it right.

When designing a markup language, there are many questions to answer: What constitutes a document? How detailed do you need it to be? How will it be generated? Is it flexible enough to handle every expected situation? Is it generic enough to support different formatting options and modes? Your decisions will help answer the most basic question which is, how can you represent a piece of information as XML? This problem is part of the important topic of data modeling.

In this chapter, we look at the ways in which different kinds of data are modelled using XML. First, I'll show you the most basic kinds of documents, simple collections of preferences for software applications. The next category covers narrative documents with characteristics such as text flows, block and inline elements, and titled sections. Lastly, under the broad umbrella of "complex" data, I'll talk about the myriad specialized markup languages for everything from vector graphics to remote procedure calls.

## Simple Data Storage

XML can be used like an extremely basic database. Since the early days of computer operating systems, data has been stored in files as tables, like the venerable */etc/ passwd* file:

```
nobody:*:-2:-2:Unprivileged User:/nohome:/noshell
root:*:0:0:System Administrator:/var/root:/bin/tcsh
daemon:*:1:1:System Services:/var/root:/noshell
smmsp:*:25:25:Sendmail User:/private/etc/mail:/noshell
```

Data like this isn't too hard to parse, but it has problems, too. Certain characters aren't allowed. Each record lives on a separate line, so data can't span lines. A syntax error is easy to create and may be difficult to locate. XML's explicit markup gives it natural immunity to these types of problems.

If you are writing a program that reads or saves data to a file, there are good reasons to go with XML. Parsers have been written to parse it already, so all you need to do is link to a library and use one of several easy interfaces: SAX, DOM, or XPath. Syntax errors are easy to catch, and that too is automated by the parser. Technologies like DTDs and Schema even check the structure and contents of elements for you, to ensure completeness and ordering.

## Dictionaries

A dictionary is a simple one-to-one mapping of properties to values. A property has a name, or *key*, which is a unique identifier. A dictionary is kind of like a table with two columns. It's a simple but very effective way to serialize data.

In the Macintosh OS X operating system, Apple selected XML as its format for preference files (called property lists). For the Chess program, the property list is in a file called *com.apple.Chess.plist*, shown here:

```
<?xml version="1.0" encoding="UTF-8"?>
<!DOCTYPE plist SYSTEM "file://localhost/System/Library/DTDs/PropertyList.dtd">
<plist version="0.9">
  <dict>
    <!--     KEY                    VALUE    -->
    <key>BothSides</key>           <false/>
    <key>Level</key>               <integer>1</integer>
    <key>PlayerHasWhite</key>      <true/>
    <key>SpeechRecognition</key>   <false/>
  </dict>
</plist>
```

Here the data is stored in a tabular form within a dict (dictionary) element. Each "row" is a pair of elements, the first a key (the name of a property), and the second a value. Values come in different types, such as the Boolean (true or false) and integer values you see here. The property SpeechRecognition is assigned the boolean value FALSE, which means that this feature is turned off in the program. The property Level (difficulty level) is set to 1 because I'm a lousy chess player.

Here's a more complex example. It's the property list for system sounds, *com.apple. soundpref.plist*:

```
<?xml version="1.0" encoding="UTF-8"?>
<!DOCTYPE plist PUBLIC "-//Apple Computer//DTD PLIST 1.0//EN" "http://www.apple.com/
DTDs/PropertyList-1.0.dtd">
<plist version="1.0">
```

```
<dict>
  <key>AlertsUseMainDevice</key>   <integer>1</integer>
  <key>Devices</key>
  <dict>
    <key>InputDevices</key>
    <dict>
      <key>AppleDBDMAAudioDMAEngine:0</key>
      <dict>
        <key>Balance</key>            <real>0.0</real>
        <key>DeviceLevels</key>       <array>
                                        <real>0.5</real>
                                        <real>0.5</real>
                                      </array>
        <key>Level</key>              <real>0.5</real>
      </dict>
    </dict>
    <key>OutputDevices</key>
    <dict>
      <key>AppleDBDMAAudioDMAEngine:0</key>
      <dict>
        <key>Balance</key>            <real>0.0</real>
        <key>DeviceLevels</key>       <array>
                                        <real>1</real>
                                        <real>1</real>
                                      </array>
        <key>Level</key>              <real>1</real>
      </dict>
    </dict>
  </dict>
</dict>
</plist>
```

In this example, the structure is recursive. A dict can be a value, allowing you to associate a key with a whole set of settings. This allows for better organization by creating categories like Devices and, under that, subcategories like InputDevices and OutputDevices. Notice also the array type, which associates multiple values to one key. Here, arrays are used to set the left and right volume levels.

I really like this way of storing preferences because it gives me two ways to access the data. I can fiddle with settings in the program's preferences window. The program would then update this XML file the moment I click on the "OK" button. Alternatively, I can edit the file myself. This may be an easier way to affect changes, especially if some features aren't addressed in the GUI. I can edit it in a text editor, or in the special application included with the Macintosh OS called *Property List Editor*, whose interface is very easy to use, as shown in Figure 3-1.

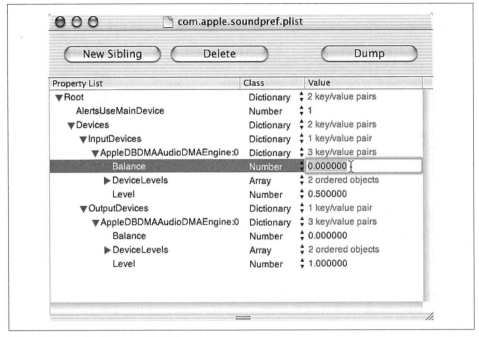

*Figure 3-1. Apple's Property List Editor*

# Records

A database typically stores information in *records*, packages of data that follow the same pattern as dictionaries. There are lots of records, each with the same set of data fields, sometimes accessed by a unique identifier. For example, a personnel database would have a record for each employee. Example 3-1 is a simple record-style XML document used for expense tracking.

*Example 3-1. A checkbook document*

```
<?xml version="1.0"?>
<checkbook balance-start="2460.62">
<title>expenses: january 2002</title>

  <debit category="clothes">
    <amount>31.19</amount>
    <date><year>2002</year><month>1</month><day>3</day></date>
    <payto>Walking Store</payto>
    <description>shoes</description>
  </debit>

  <deposit category="salary">
    <amount>1549.58</amount>
    <date><year>2002</year><month>1</month><day>7</day></date>
    <payor>Bob's Bolts</payor>
```

*Example 3-1. A checkbook document (continued)*

```
    </deposit>

    <debit category="withdrawal">
      <amount>40</amount>
      <date><year>2002</year><month>1</month><day>8</day></date>
      <description>pocket money</description>
    </debit>

    <debit category="savings">
      <amount>25</amount>
      <date><year>2002</year><month>1</month><day>8</day></date>
    </debit>

    <debit category="medical" check="855">
      <amount>188.20</amount>
      <date><year>2002</year><month>1</month><day>8</day></date>
      <payto>Boston Endodontics</payto>
      <description>cavity</description>
    </debit>

    <debit category="supplies">
      <amount>10.58</amount>
      <date><year>2002</year><month>1</month><day>10</day></date>
      <payto>Exxon Saugus</payto>
      <description>gasoline</description>
    </debit>

    <debit category="car">
      <amount>909.56</amount>
      <date><year>2002</year><month>1</month><day>14</day></date>
      <payto>Honda North</payto>
      <description>car repairs</description>
    </debit>

    <debit category="food">
      <amount>24.30</amount>
      <date><year>2002</year><month>1</month><day>15</day></date>
      <payto>Johnny Rockets</payto>
      <description>lunch</description>
    </debit>
</checkbook>
```

Each record is either a debit (expense) or a deposit (income). It contains information about the expense/income category, to whom I paid money (or received money from), the date it happened, and a brief description. I have used documents like this to balance my checkbook and summarize expenses in tables so I can figure out where all my money goes.

How can you do this? I'll show you a quick program you can write in Perl to calculate the ending balance in the previous example. Example 3-2 shows a program that spits out a number on the command line.

*Example 3-2. A tabulate program*

```perl
#!/usr/bin/perl
use XML::LibXML;
my $parser = new XML::LibXML;
my $doc = $parser->parse_file( shift @ARGV );
my $balance = $doc->findvalue( '/checkbook/@balance-start' );
foreach my $record ( $doc->findnodes( '//debit' )) {
    $balance -= $record->findvalue( 'amount' );
}
foreach my $record ( $doc->findnodes( '//deposit' )) {
    $balance += $record->findvalue( 'amount' );
}
print "Current balance: $balance\n";
```

The library XML::LibXML parses the document and stores it in an object tree called $doc. This object supports two interfaces: DOM and XPath. I used XPath queries as arguments to the methods findnodes( ) and findvalue( ) to reach into parts of the document and pull out elements and character data. What could be easier?

Run the above program on the data file and you'll get:

```
$ tab data
Current balance: 2781.37
```

This example shows how XML makes reading and accessing data easy for the programmer. What's more, the XML is flexible enough to allow you to restructure the data without rewriting the program. Adding new fields, such as an ID attribute or a time element, wouldn't affect the program a bit. With an ad hoc solution like the colon-delimited */etc/passwd* file, you would not have that kind of flexibility.

## XML and Databases

XML is very good at modelling simple data structures like the examples you've seen so far. We've seen all kinds of data types represented: strings, integers, real numbers, arrays, dictionaries, records. XML is easier to modify than flat files, with minimal impact on processing software, so you can add or remove fields as you like. Writing programs to process the data is easy, since much of the parsing work has been abstracted out, and plenty of interfaces are available. Since XML support is ubiquitous, there are many ways to modify the data.

The downside is that XML is not optimized for rapid, repetitive access. An XML parser has to read the entire document to pick out even a single detail, a huge overhead for one lookup. As the document grows, the access time gets longer. Storing it in memory isn't much better, since searches are not optimized for finding records by unique identifier. It's not as bad as doing an exhaustive search through many files, but not as good as a true database.

Dedicated databases are designed to store data in a way that is independent of the size and number of records. They are fast, but they lack the flexibility and ease of access of XML. A data processing program must access the data indirectly, through an interface like SQL. This can be cumbersome because data is stored in separate rows of a table, and it may take several queries to reach the right data point. Even worse, no two databases work the same way. Each has its quirks and refinements that make it difficult or impossible to write universal software without some kind of middleware adapter.

Storing data as XML versus storing it in a database does not have to be an exclusive choice. There is no reason why you can't do both at once. One technique I have used is to store XML in a database. Consider the document in Example 3-3. It contains a number of villain elements, each with an id attribute containing a unique identifier.

*Example 3-3. An XML document to put in a database*

```
<villain-database>
  <villain id="v1">
    <name>Darth Vader</name>
    <evil>8</evil>
    <intelligence>9</intelligence>
    <fashion>5</fashion>
  </villain>
  <villain id="v3">
    <name>Doctor Evil</name>
    <evil>6</evil>
    <intelligence>6</intelligence>
    <fashion>8</fashion>
  </villain>
  <villain id="v4">
    <name>Scorpius</name>
    <evil>9</evil>
    <intelligence>9</intelligence>
    <fashion>4</fashion>
  </villain>
</villain-database>
```

You want to be able to access a villain by id attribute. As an XML document, this access would be slow. If the record is near the bottom, the XML processor needs to read through most of the document before it gets there. With thousands of villain elements, that search could take a very long time.

Now let us create a database with a table that matches the following schema. I will use SQL data types.

| Field | Data type |
|---|---|
| id | varchar(8) |
| content | text |

You can store the information from Example 3-3 in the database. Each villain element will be a row in the table we just created. Get the id from the attribute in villain, and put the rest of the element in the content field. Here is what the table would look like:

| id | content |
| --- | --- |
| v1 | `<villain> <name>Darth Vader</name> <evil>8</evil> <intelligence>9</intelligence> <fashion>5</fashion> </villain>` |
| v3 | `<villain> <name>Doctor Evil</name> <evil>6</evil> <intelligence>6</intelligence> <fashion>8</fashion> </villain>` |
| v4 | `<villain> <name>Scorpius</name> <evil>9</evil> <intelligence>9</intelligence> <fashion>4</fashion> </villain>` |

In this arrangement, you can search quickly for records using the id as a primary key. The content field still contains the content of each record as XML. An advantage to keeping XML in a field is that you can add or remove elements any time without affecting the rest of the database. A disadvantage to storing data in elements instead of fields is that you can't use the database's built-in functionality, such as searching on one of those fields or checking the validity of an element's value. If you only need to search for a record using the id and will validate the content on your own, then this method works well. A good application of this arrangement is a web content management system, where the content is HTML to be served as a page.

Another way to combine the performance of databases with the convenience of XML is to convert database queries into XML. You store the data exclusively in the database's native field types, but when you retrieve information, a piece of code translates it into XML in real time. For example, someone may write a SAX driver tailored to the particular brand of database you are using. It would be simple to write a program that interfaces with this driver to assemble an XML document containing requested data. We will go over SAX in Chapter 10.

## Narrative Documents

Now let's look at an important category of XML. A *narrative document* contains text meant to be read by people rather than machines. Web pages, books, journals, articles, and essays are all narrative documents. These documents have some common traits. First, order of elements is inviolate. Try reading a book backward and you'll agree it's much less interesting that way (and it gives away the ending). The text runs in a single path called a *flow*, which the reader follows from beginning to end.

Another key feature of narrative documents is specialized element groups, including sections, blocks, and inlines. Sections are what you would imagine: elements that break up the document into parts like chapters, subsections, and so on. Blocks are rectangular regions such as titles and paragraphs. Inlines are strings inside those blocks specially marked for formatting. Figure 3-2 shows how a typical formatted document would render these elements.

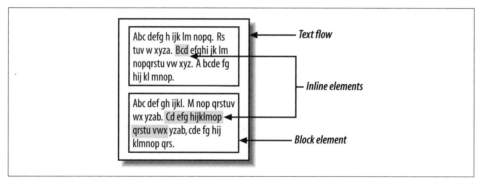

*Figure 3-2. Flows, blocks, inlines*

## Flows and Sections

A narrative document contains at least one *flow*, a stream of text to be read continuously from start to finish. If there are multiple flows, one will be dominant, branching occasionally into short tangential flows like sidebars, notes, tips, warnings, footnotes, and so on. The main flow is typically formatted as a column, while other flows are often in boxes interrupting the main flow, or moved to the side or the very end, with some kind of link (e.g., a footnote symbol).

Markup for flows are varied. Some XML applications like XHTML do not support more than one flow. Others, like DocBook, have rich support for flows, encapsulating them as elements inside the main flow. The best representations allow flows to be moved around, floated within the confines of the formatted page.

The main flow is broken up into *sections*, which are hierarchical divisions that organize the document by topics, usually with titles or *heads*. For example, a book is divided into chapters, which are subdivided into sections and subsections and subsubsections. It is often convenient to treat these divisions as separate entities which can be stored in their own files and imported using the external entity mechanism. This is useful if different people are working on sections in parallel, such as with articles of a journal.

Sections are coded in two common ways. In the first (and less flexible) scheme, the section head is tagged, but no element is used to denote the boundary of the section, like this:

```
<bighead>A major section</bighead>
<head>A cute little section</head>
<paragraph>Some text...</paragraph>
<head>Another cute little section</head>
<paragraph>Some text...</paragraph>
```

In the other (better) scheme, the section has definite boundaries created by a container element:

```
<section>
  <head>A major section</head>
  <subsection>
    <head>A cute little section</head>
    <paragraph>Some text...</paragraph>
  </subsection>
  <subsection>
    <head>Another cute little section</head>
    <paragraph>Some text...</paragraph>
  </subsection>
</section>
```

The first is called a *flat* structure. It is less desirable because it relies on presentational details to divine where parts of the document begin and end. In this case, a bigger head means a larger section is beginning, and a small head indicates a subsection is starting. It's harder to write software to recognize the details of flat structures than of *hierarchical* structures. XHTML, for example, is typically flat. In contrast, the markup language DocBook is hierarchical. We'll see examples of these shortly.

## Blocks and Inlines

A *block* is a type of element that contains a segment of a flow and is typically formatted as a rectangular region, separated from other blocks by space above and below. Unlike sections, blocks hold mixed content, both character data and elements. Examples of blocks are paragraphs, section heads, and list items.

Elements inside blocks are called *inline elements* because they follow the line of text. They begin and end within the lines scanning from left to right (or right to left, if we're reading Arabic). Inlines are used to mark words or phrases for special formatting from the surrounding text in the block. Examples include emphasis, glossary terms, and important names.

Here is an example of a block with inlines:

```
<para><person>R. Buckminster Fuller</person> once
said, <quote>When people learned to do <emphasis>more</emphasis> with
<emphasis>less</emphasis>, it was their lever to industrial
success.</quote></para>
```

The element para is a block, containing a whole paragraph of text. Inside it are three inline element types: person, quote, and emphasis. The quote element contains elements itself (the two emphasis elements), but is still considered an inline, since it begins and ends within the text line of the block.

There are different reasons to use inlines. One is to control how the text formats. In this case, a formatter will probably replace the quote start and end tags with quotation marks. For emphasis elements, it might render the contents in italic, underline, or bold.

Another role for inlines is to mark text for special processing. The person element may have no special treatment by the formatter, but could be useful in other ways. Marking items as "person," "place," "definition," or whatever, makes it possible to mine data from the document to generate indexes, glossaries, search tables, and much more.

## Complex Structures

Not all structures found in narrative documents can be so readily classified as blocks or inlines. A table is not really a block, but an array of blocks. An illustration has no character data so it can't be considered a block. Lists also have their own rules, with indentation, autonumbering or bullets, and nesting. Objects like these are necessary complications for the narrative model.

Handling these structures properly is a tricky subject, but you can make some assumptions. For one thing, these structures usually remain inside the flow, interrupting the surrounding text briefly. It's as if the XML is an ocean of narrative-style markup broken up with little islands of complex markup.

Structures like figures and tables may *float* within the flow, meaning that the formatter has some leeway in placing the objects to produce the best page layout. If a figure would cross a pagebreak in one place, the formatter may be able to reposition it elsewhere. For this reason, such objects usually have captions with references in the text that sound like "the data is summarized in Table 3-5." A simple attribute like float="yes" may be sufficient to represent this capability in the markup.

Complex objects behave a little like blocks in that they are usually separated vertically from each other and the surrounding text. They may have some of the spacing and padding properties as well. These details are usually settled in a stylesheet; XML doesn't (or shouldn't) tangle with presentational aspects any more than it has to.

## Metadata

*Metadata* is information about the document that is not part of the flow. It's useful to keep with the rest of the document, but it's not formatted, or else it's formatted in a special way, such as on a title page. Examples include author name, copyright date, publisher, revision history, ISBN, and catalog number.

In XHTML, for example, a whole part of the document, the head element, is reserved to hold metadata like the title, descriptive terms for search engines, links to stylesheets, and so on. In DocBook, metadata can be associated with individual sections, which is useful to associate authors with individual articles, for example.

## Linked Objects

The last bunch of oddball elements often found in narrative documents can be classified as *linked objects*. These are elements that act as bookmarks in a document. The
way you might stick a paperclip on a page or bend over the corner to mark the page
is how they work.

First, there is the *cross reference*, an element that refers to a section or object somewhere else in the document. When formatted, it may be replaced with generated
text, such as the section number or title of the referred object. It may be turned into a
hyperlink, which when clicked transports the user directly to the object.

Another kind of linked object is an invisible marker. It has no overt function in the
flow other than to mark a location so that later, when generating an index, you can
calculate a page number or create a hyperlink. Index items often span a range of
pages, so you might want to capture the range with two markers, one at the beginning and one at the end.

## XHTML

Good old HTML is the markup language we are all familiar with. Simple, pretty,
easy to learn, it has turned the Internet from an obscure plaything of a few academ-
ics to a must-have utility for everyone. Its success can be attributed to the "good
enough" principle of web design. It's good enough to model almost any simple document as long as you don't mind its limitations: single-column format, flat structure,
and lack of page-oriented features.

The simplicity that made HTML so popular with novice publishers is frustrating to
professionals. Graphic designers crave better page layout capability and stylesheet
granularity. Web developers want better structure and navigation. Librarians and
researchers want more detailed metadata and search capability. Users with special
needs want more localization and customization. Poor HTML has been pushed to do
far more than it was ever designed to do.

None of this makes HTML a bad markup language. It will not go away anytime
soon, because it does its job well. It is a basic markup language for electronic display
and cross-document linking. However, it is now just one star in a constellation of
XML languages. If you need to do more, you can select other kinds of narrative
markup languages such as DocBook, which we will discuss later in the chapter.

First, let me clear up something that might be confusing to you. I use the terms
HTML and XHTML interchangeably. HTML is older than XML, so its earlier incar-
nations do not follow all the rules of well-formed XML documents. However, XML
was designed to make it as easy as possible to get HTML documents into good XML
form. HTML that is well-formed XML is simply called XHTML. From now on, when
I use the term *HTML*, I mean *XHTML*.

The best feature of HTML—so great it's responsible for half of the acronym—is *hypertext*: text that spans documents. Where the Web is concerned, the boundaries of documents are quite blurred. As a result, documents are typically small and with many nonlinear flows. It's easy to get lost, so navigation aids such as links at the top, bottom, or margin are required. But the basics, blocks and inlines, are the same as in XML.

Example 3-4 is a short XHTML document. I've taken the content of a manual page for the Unix command *cat* and reformatted it as HTML. In this example, pay attention to the blocks, inlines, and complex objects like lists.

*Example 3-4. An XHTML document*

```
<?xml version="1.0"?>
<!DOCTYPE html PUBLIC "-//W3C//DTD XHTML 1.0 Transitional//EN"
    "http://www.w3.org/TR/xhtml1/DTD/xhtml1-transitional.dtd">
<html>
  <head>
    <title>CAT(1) System General Commands Manual</title>
  </head>
  <body>
    <h1>CAT(1) System General Commands Manual</h1>
    <h2>NAME</h2>
    <p>cat - concatenate and print files</p>
    <h2>SYNOPSIS</h2>
    <p>cat [-benstuv] [-] [<em>file</em>...]</p>
    <h2>DESCRIPTION</h2>
    <p>
The <i>cat</i> utility reads files sequentially, writing them to the
standard output. The file operands are processed in command line
order. A single dash represents the standard input.
    </p>
    <p>
The options are as follows:
    </p>
    <dl>
      <dt>-b</dt>
      <dd>
Implies the <tt>-n</tt> option but doesn't number blank lines.
      </dd>
      <dt>-e</dt>
      <dd>
Implies the <tt>-v</tt> option, and displays a dollar sign ($) at
the end of each line as well.
      </dd>
      <dt>-n</dt>
      <dd>Numbers the output lines, starting at 1.</dd>
      <dt>-s</dt>
      <dd>
Squeezes multiple adjacent empty lines, causing the output to be single
spaced.
      </dd>
```

*Example 3-4. An XHTML document (continued)*

```
      <dt>-t</dt>
      <dd>
Implies the <tt>-v</tt> option, and displays tab characters as
<tt>^I</tt> as well.
      </dd>
      <dt>-u</dt>
      <dd>
The <tt>-u</tt> option guarantees that the output is unbuffered.
      </dd>
      <dt>-v</dt>
      <dd>
Displays non-printing characters so they are visible. Control
characters print as <tt>^X</tt> for control-X; the delete character
(octal 0177) prints as <tt>^?</tt> Non-ascii characters (with the high
bit set) are printed as <tt>M-</tt> (for meta) followed by the
character for the low 7 bits.
      </dd>
    </dl>
    <p>
The <i>cat</i> utility exits 0 on success, and &gt;0 if an error occurs.
    </p>
    <h2>BUGS</h2>
    <p>
Because of the shell language mechanism used to perform output
redirection, the command <tt>cat file1 file2 &gt; file1</tt> will cause
the original data in file1 to be destroyed!
    </p>
    <h2>SEE ALSO</h2>
    <ul>
      <li><a href="head.html">head(1)</a></li>
      <li><a href="more.html">more(1)</a></li>
      <li><a href="pr.html">pr(1)</a></li>
      <li><a href="tail.html">tail(1)</a></li>
      <li><a href="vis.html">vis(1)</a></li>
    </ul>
    <p>
Rob Pike, <i>UNIX Style, or cat -v Considered Harmful</i>, USENIX Summer
Conference Proceedings, 1983.
    </p>
    <h3>HISTORY</h3>
    <p>
A <i>cat</i> utility appeared in Version 6 AT&T UNIX.
    </p>
    <p>3rd Berkeley Distribution, May 2, 1995</p>
  </body>
</html>
```

This is a flat document structure. No elements were used to contain and divide sections. HTML does have an element called div that can be used as a section container; however, it is not specifically designed as such, nor is it used often in HTML documents.* div is more often used to divide regions for special formatting. So I stand by my assertion that HTML is essentially a flat-structured language.

Now direct your attention to the inlines in the example, tt and i. The names are abbreviations for presentational terms, "teletype" and "italic." Right there, you know something's wrong. HTML has few element types, but is meant to be used for many different types of document. So the inventors picked elements that are generic and style-oriented. As a result we're forced to mark up terms the way we want them to look rather than by what they are.

HTML does supply an inline element called span, which can be supplemented with attributes to fit all kinds of roles. For example, I could have used <span class="command"> for the *cat* command and <span class="citation"> for the reference to "UNIX Style...". This would allow some flexibility in designing a stylesheet, but it's really not using the full power of XML. It's just one element being stretched into many different roles.

Even some of the blocks have been forced into generic roles. The paragraph under the head "SYNOPSIS" isn't really a paragraph, is it? It's really something different, and I would prefer to use an element strictly for synopses or code listings. But HTML provides very few types of block elements and I am obligated to use whatever is available.

Using HTML for this example has good and bad points. The good side is that HTML is easy to use, so I was able to mark up the manual page in only a few minutes. With only a few element types to remember, I don't have to look in a book to know which one to use and how it will look when formatted. The downside is that now I have a document fit for only one purpose: displaying in a web browser. A printout is likely to look primitive. And for other purposes, like searching and indexing, the lack of granularity is likely to prevent me from doing anything truly useful.

Until I need the extra functionality, I'm happy with HTML. But if I ever plan to use a document in more than one way, I'll need to explore other options. Something more specific to my brand of data will fit better and give me more options. What I will show you next is a markup language specifically designed for the kind of information shown in the last example.

## DocBook

DocBook is a markup language designed specifically for technical documentation, modelling everything from one-page user manuals to thousand-page tomes. Like HTML, it predates XML and was first an SGML application. Also like HTML, it has migrated to XML and works very well in that framework.

---

* XHTML 2.0 is introducing new elements section and h, which will fill this gap.

Unlike HTML, DocBook is very large and comes with a steep learning curve. Its elements are very specialized. It has blocks for different kinds of code listings, scores of inlines for technical terms, and many kinds of sections. Some users of DocBook think that it may be too big. Others feel it's too loose, allowing for so many kinds of documents (within the technical documentation realm) that it suffers from the ambiguity that hinders HTML. Despite these complaints, DocBook is and always has been the best markup language for technical documentation.

It's not hard to find tools and support for DocBook. Many XML editors (XMetaL and Adept, for example) come with DocBook packages already configured. Lots of stylesheets, schema, DTDs, and other aids are also available. This support is likely to continue as various groups, from publishers to the Linux Documentation Project, adopt DocBook as their default standard.

The first incarnation (Example 3-5) is a reformulation of the previous example. You'll see that the markup is a better fit for this type of data, and the element types are much more specific. Also note the introduction of section elements.

*Example 3-5. A DocBook reference page*

```
<?xml version="1.0"?>
<!DOCTYPE refentry PUBLIC "-//OASIS//DTD DocBook XML V4.1//EN"
    "/usr/local/dtds/docbook41/docbookx.dtd">
<refentry>
  <refnamediv>
    <refname>cat</refname>
    <manvolnum>1</manvolnum>
    <refmeta role="edition">
3rd Berkeley Distribution, May 2, 1995
    </refmeta>
    <refpurpose>concatenate and print files</refpurpose>
  </refnamediv>
  <refsynopsisdiv>
    <synopsis>cat [-benstuv] [-]
  [<replaceable>file</replaceable>...]</synopsis>
  </refsynopsisdiv>
  <refsect1><title>Description</title>
    <para>The <command>cat</command> utility reads files sequentially, writing
them to the standard output. The file operands are processed in
command line order. A single dash represents the standard input.</para>
    <para>The options are as follows:</para>
    <variablelist>
      <varlistentry><term><option>-b</option></term>
        <listitem><para>Implies the <option>-n</option> option but doesn't number blank
lines.</para></listitem>
      </varlistentry>
      <varlistentry><term><option>-e</option></term>
        <listitem><para>Implies the <option>-v</option> option, and displays a dollar sign
($) at the end of each line as well.</para></listitem>
      </varlistentry>
      <varlistentry><term><option>-n</option></term>
```

*Example 3-5. A DocBook reference page (continued)*

```
            <listitem><para>Numbers the output lines, starting at 1.</para></listitem>
          </varlistentry>
          <varlistentry><term><option>-s</option></term>
            <listitem><para>Squeezes multiple adjacent empty lines, causing the output to be
single spaced.</para></listitem>
          </varlistentry>
          <varlistentry><term><option>-t</option></term>
            <listitem><para>Implies the <option>-v</option> option, and displays tab
characters as <keysym>^I</keysym> as well.</para></listitem>
          </varlistentry>
          <varlistentry><term><option>-u</option></term>
            <listitem><para>The <option>-u</option> option guarantees that the output is
unbuffered.</para></listitem>
          </varlistentry>
          <varlistentry><term><option>-v</option></term>
            <listitem><para>Displays non-printing characters so they are visible. Control
characters print as <keysym>^X</keysym> for control-X; the delete
character (octal 0177) prints as <keysym>^?</keysym> Non-ascii
characters (with the high bit set) are printed as
<literal>M-</literal> (for meta) followed by the character for the low
7 bits.</para></listitem>
          </varlistentry>
        </variablelist>
        <para>The <command>cat</command> utility exits 0 on success, and &gt;0 if an
error occurs.</para>
      </refsect1>
      <refsect1><title>Bugs</title>
        <para>Because of the shell language mechanism used to perform output
redirection, the command <command>cat file1 file2 &gt; file1</command>
will cause the original data in file1 to be destroyed!</para>
      </refsect1>
      <refsect1><title>See also</title>
        <simplelist>
          <member><link href="head.xml">head(1)</link></member>
          <member><link href="more.xml">more(1)</link></member>
          <member><link href="pr.xml">pr(1)</link></member>
          <member><link href="tail.xml">tail(1)</link></member>
          <member><link href="vis.xml">vis(1)</link></member>
        </simplelist>
        <para>Rob Pike, <citetitle>UNIX Style, or cat -v Considered
Harmful</citetitle>, USENIX Summer Conference Proceedings, 1983.</para>
      </refsect1>
      <refsect1><title>History</title>
        <para>A <command>cat</command> utility appeared in Version 6 AT&T UNIX.</para>
      </refsect1>
</refentry>
```

The first thing you'll notice is that DocBook is a lot more verbose than HTML. The variablelist cousin to HTML's definition list is a chore to type out. But there certainly is no doubt about what an element stands for, which is necessary in a markup language with so many elements. If every tag name was an abbreviation of two letters, there'd be no hope of ever memorizing a fraction of the language.

The structure of the document element, refentry is highly specialized. Whereas HTML adopts a strategy where every document has the same overall structure, Doc-Book is very closely bound to the type of document you're authoring. If this document were a book, for example, it would look completely different. The metadata is specific to reference pages, and even the sections are called refsect1, meaning that they are specific to a reference entry.

The types of inlines are much more numerous than in HTML, with highly specific names like option, command, and citetitle. The blocks, too, are more differentiated. Notice that we now have a synopsis element to address a complaint I made about the HTML example.

The tradeoffs of HTML are reversed here. DocBook is much more complex and intricate than HTML, making it harder to learn and use. But the more specific vocabulary of this markup language makes it much more flexible in terms of formatting and processing. With flexibility may come more work, however, since someone will have to set up a big stylesheet to handle all the elements. If you purchase a package solution, as is possible with many high-end XML editors, much of this work may be done for you.

This example only shows a small part of DocBook. I'd like to give you another taste, so that you can see the breadth of its capabilities. Example 3-6 shows a more traditional narrative document, a book. Here you will see a wide variety of section elements (chapters, sections) and complex structures (table, figure, list). After the example, I've made notes to explain some of the elements.

*Example 3-6. A DocBook book*

```
<?xml version="1.0" encoding="utf-8"?>
<!DOCTYPE book SYSTEM "/xmlstuff/dtds/barebonesdb.dtd"
[
  <!ENTITY companyname "Cybertronix">             <!-- SEE NOTE 1 -->
  <!ENTITY productname "Sonic Screwdriver 9000">
]>

<book>
  <title>&productname; User Manual</title>     <!-- SEE NOTE 2 -->
  <author>Indigo Riceway</author>

  <preface id="preface">
    <title>Preface</title>

    <sect1 id="about">
      <title>Availability</title>
      <para>The information in this manual is available in the following forms:</para>

      <orderedlist>                              <!-- SEE NOTE 3 -->
        <listitem><para>Instant telepathic injection</para></listitem><listitem><para>
Lumino-goggle display</para></listitem><listitem><para>Ink on compressed, dead, arboreal
matter</para></listitem><listitem><para>Cuneiform etched in clay tablets</para></listitem>
      </orderedlist>
```

*Example 3-6. A DocBook book (continued)*

```
        <para>The &productname; is sold in galactic pamphlet boutiques or wherever
&companyname; equipment can be purchased. For more information, or
to order a copy by hyperspacial courier, please visit our universe-wide
Web page at <systemitem
role="url">http://www.cybertronix.com/sonic_screwdrivers.html</systemitem>.</para>
    </sect1>                        <!-- SEE NOTE 4 -->
  </preface>

  <chapter id="intro">            <!-- SEE NOTE 5 -->
    <title>Introduction</title>
    <para>Congratulations on your purchase of one of the most valuable tools in
the universe! The &companyname; &productname; is
equipment no hyperspace traveler should be without. Some of the
myriad tasks you can achieve with this device are:</para>

    <itemizedlist>
      <listitem><para>Pick locks in seconds. Never be locked out of your tardis
again. Good for all makes and models including Yale, Dalek, and
Xngfzz.</para></listitem>
      <listitem><para>Spot-weld metal, alloys, plastic, skin lesions, and virtually any
other material.</para></listitem>
      <listitem><para>Rid your dwelling of vermin. Banish insects, rodents, and computer
viruses from your time machine or spaceship.</para></listitem>
      <listitem><para>Slice and process foodstuffs from tomatoes to brine-worms. Unlike a
knife, there is no blade to go dull.</para></listitem>
    </itemizedlist>

    <para>Here is what satisfied customers are saying about their &companyname;
&productname;:</para>

    <comment>                        <!-- SEE NOTE 6 -->
Should we name the people who spoke these quotes?  --Ed.
    </comment>

    <blockquote>
      <para>"It helped me escape from the prison planet Garboplactor VI. I
wouldn't be alive today if it weren't for my Cybertronix 9000."</para>
    </blockquote>

    <blockquote>
      <para>"As a bartender, I have to mix martinis <emphasis>just
</emphasis>
<emphasis>right</emphasis>. Some of my customers get pretty cranky if I slip
up. Luckily, my new sonic screwdriver from Cybertronix is so accurate,
it gets the mixture right every time. No more looking down the barrel
of a kill-o-zap gun for this bartender!"</para>
    </blockquote>

  </chapter>

  <chapter id="controls">
    <title>Mastering the Controls</title>
```

*Example 3-6. A DocBook book (continued)*

```
    <sect1>
      <title>Overview</title>
      <para><xref linkend="controls-diagram"/> is a diagram of the parts of your
&productname;.</para>

        <figure id="controls-diagram">      <!-- SEE NOTE 7 -->
          <title>Exploded Parts Diagram</title>
          <graphic fileref="parts.png"/>
        </figure>

        <para><xref linkend="controls-table"/>          <!-- SEE NOTE 8 -->
lists the function of the parts labeled in the diagram.</para>

        <table id="controls-table">          <!-- SEE NOTE 9 -->
          <title>Control Descriptions</title>
          <tgroup cols="2">
            <thead>
              <row>
                <entry>Control</entry>
                <entry>Purpose</entry>
              </row>
            </thead>
            <tbody>
              <row>
                <entry>Decoy Power Switch</entry>
                <entry><para>Looks just like an on-off toggle button, but only turns on a
small flashlight when pressed. Very handy when your &productname; is misplaced
and discovered by primitive aliens who might otherwise accidentally
injure themselves.</para></entry>
              </row>
              <row>
                <entry><emphasis>Real</emphasis> Power Switch</entry>
                <entry><para>An invisible fingerprint-scanning capacitance-sensitive on/off
switch.</para></entry>
              </row>
              &vellip;
              <row>
                <entry>The "Z" Twiddle Switch</entry>
                <entry><para>We're not entirely sure what this does. Our lab testers have
had various results from teleportation to spontaneous
liquification. <emphasis role="bold">Use at your own risk!</emphasis></para></entry>
              </row>
            </tbody>
          </tgroup>
        </table>

        <note>                          <!-- SEE NOTE 10 -->
          <para>A note to arthropods: Stop forcing your inflexible appendages to adopt
un-ergonomic positions. Our new claw-friendly control template is
available.</para>
        </note>
    </sect1>
```

*Example 3-6. A DocBook book (continued)*

```
    <sect1>
      <title>The View Screen</title>
      <para>The view screen displays error messages and warnings, such as a
<errorcode>LOW-BATT</errorcode> (low battery) message.

        <footnote>                              <!-- SEE NOTE 11 -->
          <para>The advanced model now uses a direct psychic link to the user's
visual cortex, but it should appear approximately the same as the more
primitive liquid crystal display.</para>
        </footnote>

When your &productname; starts up, it should
show a status display like this:</para>

        <screen>STATUS DISPLAY            <!-- SEE NOTE 12 -->
BATT: 1.782E8 V
TEMP: 284 K
FREQ: 9.32E3 Hz
WARRANTY: ACTIVE</screen>
    </sect1>

    <sect1>
      <title>The Battery</title>
      <para>Your &productname; is capable of generating tremendous amounts of
energy. For that reason, any old battery won't do. The power source is
a tiny nuclear reactor containing a piece of ultra-condensed plutonium
that provides up to 10 megawatts of power to your device. With a
half-life of over 20 years, it will be a long time before a
replacement is necessary.</para>
    </sect1>
  </chapter>
</book>
```

## Notes

1. I'm taking the opportunity to declare some entities in the internal subset. This will save me some typing later.

2. Notice that all the major components (preface, chapter, sections) start with a title element. This is an example of how an element can be used in different contexts. In a formatted copy of this document, titles in different levels will be rendered differently. A stylesheet will use the hierarchical information (i.e., what is the ancestor of this title) to determine how to format it.

3. orderedlist is one of many types of lists available in DocBook. It produces the equivalent of HTML's ol element which formats with numbers. The formatter will generate numbers automatically, so you don't need to know how to count.

4. The systemitem inline element is rather generic, allowing for several types of "system" item, including computer domain names, URLs, FTP sites, and more.

5. It's a good idea to give sections ID attributes. Later, you may want to make a cross-reference to one of them. Remember that each ID attribute must have a unique value.

6. A `comment` element allows you to insert a message that is not part of the narrative, and will be removed before the final revision of the document is formatted. It's better than an actual XML comment object because it can be included in formatting for a draft printout.

7. This element constructs a figure, consisting of a title and an empty element that imports a graphic file.

8. The `xref` element is a cross-reference to another element in the document. The formatter will decide, based on the type of element referenced, what to put in its place. In this case, the object is a table, so we might expect to see something like "Table 3-1."

9. Here is another complex object, a table. DocBook's DTD doesn't define this element directly, but instead imports the definition from another DTD, an XML application called CALS (Continuous Acquisition and Life-Cycle Support). CALS was a Department of Defense project that made early use of SGML to improve its documentation. The CALS table model is very flexible and robust, so the DocBook framers felt it easier to borrow it than to reinvent the wheel.

10. A `note` is a new flow, similar to a sidebar. A formatter may or may not move it from this location, with no damage to the narrative, but it should stay relatively close to its origin.

11. This is how to code a footnote, another new flow. Footnotes are usually placed at the bottom of the page, but that notion is not clear when talking about web pages.

12. This element contains significant extra whitespace that needs to be preserved. The DTD has specified this for us, so we don't need to insert an `xml:space` attribute.

There are a lot of tools available for working with DocBook. For more information, see *http://docbook.org*.

# Complex Data

XML really shines when data is complex. It turns the most abstract concepts into concrete databases ready for processing by software. Multimedia formats like Scalable Vector Graphics (SVG) and Synchronized Multimedia Integration Language (SMIL) map pictures and movies into XML markup. Complex ideas in the scientific realm are just as readily coded as XML, as proven by MathML (equations), the Chemical Markup Language (chemical formulae), and the Molecular Dynamics Language (molecule interactions).

# Elements as Objects

The reason XML is so good at modelling complex data is that the same building blocks for narrative documents—elements and attributes—can apply to any composition of objects and properties. Just as a book breaks down into chapters, sections, blocks, and inlines, many abstract ideas can be deconstructed into discrete and hierarchical components. Vector graphics, for example, are composed of a finite set of shapes with associated properties. You can represent each shape as an element and use attributes to hammer down the details.

SVG is a good example of how to represent objects as elements. Take a gander at the simple SVG document in Example 3-7. Here we have three different shapes represented by as many elements: a common rectangle, an ordinary circle, and an exciting polygon. Attributes in each element customize the shape, setting color and spatial dimensions.

*Example 3-7. An SVG document*

```
<?xml version="1.0"?>
<svg>
  <desc>Three shapes</desc>
  <rect fill="green" x="1cm" y="1cm" width="3cm" height="3cm"/>
  <circle fill="red" cx="3cm" cy="2cm" r="4cm"/>
  <polygon fill="blue" points="110,160 50,300 180,290"/>
</svg>
```

Vector graphics are scalable, meaning you can stretch the image vertically or horizontally without any loss of sharpness. The image processor just recalculates the coordinates for you, leaving you to concentrate on higher concepts like composition, color, and grouping.

SVG adds other benefits too. Being an XML application, it can be tested for well-formedness, can be edited in any generic XML editor, and is easy to write software for. DTDs and Schema are available to check for missing information, and they provide an easy way to distinguish between versions.

Are there limitations? Of course. XML is not so good when it comes to raster graphics. This category of graphics formats, which includes TIFF, GIF and JPEG, renders an image based on pixel data. Instead of a conceptual representation based on shapes, it's a big fat array of numbers. You could store this in XML, certainly, but the benefits of markup are irrelevant since elements would only increase the document's size without organizing the data well. Furthermore, these formats typically use compression to force the huge amount of data into more manageable sizes, something markup would only complicate. (Video presents similar, larger, problems.)

What other concepts are ideally suited to XML representation? How about chemicals? Every molecule has a unique blueprint consisting of some combination of atoms and bonds. Languages like the Chemical Markup Language (CML) and

Molecular Dynamics Language (MoDL) follow a similar strategy to encode molecules.

Example 3-8 shows how a water molecule would be coded in MoDL. Notice the separation of head and body that is reminiscent of HTML. The head is where we define atomic types, giving them size and color properties for rendering. The body is where we assemble the molecule using definitions from the head.

*Example 3-8. A molecule definition in MoDL*

```
<?xml version="1.0"?>
<modl>
  <head>
    <meta name="title" content="Water" />
    <DEFINE name="Hydrogen">
      <atom radius="0.2" color="1 1 0" />
    </DEFINE>
    <DEFINE name="Oxygen">
      <atom radius="0.5" color="1 0 1" />
    </DEFINE>
  </head>
  <body>
    <atom id="H0" type="Hydrogen" position="1 0 0" />
    <atom id="H1" type="Hydrogen" position="0 0 1" />
    <atom id="O" type="Oxygen" position="0 1 0" />
    <bond atom1="O" atom2="H0" color="0 0 1" />
    <bond atom1="O" atom2="H1" color="0 0 1" />
  </body>
</modl>
```

For each atom instance, there is an element describing its type, position, and a unique identifier (e.g., "H0" for the first hydrogen atom). Each bond between atoms also has its own element, specifying color and the two atoms it joins. Notice the interplay between atoms and bonds. The unique identifiers in the first group are the "hooks" for the second group, which use attributes that refer to them. Unique identifiers are another invaluable technique in expressing relationships between concepts.

MoDL is a project by Swami Manohar and Vijay Chandru of the Indian Institute of Science. The goal is not just to model molecules, but to model their interactions. The language contains elements to express motion as well as the static initial positions. Elements can represent actions applied to molecules, including translate and rotate.

Software developed for this purpose converts MoDL documents into a temporal-spatial format called Virtual Reality Markup Language (VRML). When viewed in a VRML reader, molecules dance around and bump into each other! Read more about MoDL at *http://violet.csa.iisc.ernet.in/~modl/* and VRML at *http://www.web3d.org*.

Again, there are limitations. Movies, just like graphics, can be vector-based or rasterized. Formats like MPEG and MOV are compressed sequences of bitmaps, a huge amount of pixel information that XML would not be good at organizing. Simple shapes bouncing around in space are one thing, but complex scenes involving faces and puppy dogs are probably never going to involve XML.

## Presentation Versus Conceptual Encoding

Moving up in complexity is mathematics. The Mathematics Markup Language (MathML) attacks this difficult area with two different modes of markup: presentational and conceptual. If we were describing an equation, we could do it in two ways. I could say "the product of A and B" or I could write on a chalkboard the more compact "A × B," both conveying the same idea. MathML allows you to use either style and mix them together in a document.

Consider the mathematical expression in Figure 3-3. This example was generated with MathML and displayed with Mozilla, which recognizes MathML as of version 1.1.

$$1 - \cfrac{1}{1 - \cfrac{1}{1 - \cfrac{1}{x}}}$$

*Figure 3-3. A complex fraction*

Example 3-9 is the MathML document used to generate this figure.

*Example 3-9. Presentation encoding in MathML*

```
<?xml version="1.0"?>
<math xmlns="http://www.w3.org/1998/Math/MathML">
  <mn>1</mn><mo>-</mo>
  <mfrac><mrow><mn>1</mn></mrow>
    <mrow><mn>1</mn><mo>-</mo>
      <mfrac><mrow><mn>1</mn></mrow>
        <mrow><mn>1</mn><mo>-</mo>
          <mfrac><mrow><mn>1</mn></mrow>
            <mrow><mi>x</mi></mrow>
          </mfrac>
        </mrow>
      </mfrac>
    </mrow>
  </mfrac>
</math>
```

mfrac, as you may have guessed, sets up a fraction. It contains two elements called mrow, one each for the top and bottom. Notice how the denominator can itself contain a fraction. Take this recursively as far as you wish and it's perfectly legal in MathML. At the atomic level of expression are numbers, variables, and operators, which are marked up with the simple elements mn (number), mi (identifier), and mo (operator).

Conceptual encoding (also known as *content encoding*) is the name given for the other mode of MathML. It resembles functional programming, notably LISP, in that every sum, fraction, and product is represented as an operator followed by arguments all wrapped up in an apply element. Example 3-10 shows how the equation $(2a + b)^3$ looks in MathML's content mode.

*Example 3-10. Content encoding in MathML*

```
<?xml version="1.0"?>
<math xmlns="http://www.w3.org/1998/Math/MathML">
  <apply><power/>
    <apply><plus/>
      <apply><times/>
        <cn>2</cn>
        <ci>a</ci>
      </apply>
      <ci>b</ci>
    </apply>
    <cn>3</cn>
  </apply>
</math>
```

Why the two modes of MathML? One reason is flexibility of authoring. But a more important reason is that each lends itself to a different means of processing. Presentational encoding is easier to render visually, and so is better supported in browsers and such. Content encoding, because it's more regular and closer to the meaning of the expression, is easier to process by calculator-type programs.

With support for MathML in browsers and other programs increasing, its popularity is growing. For more information, read *A Gentle Introduction to MathML* by Robert Miner and Jeff Schaeffer at *http://www.dessci.com/en/support/tutorials/mathml/*.

## Documents Describing Documents

Many XML documents contain metadata, information about themselves that help search engines to categorize them. But not everyone takes advantage of the possibilities of metadata. And, unless you're using an exhaustive program that spiders through an entire document collection, it's difficult to summarize the set and choose a particular article from it. Making matters worse, not all documents have the capability to describe themselves, such as sound and graphics files. To address these problems, a class of documents evolved that specialize in describing other documents.

To fully describe different kinds of documents, these markup languages have some interesting features in common. They list the time documents have been updated using standard time formats. They label the content type, be it text, image, sound, or something else. They may contain text descriptions for a user to peruse. For international documents, they may track the language encodings. Also interesting is the way documents are uniquely identified: using a physical address or some non-physical identifier.

## Describing Media

Rich Site Summary (or Really Simple Syndication, depending on whom you talk to) was created by Netscape Corp. to describe content on web sites. They wanted to make a portal that was customizable, allowing readers to subscribe to particular subject areas or *channels*. Each time they returned to the site, they would see updates on their favorite topics, saving them the trouble of hunting around for this news on their own. Thus was born the service known as *content aggregation*.

Since the time when there were a few big content aggregators like Netscape and Userland, the landscape has shifted to include hundreds of smaller, more granular services. Instead of subscribing to channels that mix together lots of different sources, you can subscribe to individual sites for an even higher level of customization. Everything from the BBC to a swarm of one-person weblogs are at your disposal. Publishing has never been easier.

RSS works like the cover of a magazine, beckoning to you from the newsstand. Splashed all over the cover graphic are the titles of articles, like "Lose Weight with the Ice Cream Diet" and "Ten Things the Government Doesn't Want You to Know About UFOs." At a glance, you can decide whether you must have this issue or *National Geographic* instead. It saves you time and keeps the newsstand owner from yelling at you for reading without buying.

There are a few different models of publishing with RSS. The *pull* model is where a content aggregator checks an RSS file periodically to see if anything has been updated, pulling in new articles as they appear. In the *push* model, also called *publish and subscribe*, the information source informs the content aggregator when it has something new to offer. In both cases, RSS serves as a menu for the aggregator (or the user logged into it) to decide whether the articles are of interest.

Example 3-11 shows a sample of RSS describing a fictional web site. The owner of a web site will register this file with all the aggregators it wants to be listed under and hope that people will be convinced by the descriptions that it's interesting enough to subscribe to.

*Example 3-11. RSS describing a web site*

```
<?xml version="1.0" encoding="ISO-8859-1" standalone="yes"?>
<rss version="2.0">
  <channel>
    <title>Lifestyles of the Foolhardy</title>
    <link>http://www.foolhardy.org/</link>
    <description>
Incredibly bold or just plain stupid? Tips and tricks for folks who
```

*Example 3-11. RSS describing a web site (continued)*

```
just don't have time to think about safety.
    </description>
    <language>en-us</language>
    <copyright>Copyright 2002 Liv Dangerously</copyright>
    <lastBuildDate>Fri, 20 Sep 2002 11:05:02 GMT</lastBuildDate>
    <managingEditor>liv@foolhardy.org (Liv Dangerously)</managingEditor>
    <item>
      <title>Using a Hair Dryer in the Bathtub.</title>
      <pubDate>Fri, 20 Sep 2002 11:05:02 GMT</pubDate>
      <link>http://www.foolhardy.org/art/tub.html</link>
      <description>
Don't wait till bathtime is over to dry your hair. Save time and do
both at once.
      </description>
    </item>
    <item>
      <description>
Sounds of someone falling down the stairs; a brave soul proving that
rollerskates aren't just for flat surfaces.
      </description>
      <pubDate>Fri, 20 Sep 2002 10:28:19 GMT</pubDate>
      <enclosure url="http://www.foolhardy.org/sounds/stairs.mp3"
                 length="44456" type="audio/mpeg"/>
    </item>
  </channel>
</rss>
```

The first thing inside the document element rss is a channel element giving a general overview of the site. In it, we find:

- Descriptive text including a short title and longer paragraph.

- Administrative details: contact information, link to the main page, copyright.

- Language identifier en-us, which means that it uses the American variant of English (more about language encodings in Chapter 9).

- Time of last update, using a standard time format (RFC 822) recognized all over the Internet.

After the channel comes a series of elements describing each item in the site. This example has two: a text document and a sound file. Each has a corresponding item element containing a text description, link to the resource, and the date it was posted.

The sound file has an additional element, enclosure, which provides some details about the format. The type attribute gives the *content type*, audio/mp3. The format of this description comes from the Multipurpose Internet Mail Extensions standard (RFC 2046).

For more about RSS, see Ben Hammersley's *Context Syndication with RSS* (O'Reilly & Associates, 2003)

## Templates

Describing documents is also the job of the transformation language XSLT. But in this case, we're talking about documents in the *future*. XSLT generates new documents from old ones, following rules in a transformation stylesheet. For each element in the source document, there will be a rule dictating what to do with it and its content. The rule can be explicit (defined by you) or implicit (not finding a specific rule, the processor falls back on a default one).

These rules are encoded in an XSLT document using an ingenious mechanism called a *template*, which is a sample of a piece of the result document. Some blanks need to be filled into the template, but otherwise, you can see by looking at the template how the future document will look.

Here is a typical XSLT stylesheet with a couple of templates:

```
<xsl:stylesheet
  xmlns:xsl="http://www.w3.org/1999/XSL/Transform"
  version="1.0">

  <!-- first template: how to process a <para> element -->
  <xsl:template match="para">
    <p>
      <xsl:apply-templates/>
    </p>
  </xsl:template>

  <!-- second template: how to process a <note> element -->
  <xsl:template match="note">
    <div class="note">
      <h3>NOTE</h3>
      <xsl:apply-templates/>
    </div>
  </xsl:template>
</xsl:stylesheet>
```

The first template tells the XSLT processor what to output when it comes across a para element in the source document. The second is a rule for note elements. In each case, the template element's contents mirror a piece of the document to be created.

Note the use of the namespace prefix xsl: in some of the elements. This is how the XSLT processor can tell the difference between markup to be obeyed as instructions and markup to be output. In other words, if there is no xsl: prefix, the markup is treated as data and carried to the output document as is. Some of the instruction elements, like xsl:apply-templates, control the flow of processing, making the XSLT processor recurse through the source document looking for more elements to transform.

In some ways, XML schemas are similar to XSLT. They use templates to describe parts of documents as they *should* be, instead of as they will be. In other words, a schema is a test to determine whether a document can be labeled a valid instance of a language.

Templates are a good design mechanism for documents describing documents because they are modular and easy to understand. Instead of looking at the whole document, you only have to imagine one element at a time. Templates can be imported from other files and mixed to add more flexibility.

XML schemas will be discussed in greater detail in Chapter 4, while XSLT will be discussed in greater detail in Chapter 7.

# Quality Control with Schemas

Up until now, we have been talking about the things all XML documents have in common. Well-formedness rules are universal, ensuring perfect compatibility with generic tools and APIs. This syntax homogeneity is a big selling point for XML, but equally important is the need for ways to distinguish XML-based languages from each other. A document usually attempts to conform to a language of some sort, and we need methods to test its level of conformance.

Schemas, the topic of this chapter, are the shepherds of markup languages. They keep documents from straying outside of the herd and causing trouble. For instance, an administrator of a web site can use a schema to determine which web pages are legal XHTML, and which are only pretending to be. A schema can also be used to publish a specification for a language in a succinct and unambiguous way.

## Basic Concepts

In the general sense of the word, a schema is a generic representation of a class of things. For example, a schema for restaurant menus could be the phrase "a list of dishes available at a particular eating establishment." A schema may resemble the thing it describes, the way a "smiley face" represents an actual human face. The information contained in a schema allows you to identify when something is or is not a representative instance of the concept.

In the XML context, a schema is a pass-or-fail test for documents.[*] A document that passes the test is said to *conform* to it, or be *valid*. Testing a document with a schema is called *validation*. A schema ensures that a document fulfills a minimum set of requirements, finding flaws that could result in anomalous processing. It also may

---

[*] Technically, schemas validate on an element-by-element and attribute-by-attribute basis. It is possible to test a subtree alone for validity and determine that parts are valid while others are not. This process is rather complex and beyond the scope of this book.

serve as a way to formalize an application, being a publishable object that describes a language in unambiguous rules.

## Validation

An XML schema is like a program that tells a processor how to read a document. It's very similar to a later topic we'll discuss called *transformations*. The processor reads the rules and declarations in the schema and uses this information to build a specific type of parser, called a validating parser. The validating parser takes an XML instance as input and produces a validation report as output. At a minimum, this report is a return code, true if the document is valid, false otherwise. Optionally, the parser can create a Post Schema Validation Infoset (PSVI) including information about data types and structure that may be used for further processing.

Validation happens on at least four levels:

*Structure*
> The use and placement of markup elements and attributes.

*Data typing*
> Patterns of character data (e.g., numbers, dates, text).

*Integrity*
> The status of links between nodes and resources.

*Business rules*
> Miscellaneous tests such as spelling checks, checksum results, and so on.

Structural validation is the most important, and schemas are best prepared to handle this level. Data typing is often useful, especially in "data-style" documents, but not widely supported. Testing integrity is less common and somewhat problematic to define. Business rules are often checked by applications.

## A History of Schema Languages

There are many different kinds of XML schemas, each with its own strengths and weaknesses.

### DTD

The oldest and most widely supported schema language is the Document Type Definition (DTD). Borrowed from SGML, a simplified DTD was included in the XML Core recommendation. Though a DTD isn't necessary to read and process an XML document, it can be a useful component for a document, providing the means to define macro-like entities and other conveniences. DTDs were the first widely used method to formally define languages like HTML.

## W3C XML Schema

As soon as XML hit the streets, developers began to clamor for an alternative to DTDs. DTDs don't support namespaces, which appeared after the XML 1.0 specification. They also have very weak data typing, being mostly markup-focused. The W3C formed a working group for XML Schema and began to receive proposals for what would later become their W3C XML Schema recommendation.

Following are some of the proposals made by various groups.

*XML-Data*

> Submitted by Arbortext, DataChannel, Inso Corporation, Microsoft, and the University of Edinburgh in January 1998, this technical note put forth many of the features incorporated in W3C Schema, and many others that were left out, such as a mechanism for declaring entities and object-oriented programming support. Microsoft implemented a version of this called XML-Data Reduced (XDR).

*Document Content Description (DCD)*

> IBM, Microsoft, and Textuality submitted this proposal in July 1998 as an attempt to integrate XML-Data with the Resource Description Framework (RDF). It introduced the idea of making elements and attributes interchangeable.

*Schema for Object-Oriented XML (SOX)*

> As the name implies, this technical note was influenced by programming needs, incorporating concepts as interfaces and parameters. It was submitted in July 1998 by Veo Systems/Commerce One. They have created an implementation that they use today.

*Document Definition Markup Language (DDML)*

> This proposal came out of discussions on the XML-Dev mailing list. It took the information expressed in a DTD and formatted it as XML, leaving support for data types to other specifications.

Informed by these proposals, the W3C XML Schema Working Group arrived at a recommendation in May 2001, composed of three parts (XMLS0, XMLS1, and XMLS2) named Primer, Structures, and Datatypes, respectively. Although some of the predecessors are still in use, all involved parties agreed that they should be retired in favor of the one, true W3C XML Schema.

## RELAX NG

An independent effort by a creative few coalesced into another schema language called RELAX NG (pronounced "relaxing"). It is the merging of Regular Language Description for XML (RELAX) and Tree Regular Expressions for XML (TREX). Like W3C Schema, it supports namespaces and datatypes. It also includes some unique innovations, such as interchangeability of elements and attributes in content descriptions and more flexible content models.

RELAX, a product of the Japanese Standard Association's INSTAC XML Working Group, led by Murata Makoto, was designed to be an easy alternative to XML Schema. "Tired of complex specifications?" the home page asks. "You can relax!" Unlike W3C Schema, with its broad scope and high learning curve, RELAX is simple to implement and use.

You can think of RELAX as DTDs (formatted in XML) plus datatypes inherited from W3C Schema's datatype set. As a result, it is nearly painless to migrate from DTDs to RELAX and, if you want to do so later, fairly easy to migrate from RELAX to W3C Schemas. It supported two levels of conformance. "Classic" is just like DTD validation plus datatype checking. "Fully relaxed" added more features.

The theoretical basis of RELAX is Hedge Automata tree processing. While you don't need to know anything about Hedge Automata to use RELAX or RELAX NG, these mathematical foundations make it easier to write efficient code implementing RELAX NG. Murata Makoto has demonstrated a RELAX NG implementation which occupies 27K on a cell phone, including both the schema and the XML parser.

At about the same time RELAX was taking shape, James Clark of Thai Opensource Software was developing TREX. It came out of work on XDuce, a typed programming language for manipulating XML markup and data. XDuce (a contraction of "XML" and "transduce") is a transformation language which takes an XML document as input, extracts data, and outputs another document in XML or another format. TREX uses XDuce's type system and adds various features into an XML-based language. XDuce appeared in March 2000, followed by TREX in January 2001.

Like RELAX, TREX uses a very clear and flexible language that is easy to learn, read, and implement. Definitions of elements and attributes are interchangeable, greatly simplifying the syntax. It has full support for namespaces, mixed content, and unordered content, things that are missing from, or very difficult to achieve, with DTDs. Like RELAX, it uses the W3C XML Schema datatype set, reducing the learning curve further.

RELAX NG (new generation) combines the best features from both RELAX and TREX in one XML-based schema language. First announced in May 2001, an OASIS Technical Committee headed by James Clark and Murata Makoto oversees its development. It was approved as a Draft International Standard by the ISO/IEC.

### Schematron

Also worth noting is Schematron, first proposed by Rick Jelliffe of the Academia Sinicia Computing Centre in 1999. It uses XPath expressions to define validation rules and is one of the most flexible schema languages around.

# Do You Need Schemas?

It may seem like schemas are a lot of work, and you'd be right to think so. In designing a schema, you are forced to think hard about how your language is structured. As your language evolves, you have to update your schema, which is like maintaining a piece of software. There will be bugs, version tracking, usability issues, and even the occasional overhaul to consider. So with all this overhead, is it really worth it?

First, let's look at the benefits:

- A schema can function as a publishable specification. There is simply no better way to describe a language than with a schema. A schema is, after all, a "yes or no" test for document conformance. It's designed to be readable by humans and machines alike. DTDs are very reminiscent of Backus-Naur Form (BNF) grammars which are used to describe programming languages. Other schemas, such as RELAX NG, are intuitive and very easy to read. So if you need to disseminate information on how to use a markup language, a schema is not a bad way to do it.

- A schema will catch higher-level mistakes. Sure, there are well-formedness rules to protect your software from errors in basic syntax, but do they go far enough? What if a required field of information is missing? Or someone has consistently misspelled an element name? Or a date was entered in the wrong format? These are things only a validating parser can detect.

- A schema is portable and efficient. Writing a program to test a document is an option, but it may not be the best one. Software can be platform-dependent, difficult to install, and bulky to transfer. A schema, however, is compact and optimized for one purpose: validation. It's easy to hand someone a schema, and you know it has to work for them because its syntax is governed by a standard specification. And since many schemas are based on XML, they can be edited in XML editors and tested by well-formedness checkers.

- A schema is extensible. Schemas are designed to support modularity. If you want to maintain a set of similar languages, or versions of them, they can share common components. For example, DTDs allow you to declare general entities for special characters or frequently used text. They may be so useful that you want to export them to other languages.

Using a schema also has some drawbacks:

- A schema reduces flexibility. The expressiveness of schemas varies considerably, and each standard tends to have its flaws. For example, DTDs are notorious for their incompatibility with namespaces. They are also inefficient at specifying a content model that contains required children that may appear in any order. While other schema languages improve upon DTDs, they will always have limitations of one sort or another.

- Schemas can be obstacles for authors. In spite of advances in XML editors with fancy graphical interfaces, authoring in XML will never be as easy as writing in a traditional word processor. Time spent thinking about which element to use in a given context is time not spent on thinking about the document's content, which is the original reason for writing it. Some editors supply a menu of elements to select from that changes depending on the context. Depending on the language and the tools, it still can be confusing and frustrating for the lay person.

- You have to maintain it. With a schema, you have one more tool to debug and update. Like software, it will have bugs, versions, and even its own documentation. It's all too easy to damage a schema by deleting an imported component or introducing a syntax error. Older documents may not validate if you update the schema, forcing you to make retroactive changes to them. One silver lining is that, except for DTDs, most schema languages are based on XML, which allows you to use XML editors to make changes.

- Designing it will be hard. Schemas are tricky documents to compose. You have to really think about how each element will fit together, what kinds of data will be input, whether there are special cases to accommodate. If you're just starting out with a language, there are many needs you don't know about until you start using it, creating a bit of a bootstrapping problem.

To make the decision easier, think about it this way. A schema is basically a quality-control tool. If you are reasonably certain that your documents are good enough for processing, then you have no need for schemas. However, if you want extra assurance that your documents are complete and structurally sound, and the work you save fixing mistakes outweighs the work you will spend maintaining a schema, then you should look into it.

One thing to consider is whether a human will be involved with producing a document. No matter how careful we are, we humans tend to make a lot of mistakes. Validation can find those problems and save frustration later. But software-created documents tend to be very predictable and probably never need to be validated.

The really hard question to answer is not whether you need a schema, but which standard to use. There are a few very valuable choices that I will be describing in the rest of the chapter. I hope to provide you with enough information to decide which one is right for your application.

# DTDs

The original XML document model is the Document Type Definition (DTD). DTDs actually predate XML; they are a reduced hand-me-down from SGML with the core syntax almost completely intact. The following describes how a DTD defines a document type.

- A DTD declares a set of allowed elements. You cannot use any element names other than those in this set. Think of this as the "vocabulary" of the language.

- A DTD defines a *content model* for each element. The content model is a pattern that tells what elements or data can go inside an element, in what order, in what number, and whether they are required or optional. Think of this as the "grammar" of the language.

- A DTD declares a set of allowed attributes for each element. Each attribute declaration defines the name, datatype, default values (if any), and behavior (e.g., if it is required or optional) of the attribute.

- A DTD provides a variety of mechanisms to make managing the model easier, for example, the use of parameter entities and the ability to import pieces of the model from an external file.

## Document Prolog

According to the XML Recommendation, all external parsed entities (including DTDs) should begin with a text declaration. It looks like an XML declaration except that it explicitly excludes the standalone property. If you need to specify a character set other than the default UTF-8 (see Chapter 9 for more about character sets), or to change the XML version number from the default 1.0, this is where you would do it.

 If you specify a character set in the DTD, it won't automatically carry over into XML documents that use the DTD. XML documents have to specify their own encodings in their document prologs.

After the text declaration, the resemblance to normal document prologs ends. External parsed entities, including DTDs, must not contain a document type declaration.

## Declarations

A DTD is a set of rules or *declarations*. Each declaration adds a new element, set of attributes, entity, or notation to the language you are describing. DTDs can be combined using parameter entities, a technique called *modularization*. You can also add declarations inside the internal subset of the document.

The order of the declarations is important in two situations. First, if there are redundant entity declarations, the first one that appears takes precedence and all others are ignored.* This is important to know if you are going to override declarations, either

---

* Entity declarations are the only kind of declaration that can appear redundantly without triggering a validity error. If an element type is declared more than once, it will render the DTD (and any documents that use it) invalid.

in the internal subset or by cascading DTDs. Second, if parameter entities are used in declarations, they must be declared before they are used as references.

Declaration syntax is flexible when it comes to whitespace. You can add extra space anywhere except in the string of characters at the beginning that identifies the declaration type.

For example, these are all acceptable:

```
<!ELEMENT          thingie     ALL>
<!ELEMENT
  thingie
  ALL>
<!ELEMENT thingie (          foo     |
                             bar     |
                             zap     )*>
```

## An Example

Imagine a scenario where you are collecting information from a group of people. The data you receive will be fed to a program that will process it and store it in a database. You need a quick way to determine whether all the required information is there before you can accept a submission. For this, we will use a DTD.

The information in this example will be census data. Your staff is roaming around the neighborhood interviewing families and entering data on their laptop computers. They are using an XML editor configured with a DTD that you've created to model your language, CensusML. Later, they will upload all the CensusML documents to the central repository to be processed overnight.

Example 4-1 shows how a typical valid CensusML document should look, minus the document prolog. A document represents an interview with one family. It contains a date, an address, and a list of people residing there. For each person, we are interested in taking their full name, age, employment status, and gender. We also use identification numbers for people, to ensure that we don't accidentally enter in somebody more than once.

*Example 4-1. A typical CensusML document*

```
<census-record taker="3163">
  <date><year>2003</year><month>10</month><day>11</day></date>
  <address>
    <street>471 Skipstone Lane <unit>4-A</unit></street>
    <city>Emerald City</city>
    <county>Greenhill</county>
    <country>Oz</country>
    <postalcode>885JKL</postalcode>
  </address>
  <person employed="fulltime" pid="P270405">
    <name>
      <first>Meeble</first>
```

*Example 4-1. A typical CensusML document (continued)*

```
      <last>Bigbug</last>
      <junior/>
    </name>
    <age>39</age>
    <gender>male</gender>
  </person>
  <person employed="parttime" pid="P273882">
    <name>
      <first>Mable</first>
      <last>Bigbug</last>
    </name>
    <age>36</age>
    <gender>female</gender>
  </person>
  <person pid="P472891">
    <name>
      <first>Marble</first>
      <last>Bigbug</last>
    </name>
    <age>11</age>
    <gender>male</gender>
  </person>
</census-record>
```

Let's start putting together a DTD. The first declaration is for the document element:

```
<!ELEMENT census-record
(date, address, person+)>
```

This establishes the first rules for the CensusML language: (1) there is an element named census-record and (2) it must contains one date element, one address element, and at least one person element. If you leave any of these elements out, or put them in a different order, the document will be invalid.

Note that the declaration doesn't actually specify that the census-record must be used as the document element. In fact, a DTD can't single out any element to be the root of a document. You might view this as a bad thing, since you can't stop someone from submitting an incomplete document containing only a person element and nothing else. On the other hand, you could see it as a feature, where DTDs can contain more than one model for a document. For example, DocBook relies on this to support many different models for documents; a book would use the book element as its root, while an article would use the article element. In any case, be aware of this loophole.

Now we should declare the attributes for this element. There is only one, taker, identifying the census taker who authored this document. Its type is CDATA (character data). We will make it required, because it's important to know who is submitting the data just to make sure no mischievous people submit fraudulent records. Here is the attribute list for census-record:

```
<!ATTLIST census-record
   taker   CDATA   #REQUIRED>
```

Next declare the date element. The order of element declarations doesn't really matter. All the declarations are read into the parser's memory before any validation takes place, so all that is necessary is that every element is accounted for. But I like things organized and in the approximate order, so here's the next set of declarations:

```
<!ELEMENT date (year, month, day)>
<!ELEMENT year #PCDATA>
<!ELEMENT month #PCDATA>
<!ELEMENT day #PCDATA>
```

The #PCDATA literal represents character data. Specifically, it matches zero or more characters. Any element with a content model #PCDATA can contain character data but not elements. So the elements year, month, and day are what you might call data fields. The date element, in contrast, must contain elements, but not character data.*

Now for the address bit. address is a container of elements just like date. For the most part, its subelements are plain data fields (their content is character data only), but one element has mixed content: street. Here are the declarations:

```
<!ELEMENT address
   (street, city, county, country, postalcode)>
<!ELEMENT street (#PCDATA | unit)*>
<!ELEMENT city #PCDATA>
<!ELEMENT county #PCDATA>
<!ELEMENT country #PCDATA>
<!ELEMENT postalcode #PCDATA>
<!ELEMENT unit #PCDATA>
```

The declaration for street follows the pattern used by all mixed-content elements. The #PCDATA must come first followed by all the allowed subelements separated by vertical bars (|). The asterisk (*) here is required. It means that there can be zero or more of whatever comes before it. The upshot is that character data is optional, along with all the elements that can be interspersed within it.

Alas, there is no way to *require* that an element with mixed content contains character data. The census taker could just leave the street element blank and the validating parser would be happy with that. Changing that asterisk (*) to a plus (+) to require some character data is not allowed. To make validation simple and fast, DTDs never concern themselves with the actual details of character data.

Our final task is to declare the elements and attributes making up a person. Here is a crack at the element declarations:

```
<!ELEMENT person (name, age, gender)>
<!ELEMENT name (first, last, (junior | senior)?)>
```

---

* Whitespace is allowed to make the markup more readable, but would be ignored for the purpose of validation.

```
<!ELEMENT age #PCDATA>
<!ELEMENT gender #PCDATA>
<!ELEMENT first #PCDATA>
<!ELEMENT last #PCDATA>
<!ELEMENT junior EMPTY>
<!ELEMENT senior EMPTY>
<!ATTLIST person
    pid       ID                    #REQUIRED
    employed  (fulltime|parttime)   #IMPLIED>
```

The content model is a little more complex for this container. The first and last names are required, but there is an option to follow these with a qualifier ("Junior" or "Senior"). The qualifiers are declared as empty elements here using the keyword EMPTY and the question mark makes them optional, as not everyone is a junior or senior. Perhaps it would be just as easy to make an attribute called qualifier with values junior or senior, but I decided to do it this way to show you how to declare empty elements. Also, using an element makes the markup less cluttered, and we already have two attributes in the container element.

The first attribute declared is a required pid, a person identification string. Its type is ID, which to validating parsers means that it is a unique identifier within the scope of the document. No other element can have an ID-type attribute with that value. This means that if the census taker accidentally puts in a person twice, the parser will catch the error and report the document invalid. The parser can only check within the scope of the document, however, so there is nothing to stop a census taker from entering the same person in another document.

ID-type attributes have another limitation. There is one identifier-space for all of them, so even if you want to use them in different ways, such as having an identifier for the address and another for people, you can't use the same string in both element types. A solution to this might be to prefix the identifier string with a code like "HOME-38225" for address and "PID-489294" for person, effectively creating your own separate identifier spaces. Note that ID-type attributes must always begin with a letter or underscore, like XML element and attribute names.

The other attribute, employed, is optional as denoted by the #IMPLIED keyword. It's also an enumerated type, meaning that there is a set of allowed values (fulltime and parttime). Setting the attribute to anything else would result in a validation error.

Example 4-2 shows the complete DTD.

*Example 4-2. The CensusML DTD*

```
<!--
Census Markup Language
(use <census-record> as the document element)
-->
<!ELEMENT census-record (date, address, person+)>
<!ATTLIST census-record
  taker   CDATA   #REQUIRED>
```

*Example 4-2. The CensusML DTD (continued)*

```
<!-- date the info was collected -->
<!ELEMENT date (year, month, day)>
<!ELEMENT year #PCDATA>
<!ELEMENT month #PCDATA>
<!ELEMENT day #PCDATA>

<!-- address information -->
<!ELEMENT address
   (street, city, county, country, postalcode)>
<!ELEMENT street (#PCDATA | unit)*>
<!ELEMENT city #PCDATA>
<!ELEMENT county #PCDATA>
<!ELEMENT country #PCDATA>
<!ELEMENT postalcode #PCDATA>
<!ELEMENT unit #PCDATA>

<!-- person information -->
<!ELEMENT person (name, age, gender)>
<!ELEMENT name (first, last, (junior | senior)?)>
<!ELEMENT age #PCDATA>
<!ELEMENT gender #PCDATA>
<!ELEMENT first #PCDATA>
<!ELEMENT last #PCDATA>
<!ELEMENT junior EMPTY>
<!ELEMENT senior EMPTY>
<!ATTLIST person
    pid      ID               #REQUIRED
    employed (fulltime|parttime) #IMPLIED>
```

# Tips for Designing and Customizing DTDs

DTD design and construction is part science and part art form. The basic concepts are easy enough, but managing a large DTD—maintaining hundreds of element and attribute declarations while keeping them readable and bug-free—can be a challenge. This section offers a collection of hints and best practices that you may find useful. The next section shows a concrete example that uses these practices.

### Keeping it organized

DTDs are notoriously hard to read, but good organization always helps. A few extra minutes spent tidying up and writing comments can save you hours of scrutinizing later. Often a DTD is its own documentation, so if you expect others to use it, clean code is doubly important.

*Organizing declarations by function*

   Keep declarations separated into sections by their purpose. In small DTDs, this helps you navigate the file. In larger DTDs, you might even want to break the declarations into separate modules. Some categories to group by are blocks, inlines, hierarchical elements, parts of tables, lists, etc. In Example 4-4, the declarations are divided by function (block, inline, and hierarchical).

*Whitespace*

Pad your declarations with lots of whitespace. Content models and attribute lists suffer from dense syntax, so spacing out the parts, even placing them on separate lines, helps make them more understandable. Indent lines inside declarations to make the delimiters more clear. Between logical divisions, use extra space and perhaps a comment with a row of dark characters to add separation. When you quickly scroll through the file, you will find it is much easier to navigate.

*Comments*

Use comments liberally—they are signposts in a wilderness of declarations. First, place a comment at the top of each file that explains the purpose of the DTD or module, gives the version number, and provides contact information. If it is a customized frontend to a public DTD, be sure to mention the original that it is based on, give credit to the authors, and explain the changes that you made. Next, label each section and subsection of the DTD.

Anywhere a comment might help to clarify the use of the DTD or explain your decisions, add one. As you modify the DTD, add new comments describing your changes. Comments are part of documentation, and unclear or outdated documentation can be worse than useless.

*Version tracking*

As with software, your DTD is likely to be updated as your requirements change. You should keep track of versions by numbering them; to avoid confusion, it's important to change the version number when you make a change to the document. By convention, the first complete public release is 1.0. After that, small changes earn decimal increments: 1.1, 1.2, etc. Major changes increment by whole numbers: 2.0, 3.0, etc. Document the changes from version to version. Revision control systems are available to automate this process. On Unix-based systems, the RCS and CVS packages have both been the trusted friends of developers for years.

*Parameter entities*

Parameter entities can hold recurring parts of declarations and allow you to edit them in one place. In the external subset, they can be used in element-type declarations to hold element groups and content models, or in attribute list declarations to hold attribute definitions. The internal subset is a little stricter; parameter entities can hold only complete declarations, not fragments.

For example, assume you want every element to have an optional ID attribute for linking and an optional class attribute to assign specific role information. Parameter entities, which apply only in DTDs, look much like ordinary general entities, but have an extra % in the declaration. You can declare a parameter entity to hold common attributes like this:

```
<!ENTITY % common.atts "
  id      ID       #IMPLIED
  class   CDATA    #IMPLIED"
 >
```

That entity can then be used in attribute list declarations:

```
<!ATTLIST foo %common.atts;>
<!ATTLIST bar %common.atts;
   extra    CDATA    #FIXED "blah"
 >
```

Note that parameter entity references start with % rather than &.

### Attributes versus elements

Making a DTD from scratch is not easy. You have to break your information down into its conceptual atoms and package it as a hierarchical structure, but it's not always clear how to divide the information. The book model is easy, because it breaks down readily into hierarchical containers such as chapters, sections, and paragraphs. Less obvious are the models for equations, molecules, and databases. For such applications, it takes a supple mind to chop up documents into the optimal mix of elements and attributes. These tips are principles that can help you design DTDs:

- Choose names that make sense. If your document is composed exclusively of elements like thing, object, and chunk, it's going to be nearly impossible to figure out what's what. Names should closely match the logical purpose of an element. It's better to create specific elements for different tasks than to overload a few elements to handle many different situations. For example, the DIV and SPAN HTML elements aren't ideal because they serve many different roles.

- Hierarchy adds information. A newspaper has articles that contain paragraphs and heads. Containers create boundaries to make it easier to write stylesheets and processing applications. And they have an implied ownership that provides convenient handles and navigation aids for processors. Containers add depth, another dimension to increase the amount of structure.

  Strive for a tree structure that resembles a wide, bushy shrub. If you go too deep, the markup begins to overwhelm the content and it becomes harder to edit a document; too shallow and the information content is diluted. Think of documents and their parts as nested boxes. A big box filled with a million tiny boxes is much harder to work with than a box with a few medium boxes, and smaller boxes inside those, and so on.

- Know when to use elements over attributes. An element holds content that is part of your document. An attribute modifies the behavior of an element. The trick is to find a balance between using general elements with attributes to specify purpose and creating an element for every single contingency.

## Modularization

There are advantages to splitting a monolithic DTD into smaller components, or *modules*. The first benefit is that a modularized DTD can be easier to maintain, for reasons of organization mentioned earlier and because parts can be edited separately or "turned off" for debugging purposes. Also, the DTD becomes configurable. Modules in separate files can be swapped with others as easily as redefining a single parameter entity. Even within the same file, they can be marked for inclusion or exclusion.

XML provides two ways to modularize your DTD. The first is to store parts in separate files, then import them with external parameter entities. The second is to use a syntactic device called a *conditional section*. Both are powerful ways to make a DTD more flexible.

### Importing modules from external sources

A DTD does not have to be stored in a single file. In fact, it often makes sense to store it in multiple files. You may wish to borrow from someone else, importing their DTD into your own as a subset. Or you may just want to make the DTD a little neater by separating pieces into different files.

To import whole DTDs or parts of DTDs, use an external parameter entity. Here is an example of a complete DTD that imports its pieces from various modules:

```
<!ELEMENT catalog (title, metadata, front, entries+)>
<!ENTITY % basic.stuff   SYSTEM "basics.mod">
%basic.stuff;
<!ENTITY % front.matter  SYSTEM "front.mod">
%front.matter;
<!ENTITY % metadata      PUBLIC "-//Standards Stuff//DTD Metadata
  v3.2//EN" "http://www.standards-stuff.org/dtds/metadata.dtd">
%metadata;
```

This DTD has two local components, which are specified by system identifiers. Each component has a *.mod* filename extension, which is a traditional way to show that a file contains declarations but should not be used as a DTD on its own. The last component is a DTD that can stand on its own; in fact, in this example, it's a public resource.

There is one potential problem with importing DTD text. An external parameter entity imports *all* the text in a file, not just a part of it. You get all the declarations, not just a few select ones. Worse, there is no concept of local scope, in which declarations in the local DTD automatically override those in the imported file. The declarations are assembled into one logical entity, and any information about what was imported from where is lost before the DTD is parsed.

There are a few ways to get around this problem. You can override entity declarations by redeclaring them or, to be more precise, predeclaring them. In other words, if an entity is declared more than once, the first declaration will take precedence. So you can override any entity declaration with a declaration in the internal subset of your document, since the internal subset is read before the external subset.

Overriding an element declaration is more difficult. It is a validity error to declare an element more than once. (You can make multiple ATTLIST declarations for the same element, and the first one is accepted as the right one.) So, the question is, how can you override a declaration such as this:

```
<!ELEMENT polyhedron (side+, angle+)>
```

with a declaration of your own like this:

```
<!ELEMENT polyhedron (side, side, side+, angle, angle, angle+)>
```

To be able to override element and attribute declarations is not possible with what you know so far. I need to introduce you a new syntactic construct called the conditional section.

## Conditional sections

A *conditional section* is a special form of markup used in a DTD to mark a region of text for inclusion or exclusion in the DTD.* If you anticipate that a piece of your DTD may someday be an unwanted option, you can make it a conditional section and let the end user decide whether to keep it or not. Note that conditional sections can be used only in external subsets, not internal subsets.

Conditional sections look similar to CDATA sections. They use the square bracket delimiters, but the CDATA keyword is replaced with either INCLUDE or IGNORE. The syntax is like this:

```
<![switch[DTD text]]>
```

where *switch* is like an on/off switch, activating the *DTD text* if its value is INCLUDE, or marking it inactive if it's set to IGNORE. For example:

```
<![INCLUDE[
<!-- these declarations will be included -->
<!ELEMENT foo (bar, caz, bub?)>
<!ATTLIST foo crud CDATA #IMPLIED)>
]]>
<![IGNORE[
<!-- these declarations will be ignored -->
<!ELEMENT blah #PCDATA>
<!ELEMENT glop (flub|zuc) 'zuc')>
]]>
```

---

* In SGML, you can use conditional sections in documents as well as in DTDs. XML restricts its use to DTDs only. I personally miss them because I think they are a very powerful way to conditionally alter documents.

Using the hardcoded literals INCLUDE and IGNORE isn't all that useful, since you have to edit each conditional section manually to flip the switch. Usually, the switch is a parameter entity, which can be defined anywhere:

```
<!ENTITY % optional.stuff "INCLUDE">
<![%optional.stuff;[
<!-- these declarations may or may not be included -->
<!ELEMENT foo (bar, caz, bub?)>
<!ATTLIST foo crud CDATA #IMPLIED)>
]]>
```

Because the parameter entity optional.stuff is defined with the keyword INCLUDE, the declarations in the marked section will be used. If optional.stuff had been defined to be IGNORE, the declarations would have been ignored in the document.

This technique is especially powerful when you declare the entity inside a document subset. In the next example, our DTD declares a general entity that is called disclaimer. The actual value of the entity depends on whether use-disclaimer has been set to INCLUDE:

```
<![%use-disclaimer;[
  <!ENTITY disclaimer "<p>This is Beta software. We can't promise it
  is free of bugs.</p>">
]]>
<!ENTITY disclaimer "">
```

In documents where you want to include a disclaimer, it's a simple step to declare the switching entity in the internal subset:

```
<?xml version="1.0"?>
<!DOCTYPE manual SYSTEM "manual.dtd" [
  <!ENTITY % use-disclaimer "IGNORE">
]>

<manual>
  <title>User Guide for Techno-Wuzzy</title>

  &disclaimer;
  ...
```

In this example, the entity use-disclaimer is set to IGNORE, so the disclaimer is declared as an empty string and the document's text will not contain a disclaimer. This is a simple example of customizing a DTD using conditional sections and parameter entities.

Now, returning to our previous problem of overriding element or attribute declarations, here is how to do it with conditional sections. First, the DTD must be written to allow parameter entity switching:

```
<!ENTITY % default.polyhedron "INCLUDE">
<![%default.polyhedron;[
<!ELEMENT polyhedron (side+, angle+)>
]]>
```

Now, in your document, you declare this DTD as your external subset, then redeclare the parameter entity default.polyhedron in the internal subset:

```
<!DOCTYPE picture SYSTEM "shapes.dtd" [
  <!ENTITY % default.polyhedron "IGNORE">
  <!ELEMENT polyhedron (side, side, side+, angle, angle, angle+)>
]>
```

Since the internal subset is read before the external subset, the parameter entity declaration here takes precedence over the one in the DTD. The conditional section in the DTD will get a value of IGNORE, masking the external element declaration for polyhedron. The element declaration in the internal subset is valid and used by the parser.

Conditional sections can be nested, but outer sections override inner ones. So if the outer section is set to IGNORE, its contents (including any conditional sections inside it) are completely turned off regardless of their values. For example:

```
<![INCLUDE[
<!-- text in here will be included -->
  <![IGNORE[
  <!-- text in here will be ignored -->
  ]]>
]]>
<![IGNORE[
<!-- text in here will be ignored -->
  <![INCLUDE[
  <!-- Warning: this stuff will be ignored too! -->
  ]]>
]]>
```

Public DTDs often make heavy use of conditional sections to allow the maximum level of customization. For example, the DocBook XML DTD Version 1.0 includes the following:

```
<!ENTITY % screenshot.content.module "INCLUDE">
<![%screenshot.content.module;[
<!ENTITY % screenshot.module "INCLUDE">
<![%screenshot.module;[
<!ENTITY % local.screenshot.attrib "">
<!ENTITY % screenshot.role.attrib "%role.attrib;">
<!ELEMENT screenshot (screeninfo?, (graphic|graphicco))>
<!ATTLIST screenshot
                %common.attrib;
                %screenshot.role.attrib;
                %local.screenshot.attrib;
>
<!--end of screenshot.module-->]]>

<!ENTITY % screeninfo.module "INCLUDE">
<![%screeninfo.module;[
<!ENTITY % local.screeninfo.attrib "">
<!ENTITY % screeninfo.role.attrib "%role.attrib;">
```

```
<!ELEMENT screeninfo (%para.char.mix;)*>
<!ATTLIST screeninfo
                %common.attrib;
                %screeninfo.role.attrib;
                %local.screeninfo.attrib;
>
<!--end of screeninfo.module-->]]>
<!--end of screenshot.content.module-->]]>
```

The outermost conditional section surrounds declarations for screenshot and also screeninfo, which occurs inside it. You can completely eliminate both screenshot and screeninfo by setting screenshot.content.module to IGNORE in your local DTD before the file is loaded. Alternatively, you can turn off only the section around the screeninfo declarations, perhaps to declare your own version of screeninfo. (Turning off the declarations for an element in the imported file avoids warnings from your parser about redundant declarations.) Notice that there are parameter entities to assign various kinds of content and attribute definitions, such as %common.attrib;. There are also hooks for inserting attributes of your own, such as %local.screenshot. attrib;.

Skillful use of conditional sections can make a DTD extremely flexible, although it may become harder to read. You should use them sparingly in your personal DTDs and try to design them to fit your needs from the beginning. Later, if the DTD becomes a public resource, it will make sense to add conditional sections to allow end user customization.

### Using the internal subset

Recall from the section "Declarations" earlier in this chapter that the internal subset is the part of an XML document that can contain entity declarations. Actually, it's more powerful than that: you can put any declarations that would appear in a DTD into the internal subset. The only things that are restricted are conditional sections (can't use them) and parameter entities (they can hold only complete declarations, not fragments). This is useful for overriding or turning on or off parts of the DTD. Here's the general form:

```
<!DOCTYPE root-element URI [ declarations ]>
```

When a parser reads the DTD, it reads the internal subset first, then the external subset. This is important because the first declaration of an entity takes precedence over all other declarations of that entity. So you can override entity declarations in the DTD by declaring them in the internal subset. New elements and attributes can be declared in the internal subset, but you may not override existing declarations in the DTD. Recall that the mechanism for redefining an element or attribute is to use a parameter entity to turn off a conditional section containing the DTD's declaration.

This example shows some correct uses of the internal subset:

```
<!DOCTYPE inventory SYSTEM "InventoryReport.dtd" [

<!-- add a new "category" attribute to the item element -->
<!ATTLIST item category (screw | bolt | nut) #REQUIRED>

<!-- redefine the general entity companyname -->
<!ENTITY companyname "Crunchy Biscuits Inc.">

<!-- redefine the <price> element by redefining the price.module
     parameter entity -->
<!ELEMENT price (currency, amount)>
<!ENTITY % price.module "IGNORE">

<!-- use a different module for figures than what the DTD uses -->
<!ENTITY % figs SYSTEM "myfigs.mod">
]>
```

The attribute list declaration in this internal subset adds the attribute category to the set of attributes for item. As long as the DTD doesn't also declare a category attribute for item, this is okay.

The element declaration here clashes with a declaration already in the DTD. However, the next line switches off a conditional section by declaring the parameter entity price.module to be IGNORE. So the DTD's declaration will be hidden from the parser.

The last declaration overrides an external parameter entity in the DTD that imports a module, causing it to load the file *myfigs.mod* instead.

 You're only allowed to declare an element once in a DTD, so while you can override declarations for attributes, don't declare an element in the internal subset if it's already declared elsewhere.

## SimpleDoc: A Narrative Example

In the section "An Example" we developed a simple DTD for a data markup language. Narrative applications tend to be a little more complex, since there is more to human languages than simple data structures. Let's experiment now with a DTD for a more complex, narrative application.

Inspired by DocBook, I've created a small, narrative application called SimpleDoc. It's much smaller and doesn't attempt to do even a fraction of what DocBook can do, but it touches on all the major concepts and so is suitable for pedagogical purposes. Specifically, the goal of SimpleDoc is to mark up small, simple documents such as the one in Example 4-3.

*Example 4-3. A sample SimpleDoc document*

```
<?xml version="1.0"?>
<!DOCTYPE doc SYSTEM "simpledoc.dtd">
<doc>
  <title>Organism or Machine?</title>
```

*Example 4-3. A sample SimpleDoc document (continued)*

```
  <section id="diner">
    <title>Sam's Diner</title>
    <para>A huge truck passed by, eating up four whole lanes with its girth.
The whole back section was a glitzy passenger compartment trimmed in
chrome and neon. The roof sprouted a giant image of a hamburger with
flashing lights and the words, "Sam's Scruvi Soul Snax Shac". As it
sped past at foolhardy speed, I saw a bevy of cars roped to the back,
swerving back and forth.</para>
    <para>Included among these were:</para>
    <list>
      <listitem><para>a diesel-powered unicycle,</para></listitem>
      <listitem><para>a stretch limousine about 50 yards
      long,</para></listitem>
      <listitem><para>and the cutest little pod-cars shaped like spheres,
      with caterpillar tracks on the bottoms.</para></listitem>
    </list>
    <para>I made to intercept the truck, to hitch up my vehicle and climb
aboard.</para>
    <note>
      <para>If you want to chain up your car to a moving truck, you had better
know what you are doing.</para>
    </note>
  </section>
</doc>
```

Example 4-4 is the SimpleDoc DTD.

*Example 4-4. The SimpleDoc DTD*

```
<!--
SimpleDoc DTD
-->

<!-- ============================================================================
              Parameter Entities
     ======================================================================== -->

<!-- Attributes used in all elements -->
<!ENTITY % common.atts "
      id         ID         #IMPLIED
      class      CDATA      #IMPLIED
      xml:space (default | preserve) 'default'
">

<!-- Inline elements -->
<!-- Block and complex elements -->
<!ENTITY % block.group "
        author
      | blockquote
      | codelisting
      | example
      | figure
```

*Example 4-4. The SimpleDoc DTD (continued)*

```
        | graphic
        | list
        | note
        | para
        | remark
">

<!ENTITY % inline.group "
        acronym
        | citation
        | command
        | date
        | emphasis
        | filename
        | firstterm
        | literal
        | quote
        | ulink
        | xref
">

<!-- ============================================================================
                Hierarchical Elements
    ========================================================================= -->

<!-- The document element -->
<!ELEMENT doc (title, (%block.group)*, section+)>
<!ATTLIST doc %common.atts;>

<!-- Section to break up the document -->
<!ELEMENT section (title, (%block.group)*, section*)>
<!ATTLIST section %common.atts;>

<!-- ============================================================================
                Block Elements
    ========================================================================= -->

<!-- place to put the author's name -->
<!ELEMENT author #PCDATA>
<!ATTLIST author %common.atts;>

<!-- region of quoted text -->
<!ELEMENT blockquote (para+)>
<!ATTLIST blockquote %common.atts;>

<!-- formal codelisting (adds title) -->
<!ELEMENT example (title, codelisting)>
<!ATTLIST example %common.atts;>

<!-- formal picture (adds title) -->
<!ELEMENT figure (title, graphic)>
<!ATTLIST figure %common.atts;>
```

*Example 4-4. The SimpleDoc DTD (continued)*

```
<!-- out-of-flow note -->
<!ELEMENT footnote (para+)>
<!ATTLIST footnote %common.atts;>

<!-- picture -->
<!ELEMENT graphic EMPTY>
<!ATTLIST graphic
        fileref   CDATA     #REQUIRED
        %common.atts;
>

<!-- sequence of items -->
<!ELEMENT list (term?, listitem)+>
<!ATTLIST list
    type      (numbered|bulleted|definition)      "numbered"
    %common.atts;
>

<!-- component of a list -->
<!ELEMENT listitem (%block.group;)+>
<!ATTLIST listitem %common.atts;>

<!-- in-flow note -->
<!ELEMENT note (para+)>
<!ATTLIST note %common.atts;>

<!-- basic paragraph -->
<!ELEMENT para (#PCDATA | %inline.group; | footnote)*>
<!ATTLIST para %common.atts;>

<!-- code listing -->
<!ELEMENT codelisting (#PCDATA | %inline.group;)*>
<!ATTLIST codelisting
    xml:space (preserve) #FIXED 'preserve'
    %common.atts;
>

<!-- visible comment -->
<!ELEMENT remark (#PCDATA | %inline.group;)*>
<!ATTLIST remark %common.atts;>

<!-- document or section label -->
<!ELEMENT title (#PCDATA | %inline.group;)*>
<!ATTLIST title %common.atts;>

<!-- term in a definition list -->
<!ELEMENT term (#PCDATA | %inline.group;)*>
<!ATTLIST term %common.atts;>

<!-- =========================================================================
                Inline Elements
```

*Example 4-4. The SimpleDoc DTD (continued)*

```
     =========================================================================== -->

<!ENTITY % inline.content "#PCDATA">

<!ELEMENT acronym %inline.content;>
<!ATTLIST acronym %common.atts;>

<!ELEMENT citation %inline.content;>
<!ATTLIST citation %common.atts;>

<!ELEMENT command %inline.content;>
<!ATTLIST command %common.atts;>

<!ELEMENT date %inline.content;>
<!ATTLIST date %common.atts;>

<!ELEMENT emphasis %inline.content;>
<!ATTLIST emphasis %common.atts;>

<!ELEMENT filename %inline.content;>
<!ATTLIST filename %common.atts;>

<!ELEMENT firstterm %inline.content;>
<!ATTLIST firstterm %common.atts;>

<!ELEMENT literal %inline.content;>
<!ATTLIST literal %common.atts;>

<!ELEMENT quote %inline.content;>
<!ATTLIST quote %common.atts;>

<!ELEMENT ulink %inline.content;>
<!ATTLIST ulink
        href       CDATA    #REQUIRED
        %common.atts;
>

<!ELEMENT xref EMPTY>
<!ATTLIST xref
        linkend    ID       #REQUIRED
        %common.atts;
>

<!-- ===========================================================================
                  Useful Entities
     =========================================================================== -->

<!ENTITY % isolat1
    PUBLIC "ISO 8879:1986//ENTITIES Added Latin 1//EN//XML"
    "isolat1.ent"
>
%isolat1;
```

*Example 4-4. The SimpleDoc DTD (continued)*

```
<!ENTITY % isolat2
    PUBLIC "ISO 8879:1986//ENTITIES Added Latin 2//EN//XML"
    "isolat2.ent"
>
%isolat2;
<!ENTITY % isomath
    PUBLIC "ISO 8879:1986//ENTITIES Added Math Symbols: Ordinary//EN//XML"
    "isoamso.ent"
>
%isomath;
<!ENTITY % isodia
    PUBLIC "ISO 8879:1986//ENTITIES Diacritical Marks//EN//XML"
    "isodia.ent"
>
%isodia;
<!ENTITY % isogreek
    PUBLIC "ISO 8879:1986//ENTITIES Greek Symbols//EN//XML"
    "isogrk3.ent"
>
%isogreek;
```

# W3C XML Schema

DTDs are chiefly directed toward describing how elements are arranged in a document. They say very little about the content in the document, other than whether an element can contain character data. Although attributes can be declared to be of different types (e.g. ID, IDREF, enumerated), there is no way to constrain the type of data in an element.

Returning to the example in "An Example," we can see how this limitation can be a serious problem. Suppose that a census taker submitted the document in Example 4-5.

*Example 4-5. A bad CensusML document*

```
<census-record taker="9170">
  <date><month>?</month><day>110</day><year>03</year></date>
  <address>
    <city>Munchkinland</city>
    <street></street>
    <county></county>
    <country>Here, silly</country>
    <postalcode></postalcode>
  </address>
  <person employed="fulltime" pid="?">
    <name>
      <last>Burgle</last>
      <first>Brad</first>
    </name>
    <age>2131234</age>
```

*Example 4-5. A bad CensusML document (continued)*

```
   <gender>yes</gender>
 </person>
</census-record>
```

There are a lot of things wrong with this document. The date is in the wrong format. Several important fields were left empty. The stated age is an impossibly large number. The gender, which ought to be "male" or "female," contains something else. The personal identification number has a bad value. And yet, to our infinite dismay, the DTD would pick up none of these problems.

It isn't hard to write a program that would check the data types, but that's a low-level operation, prone to bugs and requiring technical ability. It's also getting away from the point of DTDs, which is to create a kind of metadocument, a formal description of a markup language. Programming languages aren't portable and don't work well as a way of conveying syntactic and semantic details. So we have to conclude that DTDs don't go far enough in describing a markup language.

To make matters worse, what the DTD will reject as bad markup are often trivial things. For example, the contents of date and name are not in the specific order required by their element declarations. This seems unnecessarily picayune, but it's actually very difficult to write a content model that allows its children to appear in any order.

To illustrate the problem, let's try to make the date more flexible, so that it accepts children in any order. The best I can think of is to write the declaration like this:

```
<!ELEMENT date (
        (year,  ((month, day)  | (day, month)))
      | (month, ((year, day)   | (day, year)))
      | (day,   ((month, year) | (year, month)))
  )>
```

Pretty ugly, isn't it? And that's only with three child elements. This is another serious drawback of DTDs.

Perhaps the most damaging limitation of DTDs is the lockdown of namespace. Any element in a document has to have a corresponding declaration in the DTD. No exceptions. This is fundamentally at odds with XML namespaces, which allow you to import vocabularies from anywhere. Granted, there are good reasons to want to limit the kinds of elements used: more efficient validation and preventing illegal elements from appearing. But there's no way to turn this feature off if you don't want it.[*]

To address problems like these, a new validation system was invented called *schema*. Like DTDs, schemas contain rules that all must be satisfied for a document to be

---

[*] There is a complex parameter entity hack for creating DTDs that can cope with namespaces. Although the W3C has used it for both XHTML and SVG modularization, it's both fragile and a huge readability problem.

considered valid. Unlike DTDs, however, schemas are not built into the XML specification. They are an add-on technology that you can use, provided you have access to parsers that will support it.

There are several competing kinds of schema. The one that is sanctioned by the W3C is called XML Schema. Another proposal, called RELAX NG, adds capabilities not found in XML Schema, such as regular expression matching in character data. Yet another popular alternative is Schematron. We'll focus on the W3C variety in this section and visit alternatives in later sections.

XML Schemas are themselves XML documents. That's a nice convenience, allowing you to check well-formedness and validity when you make modifications to a schema. It's more verbose than a DTD, but still pretty readable and vastly more flexible.

From the census example, here is how you would define the county element:

```
<xs:schema xmlns:xs="http://www.w3.org/2001/XMLSchema">
  <xs:element name="county" type="xs:string"/>
</xs:schema>
```

The xs:element element acts like an !ELEMENT declaration in a DTD. Its name attribute declares a name ("county"), and its type attribute defines a content model by referring to a *data type* identifier. Instead of using a compact string of symbols to define a content model, schemas define content models in a separate place, then refer to them inside the element definition. This is kind of like using parameter entities, but as we will see it's more flexible in schemas.

xs:string refers to a *simple type* of element, one that is built in to the Schema specification. In this case, it's just a string of character data, about as simple as you can get. An alternative to xs:string is xs:token. It also contains a string, but normalizes the space (strips out leading and trailing space and collapses extra space characters) for you. Table 4-1 lists other simple types which are commonly used in schemas. There are many more types in W3C XML Schema Part 2: Datatypes, but this core covers most frequent needs and will get you started.

*Table 4-1. Simple types commonly used in schemas*

| Type | Usage |
| --- | --- |
| xs:string | Contains any text. |
| xs:token | Contains textual tokens separated by whitespace. |
| xs:QName | Contains a namespace-qualified name. |
| xs:decimal | Contains a decimal number of arbitrary precision. (Processors must support a minimum of 18 digits.) "3.252333", "−1.01", and "+20" are all acceptable values. |
| xs:integer | Contains an integer number, like "0", "35", or "−1433322" |
| xs:float | Contains a 32-bit IEEE 754 floating point number. |
| xs:ID, xs:IDREF, xs:IDREF | Behave the same as the ID, IDREF, IDREFS in DTDs. |

*Table 4-1. Simple types commonly used in schemas (continued)*

| Type | Usage |
|---|---|
| xs:boolean | Contains a true or false value, expressed as "true" or "false" or "1" or "0". |
| xs:time | Contains a time in ISO 8601 format (*HH:MM:SS—Timezone*), like 21:55:00—06:00. |
| xs:date | Contains a date in ISO 8601 format (CCYY-MM-DD), like 2004-12-30. |
| xs:dateTime | Contains a date/time combination in ISO 8601 format (*CCYY-MM-DDTHH:MM:SS—Timezone*), like 2004-12-30T21:55:00—06:00. |

Most elements are not simple, however. They can contain elements, attributes, and character data with specialized formats. So schemas also contain complex element definitions. Here's how you could define the date element:

```
<xs:element name="date">
  <xs:complexType>
    <xs:all>
      <xs:element ref="year"/>
      <xs:element ref="month"/>
      <xs:element ref="day"/>
    </xs:all>
  </xs:complexType>
</xs:element>
<xs:element name="year" type="xs:integer"/>
<xs:element name="month" type="xs:integer"/>
<xs:element name="day" type="xs:integer"/>
```

The date element is a *complex type* because it has special requirements that you must explicitly define. In this case, the type is a group of three elements (in any order), referred to by name using the ref attribute. These referred elements are defined at the bottom to be of type integer.

It is possible to refine the date even further. Although the schema will guarantee that each of the subfields year, month, and day are integer values, it will allow some values we don't want. For example, –125724 is a valid integer, but we wouldn't want that to be used for month.

The way to control the range of a data type is to use *facets*. A facet is an additional parameter added to a type definition. You can create a new data type for the <month> element like this:

```
<xs:simpleType name="monthNum">
  <xs:restriction base="xs:integer">
    <xs:minInclusive value="1"/>
    <xs:maxInclusive value="12"/>
  </xs:restriction>
</xs:simpleType>
<xs:element name="month" type="monthNum"/>
```

Here, we created a named type and named it monthNum. Named types are not bound to any particular element, so they are useful if you'll be using the same type over and over. In this type definition is an xs:restriction element from which we will derive a more specific type than the loose xs:integer. Inside are two facets, minInclusive and maxInclusive, setting the lower and upper bounds respectively. Any element set to the type monthNum will be checked to ensure its value is a number that falls inside that range.

Besides setting ranges, facets can create fixed values, constrain the length of strings, and match patterns with regular expressions. For example, say you want the postal code to be any string that contains three digits followed by three letters, as in the census example:

```
<postalcode>885JKL</postalcode>
```

A pattern to match this is [0-9][0-9][0-9][A-Z][A-Z][A-Z]. Even better: [0-9]{3}[A-Z]{3}. Here is how the schema element might look:

```
<xs:element name="postalcode" type="pcode"/>
<xs:simpleType name="pcode">
  <xs:restriction base="xs:token">
    <xs:pattern value="[0-9]{3}[A-Z]{3}"/>
  </xs:restriction>
</xs:simpleType>
```

Another way to define a type is by *enumeration*, defining a set of allowed values. The gender element, for example, may only contain two values: female or male. Here's a gender type:

```
<xs:simpleType name="genderType">
  <xs:restriction base="xs:token">
    <xs:enumeration value="female"/>
    <xs:enumeration value="male"/>
  </xs:restriction>
</xs:simpleType>
```

Now, let me show you how I would write a schema for the CensusML document type. Example 4-6 shows my attempt.

*Example 4-6. A schema for CensusML*

```
<xs:schema xmlns:xs="http://www.w3.org/2001/XMLSchema">
  <!-- document element -->
  <xs:element name="census-record">
    <xs:complexType>
      <xs:sequence>
        <xs:element ref="date"/>
        <xs:element ref="address"/>
        <xs:element ref="person" maxOccurs="unbounded"/>
      </xs:sequence>
      <xs:attribute ref="taker"/>
    </xs:complexType>
  </xs:element>

  <!-- Number identifying the census taker (1-9999) -->
```

*Example 4-6. A schema for CensusML (continued)*

```
<xs:attribute name="taker">
  <xs:simpleType>
    <xs:restriction base="integer">
      <xs:minInclusive value="1"/>
      <xs:maxInclusive value="9999"/>
    </xs:restriction>
  </xs:simpleType>
</xs:attribute>

<!-- structure containing date information -->
<!-- this is a simplification over the previous definition using -->
<!-- three subelements. -->
<xs:element name="date" type="date"/>

<!-- structure containing address information -->
<xs:element name="address">
  <xs:complexType>
    <xs:all>
      <xs:element ref="street"/>
      <xs:element ref="city"/>
      <xs:element ref="county"/>
      <xs:element ref="country"/>
      <xs:element ref="postalcode"/>
    </xs:all>
  </xs:complexType>
</xs:element>

<xs:element name="street" type="string"/>
<xs:element name="city" type="string"/>
<xs:element name="county" type="string"/>
<xs:element name="country" type="string"/>

<!-- postalcode element: uses format 123ABC -->
<xs:element name="postalcode">
  <xs:simpleType>
    <xs:restriction base="string">
      <xs:pattern value="[0-9]{3}[A-Z]{3}"/>
    </xs:restriction>
  </xs:simpleType>
</xs:element>

<!-- structure containing data for one resident of the household -->
<xs:element name="person">
  <xs:complexType>
    <xs:all>
      <xs:element ref="name"/>
      <xs:element ref="age"/>
      <xs:element ref="gender"/>
    </xs:all>
    <xs:attribute ref="employed"/>
    <xs:attribute ref="pid"/>
  </xs:complexType>
```

*Example 4-6. A schema for CensusML (continued)*

```
  </xs:element>

  <!-- Employment status: fulltime, parttime, or none -->
  <xs:attribute name="employed">
    <xs:simpleType>
      <xs:restriction base="string">
        <xs:enumeration value="fulltime"/>
        <xs:enumeration value="parttime"/>
        <xs:enumeration value="none"/>
      </xs:restriction>
    </xs:simpleType>
  </xs:attribute>

  <!-- Number identifying the person (1-999999) -->
  <xs:attribute name="pid">
    <xs:simpleType>
      <xs:restriction base="integer">
        <xs:minInclusive value="1"/>
        <xs:maxInclusive value="999999"/>
      </xs:restriction>
    </xs:simpleType>
  </xs:attribute>

  <!-- Age (0-200) -->
  <xs:element name="age">
    <xs:complexType>
      <xs:restriction base="integer">
        <xs:minInclusive value="0"/>
        <xs:maxInclusive value="200"/>
      </xs:restriction>
    </xs:complexType>
  </xs:element>

  <!-- Enumerated type: male or female -->
  <xs:element name="gender">
    <xs:simpleType>
      <xs:restriction base="string">
        <xs:enumeration value="female"/>
        <xs:enumeration value="male"/>
      </xs:restriction>
    </xs:simpleType>
  </xs:element>

  <!-- structure containing the name; note the choice element
       that allows an optional junior OR senior element -->
  <xs:element name="name">
    <xs:complexType>
      <xs:all>
        <xs:element ref="first"/>
        <xs:element ref="last"/>
      </xs:all>
      <xs:choice minOccurs="0">
```

*Example 4-6. A schema for CensusML (continued)*

```
      <xs:element ref="junior"/>
      <xs:element ref="senior"/>
    </xs:choice>
  </xs:complextype>
</xs:element>

<xs:element name="junior" type="emptyElem"/>
<xs:element name="senior" type="emptyElem"/>

<!-- Defining a type of element that is empty -->
<xs:complexType name="emptyElem"/>

</xs:schema>
```

Some notes:

- Since XML Schema supports a variety of date formats for character data, it makes sense to replace the cumbersome date container and its three child elements with one that takes only text content. This simplifies the schema and supporting software for the census application.

- I used an attribute maxOccurs to allow an unlimited number of person elements. Without it, the schema would allow no more than one such element.

- A choice element is the opposite of all. Instead of requiring all the elements to be present, it will allow only one of the choices to appear. In this case, I wanted at most one of <junior/> or <senior/> to appear.

- I set the minOccurs attribute in the choice to zero to make it optional. You can choose to use <junior/> or <senior/>, but you don't have to.

- Curiously, there is no type for empty elements. That's why I had to define one, emptyElem for the elements junior and senior.

> This is only scratching the surface of XML Schema, which offers an enormous variety of features, including type extension and restriction, lists, unions, namespace features, and much more. For more information on XML Schema, see Eric van der Vlist's *XML Schema* (O'Reilly & Associates, 2002).

# RELAX NG

RELAX NG is a powerful schema validation language that builds on earlier work including RELAX and TREX. Like W3C Schema, it uses XML syntax and supports namespaces and data typing. It goes further by integrating attributes into content models, which greatly simplifies the structure of the schema. It offers superior handling of unordered content and supports context-sensitive content models.

In general, it just seems easier to write schemas in RELAX NG than in W3C Schema. The syntax is very clear, with elements like zeroOrMore for specifying optional repeating content. Declarations can contain other declarations, leading to a more natural representation of a document's structure.

Consider the simple schema in Example 4-7 which models a document type for logging work activity. It's easy to read this schema and understand the structure of a typical document.

*Example 4-7. A simple RELAX NG schema*

```
<element name="worklog"
        xmlns="http://relaxng.org/ns/structure/1.0"
        xmlns:ann="http://relaxng.org/ns/compatibility/annotations/1.0">
  <ann:documentation>A document for logging work activity, broken down
        into days, and further into tasks.</ann:documentation>
  <zeroOrMore>
    <element name="day">
      <attribute name="date">
        <text/>
      </attribute>
      <zeroOrMore>
        <element name="task">
          <element name="description">
            <text/>
          </element>
          <element name="time-start">
            <text/>
          </element>
          <element name="time-end">
            <text/>
          </element>
        </element>
      </zeroOrMore>
    </element>
  </zeroOrMore>
</element>
```

The same thing would look like this as a DTD:

```
<!ELEMENT worklog (day*)>
<!ELEMENT day (task*)>
<!ELEMENT task (description, time-start, time-end)>
<!ELEMENT description #PCDATA>
<!ELEMENT time-start #PCDATA>
<!ELEMENT time-end #PCDATA>
<!ATTLIST day date CDATA #REQUIRED>
```

Although the DTD is more compact, it relies on a special syntax that is decidedly not XML-ish. RELAX NG accomplishes the same thing with more readability.

RELAX NG also offers a compact syntax that looks somewhat like a DTD but offers all the features of RELAX NG. For a brief introduction, see *http://www.xml.com/pub/a/2002/06/19/rng-compact.html*. James Clark's Trang program, available at *http://www.thaiopensource. com/relaxng/trang.html*, makes it easy to convert between RELAX NG, RELAX NG Compact Syntax, and DTDs, as well as create W3C XML Schema from any of these formats.

The basic component of a RELAX NG schema is a *pattern*. A pattern denotes any construct that describes the order and types of structure and content. It can be an element declaration, an attribute declaration, character data, or any combination. Elements in the schema are used to group, order, and parameterize these patterns.

Note that any element or attribute in a namespace other than the RELAX NG namespace (*http://relaxng.org/ns/structure/1.0*) is simply ignored by the parser. That gives us a mechanism for putting in comments or annotations, which explains why I created the ann namespace in the previous example.

## Elements

The element construct is used both to declare an element and to establish where the element can appear (when placed inside another element declaration). For example, the following schema declares three elements, report, title, and body, and specifies that the first element contains the other two in the exact order and number that they appear:

```
<element name="report"
      xmlns="http://relaxng.org/ns/structure/1.0">
  <element name="title">
    <text/>
  </element>
  <element name="body">
    <text/>
  </element>
</element>
```

Whitespace between these elements is allowed, as it would be for a DTD. The text element, which is always empty, restricts the content of the inner elements to character content.

### Repetition

To allow for repeating children, RELAX NG provides two modifier elements, zeroOrMore and oneOrMore. They function like DTD's star (*) and plus (+) operators, respectively. In this example, the body element has been modified to allow an arbitrary number of para elements:

```
<element name="report"
      xmlns="http://relaxng.org/ns/structure/1.0">
```

```
<element name="title">
  <text/>
</element>
<element name="body">
  <zeroOrMore>
    <element name="para">
      <text/>
    </element>
  </zeroOrMore>
</element>
</element>
```

### Choices

The question mark (?) operator in DTDs means that an element is optional (zero or one in number). In RELAX NG, you can achieve that effect with the optional modifier. For example, this schema allows you to insert an optional authorname element after the title:

```
<element name="report"
      xmlns="http://relaxng.org/ns/structure/1.0">
  <element name="title">
    <text/>
  </element>
  <optional>
    <element name="authorname">
      <text/>
    </element>
  </optional>
  <element name="body">
    <text/>
  </element>
</element>
```

It is also useful to offer a choice of elements. Corresponding to DTD's vertical bar (|) operator is the modifier choice. Here, we require either an authorname or a source element after the title:

```
<element name="report"
      xmlns="http://relaxng.org/ns/structure/1.0">
  <element name="title">
    <text/>
  </element>
  <choice>
    <element name="authorname">
      <text/>
    </element>
    <element name="source">
      <text/>
    </element>
  </choice>
  <element name="body">
    <text/>
```

```
      </element>
    </element>
```

This declaration combines choice with zeroOrMore to create a container that can have mixed content (text plus elements, in any order):

```
<element name="paragraph"
      xmlns="http://relaxng.org/ns/structure/1.0">
  <zeroOrMore>
    <choice>
      <text/>
      <element name="emphasis">
        <text/>
      </element>
    </choice>
  </zeroOrMore>
</element>
```

### Grouping

For a required sequence of children, you can use the group modifier, which functions much like parentheses in DTDs. For example, here the (now required) authorname is either plain text or a sequence of elements:

```
<element name="report"
      xmlns="http://relaxng.org/ns/structure/1.0">
  <element name="title">
    <text/>
  </element>
  <element name="authorname">
    <choice>
      <text/>
      <group>
        <element name="first"><text/></element>
        <element name="last"><text/></element>
      </group>
    </choice>
  </element>
  <element name="body">
    <text/>
  </element>
</element>
```

The group container is necessary because without it the first and last elements would be part of the choice and become mutually exclusive.

DTDs provide no way to require a group of elements in which order is *not* significant but contents are required. RELAX NG provides a container called interleave which does just that. It requires all the children to be present, but in any order. In the following example, title can come before authorname, or it can come after:

```
<element name="report"
      xmlns="http://relaxng.org/ns/structure/1.0">
```

```
<interleave>
  <element name="title">
    <text/>
  </element>
  <element name="authorname">
    <text/>
  </element>
</interleave>
<element name="body">
  <text/>
</element>
</element>
```

## Nonelement content descriptors

The `text` content descriptor is only one of several options for describing non-element content. Here's the full assortment:

| Name | Content |
| --- | --- |
| empty | No content at all |
| text | Any string |
| value | A predetermined value |
| data | Text following a specific pattern (datatype) |
| list | A sequence of values |

The `empty` marker precludes any content. With this declaration, the element `bookmark` is not allowed to appear in any form other than as an empty element:

```
<element name="bookmark">
  <empty/>
</element>
```

RELAX NG provides the `value` descriptor for matching a string of characters. For example, here is an enumeration of values for a `size` element:

```
<element name="size">
  <choice>
    <value>small</value>
    <value>medium</value>
    <value>large</value>
  </choice>
</element>
```

By default, `value` normalizes the string, removing extra space characters. The example element below would be accepted by the previous declaration:

```
<size>  small    </size>
```

If you want to turn off normalization and require exact string matching, you need to add a type="string" attribute. The following declaration would reject the above element's content because of its extra space:

```
<element name="size">
  <choice>
    <value type="string">small</value>
    <value type="string">medium</value>
    <value type="string">large</value>
  </choice>
</element>
```

The most interesting content descriptor is data. This is the vehicle for using datatypes in RELAX NG. Its type attribute contains the name of a type defined in a datatype library. (Don't worry about what that means yet, we'll get to it in a moment.) The content of the element declared here is set to be an integer value:

```
<element name="font-size">
  <data type="integer"/>
</element>
```

One downside to using data is that it can't be mixed with elements in content, unlike text.

The list descriptor contains a sequence of space-separated tokens. A token is a special type of string consisting only of nonspace characters. Token lists are a convenient way to represent sets of discrete data. Here, one is used to encode a set of numbers:

```
<element name="vector">
  <list>
    <oneOrMore>
      <data type="float"/>
    </oneOrMore>
  </list>
</element>
```

Here is an acceptable vector:

```
<vector>44.034 19.0 -65.33333</vector>
```

Note how the oneOrMore descriptor works just as well with text as it does with elements. It's yet another example of how succinct and flexible RELAX NG is.

## Data Typing

Although RELAX NG supports datatyping, the specification only includes two built-in types: string and token. To use other kinds of datatypes, you need to import them from another specification. You do this by setting a datatypeLibrary attribute like so:

```
<element name="font-size">
  <data type="integer"
        datatypeLibrary="http://www.w3.org/2001/XMLSchema-datatypes"/>
</element>
```

This will associate the datatype definitions from the W3C Schema specification with your schema. The datatypes you can use depend on the implementation of your RELAX NG validating parser.

It isn't so convenient to put the datatypeLibrary attribute in every data element. The good news is it can be inherited from any ancestor in the schema. Here, we declare it once in an element declaration, and all the data descriptors inside call from that library:

```
<element name="rectangle"
      xmlns="http://relaxng.org/ns/structure/1.0"
      datatypeLibrary="http://www.w3.org/2001/XMLSchema-datatypes">
  <element name="width">
    <data type="double"/>
  </element>
  <element name="height">
    <data type="double"/>
  </element>
</element>
```

### String and token

Both string and token match arbitrary strings of legal XML character data. The difference is that token normalizes whitespace and string keeps whitespace as is. They correspond to the datatypes value and fixed, respectively.

### Parameters

Some datatypes allow you to specify a parameter to further restrict the pattern. This is expressed with a param element as a child of the data element. For example, the element below restricts its content to a string of no more than eight characters:

```
<element name="username"
      xmlns="http://relaxng.org/ns/structure/1.0">
  <data type="string">
    <param name="maxLength">8</param>
  </data>
</element>
```

## Attributes

Attributes are declared much the same way as elements. In this example, we add a date attribute to the report element:

```
<element name="report"
      xmlns="http://relaxng.org/ns/structure/1.0">
  <attribute name="date">
    <text/>
  </attribute>
  <element name="title">
```

```
    <text/>
  </element>
  <element name="body">
    <text/>
  </element>
</element>
```

Unlike elements, the order of attributes is not significant. In this next example, the attributes for any alert element can appear in any order, even though we are not using a choice element:

```
<element name="alert"
      xmlns="http://relaxng.org/ns/structure/1.0">
  <attribute name="priority">
    <value>emergency</value>
    <value>important</value>
    <value>warning</value>
    <value>notification</value>
  </attribute>
  <attribute name="icon">
    <value>bomb</value>
    <value>exclamation-mark</value>
    <value>frown-face</value>
  </attribute>
  <element name="body">
    <text/>
  </element>
</element>
```

Element and attribute declarations are interchangeable. Here, we use a choice element to provide two cases: one with an icon attribute and another with an icon element. The two are mutually exclusive:

```
<element name="alert"
      xmlns="http://relaxng.org/ns/structure/1.0">
  <choice>
    <attribute name="icon">
      <value>bomb</value>
      <value>exclamation-mark</value>
      <value>frown-face</value>
    </attribute>
    <element name="icon">
      <value>bomb</value>
      <value>exclamation-mark</value>
      <value>frown-face</value>
    </element>
  </choice>
  <element name="body">
    <text/>
  </element>
</element>
```

Another difference with element declarations is that there is a shorthand form in which the lack of any content information defaults to text. So, for example, this declaration:

```
<element name="emphasis">
  <attribute name="style"/>
</element>
```

...is equivalent to this:

```
<element name="emphasis">
  <attribute name="style">
    <text/>
  </attribute>
</element>
```

This interchangeability between element and attribute declarations makes the schema language much simpler and more elegant.

## Namespaces

RELAX NG is fully namespace aware. You can include namespaces in any name attribute using the xmlns attribute:

```
<element name="poem"
        xmlns="http://relaxng.org/ns/structure/1.0">
        xmlns:foo="http://www.mystuff.com/commentary">
  <optional>
    <attribute name="xml:space">
      <choice>
        <value>default</value>
        <value>preserve</value>
      </choice>
    </attribute>
  </optional>
  <zeroOrMore>
    <choice>
      <text/>
      <element name="foo:comment"><text/></element>
    </choice>
  </zeroOrMore>
</element>
```

Add the attribute ns to any element or attribute declaration to set an implicit namespace context. For example, this declaration:

```
<element name="vegetable" ns="http://www.broccoli.net"
      xmlns="http://relaxng.org/ns/structure/1.0">
  <empty/>
</element>
```

would match either of these:

```
<food:vegetable xmlns:food="http://www.broccoli.net"/>
<vegetable xmlns="http://www.broccoli.net"/>
```

...but fail to match these:

```
<vegetable/>
<food:vegetable xmlns:food="http://www.uglifruit.org"/>
```

The namespace setting is inherited, allowing you to set it once at a high level. Here, the inner element declarations for title and body implicitly require the namespace http://howtowrite.info:

```
<element name="report" ns="http://howtowrite.info"
      xmlns="http://relaxng.org/ns/structure/1.0">
  <element name="title"><text/></element>
  <element name="body"><text/></element>
</element>
```

## Name Classes

A *name class* is any pattern that substitutes for a set of element or attribute types. We've already seen one, choice, which matches an enumerated set of elements and attributes. Even more permissive is the name class anyName, which allows any element or attribute type to have the described content model.

For example, this pattern matches any well-formed document:

```
<grammar
      xmlns="http://relaxng.org/ns/structure/1.0">
  <start>
    <ref name="all-elements"/>
  </start>
  <define name="all-elements">
    <element>
      <anyName/>        <!-- use in place of the "name" attribute -->
      <zeroOrMore>
        <choice>
          <ref name="anyElement"/>
          <text/>
          <attribute><anyName/></attribute>
        </choice>
      </zeroOrMore>
    </element>
  </define>
</grammar>
```

The anyName appears inside the element instead of a name attribute. The zeroOrMore is required here because each name class element matches exactly one object.

The nsName class matches any element or attribute in a namespace specified by an ns attribute. For example:

```
<element
      xmlns="http://relaxng.org/ns/structure/1.0">
  <nsName ns="http://fakesite.org" />
  <empty/>
</element>
```

This will set any element in the namespace `http://fakesite.org` to be an empty element. If you leave out the `ns` attribute, `nsName` will inherit the namespace from the nearest ancestor that defines one. So this will also work:

```
<element ns="http://fakesite.org"
      xmlns="http://relaxng.org/ns/structure/1.0">
  <nsName />
  <empty />
</element>
```

If you don't want to let *everything* through, trim down the set using except. Use it as a child to anyName or nsName to list classes of elements or attributes you don't want to allow. Here, only elements not in the current namespace are declared empty:

```
<element ns="http://fakesite.org"
      xmlns="http://relaxng.org/ns/structure/1.0">
  <anyName>
    <except>
      <nsName />
    </except>
  </anyName>
  <empty />
</element>
```

The only place you cannot use a name class is as the child of a `define` element. This is wrong:

```
<define name="too-ambiguous">
  <anyName/>
</define>
```

We'll discuss `define` elements in the next section.

 As this book was going to press, James Clark announced the Namespace Routing Language (NRL), which provides enormous flexibility for describing how content in different namespaces should be validated and processed. See *http://www.thaiopensource.com/relaxng/nrl.html* for more information and an implementation.

## Named Patterns

The patterns we have seen so far are monolithic. All the declarations are nested inside one big one. This is fine for simple documents, but as complexity builds, it can be hard to manage. *Named patterns* allow you to move declarations outside of the main pattern, breaking up the schema into discrete parts that are more easily handled. It also allows for reusing patterns that recur in many places.

A schema that uses named patterns follows this layout:

```
<grammar>
  <start>
    main pattern
```

```
    main pattern
  </start>
  <define name="identifier">
    pattern
  </define>
  more pattern definitions
</grammar>
```

The outermost grammar element encloses both the main pattern and a set of named pattern definitions. It contains exactly one start element with the primary pattern, and any number of define elements, each defining a named pattern. Named patterns are imported into a pattern using a ref element. For example:

```
<grammar
    xmlns="http://relaxng.org/ns/structure/1.0">

  <start>
    <element name="report">
      <ref name="head"/>
      <ref name="body"/>
    </element>
  </start>

  <define name="head">
    <element name="title">
      <text/>
    </element>
    <element name="authorname">
      <text/>
    </element>
  </define>

  <define name="body">
    <zeroOrMore>
      <element name="paragraph">
        <text/>
      </element>
    </zeroOrMore>
  </define>

</grammar>
```

The start element must contain exactly one pattern. However, a define may contain any number of children, since its contents will be copied into another pattern.

You can write a grammar to fit the style of DTDs, with one definition per element:[*]

```
<grammar
    xmlns="http://relaxng.org/ns/structure/1.0">
```

---

[*] This is how DTDs can be mapped directly into RELAX NG schema. This kind of backward compatibility is important, since most people are still using DTDs. So this is a good way to upgrade to RELAX NG.

```
<start>
  <element name="report">
    <ref name="title"/>
    <ref name="authorname"/>
    <zeroOrMore>
      <ref name="paragraph"/>
    </zeroOrMore>
  </element>
</start>

<define name="title">
  <element name="title">
    <text/>
  </element>
</define>

<define name="authorname">
  <element name="authorname">
    <text/>
  </element>
</define>

<define name="paragraph">
  <element name="paragraph">
    <text/>
  </element>
</define>

</grammar>
```

## Recursive definitions

Recursive definitions are allowed, as long as the ref is enclosed inside an element. This pattern describes a section element that can contain subsections arbitrarily deep:

```
<grammar
     xmlns="http://relaxng.org/ns/structure/1.0">

  <start>
    <element name="report">
      <element name="title"><text/></element>
      <zeroOrMore>
        <ref name="paragraph">
      </zeroOrMore>
      <zeroOrMore>
        <ref name="section"/>
      </zeroOrMore>
    </element>
  </start>

  <define name="paragraph">
    <element name="paragraph">
```

```
        <text/>
      </element>
    </define>

    <define name="section">
      <element name="section">
        <zeroOrMore>
          <ref name="paragraph"/>
        </zeroOrMore>
        <zeroOrMore>
          <ref name="section"/>
        </zeroOrMore>
      </element>
    </define>

  </grammar>
```

Failing to put the ref inside an element in a recursive definition would set up a logical infinite loop. So this is illegal:

```
<define name="foo">
  <choice>
    <ref name="bar"/>
    <ref name="foo"/>
  </choice>
</define>
```

The order of definitions for named patterns doesn't matter. As long as every referenced pattern has a definition within the same grammar, everything will be kosher.

### Aggregate definitions

Multiple pattern definitions with the same name are illegal unless you use the combine attribute. This tells the processor to merge the definitions into one, grouped with either a choice or an interleave container. The value of this attribute describes how to combine the parts. For example:

```
<define name="block.class" combine="choice">
  <element name="title">
    <text/>
  </element>
</define>

<define name="block.class" combine="choice">
  <element name="para">
    <text/>
  </element>
</define>
```

...which is equivalent to this:

```
<define name="block.class"
    xmlns="http://relaxng.org/ns/structure/1.0">
  <choice>
    <element name="title">
```

```
        <text/>
      </element>
      <element name="para">
        <text/>
      </element>
    </choice>
  </define>
```

The usefulness of aggregate definitions becomes more clear when used with patterns in other files.

# Modularity

Good housekeeping of schemas often requires putting pieces in different files. Not only will it make parts smaller and easier to manage, but it allows them to be shared between schemas.

### External references

The pattern externalRef functions like ref and uses the attribute href to locate the file containing a grammar. externalRef references the whole grammar, not a named pattern inside it.

Suppose we have a file *section.rng* containing this pattern:

```
<grammar
    xmlns="http://relaxng.org/ns/structure/1.0">
  <start>
    <ref name="section"/>
  </start>
  <define name="section">
    <element name="section">
      <zeroOrMore>
        <ref name="paragraph"/>
      </zeroOrMore>
      <zeroOrMore>
        <ref name="section"/>
      </zeroOrMore>
    </element>
  </define>
  <define name="paragraph">
    <text/>
  </define>
</grammar>
```

We can link it to a pattern in another file like this:

```
<element name="report"
    xmlns="http://relaxng.org/ns/structure/1.0">
  <element name="title"><text/></element>
  <oneOrMore>
    <externalRef href="section.rng"/>
  </oneOrMore>
</element>
```

## Nested grammars

One consequence of external referencing is that grammars effectively contain other grammars. To prevent name clashes, each `grammar` has its own scope for named patterns. The named patterns in a parent are not automatically available to its child grammars. Instead, `ref` will only reference a definition from inside the current grammar.

To get around that limitation, you can use `parentRef`. It functions like `ref` but looks for definitions in the grammar one level up. For example, consider this case where two grammars reference each other. I am defining one element, `para`, as a paragraph that can include footnotes. The footnote element contains some number of paras. They are stored in files *para.rng* and *footnote*, respectively, and shown in Examples 4-8 and 4-9.

*Example 4-8. para.rng*

```
<grammar
      xmlns="http://relaxng.org/ns/structure/1.0">
  <start>
    <element name="para">
      <zeroOrMore>
        <choice>
          <ref name="para.content"/>
          <externalRef name="footnote.rng"/>
        </choice>
      </zeroOrMore>
    </element>
  </start>
  <define name="para.content">
    <text/>
  </define>
</grammar>
```

*Example 4-9. footnote.rng*

```
<grammar
      xmlns="http://relaxng.org/ns/structure/1.0">
  <start>
    <element name="footnote">
      <oneOrMore>
        <parentRef name="para.content"/>
      </oneOrMore>
    </element>
  </start>
</grammar>
```

The footnote pattern relies on its parent grammar to define a pattern for para.

## Merging grammars

You can merge grammars from external sources by using include as a child of grammar. Like externalRef, include uses an href attribute to source in the definitions. However, it actually incorporates them in the same context, unlike externalRef which keeps scopes for named patterns separate.

One use for include is to augment an existing definition with more patterns. Suppose, for example, this pattern is located in *block.rng*:

```
<grammar
      xmlns="http://relaxng.org/ns/structure/1.0">
  <start>
    <ref name="block.class"/>
  </start>
  <define name="block.class">
    <choice>
      <element name="title">
        <text/>
      </element>
      <element name="para">
        <text/>
      </element>
    </choice>
  </define>
</grammar>
```

I can add more items to this class by including it like so:

```
<grammar
      xmlns="http://relaxng.org/ns/structure/1.0">
  <include href="block.rng">
  <start>
    <oneOrMore>
      <element name="section">
        <ref name="block.class"/>
      </element>
    </oneOrMore>
  </start>
  <define name="block.class" combine="choice">
    <element name="poem">
      <text/>
    </element>
  </define>
</grammar>
```

The combine attribute is necessary to tell the processor how to incorporate the new definition with the previous one imported from *block.rng*. Note that for multiply defined patterns of the same name, one is allowed to leave out the combine attribute, as is the case in the file *block.rng*.

### Overriding imported definitions

You can override some definitions that you import by including new ones inside the include element. Say we have a file *report.rng* defined like this:

```
<grammar
      xmlns="http://relaxng.org/ns/structure/1.0">
  <start>
    <element name="report">
      <ref name="head"/>
      <ref name="body"/>
    </element>
  </start>

  <define name="head">
    <element name="title"><text/></element>
  </define>

  <define name="body">
    <element name="section">
      <oneOrMore>
        <element name="para"><text/></element>
      </oneOrMore>
    </element>
  </define>
</grammar>
```

We wish to import this grammar, but adjust it slightly. Instead of just a title, we want to allow a subtitle as well. Rather than rewrite the whole grammar, we can just redefine head:

```
<grammar
      xmlns="http://relaxng.org/ns/structure/1.0">
  <include href="report.rng">
    <define name="head">
      <element name="title"><text/></element>
      <optional>
        <element name="subtitle"><text/></element>
      </optional>
    </define>
  </include>
  <start>
    <ref name="report">
  </start>
</grammar>
```

This is a good way to customize a schema to suit your own particular taste.

## CensusML Example

In case you are curious, let's go back to the CensusML example from the section "W3C XML Schemas" and try to do it as a RELAX NG schema. The result is Example 4-10.

*Example 4-10. A RELAX NG schema for CensusML*

```
<element name="census-record">
        xmlns="http://relaxng.org/ns/structure/1.0"
        datatypeLibrary="http://www.w3.org/2001/XMLSchema-datatypes">
  <attribute name="taker">
    <data type="integer">
      <param name="minInclusive">1</param>
      <param name="maxInclusive">9999</param>
    </data>
  </attribute>
  <element name="date">
    <data type="date"/>
  </element>
  <element name="address">
    <interleave>
      <element name="street"><text/></element>
      <element name="city"><text/></element>
      <element name="county"><text/></element>
      <element name="postalcode">
        <data type="string">
          <param name="pattern">[0-9][0-9][0-9][A-Z][A-Z][A-Z]</param>
        </data>
      </element>
    </interleave>
  </element>
  <oneOrMore>
    <element name="person">
      <interleave>
        <attribute name="employed">
          <choice>
            <value>fulltime</value>
            <value>parttime</value>
            <value>none</value>
          </choice>
        </attribute>
        <attribute name="pid">
          <data type="integer">
            <param name="minInclusive">1</param>
            <param name="maxInclusive">999999</param>
          </data>
        </attribute>
        <element name="age">
          <data type="integer">
            <param name="minInclusive">0</param>
            <param name="maxInclusive">200</param>
          </data>
        </element>
        <element name="gender">
          <choice>
            <value>male</value>
            <value>gender</value>
          </choice>
        </element>
        <element name="name">
```

*Example 4-10. A RELAX NG schema for CensusML (continued)*

```
          <interleave>
            <element name="first"><text/></element>
            <element name="last"><text/></element>
            <optional>
              <choice>
                <element name="junior"><empty/></element>
                <element name="senior"><empty/></element>
              </choice>
            </optional>
          </interleave>
        </element>
      </interleave>
    </element>
  </oneOrMore>
</element>
```

This schema certainly looks a lot cleaner than the W3C Schema version. Enumerations and complex types are much more clear. The grouping structures are very easy to read. Personally, I think RELAX NG is just more intuitive all around.

# Schematron

Schematron takes a different approach from the schema languages we've seen so far. Instead of being prescriptive, as in "this element has the following content model," it relies instead on a series of Boolean tests. Depending on the result of a test, the schema will output some predetermined message.

The tests are based on XPath, which is a very granular and exhaustive set of node examination tools. Relying on XPath is clever, taking much of the complexity out of the schema language. XPath, which is used in places such as XSLT and some implementations of DOM, can scratch an itch that more blunt tools like DTDs can't reach. As the creator of Schematron, Rick Jelliffe, says it's like "a feather duster for the furthest corners of a room where the vacuum cleaner (DTD) cannot reach."

## Overview

The basic structure of a Schematron schema is this:

```
<schema xmlns="http://www.ascc.net/xml/schematron">
  <pattern>
    <rule context="XPath Expression">
      <assert test="XPath Expression">
        message
      </assert>
      <report test="XPath Expression">
        message
      </report>
      ...more tests...
```

```
    </rule>
    ...more rules...
  </pattern>
  ...more patterns...
</schema>
```

A pattern in Schematron does not carry the same meaning as patterns in RELAX NG. Here, it's just a logical grouping of rules. If your schema is testing books, one pattern may hold rules for chapters while another groups rules for appendixes. So think of this as more of a higher-level, conceptual testing pattern, rather than as a specific node-matching pattern.

The context for each test is determined by a rule. Its context attribute contains an XSLT pattern that matches nodes. Each node found becomes the *context node*, on which all tests inside the rule are applied.

The children of a rule, report and assert, each apply a test to the context node. The test is another XPath expression, stored in a test attribute. report's contents will be output if its XPath expression evaluates to "true." assert is just the opposite, outputting its contents if its test evaluates to "false."

XPath expressions are very good at describing XML nodes and reasonably good at matching text patterns. Here's how you might test an email address:

```
<rule context="email">
  <p>Found an email address...</p>
  <assert test="contains(.,'@')">Error: no @ in email</assert>
  <assert test="contains(.,'.')">Error: no dot in email</assert>
  <report test="length(.)>20">Warning: email is unusually long</report>
</rule>
```

To summarize, running a Schematron validator on a document works like this. First, parse the document to build a document tree in memory. Then, for each rule, obtain a context node using its XPath locator expression. For each assert or report in the rule, evaluate the XPath expression for a Boolean value, and conditionally output text. The idea is that whenever something is found that is not right with the document, the Schematron processor should output a message to that effect. You can think of Schematron as a language for generating validation reports.

One interesting feature of Schematron is that its documentation is a part of the language itself. Rather than rely on comments or the namespace hack from RELAX NG, this language explicitly defines elements and attributes to hold commentary. The root element, schema has an optional child title to name the schema, and pattern elements have a name attribute for identifying rule groups. A Schematron validator will use that attribute to label each pattern of testing in output. There is also a set of tags for formatting text, borrowed from HTML, such as p and span.

Let's look at an example. Below is a schema to test a report document. There are two kinds of reports we allow: one with a body and another with a set of at least three sections.

```
<schema xmlns="http://www.ascc.net/xml/schematron">
  <title>Test: Report Document Validity</title>

  <pattern name="Type 1">
    <p>Type 1 reports should have a title and a body.</p>
    <rule context="/">
      <assert test="report">Wrong root element. This isn't a report.</assert>
    </rule>
    <rule context="report">
      <assert test="title">Darn! It's missing a title.</assert>
      <report test="title">Yup, found a title.</assert>
      <assert test="body">Yikes! It's missing a body.</assert>
      <report test="body">Yup, found a body.</report>
    </rule>
  </pattern>

  <pattern name="Type 2">
    <p>Type 2 reports should have a title and <em>at least
      three</em> sections.</p>
    <rule context="/">
      <assert test="report">Wrong root element. This isn't a report.</assert>
    </rule>
    <rule context="report">
      <assert test="title">Darn! It's missing a title.</assert>
      <report test="title">Yup, found a title.</assert>
      <assert test="count(section)&gt;2">There are not enough section
        elements in this report.</assert>
      <report test="count(section)&gt;2">Plenty of sections, so I'm
        happy.</report>
    </rule>
  </pattern>
</schema>
```

Now, let's run the Schematron validator on this document:

```
<report>
  <title>A ridiculous report</title>
  <body>
    <para>Here's a paragraph.</para>
    <para>Here's a paragraph.</para>
  </body>
</report>
```

I used a version of Schematron that outputs its report in HTML form. Figure 4-1 shows how it looks in my browser.

## Abstract Rules

An *abstract rule* allows you to reuse rules when they are likely to appear often in the schema. The syntax is the same, with the additional attribute abstract set to yes and an id with some unique value. Another rule will reference the id with a rule attribute in an extends child element. See the following example.

```
┌─────────────────────────────────────────────────┐
│              pattern: Type 1                     │
├─────────────────────────────────────────────────┤
│ Type 1 reports should have a title and a body.   │
│                                                  │
│ Yup, found a title.                              │
│ Yup, found a body.                               │
└─────────────────────────────────────────────────┘

┌─────────────────────────────────────────────────┐
│              pattern: Type 2                     │
├─────────────────────────────────────────────────┤
│ Type 2 reports should have a title and at least three sections. │
│                                                  │
│ Yup, found a title.                              │
│ There are not enough section elements in this report. │
└─────────────────────────────────────────────────┘
```

*Figure 4-1. A Schematron report*

```
<rule id="inline" abstract="yes">
  <report test="*">Error! Element inside inline.</report>
  <assert test="text">Strange, there's no text inside this inline.</assert>
</rule>
<rule context="bold">
  <extends rule="inline"/>
</rule>
<rule context="emphasis">
  <extends rule="inline"/>
</rule>
<rule context="quote">
  <extends rule="inline"/>
</rule>
```

# Schemas Compared

Each of the schemas we've looked at has compelling features and significant flaws. Some of the important points are listed Table 4-2.

*Table 4-2. A comparison of schema*

| Feature | DTD | W3C Schema | RELAX NG | Schematron |
|---|---|---|---|---|
| XML syntax | No | Yes | Yes | Yes |
| Namespace compatible | No | Yes | Yes | Yes |
| Declares entities | Yes | No | No | No |
| Tests datatypes | No | Yes | Yes | Yes |
| Default attribute values | Yes | Yes | No[a] | No |
| Notations | Yes | Yes | No | No |
| Unordered content | No | Yes | Yes | Yes |
| Modular | Yes | Yes | Yes | No |
| Element-attribute interchangeability | No | Yes | Yes | Yes |
| Specifies how to associate with a document | Yes | Yes | No | No |

[a] Added later in the RELAX NG DTD Compatibility specification.

DTDs have been around the longest, so as you would expect they have the widest support in literature and software. They also have the advantage of being the only way to declare entities at the moment. The syntax for DTDs is very easy to learn, although its readability often leaves much to be desired. Try reading the DocBook-XML DTD sometime and you'll see what I mean. After a fashion, it is modular, but I find the parameter entities are often a nuisance, especially when you want to override imported declarations.

W3C XML Schema has the advantage of being blessed by the W3C, so you can be sure it will win many converts. Software support is growing quickly. I think it's pretty decent, but it has a clunkiness to it that can make schema design a chore. The datatypes will become a de facto standard, as they are already borrowed upon by the likes of RELAX NG. In general, this is a good step forward, but be aware that there will always be contenders for the throne.

RELAX NG has won my admiration for its elegance and simplicity. Writing schemas is easy and reading them even easier. It is easily translated into other schema languages such as W3C Schema and DTDs (using Trang), making it an ideal starting point for schema development. Niceties like interleave and nested grammars are not to be overlooked. It would be nice to see more built-in types defined in the specification, but it is likely most implementers will just extend them using the types in the W3C Schema recommendation, so no worries there.

By itself, Schematron is not nearly as useful as the other validation tools we saw in this chapter. One could do some simple tests with XPath, but it has no support for regular expressions to match elements or character data, and its dependence on a flat set of rules makes schema clunky and hard to develop. However, when used in conjunction with other validation tools, Schematron can really shine. "The real win with Schematron," writes XML expert Jeni Tennison, "is when you use it in tandem with another schema language, particularly W3C XML Schema. There is no way that you should use it for a standalone schema, but to test co-occurrence constraints once the initial validation is done with W3C XML Schema or RELAX NG, it's a godsend."

There was a time when all we had to work with were DTDs. With time, more and more XML tools become available, and we should all be thankful for the tireless efforts of many developers. It's worth taking time to become familiar with different schema types in order to find one that will fit your needs best.

# CHAPTER 5

# Presentation Part I: CSS

As the Web exploded in popularity in the mid-1990s, everyone wanted their own web site. I remember learning HTML from friends and the excitement I felt when I saw my virtual homestead suddenly become accessible to thousands of computer users. Back then, I had only a very limited understanding of things like "good design," "standards," and "best practices." They seemed like lofty concepts with little relation to me and my happy experiments. So, like everyone else, I cut corners, sacrificed good taste, and ignored rules because all that mattered was seeing something display reasonably well in a browser.

Since then, the novelty has worn off and my situation is vastly different. My concern has shifted from "How can I get something to display at all?" to "How can I make my information available to everyone who tries to look at it, regardless of what software they are using, on what platform, and in which media format?" And instead of asking "How can I create an HTML page?", I now ask, "How can I make this vast amount of information easier to update, store, and publish?" And where before I might wonder how to achieve some effect in HTML, like making some lines of text larger than other lines, I now have to cope with a variety of different XML formats and extremely detailed design needs.

Cascading Style Sheets (CSS) are the first piece of this puzzle. They have been around for a long time, but for several reasons they were slow to take off. Now sites like *wired.com* are totally based on CSS and they actually look pretty good, while sites like *http://csszengarden.com/* show off more CSS capabilities. Although originally designed to augment HTML, CSS can complement XML as well. In this chapter, we will see how it can be used for web pages as well as XML documents for human consumption.

## Stylesheets

XML and stylesheets go together like naked people and clothes. Let's take a moment to familiarize ourselves with the general concepts behind stylesheets. First, why do you want them? Second, how do they work? Finally, are there limitations, and what can we do about them?

## Why We Need Them

I can rant about why it's important to keep information pure and separate presentation into stylesheets, but this would ignore a critical question: if it's easier to write in presentational markup—and I admit that it is—why would you want to bother with stylesheets? After all, the Web itself testifies to the fact that presentational markup is working quite well for what it was designed to do. For that matter, what's wrong with plain text?

If you are already familiar with the sermon, then skip this section, because I'm going to preach the religion of stylesheets now.

XML was inspired, to a large extent, by the limitations of HTML. Tim Berners-Lee, the inventor of HTML, always had stylesheets in mind, but for some reason, they had been forgotten in the huge initial surge of webification. Although HTML had only limited presentational capabilities built in, it was enough to satisfy the hordes of new web authors. Easy to implement and even easier to learn, HTML was soon stretched far beyond its original intentions as a simple report-formatting language, forced to encode everything from product catalogs to corporate portals. But the very thing that led to its rapid uptake, presentational markup, is also holding HTML back.

Here are some problems associated with presentational markup and some solutions provided by stylesheets:

*Low information content*

Presentational markup is not much better than plain text. A machine can't understand the difference between a typical body paragraph and a poem or code sample. Nor does it know that one thing is marked bold because it's a stock price and another is bold because it's the name of a town. Consequently, you can't easily mine pages for information. Search engines can only try to match character strings, since any sense of context is missing from the markup.

With stylesheets, you are free to mark up a document in a way that preserves information. XML markup languages are tailored for their data, using element names that describe what things are rather than how they should look. This makes it possible to create data mining software or search engines that use markup information in addition to content.

*Management nightmare*

When your markup is presentational, the design details are inextricably mixed with the content. You have to get into the document itself anytime you need to make a change to the design. This can be quite laborious. For example, to change italicized proper nouns to bold typeface means editing each case manually, since no automatic search-and-replace utility can recognize a proper noun from an emphasized phrase.

Stylesheets untangle presentation details from the document and store them in a separate place. If you need to make a change to the design of a document, you can change one place in the stylesheet, rather than manually fix every hard-coded tag in the markup. What's more, since one stylesheet can be used for many documents (see Figure 5-1), one simple change can affect many pages. In a setting where design changes occur frequently, this is a godsend.

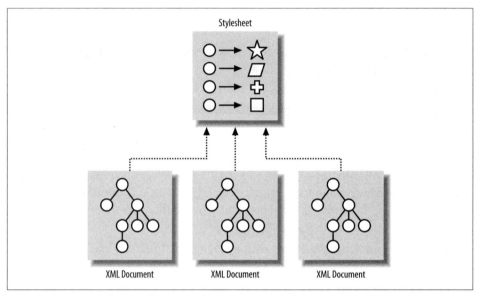

*Figure 5-1. One stylesheet used by many documents*

*Dubious vendor extensions*

Seeking to extend their market share by addressing the frustrations of web authors, some tool vendors have taken the initiative of extending HTML on their own, circumventing the standards process. Differentiating their products this way seems good at first, but it leads to a horrible fracturing of your audience. People have to use the same tools as you in order to view your information. Web pages with messages like "best when viewed by browser X" have fallen into this trap.

Stylesheets are regulated by standards bodies. Instead of inventing ad hoc extensions that fragment the community, vendors instead are encouraged to implement the same standards as everyone else. If something that people need is missing, it's better to tell the standard maintaining body than to go it alone. (That's the theory, anyway. In practice, it doesn't always work. CSS has been around for a long time, and to date no one has completely implemented it correctly. There are also a few vendor extensions.)

*Device dependence*

Designers often focus too much on getting something to look *just right* instead of making it good enough for a range of uses. In the process, they end up making their document too inflexible for viewers. For example, it's tempting to set the column widths of a table with absolute widths. It may look terrific on the designer's 17-inch screen, but simply awful on a smaller, 14-inch monitor, not to mention PDAs and cell phones.

Instead of trying to exploit side-effects of tags or tinkering with minute details in markup to get the right effect, designers now can work with a stylesheet. Stylesheets typically are designed with multiple purposes in mind. For example, typeface selection is flexible, taking into account the capabilities of the reader's local system. Stylesheets supply more options for specifying sizes, lengths, colors, margins, and other properties, usually with the option for flexible, relative dimensions.

*Limited reusability*

Sometimes you want your document to be used in different ways, but are limited by the hardwired presentation details. Write a document in HTML and it's only good for viewing online. You can print it out, but the typeface looks big and blocky because it's designed for a computer screen. You could cut and paste the content into another program, but then you'd lose design information or you'd carry in some unwanted artifacts (spurious whitespace for example).

Again, the separation of stylesheet from document will help you here. You can write as many stylesheets as you want for different purposes (see Figure 5-2). In the document, you only need to change a simple setting to associate it with a different stylesheet. A web server can detect what device is requesting a page and select an appropriate stylesheet. The user can also make changes to the presentation, substituting their own stylesheet, or just overriding a few styles.

To summarize, the three principle ways in which stylesheets help you are:

- Making design changes easier by disentangling the details from the document.
- Enabling multiple uses for one document.
- Giving the end user more control and accessibility.

The key to all this is what we in XML intellectual circles call *late binding*. Keep the document as far away from its final product as possible, and you maximize its flexibility. The stylesheet extends the information into a particular realm, be it online viewing or print or spoken text.

## How They Work

Think of applying a stylesheet to a document as preparing a meal from a cookbook. Your XML document is a bunch of raw, unprocessed ingredients; the stylesheet is a recipe, telling the chef how to handle each ingredient and how to combine them. The

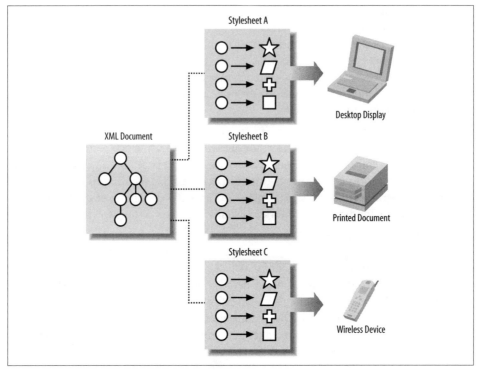

*Figure 5-2. Mixing and matching stylesheets for different purposes*

software that transmutes XML into another format, based on the stylesheet's instructions, is the chef in our analogy. After the dicing, mixing, and baking, we have something palatable and easily digested.

### Applying properties

In the simplest sense, a stylesheet is like a table that maps style properties to elements in the document (see Figure 5-3). A *property* is anything that affects the appearance or behavior of the document, such as typeface, color, size, or decoration. Each mapping from element to property set is called a *rule*. It consists of a part that matches parts of a document, and another that lists the properties to use.

The software that uses a stylesheet to generate formatted output is a *stylesheet processor*. As it reads the XML document, it keeps consulting the stylesheet to find rules to apply to elements. For each element, there may be multiple rules that match, so the processor may apply them all, or it may just try to find one that is the best fit. Matching rules to elements can be a complex process in writing a stylesheet.

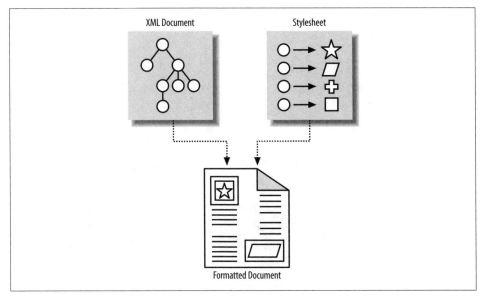

*Figure 5-3. A stylesheet used to help produce a formatted document*

### Client and server-side processing

The result of this processing is either a generated display or another document. The first case is what you would see in a web browser on screen, or a printout from the browser. It's a device-dependent result, created on the client end of the transaction. Client-side processing like this takes the load off of the server making information propagate faster. It also gives the end user more control over the appearance by being able to override some style settings.

The other kind of output from a style processor is a new document. XSLT, which we will explore in Chapter 7, is such a stylesheet language. This sort of process is also known as a *transformation* because it effectively transforms the original document into a different form. Transformations can be performed on either the server or the client end, before or during the transaction. For example, a DocBook document can be transformed into HTML for presentation on a browser. It's a very powerful technique that we will have fun talking about later.

### Cascading styles

Stylesheets can be modularized to mix and match rules. This is the source of the term "cascading" in CSS. The idea is that no stylesheet ought to be monolithic. Instead, you should be able to combine styles from different sources, create subsets, and override rules in different situations. For example, you can use a general-purpose stylesheet combined with one that fine-tunes the style settings for a specific product (see Figure 5-4).

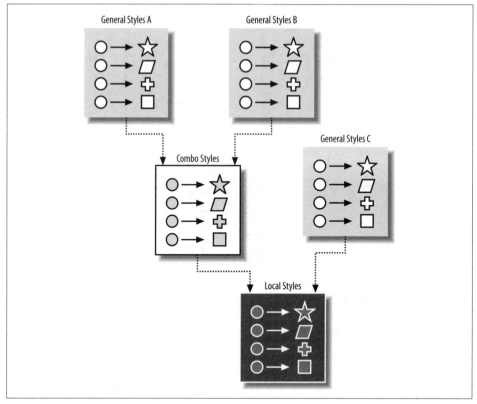

*Figure 5-4. A cascade of stylesheets*

One reason for doing this is to make it easier to manage a huge set of style rules. The fix-once-see-everywhere principle is enhanced when changes to one set of rules are inherited by many stylesheets.

Cascading rules also make it possible to change the result at any point in the transaction. All browsers in fact have a default client-side stylesheet that specifies how to render HTML in the absence of any specifications from the server. Some browsers, such as Mozilla allow you to edit this local stylesheet, or *user stylesheet*, so you can customize the appearance to suit your tastes. For example, if you think most text in pages is hard to read, you can increase the default size of fonts and save yourself some eyestrain.

### Associating a stylesheet to a document

There is no hard and fast rule for associating resources to documents in XML. Each markup language may or may not provide support for stylesheets. Some languages, like MoDL, have their own software to display or process the data, so it wouldn't make any sense to use stylesheets. In others, the language doesn't have an explicit method for association, so stylesheets are a good idea, as is the case with DocBook.

HTML happens to define an element for linking resources like stylesheets to the document. The `link` element will bind a web page to a CSS stylesheet like this:

```html
<html>
  <head>
    <title>The Behavior of Martian Bees</title>
    <link rel="stylesheet" type="text/css" href="honey.css"/>
  </head>
  ...
```

Alternatively, in HTML you can embed the stylesheet inside the document:

```html
<html>
  <head>
    <title>The Behavior of Martian Bees</title>
    <style>
      body { background-color: wheat;
             color: brown;
             font-family: sans-serif; }
      .sect { border: thin solid red;
              padding: 0.5em; }
    </style>
  </head>
  ...
```

Of course, this is more limiting, since the stylesheet can't be applied to more than one document and the document is stuck with this stylesheet. In general, I think keeping the two separate is a better idea, but there may be advantages to putting them together, such as making it easier to transport a document through email.

These two solutions work because HTML evolved together with stylesheets. Not all languages are designed with them in mind. For this purpose, XML provides a generic way to embed a stylesheet using a processing instruction named `<?xml-stylesheet?>` whose syntax is shown in Figure 5-5.

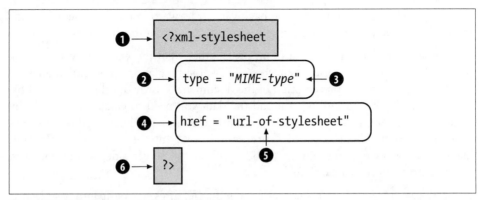

*Figure 5-5. Syntax for a stylesheet declaration*

The declaration begins with the processing instruction delimiter and target, `<?xml-stylesheet` (1). The PI (processing instruction) includes several property assignments

similar to attributes, two of which are required: `type` and `href`. `type` (2), is set to the MIME type (3) of the stylesheet (for CSS, this is `text/css`). The value of the other property, `href` (4), is the URL of the stylesheet (5), which can be on the same system or anywhere on the Internet. The declaration ends with the closing delimiter (6).

Here's how it would be used in a document:

```
<?xml version="1.0"?>
<?xml-stylesheet type="text/css" href="bookStyle.css"?>
<book>
  <title>Tom Swift's Aerial Adventures</title>
  <chapter>
    <title>The Dirigible</title>
  ...
```

Using a processing instruction for this purpose is smart for a few reasons. First, it doesn't "pollute" the language with an extra element that has to be declared in a DTD. Second, it can be ignored by processors that don't care about stylesheets, or older ones that don't know how to work with them. Third, it isn't really part of the document anyway, but rather a recommended way to work with the information.

## Limitations

Not surprisingly, there are limits to what you can do with stylesheets. Languages for stylesheets are optimized for different purposes. You need to be aware of how a stylesheet language works to use it most effectively.

CSS, for example, is designed to be compact and efficient. Documents have to be rendered quickly because people don't want to wait a long time for something to read. The stylesheet processor is on the client end, and doesn't have a lot of computing power at its disposal. So the algorithm for applying styles needs to be very simple. Each rule that matches an element can only apply a set of styles. There is no other processing allowed, no looking backward or forward in the document for extra information. You have only one pass through the document to get it right.

Sometimes, information is stored in an order other than the way you want it to be rendered. If that is the case, then you need something more powerful than CSS. XSLT works on a tree representation of the document. It provides the luxury of looking ahead or behind to pull together all the data you need to generate output. This freedom comes at the price of increased computational requirements. Although some browsers support client-side XSLT processing (e.g., Internet Explorer), it's more likely you'll want transformations to be done on the server side, where you have more control and can cache results.

Property sets are finite, so no matter how many features are built into a stylesheet language, there will always be something lacking, some effect you want to achieve but can't. When that happens, you should be open to other options, such as post-processing with custom software. In Chapter 10, I'll talk about strategies for programming with XML. This is the ultimate and most work-intensive solution, but sometimes there just is no other way to get what you want.

Unquestionably, implementation among clients has been the biggest obstacle. The pace of standards development was much faster than actual implementation. Browsers either didn't support them or had buggy and incomplete implementations. This is quite frustrating for designers who want to support multiple platforms but are stymied by differing behaviors among user agents. Not only does behavior vary among vendors, but among versions and platforms too. Internet Explorer, for example, behaves very differently on Macintosh than it does on Windows for versions that came out at the same time.

When I wrote the first edition of this book, I was quite disappointed by the level of support for CSS. Any but the most simple example would not work on more than one browser. Since then, the situation has improved a little. Mozilla has much better support for CSS now. Internet Explorer, which used to be the leader, has inexplicably remained stuck for over a year and Microsoft has suggested its development as a standalone application is complete. Sure, CSS is rich and featured, but it shouldn't be *that* difficult to implement. I think the open source movement offers the most hope, because there will always be an opportunity for some hacker, fed up with an unimplemented option, to go in and get it working; whereas with corporations, we have to wait until the marketing department deems it a high enough priority to put it on the schedule.

# CSS Basics

While CSS is a field of endeavor all its own, we'll get started with some foundations.

## The CSS Specification

Cascading Style Sheets (CSS) is a recommendation developed by the World Wide Web Consortium (W3C). It originated in 1994 when Håkon Wium Lee, working at CERN (the birthplace of HTML), published a paper titled *Cascading HTML Style Sheets*. It was a bold move at the right time. By then, the Web was four years old and growing quickly, yet there was still no consensus for a standard style description language. The architects of HTML knew that the language was in danger of becoming a style description language if something like CSS wasn't adopted soon.

The goal was to create a simple yet expressive language that could combine style descriptions from different sources. Another style description language, DSSSL, was already being used to format SGML documents. Though very powerful, DSSSL was too big and complex to be practical for the Web. It is a full programming language, capable of more precision and logical expression than CSS, which is a simple language, focused on the basic needs of small documents.

While other stylesheet languages existed when CSS was proposed, none offered the ability to combine multiple sources into one style description set. CSS makes the Web truly accessible and flexible by allowing a reader to override the author's styles to adapt a document to the reader's particular requirements and applications.

The W3C put forward the first CSS recommendation (later called CSS1) in 1996. A short time later, a W3C working group formed around the subject of "Cascading Style Sheets and Formatting Properties" to add missing functionality. Their recommendation, CSS2, increased the language's properties from around 50 to more than 120 when it was released in 1998. It also added concepts like generated text, selection by attribute, and media other than screen display. CSS3 is still a work in progress.

## Syntax

Below is a sample CSS stylesheet:

```
/* A simple example */
addressbook {
  display-type: block;
  font-family: sans-serif;
  font-size: 12pt;
  background-color: white;
  color: blue;
}
entry {
  display-type: block;
  border: thin solid black;
  padding: 5em;
  margin: 5em;
}
name, phone, email, address {
  display-type: block;
  margin-top: 2em;
  margin-bottom: 2em;
}
```

This stylesheet has three rules. The first matches any addressbook element. The name to the left of the open bracket is a *selector*, which tells the processor what element this rule matches. The items inside the brackets are the *property declaration*, a list of properties to apply.

The syntax for a CSS rule is shown in Figure 5-6. It consists of a *selector* (1) for matching elements and a *declaration* (2) for describing styles. The declaration is a list of name-value assignments (3), in which each style *property* (4) is assigned to a *value* (5) with a colon (:) separator.

CSS also has a syntax for comments. Anything inside a comment is ignored by the processor. The start delimiter is /* and the end delimiter is */. A comment can span

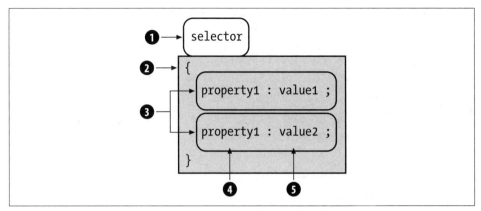

*Figure 5-6. CSS rule syntax*

multiple lines and may be used to enclose CSS rules to remove them from consideration:

```
/* this part will be ignored
gurble { color: red }
burgle { color: blue; font-size: 12pt; }
*/
```

Whitespace is generally ignored and provides a nice way to make stylesheets more readable. The exception is when spaces act as delimiters in lists. Some properties take multiple arguments separated with spaces like border below:

```
sidebar {
   border: thin solid black
}
```

## Matching Properties to Elements

Let's look more closely at this rule:

```
addressbook {
   display-type: block;
   font-family: sans-serif;
   font-size: 12pt;
   background-color: white;
   color: blue;
}
```

Qualitatively, this rule is like saying, "for every addressbook element, display it like a block, set the font family to any sans serif typeface with size 12 points, set the background color to white and make the foreground (text) blue." Whenever the CSS processor encounters an addressbook element, it will set apply these properties to the current formatting context.

To understand how it works, think of painting-by-numbers. In front of you is a canvas with outlines of shapes and numbers inside the shapes. Each number corresponds to a paint color. You go to each shape, find the paint that corresponds to the number inside it, and fill it in with that color. In an hour or so, you'll have a lovely stylized pastoral scene with a barn and wildflowers. In this analogy, the rule is a paint can with a numbered label. The color is the property and the number is the selector.

The selector can be more complex than just one element name. It can be a comma-separated list of elements. It could be qualified with an attribute, as in this example, which matches a foo element with class="flubber":

```
foo.flubber { color: green; }
```

This dot-qualified selector matches an element with a class attribute, which is supported in HTML and SVG.

The CSS processor tries to find the *best* rule (or rules) for each element. In a stylesheet, several rules may apply. For example:

```
p.big {
  font-size: 18pt;
}

p {
  font-family: garamond, serif;
  font-size: 12pt;
}

* {
  color: black;
  font-size: 10pt;
}
```

The first rule matches a p with attribute class="big". The second matches any p regardless of attributes, and the last matches any element at all. Suppose the next element to process is a p with the attribute class="big". All three rules match this element.

How does CSS decide which properties to apply? The solution to this dilemma has two parts. The first is that all rules that match are used. It's as if the property declarations for all the applicable rules were merged into one set. That means all of these properties potentially apply to the element:

```
font-size: 18pt;
font-family: garamond, serif;
font-size: 12pt;
color: black;
font-size: 10pt;
```

The second part is that redundant property settings are resolved according to an algorithm. As you can see, there are three different font-size property settings. Only one of the settings can be used, so the CSS processor has to weed out the worst two using a property clash resolution system. As a rule of thumb, you can assume that the property from the rule with the most specific selector will win out. The first font-size property originates from the rule with selector p.big, which is more descriptive than p or *, so it's the winner.

In the final analysis, these three properties will apply:

```
font-size: 18pt;
font-family: garamond, serif;
color: black;
```

## Property Inheritance

XML documents have a hierarchy of elements. CSS uses that hierarchy to pass along properties in a process called *inheritance*. Going back to our DocBook example, a sect1 contains a para. Consider the following stylesheet:

```
sect1 {
  margin-left: 25pt;
  margin-right: 25pt;
  font-size: 18pt;
  color: navy;
}

para {
  margin-top: 10pt;
  margin-bottom: 10pt;
  font-size: 12pt;
}
```

The para's set of properties is a combination of those explicitly declared for it and those it inherits from the elements in its ancestry. Not all properties are inherited. Margins are never inheritable, so in the above example, only font-size and color may be inherited. However, the font-size property is not inherited by para because it is redefined there. So the para's properties include those specifically defined for it, plus the one it inherited, color: navy.

## Combining Stylesheets

A very powerful feature of CSS is its ability to combine multiple stylesheets by importing one into another. This lets you borrow predefined style definitions so you don't have to continuously reinvent the wheel. Any style settings that you want to redefine or don't need can be overridden in the local stylesheet.

One reason to combine stylesheets is *modularity*. It may be more manageable to break up a large stylesheet into several smaller files. For example, we could store all the styles pertaining to math equations in *math.css* and all the styles for regular text in *text.css*. The command @import links the current stylesheet to another and causes the style settings in the target to be imported:

```
@import url(http://www.example.org/mystyles/math.css);
@import url(http://www.example.org/mystyles/text.css);
```

Some of the imported style rules may not suit your taste, or they may not fit the presentation. You can override those rules by redefining them in your own stylesheet. Here, we've decided that the rule for h1 elements defined in *text.css* needs to be changed:

```
@import url(http://www.example.org/mystyles/text.css);

h1: { font-size: 3em; }    /* redefinition */
```

# Rule Matching

We will delve now into the details of selector syntax and all the ways a rule can match an element or attribute. Don't worry yet about what the properties actually mean. I'll cover all that in the next section. For now, concentrate on how rules drive processing and how they interact with each other.

Figure 5-7 shows the general syntax for selectors. They typically consist of an element name (1) followed by some number of attribute tests (2) in square brackets, which in turn contain an attribute name (3) and value (4). Note that only an element or attribute is required. The other parts are optional. The element name can contain wildcards to match any element, and it can also contain chains of elements to specify hierarchical information. The attribute tests can check for the existence of an attribute (with any value), the existence of a value (for any attribute), or in the strictest case, a particular attribute-value combination.

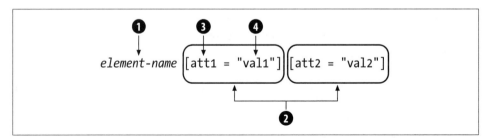

*Figure 5-7. Syntax for a CSS selector*

## Elements

Matching an element is as simple as writing its name:

```
emphasis {
  font-style: italic;
  font-weight: bold; }
```

This rule matches any emphasis element in the document. This is just the tip of the iceberg. There are many ways to qualify the selection. You can specify attribute names, attribute values, elements that come before and after, and even special conditions such as whether the cursor is currently hovering over a link, or in what language the document claims to be written.

A list of names is also allowed, letting you apply the same properties to many kinds of elements. Here, a set of three properties applies to any of the four elements, `name`, `phone`, `email`, and `address`:

```
name, phone, email, address {
  display-type: block;
  margin-top: 2em;
  margin-bottom: 2em;
}
```

Besides using definite element names, you can use an asterisk (*) as a wildcard to match any element name. It's called the *universal selector*. For example, the following rule applies to any element in a document, setting the text color to blue:

```
* { color: blue }
```

Since this is a very general selector, it takes a low precedence in the set of rules. Any other element that defines a color property will override this rule.

## Attributes

For a finer level of control, you can qualify the selection of elements by their attributes. An *attribute selector* consists of an element name immediately followed by the attribute refinement in square brackets. Varying levels of precision are available:

planet[atmosphere]

> This selector matches any `planet` element that has an `atmosphere` attribute. For example, it selects `<planet atmosphere="poisonous"/>` and `<planet atmosphere="breathable"/>`, but not `<planet/>`.
>
> You can leave out the element name if you want to accept any element that contains the attribute. The selector `[atmosphere]` matches both `<planet atmosphere="dense"/>` and `<moon atmosphere="wispy"/>`.

planet[atmosphere="breathable"]

> Adding a value makes the selector even more specific. This selector matches `<planet atmosphere="breathable"/>`, but it doesn't match `<planet atmosphere="poisonous"/>`.

planet[atmosphere~="sweet"]

> If the attribute's value is a space-separated list of strings, you can match any one of them by using the operator ~= instead of the equals sign (=). This selector matches `<planet atmosphere="breathable sweet dense"/>` or `<planet atmosphere="foggy sweet"/>`, but it does not match `<planet atmosphere="breathable stinky"/>`.

`planet[populace|="barbaric"]`

> Similar to the item-in-list matching operator, a selector with the operator |= matches an item in a hyphen-separated value list, provided it begins with the value in the selector. This matches `<planet populace="barbaric-hostile"/>`.
>
> This kind of selector is often used to distinguish between language types. The value of the XML attribute `xml:lang` is a *language identifier*, a string that looks like this: en-US. The two-character code "en" stands for "English" and the code "US" qualifies the United States variant. To match a `planet` element with an `xml:lang` attribute that specifies English, use the selector `planet[language|="en"]`. This selects both en-US and en-UK.

`planet[atmosphere="breathable"][populace="friendly"]`

> Selectors can string together multiple attribute requirements. To match, the attribute selectors must be satisfied, just as if they were bound with a logical AND operator. The above selector matches `<planet atmosphere="breathable" populace="friendly"/>` but not `<planet populace="friendly"/>`.

`#mars`

> This special form is used to match ID attributes. It matches `<planet id="mars"/>` or `<candy-bar id="mars"/>`, but not `<planet id="venus"/>`. Remember that only one element in the whole document can have an ID attribute with a given value, so this rule is very specific.

`planet.uninhabited`

> An attribute that is frequently used to designate special categories of an element for stylesheets is `class`. A shortcut for matching class attributes is the period, which stands for `class=`. The selector above matches `<planet class="uninhabited"/>` but doesn't match `<planet class="colony"/>`.

`planet:lang(en)`

> This selector form is used to match elements with a particular language specified. In pre-XML versions of HTML, language would be specified in a `lang` attribute. In XML, the attribute is `xml:lang`. The attribute values are matched in the same way as with the |= operator: a hyphenated item is a match if its name begins with a string identical to the one in the selector. The `xml:lang` attribute is an exception to XML's usual rules of case-sensitivity; values here are compared without regard to case. So in this example the selector matches `<planet lang="en"/>`, `<planet lang="EN-us"/>`, or `<planet lang="en-US"/>`, but not `<planet lang="jp"/>`.

## Contextual Selection

Selectors can also use contextual information to match elements. This information includes the element's ancestry (its parent, its parent's parent, etc.) and siblings, and is useful for cases in which an element needs to be rendered differently depending on where it occurs.

## Ancestry

You can specify that an element is a child of another element using the greater-than symbol (>). For example:

```
book > title { font-size: 24pt; }
chapter > title { font-size: 20pt; }
title { font-size: 18pt; }
```

The element to select here is title. If the title appears in a book, then the first rule applies. If it appears within a chapter, the second rule is chosen. If the title appears somewhere else, the last rule is used.

The > operator works only when there is one level separating the two elements. To reach an element at an arbitrary depth inside another element, list them in the selector, separated by spaces. For example:

```
table para { color: green }
para { color: black }
```

The first rule matches a para that occurs somewhere inside a table, like this:

```
<table>
  <title>A plain ol' table</title>
  <tgroup>
    <tbody>
      <row>
        <entry>
          <para>Hi! I'm a table cell paragraph.</para>
      ...
```

There's no limit to the number of elements you can string in a row. This is useful if you ever need to go far back into the ancestry to gather information. For example, say you want to use a list inside a list, perhaps to create an outline. By convention, the inner list should be indented more than the outer list. The following rules would provide you with up to three levels of nested lists:

```
list { indent: 3em }
list > list { indent: 6em }
list > list > list { indent: 9em }
```

The universal selector (*) can be used anywhere in the hierarchy. For example, given this content:

```
<chapter><title>Classification of Bosses</title>
  <sect1><title>Meddling Types</title>
    <sect2><title>Micromanagers</title>
      ...
```

You can match the last two title elements with this selector:

```
chapter * title
```

The first title is not selected, since the universal selector requires at least one element to sit between chapter and title.

## Position

Often, you need to know where an element occurs in a sequence of same-level elements. For example, you might want to treat the first paragraph of a chapter differently from the rest, by making it all uppercase perhaps. To do this, add a special suffix to the element selector like this:

```
para:first-child { font-variant: uppercase; }
```

`para:first-child` matches only a `para` that is the first child of an element. A colon (:) followed by a keyword like `first-child` is called a *pseudo-class* in CSS. It provides extra information that can't be expressed in terms of element or attribute names. We saw another earlier: `:lang`.

Another way to examine the context of an element is to look at its siblings. The *sibling selector* matches an element immediately following another. For example:

```
title + para { text-indent: 0 }
```

matches every `para` that follows a `title` and turns off its initial indent. This works only for elements that are right next to each other; there may be text in between, but no other elements.

You can select parts of an element's content with *pseudo-element selectors*. `:first-line` applies to the first line of an element as it appears in a browser. (This may vary, since the extent of the line depends on unpredictable factors such as window size.) With this selector, we can set the first line of a paragraph to all-caps, achieving a nice stylistic effect to open an article. This rule transforms the first line of the first `para` of a chapter to all capitals:

```
chapter > para:first-child:first-line {
  text-transform: uppercase }
```

In a similar fashion, `:first-letter` operates solely on the first letter in an element's content, as well as any punctuation preceding the letter within the element. This is useful for drop caps and raised capitals:

```
body > p:first-child:first-letter {
  font-size: 300%;
  font-color: red }
```

With the pseudo-classes `:before` and `:after`, you can select a point just before or just after an element, respectively. This is most valuable for adding generated text: character data not present in the XML document. Figure 5-8 illustrates the following example:

```
warning > *:first-child:before {
  content: "WARNING!";
  font-weight: bold;
  color: red }
```

> **WARNING!** Do not feed
> the Lexx. If you do, it will
> go on an interplanetary
> killing spree, and we can't
> have that, can we?

*Figure 5-8. Autogenerated text in an admonition object*

## Resolving Property Conflicts

We talked before about how multiple rules can match the same element. When that happens, all unique property declarations are applied. Conflicting properties have to be resolved with a special algorithm to find the "best" match.

Consider this stylesheet:

```
* {font-family: "ITC Garamond"}
h1 { font-size: 24pt }
h2 { font-size: 18pt }
h1, h2 { color: blue }
```

The h1 element matches three of these rules. The net effect is to render it with the font ITC Garamond at 24-point size in the color blue.

What if there's a conflict between two or more values for the same property? For example, there might be another rule in this stylesheet that says:

```
h1:first-child {
    color: red
}
```

An h1 that is the first child of its parent would have conflicting values for the color property.

CSS defines an algorithm for resolving conflicts like these. The basic principle is that more specific selectors override more general selectors. The following list outlines the decision process:

1. IDs are more specific than anything else. If one rule has an ID selector and another doesn't, the one with the ID selector wins. More IDs are stronger than fewer, though given that IDs are unique within a document, a rule doesn't really need more than one.

2. More attribute selectors and pseudo-classes are stronger than fewer. This means that para:first-child is more specific than title + para, and that *[role="powerful"][class="mighty"] overrides para:first-child.

3. More specific genealogical descriptions win over less specific chains. So chapter > para has precedence over para, but not over title + para. Pseudo-elements don't count here.

4. If the selectors are still in a dead heat, there's a tie-breaking rule: the one that appears later in the stylesheet wins out.

Property value conflicts are resolved one property at a time. One rule might be more specific than another, but set only one property; other properties may be set by a less specific rule, even though one of the rule's properties has been overridden. So in our earlier example, the first h1 in an element gets the color red, not blue.

# Properties

The three levels of CSS define so many properties, I can't cover them all here. There are over 120 in level 2 alone. Instead, I'll cover the basic categories you are likely to encounter and leave more exhaustive descriptions to books specializing on the topic.

## Inheritance

CSS properties can be passed down from a container element to its child. This inheritance principle greatly simplifies stylesheet design. For example, in the document element rule, you can set a font family that will be used throughout the document. Wherever you want to use a different family, simply insert a new property for a rule and it will override the global setting.

In Figure 5-9, a para inherits some properties from a section, which in turn inherits from an article. The properties font-family and color are defined in the property set for article, and inherited by both section and para. The property font-size is not inherited by section because section's explicit setting overrides it. para does inherit this property from section.

Inheritance is forbidden for some properties where it wouldn't make sense to pass that trait on. For example, the background-image property, which causes an image to be loaded and displayed in the background, is not inherited. If every element did inherit this property, the result would be a complete mess, with every paragraph and inline element trying to display its own copy of the image in its rectangular area. It looks much better if only one element has this property and its children don't. Display type and margins are other examples.

## Units of Measurement

Many properties involve some kind of measurement: the width of a rule, a font size, or a distance to indent. These lengths can be expressed in several different kinds of units. *Absolute* measurements use units that have a predefined size, such as inches,

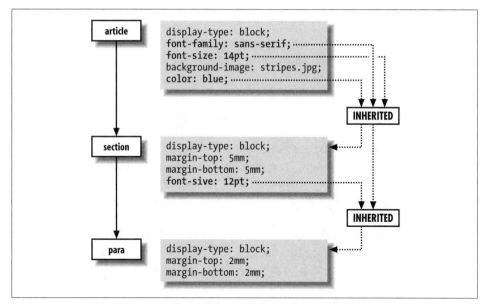

*Figure 5-9. Element-inheriting properties*

points, or picas. *Relative* measurements use percentages and fractions of some variable distance, such as the height of the current font.

You can measure an absolute length with a ruler because the units never change. A millimeter is the same no matter what font you're using or which language you're speaking. Absolute units used in CSS include millimeters (mm), centimeters (cm), and inches (in), as well as units specific to the world of print, such as points (pt) and picas (pc).

Relative units are nonfixed, scaling values that depend on some other measurement. For example, an em is defined as the size of the current font. If that font happens to be 12 points, then an em is 12 points. If the font size changes to 18 points, so does the em. Another relative unit is an ex, defined to be the *x-height* of a font (the height of a lowercase x). This is a fraction of the em, usually around a half, but it changes depending on the font. Different fonts can have different x-heights even if their em sizes are the same.

Relative measurements can also be expressed as percentages. This type of measurement relies on another element's value of the same property. For example:

```
b { font-size: 200% }
```

means that the b element has a font size that is twice its parent's.

In general, relative measurements are better than absolute. Relative units don't have to be rewritten when you adjust the default properties. It's much easier to write a stylesheet for multiple scenarios when you define the base size in only one place, and everything else is relative.

## Display Types

Most elements fit into one of three categories of formatting: *block*, *inline*, and *none*. These designations, listed here, govern how the content is packaged in the formatted document:

*block*

A block is a rectangular region of text isolated from the content preceding and following it by spacing. It begins on a new line, often after some whitespace, and it has boundaries (called margins) that keep the text in the rectangular shape. The text *wraps* at the margin, meaning it stops and then restarts on the next line. Blocks can contain other, smaller blocks, as well as inlines. Examples of blocks in traditional documents are paragraphs, titles, and sections.

*inline*

An inline is content that doesn't interrupt the flow of text in a block. It wraps at the margin of the block it resides in like ordinary character data. It can set properties that don't affect the flow, such as `font-family` and `color`, but cannot have properties related to blocks, such as text alignment and text indentation. Examples of inlines are emphasis, keywords, and hypertext links.

*none*

Any element defined as `display: none` will be skipped by the CSS processor. It's a convenient way to "turn off" large portions of a document for faster processing. It also happens to be the only display setting that is inherited, since all the children of the element are ignored too.

Every element is assigned a `display` property that tells the CSS processor how to format it. If `display` is set to `block`, the element begins on its own line. If it's set to `inline`, the element begins on the line that the previous element or character data finished on. The value `none` indicates that the element is invisible.

This model breaks down for complex objects like tables. A table is a unique formatting structure with cellular regions that can contain blocks or inlines. The discussion of this formatting is too complex for the scope of this chapter.

 Because HTML browsers have an implicit CSS stylesheet built-in, there is no need to define a display value for any HTML elements. The `p` element always displays like a block, and `tt` displays as an inline. However, the same is not true for generic XML languages. The processor has no prior knowledge of the language, so it is forced to guess. Declaring the display property for all elements is recommended.

## Blockish Properties

Around every block is an invisible box that shapes its content and keeps a healthy distance from its neighbors. Figure 5-10 shows all the parts of this *box model*.

Immediately surrounding the content of the block is a rectangular buffer of space called the *bounding box*. Its distance from the content is known as *padding*. The perimeter of this region, called the *boundary*, is sometimes displayed as a rule or border on one, two, three, or all four sides. The thickness of these rules is measured outward. Outside the boundary is another envelope of space, defined by four widths called *margins*.

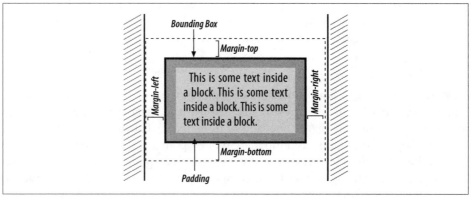

*Figure 5-10. The CSS box model*

A block's boundaries hold content while separating the block from sibling blocks. Any background image or color is confined to the area within the boundary, while text and nested boxes are confined to an even smaller area, the rectangle determined by the boundary minus padding. If the boundary is not displayed, the padding is often set to zero. Margins demarcate a rectangular region outside the box that keeps other boxes away.

## Margins

A common way to adjust space around an element is to set its margins. A margin is the distance between the bounding box of an element and that of any neighboring (or containing) element. The four sides of a box have their own margin property: margin-left, margin-right, margin-top, and margin-bottom. The value can be a length or a percentage of the containing element's width.

The margin property is shorthand for defining all four sides of the margin. Its value is a space-separated list containing between one and four lengths or percentages. If only one value is specified, that value applies to all four sides. If there are two values, the first sets the top and bottom margins and the second sets the left and right margins. If there are three values, the first assigns the top margin, the second assigns both the left and right margins, and the third assigns the bottom margin. Finally, if four values are specified, they correspond to the top, right, bottom, and left margins, respectively. Unspecified margins default to zero. Thus the following rules are equivalent:

```
para { margin-left: 10em; margin-right: 10em; margin-top: 5% }
para { margin: 5% 10em 0 }
```

In both cases, the <para> element is defined with left and right margins of 10 ems, a top margin of 5% of the containing element's height, and no bottom margin. Negative values are acceptable. The result of a negative margin is to push the bounding box outside its container's box by the value given. To create the effect of text spilling outside a colored region, we use this stylesheet for an HTML file:

```
body { background-color: silver }
p { right-margin: -15% }
```

Margins often overlap. For example, paragraphs in a column touch at their top and bottom sides. Instead of adding the margins to make a bigger space, the smaller margin is discarded and the bigger one is used in its place. This is called *collapsing* the margins. So, if a paragraph has a top margin of 24 points and a bottom margin of 10 points, the actual distance between two paragraphs is 24 points. The rules of collapsing margins are actually a little more complex than this, but a full explanation is beyond the scope of this chapter.

## Borders

It's often appealing to surround an element with a rectangular outline to make it stand out. The warning example used previously would catch readers' attention better if it were enclosed in a border. With the border property, you can create many kinds of effects, from dotted lines enclosing a block to rules on any side.

It takes three parameters to define the border you want. The width can be an absolute or relative measurement, or one of three preset values:

```
thin
medium (the default)
thick
```

The next parameter is style. Eight styles are provided in CSS2:

```
solid
dashed
dotted
groove
ridge
double
inset
outset
```

The final parameter is color. Put all the parameters together in a space-separated list, in any order. Some examples:

```
border: thin solid green;
border: red groove thick;
border: inset blue 12pt;
```

### Padding

One thing is still missing. Recall that this border is just inside the margins, putting it right against the text of the block. As a result, we need some extra space inside the border to keep it from crowding the text. The padding property lines the inside of the border with space to compact the text and keep the border from colliding into it. The value of this property is a space-separated list of between one and four length measurements. The application of lengths to sides is the same as it is with the margin property.

Let's expand on our previous warning example by giving it a border, shown in Figure 5-11:

```
warning {
    display: block;
    border: thick solid gray;
}
warning:before {
    content: "WARNING!";
    font-weight: bold;
    color: red }
```

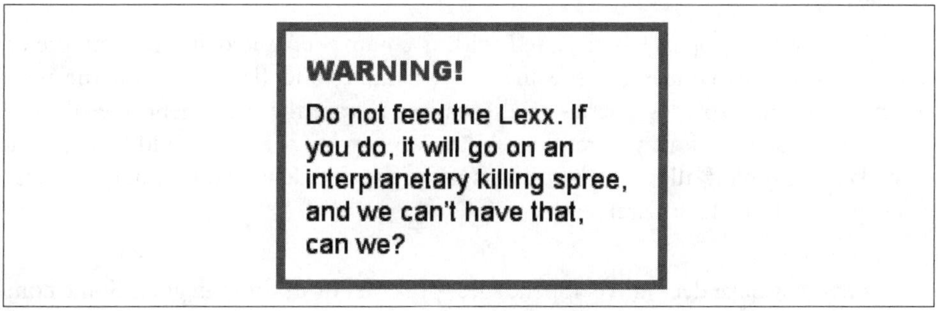

*Figure 5-11. A warning inside a border*

### Alignment and indentation

text-align is a property that defines the alignment or justification of lines in a paragraph. Sometimes you may want a crisp border on both the left and right sides of a column. At other times you may want a ragged right or left, or centered text. The following values are supported:

left
    Align text with the left border (ragged right).

`right`

Align text with the right border (ragged left).

`center`

Center each line within the block (ragged left and right).

`justify`

Expand each line to reach both left and right borders of the block.

Left justification is used by default in most CSS processors. Note that `left` and `right` are absolute and independent of text direction.

The `text-indent` property indents the first line of a block. A positive or negative absolute length can be specified, or the indent can be given as a percentage of the width of the block.

## Text Properties

So far, we've talked about blocks as containers of text. Now let's focus on the text itself. This section lists some properties for controlling how character data looks and behaves, such as font types, font styles, and color.

### Font family

A typeface has several parameters that control its appearance, such as size, weight, and style. The most important, however, is the font family (e.g., Courier, Helvetica, and Times). Each family comes in different styles and weights, such as italic, bold, and heavy.

The `font-family` property is declared with a comma-separated list of font preferences, starting with the most specific and desirable, and finishing with the most generic. This list provides a series of alternatives in case the user agent doesn't have access to the specific font you request. At the very end of the list should be a generic font class, essentially allowing the user's software to decide which font matches best. Some generic font classes are:

`serif`

Fonts that have decorative appendages, or serifs, fit in this category. Some common serif fonts include Palatino, Times, and Garamond.

`sans-serif`

These fonts, lacking serifs, are relatively plain in comparison to the serif fonts. Helvetica and Avant-Garde are in this group.

`monospace`

In these fonts each character occupies the same amount of space, unlike most fonts, where letters are packed together in varying widths. This font type is typically used to render computer programs, teletype simulations, and ASCII art.* Examples of monospace fonts are Courier and Monaco.

cursive

Fonts that connect characters in a simulation of calligraphy or handwriting fall in this group. Such typefaces are often used on wedding invitations and diplomas. Since this is not a standard font category on most systems, you should use it rarely, if ever.

fantasy

This collects all the oddball fonts like Comic Strip, Ransom Note, and Wild West. Again, most users are not likely to have access to this kind of font, so use this category sparingly.

Examples of these typefaces are shown in Figure 5-12.

Figure 5-12. Generic font families

Let's say you want to select the typeface Palatino. Zapf's Humanist 521 is generally held to be a high-quality variant of Palatino. Book Antiqua, a clone from the Monotype foundry, is not as carefully designed, but it's fairly sturdy. There are also cheap knock-offs variously called Palisades or Palestine. If neither Palatino nor any of its kin can be found, Times New Roman is a handy substitute. (It doesn't have much in common with Palatino other than being another serif font, but at least it's closer than Helvetica.) Times New Roman is sometimes found as Times Roman, TmsRmn, or Times.

Now you must decide how to order your list. There is a trade-off between including Palatino clones of doubtful quality, or keeping the list short in favor of radically different, but higher-quality, alternative typefaces. Three approaches might be:

```
font-family: Palatino, "BT Humanist 521", "Book Antiqua", Palisades,
    "Times New Roman", "Times Roman", Times, serif;

font-family: Palatino, "Times New Roman", serif;

font-family: "BT Humanist 521", Palatino, serif;
```

* See *http://www.textfiles.com/art/*.

Note that font names with spaces must be quoted. Capitalization is not necessary.

The first option offers the most alternatives, but by including Palisades it risks diminishing the appearance of the document. The second is much shorter, and says, "If I can't have Palatino, then just use Times New Roman." The third ambitiously strives for BT Humanist 521, but will settle for common Palatino. All of these include the serif generic as a last resort, letting the system pick any serif font if all else fails.

### Font size

The size of a font is determined by the font-size property. The value can be given in absolute units (points, usually) or relative units (percentages or ems of the parent's font). You can also use semi-absolute keywords:

```
xx-small
x-small
small
medium
large
x-large
xx-large
```

The CSS specification recommends that CSS processors display each size 1.2 times larger than the previous one (so that xx-large would be 3.6 times the size of xx-small), but the actual sizes are left to user preference. This provides a nice way to specify sizes relative to your audience's comfort levels, at the cost of losing absolute precision. Figure 5-13 shows how these different font sizes might look.

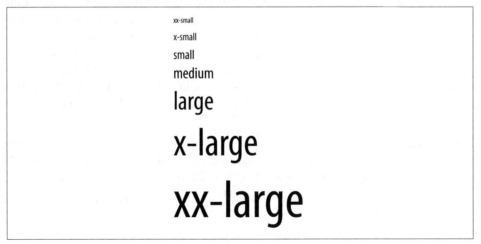

*Figure 5-13. Font sizes*

Relative keywords are also available:

```
larger
smaller
```

These move the size up or down by a size factor.

### Line height and font size adjustment

Whereas `font-size` determines the size of characters being displayed, the `line-height` property affects the total height of the font plus the whitespace above it. If the `line-height` is greater than the `font-size`, the difference is made up by adding space evenly to the top and bottom of each line. This makes the block look either looser or more condensed.

In the following example, we have specified single space, double space, and one-and-one-half space between lines:

```
para1 { line-height: 1 }
para2 { line-height: 2 }
para3 { line-height: 1.5 }
```

Fonts with the same point size can look bigger or smaller, depending on various characteristics summarily referred to as the *eye* of the font. Chief among these is the x-height, or ex. In Latin (read: European) fonts, ex is the height of a lowercase x. (Other fonts use different criteria, but it's always a fraction of the font size, or em.) As a result, some fonts appear bigger than others.

For the obsessive designer, there is a way around this problem. The `font-size-adjust` property can be used to tweak the sizes of fonts in the `font-family` property. The *aspect value* is the ratio of the x-height to the font size. If you provide the aspect value of your desired font, expressed as a decimal fraction, as the value of `font-size-adjust`, the browser can adjust substitute fonts to have the same apparent size as the desired font.

### Font style and weight

Font families contain variants that allow an author to add emphasis or meaning to parts of the text. There are two kinds of variants: font style (italic, oblique) and font weight (light, bold).

The `font-style` property has four possible settings:

`normal`
> The traditional, upright version of the font.

`italic`
> An italic version of the font, if available, or the oblique version.

oblique

> The oblique version, if available, or the normal font with a slight slant effect.

inherit

> Whatever setting the parent element has.

The CSS specification is not clear on the effect of italic on languages without a tradition of italics; as a result, it is probably best to specify an alternative typeface for other languages:

```
em { font-style: italic }
em:lang(ja) { font-family: ...;
              font-style: normal }
```

The font-weight property controls how bold or light a font is. The following keyword values are defined:

light

> A light and airy version of the font, if available. Otherwise, the user's system may generate one automatically.

normal

> The standard variant of the font.

bold

> A darker, heavier version of the font, if available. Otherwise, the user's system may generate one automatically.

There are also relative keywords, which decrease or increase the weight with respect to the parent's property:

lighter

> Decreases the weight by one increment.

bolder

> Increases the weight by one increment.

Nine weight increments are available, so lighter and bolder can fine-tune weight by 1/9 of the range. Alternatively, a numeric value can be used, ranging from 100 to 900 (in steps of 100). Not every font has nine weights, so changing the number by 100 may not have a visible effect. The value 400 corresponds to normal, and bold is set to 700. Figure 5-14 shows some font styles and weights.

*Figure 5-14. Font styles and weights*

## Color

Color is an important feature for text, especially with computer displays. Text has two color properties: color for the foreground, and background-color for the background.

There is a bevy of predefined colors you can call by name. Alternately, you can specify a color using a three-number code where the numbers correspond to values for red, green, and blue (RGB). These numbers can be percentages, integers from 0 to 255, or hexadecimal values from #000000 to #ffffff. Some examples are given in Table 5-1.

*Table 5-1. Color selections*

| Preset Name | Percentages | Integers | Hexadecimal |
| --- | --- | --- | --- |
| aqua | rgb(0%,65%,65%) | rgb(0,160,160) | #00a0a0 |
| black | rgb(0%,0%,0%) | rgb(0,0,0) | #000000 |
| blue | rgb(0%,32%,100%) | rgb(0,80,255) | #0050ff |
| fuchsia | rgb(100%,0%,65%) | rgb(255,0,160) | #ff00a0 |
| gray | rgb(65%,65%,65%) | rgb(160,160,160) | #a0a0a0 |
| green | rgb(0%,100%,0%) | rgb(0,255,0) | #00ff00 |
| lime | rgb(0%,65%,0%) | rgb(0,160,0) | #00a000 |
| maroon | rgb(70%,0%,32%) | rgb(176,0,80) | #b00050 |
| navy | rgb(0%,0%,65%) | rgb(0,0,160) | #0000a0 |
| olive | rgb(65%,65%,0%) | rgb(160,160,0) | #a0a000 |
| purple | rgb(65%,0%,65%) | rgb(160,0,160) | #a000a0 |
| red | rgb(100%,0%,32%) | rgb(255,0,80) | #ff0050 |
| silver | rgb(90%,90%,90%) | rgb(225,225,255) | #d0d0d0 |
| teal | rgb(0%,65%,100%) | rgb(0,160,255) | #00a0ff |
| white | rgb(100%,100%,100%) | rgb(255,255,255) | #ffffff |
| yellow | rgb(100%,100%,0%) | rgb(255,255,0) | #ffff00 |

## Generated Text

Automatically generating text is an important capability of stylesheets. We have seen an example where a warning sidebar was created with an automatically generated "WARNING!" header. The general form of a text-generating property is:

```
content: string1 string2 ...
```

Each string is either a quoted value (like "WARNING!") or a function that creates text. Some of these text-creating functions are:

url(*locator*)
>    This function opens a file at a URL given by *locator* and inserts the contents of the file at that point in the text. This is useful for including boilerplate text.

attr(*attname*)

   This function inserts the value of an attribute with name *attname*.

counter(*name*)

   This useful function reads the value of an internal counter with the label *name* and converts it to text.

## Counters

Counters in CSS are variables that hold numeric values. They are used for chapter numbers, ordered lists, and anything else that needs to be labeled with a number. To use a counter, you have to give it a name and tell CSS when to increment it using the property counter-increment. You can get the value of the counter any time with the counter( ) function. For example:

```
chapter { counter-increment: chapnum }
chapter > title:before { content: "Chapter " counter(chapnum) ". " }
```

Here, we create a counter called chapnum and increment it every time the CSS processor sees a new chapter. The title element is rendered with this number just before it, like this:

```
Chapter 3. Sonic the Hedgehog
```

counter-reset is another property that affects counters. It sets the counter value back to zero when the element is processed. This can be used for things like numbered lists, where you want each list to start at 1 instead of incrementing through the whole document:

```
numberedlist { counter-reset: list_item_number; }
listitem { counter-increment: list_item_number; }
listitem:before { content: counter(list_item_number) ". "; }
```

Now, each list will start counting at 1:

```
First list:
   1. Alpha
   2. Bravo
   3. Charlie
   4. Delta

Second list:
   1. Fee
   2. Fi
   3. Fo
   4. Fum
```

# Examples

Let's put what we know to use now and format a document with CSS. XHTML is a good place to start, so let's take the document in Example 3-4. To maximize the possibilities for formatting it, we should add some structure with div elements, and use span elements to increase the granularity of inlines. Example 5-1 is the improved result.

*Example 5-1. An XHTML document with DIVs and SPANs*

```
<html>
  <head>
    <title>CAT(1) System General Commands Manual</title>
    <link rel="stylesheet" type="text/css" href="style1.css" />
  </head>
  <body>
    <h1>CAT(1) System General Commands Manual</h1>
    <div class="section">
      <h2>NAME</h2>
      <p>cat - concatenate and print files</p>
    </div>
    <div class="section">
      <h2>SYNOPSIS</h2>
      <p class="code">cat [-benstuv] [-] [<em>file</em>...]</p>
    </div>
    <div class="section">
      <h2>DESCRIPTION</h2>
      <p>
The <span class="command">cat</span> utility reads files sequentially,
writing them to the standard output. The file operands are processed
in command line order. A single dash represents the standard input.
      </p>
      <p>
The options are as follows:
      </p>
      <dl>
        <dt><span class="option">-b</span></dt>
        <dd>
Implies the <span class="option">-n</span> option but doesn't number blank lines.
        </dd>
        <dt><span class="option">-e</span></dt>
        <dd>
Implies the <span class="option">-v</span> option, and displays a
dollar sign (<span class="symbol">$</span>) at the end of each line as
well.
        </dd>
        <dt><span class="option">-n</span></dt>
        <dd>Number the output lines, starting at 1.</dd>
        <dt><span class="option">-s</span></dt>
        <dd>
Squeeze multiple adjacent empty lines, causing the output to be single
spaced.
        </dd>
        <dt><span class="option">-t</span></dt>
        <dd>
Implies the <span class="option">-v</span> option, and displays tab
characters as <span class="symbol">^I</span> as well.
        </dd>
```

*Example 5-1. An XHTML document with DIVs and SPANs (continued)*

```
        <dt><span class="option">-u</span></dt>
        <dd>
The <span class="option">-u</span> option guarantees that the output
is unbuffered.
        </dd>
        <dt><span class="option">-v</span></dt>
        <dd>
Displays non-printing characters so they are visible. Control
characters print as <span class="symbol">^X</span> for control-X; the
delete character (octal 0177) prints as <span class="symbol">^?</span>
Non-ascii characters (with the high bit set) are printed as <span
class="symbol">M-</span> (for meta) followed by the character for the
low 7 bits.
        </dd>
      </dl>
      <p>
The <i>cat</i> utility exits 0 on success, and &gt;0 if an error occurs.
      </p>
    </div>
    <div class="section">
      <h2>BUGS</h2>
      <p>
Because of the shell language mechanism used to perform output
redirection, the command <span class="command">cat file1 file2 &gt;
file1</span> will cause the original data in file1 to be destroyed!
      </p>
    </div>
    <div class="section">
      <h2>SEE ALSO</h2>
      <ul>
        <li><a href="head.html">head(1)</a></li>
        <li><a href="more.html">more(1)</a></li>
        <li><a href="pr.html">pr(1)</a></li>
        <li><a href="tail.html">tail(1)</a></li>
        <li><a href="vis.html">vis(1)</a></li>
      </ul>
      <p>
Rob Pike, <span class="citation">UNIX Style, or cat -v Considered
Harmful</span>, USENIX Summer Conference Proceedings, 1983.
      </p>
    </div>
    <div class="section">
      <h3>HISTORY</h3>
      <p>
A <i>cat</i> utility appeared in Version 6 AT&T UNIX.
      </p>
      <p>3rd Berkeley Distribution, May 2, 1995</p>
    </div>
  </body>
</html>
```

Example 5-2 is a CSS stylesheet for this document.

*Example 5-2. A CSS stylesheet for an XHTML document*

```
/* GLOBAL SETTINGS */

body {
  background-color: #aa6;
  font-family: serif;
}

/* BLOCKS */

.section {
  margin: 1em;
  padding: .5em;
  background-color: wheat;
}

h1, h2, h3 {
  font-family: sans-serif;
}

dt {
  background-color: tan;
}

.code {
  padding: 1em;
  border: thin solid gray;
  font-family: monospace;
  font-weight: bold;
}

/* INLINES */

.citation {
  color: purple;
  font-family: sans-serif;
  font-style: italic;
  font-weight: bold;
}

.command {
  font-family: monospace;
  font-weight: bold;
  color: red;
}

.option {
  font-family: monospace;
  font-weight: bold;
  color: blue;
}
```

*Example 5-2. A CSS stylesheet for an XHTML document (continued)*

```
.symbol {
  font-family: monospace;
  font-weight: bold;
  color: green;
}
```

I used the body element as the stage for setting global properties. All the viewable elements will inherit these properties and optionally override them. The remaining rules are divided into the block-type element group and rules for inline elements.

In the block group, the rule matching .section will apply to all the <div class="section"> elements, separating the page into nicely separated regions using background color and margin settings.

Heads are next, with the elements h1, h2, and h3 set to override the font family of the page with sans-serif. This is an example of how a rule can match a group of elements and apply the same set of styles to each.

An interesting experiment to try is to add a font-size property setting for one of these heads. You'll probably find that, no matter what you set it to, it will not change the size of the text in most HTML browsers. I am not sure why this is the case, but it is an example of how the user agent can choose to ignore the style settings from the server.

Skip down to the rule matching .code. This is a traditional paragraph whose style has been modified to look like a code listing. In our example, there is only one line of code, but what would happen if there were more? The whitespace would be crushed into single spaces, and the code would lose its structure. So perhaps a better definition would be based on the pre element.

Figure 5-15 shows how the CSS-formatted page would look in a web browser.

This example is fairly simple due to the fact that every browser has a built-in stylesheet for HTML, so we are in fact only overriding a few default properties. We should now take a look at how a CSS stylesheet would look for another kind of XML document.

Let's return to Example 3-5, the DocBook version of a technical reference page. A stylesheet for this might look like Example 5-3. To associate this with the XML document, you first have to add this line, underneath the XML declaration:

```
<?xml-stylesheet rel="stylesheet" type="text/css" href="uri"?>
```

where *uri* is the location of the stylesheet.

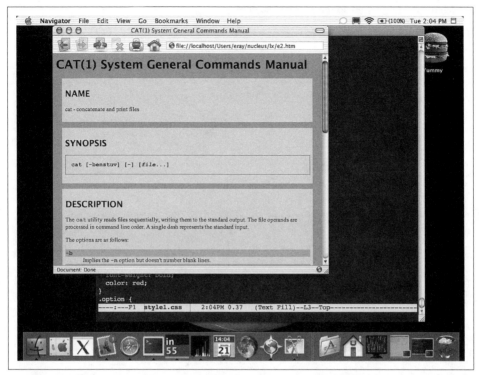

*Figure 5-15. Browser view of the XHTML document*

*Example 5-3. A CSS Stylesheet for a DocBook reference page*

```
/* GLOBAL SETTINGS */

refentry {
  display: block;
  background: silver;
  font-family: serif;
  font-size: 12pt;
}

/* SECTIONS */

refnamediv, refsynopsisdiv, refsect1 {
  display: block;
  margin-top: 1em;
  margin-bottom: 1em;
  margin-left: 0.5em;
  margin-right: 0.5em;
  padding: 0.5em;
  background: #99a;
}
```

*Example 5-3. A CSS Stylesheet for a DocBook reference page (continued)*

```
refnamediv {
  text-align: center;
  font-size: 13pt;
}

refsynopsisdiv:before {
  content: "Usage";
  font-family: sans-serif;
  font-weight: bold;
  font-size: 15pt;
}

/* BLOCKS */

listitem, member, para, refmeta, refpurpose, simplelist, synopsis,
term, title, variablelist {
  display: block;
}

listitem, member {
  margin-left: 2em;
  margin-right: 2em;
}

para { margin: 0.5em; }

refpurpose { font-style: italic; }

refsect1> title {
  margin-top: 0.5em;
  margin-bottom: 0.5em;
  font-family: sans-serif;
  font-weight: bold;
  font-size: 15pt;
}

simplelist { margin-left: 1em; }

synopsis {
  margin-top: 0.5em;
  margin-bottom: 0.5em;
  padding: 0.5em;
  font-family: monospace;
  background-color: #77f;
}

term { float: left; }

variablelist {
  margin-top: 0.5em;
  margin-bottom: 0.5em;
  margin-left: 1em;
```

*Example 5-3. A CSS Stylesheet for a DocBook reference page (continued)*

```
  margin-right: 1em;
}

/* INLINES */

citetitle, command, keysym, literal, option, manvolnum,
replaceable { display: inline; }

command, keysym, literal, option {
  font-family: monospace;
  font-weight: bold;
}

citetitle { font-style: italic; }

command {
  background: gray;
  color: black;
}

keysym {
  background: purple;
  color: yellow;
}

literal { color: brown; }

manvolnum:before { content: "("; }
manvolnum:after  { content: ")"; }

option { color: blue; }

refmeta:before { content: " - "; }

replaceable { font-style: italic; }
```

Every element in this example has its `display` property set. Although the default behavior in browsers is to set the display to `inline`, I think it's a good idea to be explicit and set them all, lest you forget. If you want to see how a document looks when everything is an inline, try taking out the display property settings. Can you say, "obfuscated"?

Notice that in this example, I took advantage of CSS's property merging feature to make things a little more organized. All the inline elements have their display property set in one rule, and any other specific properties are added in other rules.

Skip down to the rule matching `refsynopsisdiv:before`. Here's an example of generated text. As you will see in Figure 5-16, it adds a previously nonexistent head just before the synopsis element telling you that this is a "Usage" synopsis. Other elements (such as `manvolnum`) also add text to make the document more readable and correct.

The rule matching the `term` element sets a property we haven't seen before. `float` lets the block exist on the same horizontal level as another block, relaxing the requirement of vertical alignment. By setting it to `float:left`, the list terms and definitions can sit side-by-side, making a more compact and readable list.

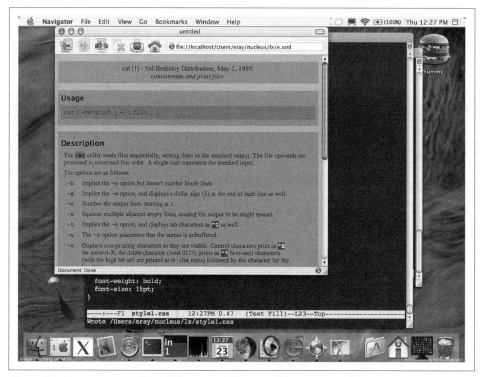

*Figure 5-16. Browser view of the CSS-formatted DocBook document*

CSS has a lot more to it than the few properties we've seen here. More and more, these features are being implemented in browsers allowing web designers more freedom to express themselves. Some things we haven't talked about are the interesting properties coming in CSS level 3. These include alternative media formats, such as speech synthesis and printed page. You will have much better control of your document in these forms as well as on screen.

As useful as CSS can be, it is still limited in many ways. We mentioned the problem of working with elements out of order. CSS can't jump ahead to grab an element at the end of the document for example. Its processing path is fixed. Lucky for us, there is another option. XSLT and XSL-FO bring to the table much more powerful formatting, allowing you incredible freedom to control the path of processing. Get ready, because they are the subjects of Chapter 7 and Chapter 8.

# XPath and XPointer

XML has often been compared to a database because of the way it packages information for easy retrieval. Ignoring the obvious issues of speed and optimization, this isn't a bad analogy. Element names and attributes put handles on data, just as SQL tables use table and field names. Element structure supplies even more information in the form of context (e.g., element A is the child of element B, which follows element C, etc.). With a little knowledge of the markup language, you can locate and extract any piece of information.

This is useful for many reasons. First, you might want to locate specific data from a known location (called a *path*) in a particular document. Given a URI and path, you ought to be able to fetch that data automatically. The other benefit is that you can use path information to get really specific about processing a class of documents. Instead of just giving element name or attribute value to configure a stylesheet as with CSS, you could incorporate all kinds of extra contextual details, including data located anywhere in the document. For example, you could specify that items in a list should use a particular kind of bullet given in a metadata section at the beginning of the document.

To express path information in a standard way, the W3C recommends the XML Path Language (also known as XPath). Quickly following on the heels of the XML recommendation, XPath opens up many possibilities for documents and facilitates technologies such as XSLT and DOM. The XML Pointer Language (XPointer) extends XPath into a wider realm, allowing you to locate information in other documents.

## Nodes and Trees

Remember in Chapter 2 when we talked about trees and XML? I said that every XML document can be represented graphically with a tree structure. The reason that is important will now be revealed. Because there is only one possible tree configuration for any given document, there is a unique path from the root (or any point inside) to any other point. XPath simply describes how to climb the tree in a series of steps to arrive at a destination.

By the way, we will be slipping into some tree-ish terminology throughout the chapter. It's assumed you read the quick introduction to trees in Chapter 2. If you hear me talking about ancestors and siblings and have no idea what that has to do with XML, go back and refresh your vocabulary.

## Node Types

Each step in a path touches a branching or terminal point in the tree called a *node*. In keeping with the arboreal terminology, a terminal node (one with no descendants) is sometimes called a *leaf*. In XPath, there are seven different kinds of nodes:

*Root*

The root of the document is a special kind of node. It's not an element, as you might think, but rather it contains the document element. It also contains any comments or processing instructions that surround the document element.

*Element*

Elements and the root node share a special property among nodes: they alone can contain other nodes. An element node can contain other elements, plus any other node type except the root node. In a tree, it would be the point where two branches meet. Or, if it is an empty element, it would be a leaf node.

*Attribute*

For simplicity's sake, XPath treats attributes as separate nodes from their element hosts. This allows you to select the element as a whole, or merely the attribute in that element, using the same path syntax. An attribute is like an element that contains only text.

*Text*

A region of uninterrupted text is treated as a leaf node. It is always the child of an element. An element may have more than one text node child, however, if it is broken up by elements or other node types. Keep that in mind if you process text in an element: you may have to check more than one node.

*Comment*

Though technically it does not contribute anything to the content of the document, and most XML processors just throw it away, an XML comment is considered a valid node. This may be a way to express a document in such a way that it can be reconstructed down to the character (although, as I will explain later, this is not strictly possible). And who knows, maybe you want to keep the comments around.

*Processing instruction*

Like comments, a processing instruction can appear anywhere in the document under the root node.

*Namespace*

You might think it strange that a namespace declaration should be treated differently from an attribute. But think about this: a namespace is actually a region of the document, not just the possession of a single element. All the descendants of that element will be affected. XML processors must pay special attention to namespaces, so XPath makes it a unique node type.

What isn't included in this list is the DTD. You can't use XPath to poke around in the internal or external subsets. XPath just considers that information to be implicit and not worth accessing directly. It also assumes that any entity references are resolved before XPath enters the tree. This is probably a good thing, because entities can contain element trees that you would probably want to be able to reach.

It isn't strictly true that XPath will maintain all the information about a document so that you could later reconstruct it letter for letter. The structure and content are preserved, however, which makes it *semantically* equivalent. What this means is, if you were to slurp up the document into a program and then rebuild it from the structure in memory, it would probably not pass a *diff* test. Little things would be changed, such as the order of attributes (attribute order is not significant in XML). Whitespace between elements may be missing or changed, and entities will all be resolved. To compare two semantically equivalent documents you'd need a special kind of tool. One that I know of in the Perl realm is the module XML::SemanticDiff, which will tell you if structure or content is the same.

To show these nodes in their natural habitat, let's look at an example. The following document contains all the node types, and Figure 6-1 shows how it looks as a tree.

```
<!-- Dee-licious! -->
<sandwich xmlns="http://www.food.org/ns">
  <ingredient type="grape">jelly</ingredient>
  <ingredient><?knife spread thickly?>
    peanut butter</ingredient>
  <ingredient>bread
    <!-- rye bread, preferably --></ingredient>
</sandwich>
```

# Trees and Subtrees

If you cut off a branch from a willow tree and plant it in the ground, chances are good it will sprout into a tree of its own. Similarly, in XML, any node in the tree can be thought of as a tree its own right. It doesn't have a root node, so that part of the analogy breaks down, but everything else is there: the node is like a document element, it has descendants, and it preserves the tree structure in a sort of fractal way. A tree fashioned from an arbitrary node is called a *subtree*.

---

* *diff* is a program in Unix that compares two text files and reports when any two lines are different. Even if one character is out of place, it will find and report that fact.

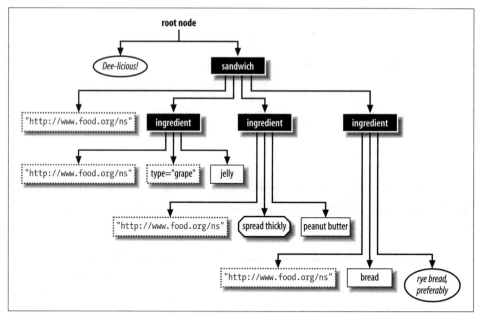

*Figure 6-1. Tree view showing all kinds of nodes*

For example, consider this XML document:

```
<?xml version="1.0"?>
<manual type="assembly" id="model-rocket">
  <parts-list>
    <part label="A" count="1">fuselage, left half</part>
    <part label="B" count="1">fuselage, right half</part>
    <part label="F" count="4">steering fin</part>
    <part label="N" count="3">rocket nozzle</part>
    <part label="C" count="1">crew capsule</part>
  </parts-list>
  <instructions>
    <step>
      Glue parts A and B together to form the fuselage.
    </step>
    <step>
      Apply glue to the steering fins (part F) and insert them into
      slots in the fuselage.
    </step>
    <step>
      Affix the rocket nozzles (part N) to the fuselage bottom with a
      small amount of glue.
    </step>
    <step>
      Connect the crew capsule to the top of the fuselage. Do not use
      any glue, as it is spring-loaded to detach from the fuselage.
    </step>
  </instructions>
</manual>
```

The whole document is a tree with `manual` as the root element (or document element); the parts-list and instructions elements are also in the form of trees, with roots and branches of their own.

XML processing techniques often rely on nested trees. Trees facilitate recursive programming, which is easier and more clear than iterative means. XSLT, for example, is elegant because a rule treats every element as a tree.

It's important to remember that you cannot take just any fragment of an XML document and expect it to form a node tree. It has to be *balanced*. In other words, there should be a start tag for every end tag. An unbalanced piece of XML is really difficult to work with in the XML environment, and certainly with XPath.

# Finding Nodes

There are still a few cultures on earth who can name their ancestors back ten generations or further. "Here is Sam, the son of Ben, the son of Andrew, the son of..." This chain of generations helps establish the identity of a person, showing that he or she is a member of such and such a clan or related to another person through some shared great-great-uncle.

XPath, too, uses chains of steps, except that they are steps in an XML tree rather than an actual family tree. The terms "child" and "parent" are still applicable. A *location path* is a chain of *location steps* that get you from one point in a document to another. If the path begins with an absolute position (say, the root node), then we call it an *absolute path*. Otherwise, it is called a *relative path* because it starts from a place not yet determined.

A location step has three parts: an *axis* that describes the direction to travel, a *node test* that specifies what kinds of nodes are applicable, and a set of optional *predicates* that use Boolean (true/false) tests to winnow down the candidates even further.

The axis is a keyword that specifies a direction you can travel from any node. You can go up through ancestors, down through descendants, or linearly through siblings. Table 6-1 lists all the types of node axes.

*Table 6-1. Node axes*

| Axis type | Matches |
| --- | --- |
| Ancestor | All nodes above the context node, including the parent, grandparent, and so on up to the root node. |
| Ancestor-or-self | The ancestor node plus the context node. |
| Attribute | Attributes of the context node. |
| Child | Children of the context node. |
| Descendant | Children of the context node, plus their children, and so on down to the leaves of the subtree. |
| Descendant-or-self | The descendant node plus the context node. |

*Table 6-1. Node axes (continued)*

| Axis type | Matches |
| --- | --- |
| Following | Nodes that follow the context node at any level in the document. This does not include any descendants of the context node, but does include its following siblings and their descendants. |
| Following-sibling | Nodes that follow the context node at the same level (i.e., that share the same parent as the context node). |
| Namespace | All the namespace nodes of an element. |
| Parent | The parent of the context node. |
| Preceding | Nodes that occur before the context node at any level in the document. This does not include any descendants of the context node, but does include its preceding siblings and their descendants. |
| Preceding-sibling | Nodes that occur before the context node at the same level (i.e., that share the same parent as the context node). |
| Self | The context node itself. |

After the axis comes a node test parameter, joined to the axis by a double colon (::). A name can be used in place of an explicit node type, in which case the node type is inferred from the axis. For the attribute axis, the node is assumed to be an attribute, and for the namespace axis, the node is assumed to be a namespace. For all other axes, the node is assumed to be an element. In the absence of a node axis specifier, the axis is assumed to be child and the node is assumed to be of type element. Table 6-2 lists the node tests.

*Table 6-2. Node tests*

| Term | Matches |
| --- | --- |
| / | The root node: not the root element but the node containing the root element and any comments or processing instructions that precede it. |
| node( ) | Matches any node. For example, the step attribute::node( ) would select all the attributes of the context node. |
| * | In the attribute axis, any attribute. In the namespace axis, any namespace. In all other axes, any element. |
| crabcake | In the attribute axis, the attribute named crabcake of the context node. In a namespace axis, it's a namespace called crabcake. In all other axes, any element named crabcake. |
| text( ) | Any text node. |
| processing-instruction( ) | Any processing instruction. |
| processing-instruction('for-web') | Any processing instruction with target for-web. |
| comment( ) | Any comment node. |

Location path steps are chained together using the slash (/) character. Each step gets you a little closer to the node you want to locate. It's sort of like giving directions to a restaurant ("Go to Davis Square, head down College Avenue; at the Powderhouse rotary, turn left and you'll see a great Vietnamese restaurant"). For example, to get from the root node to a para element inside a section inside a chapter inside a book, a path might look like this:

```
book/chapter/section/para
```

This syntax can be verbose; XPath defines some handy shortcuts as listed in Table 6-3.

*Table 6-3. Location path shortcuts*

| Pattern | Matches |
| --- | --- |
| @role | Matches an attribute named role. This is equivalent to attribute::role. |
| . | The context node. This is equivalent to self::node( ). |
| /* | Matches the document element. Any location path that starts with slash (/) is an absolute path, with the first step representing the root node. The next step is *, which matches any element. |
| parent::*/following-sibling::para | Matches all paras that follow the parent of the context node. |
| .. | Matches the parent node. The double dot (..) is shorthand for parent::node( ). |
| .//para | Matches any element of type para that is a descendant of the current node. The double slash (//) is shorthand for /descendant-or-self::node( )//. |
| //para | Matches any <para> descending from the root node. In other words, it matches all paras anywhere in the document. A location path starting with a double slash (//) is assumed to begin at the root node. |
| ../* | Matches all sibling elements (and the context node if it is an element). |

To see how axis and node tests can be used to retrieve nodes, let's now look at some examples. Consider the sample document in Example 6-1.

*Example 6-1. A sample XML document*

```
<quotelist>
  <quotation style="wise" id="q1">
    <text>Expect nothing; be ready for everything.</text>
    <source>Samurai chant</source>
  </quotation>
  <quotation style="political" id="q2">
    <text>If one morning I walked on top of the water across the Potomac
    River, the headline that afternoon would read "President Can't
    Swim".</text>
    <source>Lyndon B. Johnson</source>
  </quotation>
  <quotation style="silly" id="q3">
    <?human laugh?>
    <text>What if the hokey-pokey IS what it's all about?</text>
  </quotation>
  <quotation style="wise" id="q4">
    <text>If they give you ruled paper, write the other way.</text>
```

*Example 6-1. A sample XML document (continued)*

```
    <source>Juan Ramon Jiminez</source>
  </quotation>
  <!-- the checkbook is mightier than the sword? -->
  <quotation style="political" id="q5">
    <text>Banking establishments are more dangerous than standing
    armies.</text>
    <source>Thomas Jefferson</source>
  </quotation>
</quotelist>
```

Table 6-4 shows some location paths and what they would return.

*Table 6-4. Location path examples*

| Path | Matches |
| --- | --- |
| /quotelist/child::node( ) | All the quotation elements plus the XML comment. |
| /quotelist/quotation | All the quotation elements. |
| /*/* | All the quotation elements. |
| //comment( )/following-sibling::*/@style | The style attribute of the last quotation element. |
| id('q1')/parent::* | The first quotation element. |
| id('q2')/.. | The document element. |
| id('q1')/ancestor-or-self::* | The document element and the first quotation element. |
| id('q3')/self::aphorism | Nothing! The first step does match the third quotation element, but the next step invalidates it because it's looking for an element of type aphorism. In a context where you don't know what type the element is, this is a good way to test it. |
| //processing-instruction( )/../following::source | The source elements from the last two quotation elements. |

Note that the id( ) step will only work on attributes that have been declared to be type ID in a DTD. It is this declaration that tells a validating parser to require an attribute to have a unique value.

If the axis and node type aren't sufficient to narrow down the selection, you can use one or more predicates. A predicate is a Boolean expression enclosed within square brackets ([ ]). Every node that passes this test (in addition to the node test and axis specifier) is included in the final node set. Nodes that fail the test (the predicate evaluates to false) are not. Table 6-5 shows some examples.

*Table 6-5. XPath predicates*

| Path | Matches |
|------|---------|
| `//quotation[@id="q3"]/text` | The text element in the third `quotation` element. This is an example of an equality test, where the string value of the attribute is matched against another string. You can also test numerical and Boolean values. |
| `//quotation[source]` | All the `quotation` elements but the third, which doesn't have a `source` element. Here, the presence of a child element `source` is evaluated; if at least one node matching it is found, the value of the test is true, otherwise false. |
| `//quotation[not(source)]` | The third `quotation` element. `not( )` is true if there are no `source` elements. |
| `/*[@id="q2"]/preceding-sibling::*/source` | The `source` element with the content "Samurai Chant." |
| `//*[source='Thomas Jefferson']/text` | The `text` element in the last `quotation` element. |
| `//*[source='Thomas Jefferson'][@id='q7']` | Nothing! The two predicates are evaluated as a Boolean and function. Both have to be true or the path fails. Since there is no element matching both these tests, we are left with nothing. |
| `/*/*[position( )=last( )]` | The last `quotation` element. The `position( )` function equals the position of the most recent step among eligible candidates. The function `last( )` is equal to the total number of candidates (in this case, 5). |
| `//quotation[position( )!=2]` | All `quotation` elements but the second one. |
| `//quotation[4]` | The fourth `quotation` element. A number alone in the predicate is shorthand for `position()=...` |
| `//quotation[@type='silly' or @type='wise']` | The first, third, and fourth `quotation` elements. The `or` keyword acts as a Boolean `or` operator. |

# XPath Expressions

Location paths are a subset of a more general concept called *XPath expressions*. These are statements that can extract useful information from the tree. Instead of just finding nodes, you can count them, add up numeric values, compare strings, and more. They are much like statements in a functional programming language. There are five types, listed here:

*Boolean*
An expression type with two possible values, `true` and `false`.

*Node set*
A collection of nodes that match an expression's criteria, usually derived with a location path.

*Number*
A numeric value, useful for counting nodes and performing simple arithmetic.

*String*

A fragment of text that may be from the input tree, processed or augmented with generated text.

*Result tree fragment*

A temporary node tree that has its own root node but cannot be indexed into using location paths.

In XPath, types are determined by context. An operator or function can transform one expression type into another as needed. For this reason, there are well-defined rules to determine what values map to when transformed to another type.

XPath has a rich set of operators and functions for working with each expression type. In the following sections, I will describe these and the rules for switching between types.

## Boolean Expressions

Boolean expressions have two values: true or false. As you saw with location step predicates, anything inside the brackets that does not result in a numerical value is forced into a Boolean context. There are other ways to coerce an expression to behave as Boolean. The function boolean( ) derives a true or false value from its argument. There are also various operators that combine and compare expressions with a Boolean result.

The value derived from an expression depends on some rules listed in Table 6-6.

*Table 6-6. Boolean conversion rules*

| Expression type | Rule |
| --- | --- |
| Node set | True if the set contains at least one node, false if it is empty. |
| String | True unless the string is zero-length. |
| Number | True unless the value is zero or NaN (not a number). |
| Result tree fragment | Always true, because every fragment contains at least one node, its root node. |

Certain operators (listed in Table 6-7) compare numerical values to arrive at a Boolean value. These are *existential comparisons*, meaning that they test all the nodes in a node set to determine whether any of them satisfies the comparison.

*Table 6-7. Comparison operators*

| Operator | Returns |
| --- | --- |
| *expr* = *expr* | True if both expressions (string or numeric) have the same value, otherwise false. |
| *expr* != *expr* | True if the expressions do not have the same value (string or numeric), otherwise false. |
| *expr* < *expr*[a] | True if the value of the first numeric expression is less than the value of the second, otherwise false. |

*Table 6-7. Comparison operators (continued)*

| Operator | Returns |
|---|---|
| *expr* > *expr*[a] | True if the value of the first numeric expression is greater than the value of the second, otherwise false. |
| *expr* <= *expr*[a] | True if the value of the first numeric expression is less than or equal to the value of the second, otherwise false. |
| *expr* >= *expr*[a] | True if the value of the first numeric expression is greater than or equal to the value of the second, otherwise false. |

[a] If you use these operators inside an XML document such as an XSLT stylesheet or a Schematron schema, you must use character references &lt; and &gt; instead of < and >.

Listed in Table 6-8 are functions that return Boolean values.

*Table 6-8. Boolean functions*

| Function | Returns |
|---|---|
| *expr* and *expr* | True if both Boolean expressions are true, otherwise false. |
| *expr* or *expr* | True if at least one Boolean expression is true, otherwise false. |
| true( ) | True. |
| false( ) | False. |
| not( *expr* ) | Negates the value of the Boolean expression: true if the expression is false, otherwise false. |

# Node Set Expressions

A node set expression is really the same thing as a location path. The expression evaluates to a set of nodes. This is a set in the strict mathematical sense, meaning that it contains no duplicates. The same node can be added many times, but the set will always contain only one copy of it.

XPath defines a number of functions that operate on node sets, listed in Table 6-9.

*Table 6-9. Node set functions*

| Function | Returns |
|---|---|
| count( *node set* ) | The number of items in *node set*. For example, count(parent::*) will return the value 0 if the context node is the document element. Otherwise, it will return 1, since a node can only have one parent. |
| generate-id( *node set* ) | A string containing a unique identifier for the first node in *node set*, or for the context node if the argument is left out. This string is generated by the processor and guaranteed to be unique for each node. |
| last( ) | The number of the last node in the context node set. last( ) is similar to count( ) except that it operates only on the context node set, not on an arbitrary set. |
| local-name( *node set* ) | The name of the first node in *node set*, without the namespace prefix. Without an argument, it returns the local name of the context node. |
| name( *node set* ) | The name of the first node in node set including the namespace prefix. |

*Table 6-9. Node set functions (continued)*

| Function | Returns |
|---|---|
| namespace-uri( *node set* ) | The URI of the namespace for the first node in *node set*. Without an argument, it returns the namespace URI for the context node. |
| position( ) | The number of the context node in the context node set. |

There are also functions that create node sets, pulling together nodes from all over the document. For example, the function id( *string* ) returns the set of elements that have an ID attribute equal to the value of *string*, or an empty set if no node matches. In a valid document, only one node should be returned, because the ID type attribute must have a unique value. XPath does not require documents to be valid, however, so it is possible that more than one element will be returned.

## Numeric Expressions

XPath allows an expression to be evaluated numerically, which is useful for comparing positions in a set, adding the values of numeric elements, incrementing counters, and so forth. A number in XPath is defined to be a 64-bit floating-point number (whether it has a decimal point or not). Alternatively, a number can be specified as NaN (not a number), in case a conversion fails.

The rules for converting any expression into a numeric value are listed in Table 6-10.

*Table 6-10. Rules to convert expressions into numbers*

| Expression type | Rule |
|---|---|
| Node set | The first node is converted into a string, then the string conversion rule is used. |
| Boolean | The value true is converted to the number 1, and false to the number 0. |
| String | If the string is the literal serialization of a number (i.e., -123.5), it is converted into that number. Otherwise, the value NaN is used. |
| Result-tree fragment | Like node sets, a result-tree fragment is converted into a string, which is then converted with the string rule. |

To manipulate numeric values, there are a variety of operators and functions. These are cataloged in Table 6-11.

*Table 6-11. Numeric operators and functions*

| Function | Returns |
|---|---|
| *expr* + *expr* | The sum of two numeric expressions. |
| *expr* - *expr* | The difference of the first numeric expression minus the second. |
| *expr* * *expr* | The product of two numeric expressions. |
| *expr* div *expr* | The first numeric expression divided by the second expression. |

*Table 6-11. Numeric operators and functions (continued)*

| Function | Returns |
|---|---|
| *expr* mod *expr* | The first numeric expression modulo the second expression. |
| round( *expr* ) | The value of the expression rounded to the nearest integer. |
| floor( *expr* ) | The value of the expression rounded down to an integer value. |
| ceiling( *expr* ) | The value of the expression rounded up to an integer value. |
| sum( *node-set* ) | The sum of the values of the nodes in *node-set*. Unlike the other functions in this table, this function operates over a node set instead of expressions. |

# String Expressions

A string is a segment of character data, such as "How are you?", "990", or "z". Any expression can be converted into a string using the string( ) function following the rules in Table 6-12.

*Table 6-12. Rules to convert expressions into strings*

| Expression type | Rule |
|---|---|
| Node set | The text value of the first node is used as the string. |
| Boolean | The string is true if the expression is true, otherwise false. |
| Number | The string value is the number as it would be printed. For example, string( 1 + 5 - 9 ) evaluates to the string -3. |
| Result-tree fragment | The string value is the concatenation of the text values of all the nodes in the fragment. |

Functions that return string values are listed in Table 6-13.

*Table 6-13. Functions that create strings*

| Function | Returns |
|---|---|
| concat( *string*, *string*, …) | A string that is the concatenation of the string arguments. |
| format-number( *number*, *pattern*, *decimal-format* ) | A string containing the *number*, formatted according to *pattern*. The optional *decimal-format* argument points to a format declaration which assigns special characters like the grouping character, which separates groups of digits in large numbers for readability. In XSLT, this format declaration would be the value of the name attribute in a decimal-format element. |
| normalize-space( *string* ) | The *string* with leading and trailing whitespace removed, and all other strings of whitespace characters replaced with single spaces. The value of the context node is used if the argument is left out. |
| substring( *string*, *offset*, *range* ) | A substring of the *string* argument, starting *offset* characters from the beginning and ending *range* characters from the offset. |
| substring-after( *string*, *to-match* ) | A substring of the *string* argument, starting at the end of the first occurrence of the string *to-match* and ending at the end of *string*. |

*Table 6-13. Functions that create strings (continued)*

| Function | Returns |
|---|---|
| substring-before( *string, to-match* ) | A substring of the *string* argument, starting at the beginning of *string* and ending at the beginning of the first occurrence of the string *to-match*. |
| translate( *string, characters-to-match, characters-replace-with* ) | The *string* with all characters in the string *characters-to-match* replaced with their counterpart characters in the string *characters-replace-with*. Suppose the first argument is the string "happy days are here again.", the second argument is "ah." and the third string is "oH!". The returned result will be the string "Hoppy doys ore Here ogoin!". translate( ) only works on a per-character basis, so you can not replace arbitrary strings with it. |

Some functions operate on strings and return numeric or Boolean values. These are listed in Table 6-14.

*Table 6-14. Functions that operate on strings*

| Function | Returns |
|---|---|
| contains( *string, sub* ) | True if the substring *sub* occurs within the *string*, otherwise false. |
| starts-with( *string, sub* ) | True if the *string* begins with the substring *sub*, otherwise false. |
| string-length( *string* ) | The number of characters inside *string*. |

# XPointer

Closely related to XPath is the XML Pointer Language (XPointer). It uses XPath expressions to find points inside external parsed entities, as an extension to uniform resource identifiers (URIs). It could be used, for example, to create a link from one document to an element inside any other.

Originally designed as a component of the XML Linking Language (XLink), XPointer has become an important *fragment identifier* syntax in its own right. The XPointer Framework became a recommendation in 2003 along with the XPointer element( ) Scheme (allowing basic addressing of elements) and the XPointer xmlns( ) Scheme (incorporating namespaces). The xpointer( ) scheme itself is stuck at Working Draft, getting no further development.

An XPointer instance, which I'll just call an *xpointer*, works much like the fragment identifier in HTML (the part of a URL you sometimes see on the right side of a hash symbol). It's much more versatile than HTML's mechanism, however, as it can refer to any element or point inside text, not just to an anchor element (<a name="..."/>). By virtue of XPath, it has a few advantages over HTML fragment identifiers:

- You can create a link to the target element itself, rather than to a proxy element (e.g., <a name="foo"/>.

- You don't need to have anchors in the target document. You're free to link to any region in any document, whether the author knows about it or not.

- The XPath language is flexible enough to reach any node in the target document.

XPointer actually goes further than XPath. In addition to nodes, it has two new location types. A *point* is any place inside a document between two adjacent characters. Whereas XPath would only locate an entire text node, XPointer can be more granular and locate a spot in the middle of any sentence. The other type introduced by XPointer is a *range*, defined as all the XML information between two points. This would be useful for, say, highlighting a region of text that may start in one paragraph and end in another.

Because of these new types, the return value of an XPointer is not a node set as is the case with XPath expressions. Instead, it is a more general *location set*, where a *location* is defined as a point, range, or node. A point is represented by a pair of objects: a container node (the closest ancestor element to the point), and a numeric *index* that counts the number of characters from the start of container node's content to the point. A range is simply two points, and the information inside it is called a *sub-resource*.

The XPointer specification makes no attempt to describe the behavior of an xpointer. It simply returns a list of nodes or strings to be processed, leaving the functionality up to the developer. This is a good thing because XPointer can be used in many different ways. When used in XLink, the information it describes may be imported into the source target, or left unloaded until the user actuates the link. A completely different application might be to use xpointers as hooks for annotations, stored in a local database. The user agent may use this information to insert icons into the formatted view of the target document that, when selected, bring up another window containing commentary. So by not explaining how XPointer is meant to be used, its flexibility is enhanced.

## Syntax

The following is an example of an xpointer:

```
xpointer(id('flooby')/child::para[2])
```

If successful, it will return a node corresponding to the second `<para>` child of the element whose `id` attribute has the value `'flooby'`. If unsuccessful, it will return an empty location set.

### Schemes and chained xpointers

The keyword `xpointer` is called a *scheme*, which serves to identify a syntax method and delimit the data inside. The data for an `xpointer` scheme is an XPath expression, or a shorthand form of one. There is no need to quote the XPath expression because the parentheses are sufficient to mark the start and end.

## Whatever Happened to XLink?

Plans for XLink were announced in the early days of XML. There were great expectations for it. The limitations of HTML links were to give way to a whole new world of possibilities, from customizable navigation views to third-party collections of documents, a document soup if you will.

The recommendation is divided into two levels: simple and extended. Simple covers the traditional, inline hypertext links that we are all familiar with. Extended links are an exciting new mechanism, describing links between resources from either point, or even a third document.

Now it is two years after XLink reached recommendation status (it took four years just to reach that point), and hardly any implementations are available. None of the web browsers available today offer extended link support, and only a few support even simple links.

Why XLink failed to capture the imagination of developers and XML users may have to do with the popularity of embedded programming languages like JavaScript and Java. While XLink was slowly wending its way through the standards process, browser vendors quickly added support for various coding platforms to enable all kinds of stunts, including many of the problems XLink was meant to solve.

Had XLink appeared sooner, its chances for success might well have been better, and I suspect it would have saved a lot of headaches for web site developers. All programming languages (yes, even Java) are platform-dependent solutions. They don't always work as expected, and they aren't well suited to archiving information for a long period of time.

Perhaps XLink is an example of when the standards process does not work as advertised. Instead of inspiring developers to adopt a best practice, all it managed to inspire was a collective yawn. Whether it's because the recommendation fails to address the problem adequately, or it clashes with the marketing plans of commercial developers, or the new functionality does not justify the effort to implement it, these things do happen.

It is possible to chain together xpointers. They will be evaluated in order, until one is successful. For example:

```
xpointer(id('flooby'))xpointer(//*[@id='flooby'])
```

Here, the two xpointers semantically mean the same thing, but the first case may fail for an XPointer processor that does not implement id( ) properly. This could happen if the processor requires a DTD to tell it which attributes are of type ID, but no DTD is given. When the first expression returns an error, processing shunts over to the next xpointer as a fallback.

Besides xpointer, two other schemes are available: xmlns and element. The purpose of the xmlns scheme is to update the current evaluation environment with a new namespace declaration. Here, an xmlns declaration sets up a namespace prefix which is used in the xpointer that follows it:

```
xmlns(foo=http://www.hasenpfeffer.org/)xpointer(//foo:thingy)
```

It may seem odd, but the xmlns scheme returns an error status that forces processing to proceed on to the next part of the xpointer, using the definition of the foo namespace prefix.

The element scheme provides a syntactic shortcut. It represents the *n*th child of an element with a bare number. A string of numbers like this is called a *child sequence* and is defined in the XPointer element( ) Scheme recommendation. To find the third child of the fifth child of the element whose ID is flooby, you can use this xpointer:

```
element(flooby/5/3)
```

### Shorthand pointers

A *shorthand* xpointer only contains a string that corresponds to the form of an ID type attribute. It substitutes for the id( ) term, making code easier to read and write. These two xpointers are equivalent:

```
flooby
xpointer(id('flooby'))
```

## Points

A point inside a document is represented by two things: a container node and an index. The index counts the number of points from the start of a node, beginning with zero. If the point is inside text, the container is the text node in which it resides, not the element containing the text. The point may also lie outside of text, between two elements for instance.

Figure 6-2 shows how to find the index for points in a small piece of XML, listed here:

```
<para>These are <emphasis>strange</emphasis> times.</para>
```

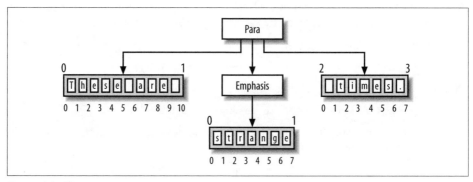

*Figure 6-2. Character points*

Inside each text node (and any node without children) are points between text characters, or *character points*. The point to the left of the first character is zero. The last point follows the last character in the text node, and its index is equal to the length of the string. It's important to note that the first point in the first text node of the example above is not equal to the first point of the element para. These are two separate points.

 XPath and XPointer use UCS character encoding, whereas DOM uses UTF-16 and XML by default is UTF-8. This could cause some confusion when doing string comparisons. For example, what is one character in an XPath string might be two in a DOM string. For more about character encoding, see Chapter 9.

Inside each container node, the point whose index is zero is called the *start point*. The point with the highest index is the *end point*. (A range also has start and end points, but they might not come from the same container node.)

## Character Escaping

XPointers have somewhat complex character escaping rules. This is a side effect of the fact that they can appear in different contexts. Inside an XML document, for example, the well-formedness rules apply. So characters like < and & must be represented with appropriate character entity references.

When using xpointers you always should be careful with three characters: left and right parentheses and the circumflex (^). Parentheses mark the beginning and end of data inside a location term, so any parenthesis that is meant to be data is liable to confuse an XPointer parser. The way to escape such a character is to precede it with a circumflex. As the circumflex is the escaping character, it too must be escaped if it appears on its own. Simply precede it with another circumflex.

If the xpointer is to be used inside a URI reference, then you need to respect the character escaping rules laid out in IETF RFC 2396. In this scheme, certain characters are represented with a percent symbol (%) and a hexadecimal number. For example, a space character would be replaced by %20 and a percent symbol by %25.

Here is an xpointer before escaping:

```
xpointer(string-range(//para,"I use parentheses (a lot)."))
```

You must at minimum escape it like so:

```
xpointer(string-range(//para,"I use parentheses ^(a lot^)."))
```

If the xpointer appears in an URI reference, some other characters need to be escaped, including the circumflexes:

```
xpointer(string-range(//para,"I%20use%20parentheses%20%5E(a%20lot%5E)."))
```

# XPointer Functions

XPointer inherits from XPath all the functions and tests defined in that recommendation. To that set it adds a few specific to points and ranges.

## Constructing ranges

The function range-to( ) creates a range starting from the context node and extending to the point given as its argument. In other words, it creates a range from the last step to the next step.

For example, suppose you have a document that defines index terms that each spans several pages. The element marking the start of the range is indexterm and has the attribute class="startofrange". The element ending the range is the same type, but has an attribute class="endofrange". The following xpointer would create a range for each pair of such elements:

```
xpointer(indexterm[@class='startofrange']/range-to(following::
indexterm[@class='endofrange']))
```

## Ranges from points and nodes

The function range( ) returns the covering range for every location in its argument, the location set. A *covering range* is the range that exactly contains a location. For a point, the range's start and end points would equal that point (a zero-length, or *collapsed*, range). The covering range for a range is the range itself (same start and end points). For any other object, the covering range starts at the point preceding it and ends at the point following it, both of which belong to the object's container node.

The function range-inside( ) changes nodes into ranges. For each node in a given location set, the function treats it as a container node and finds the start and end points. Ranges and points are passed through unchanged.

## Ranges from strings

To create ranges for arbitrary regions of text, you can use string-range( ). This function takes up to four arguments:

1. A location set, positions from which to search for strings.
2. A string, the pattern to match against.
3. An offset from the start of the match (default is 1).
4. The length of the result string, default being the length of the pattern in the second argument.

For example, this xpointer would locate the ninth occurrence of the word "excelsior" in a document:

```
xpointer(string-range(/,"excelsior")[9])
```

And this next xpointer would return a range for the eight characters following the string "username: " (with one space for padding) inside an element with id="user123". (Note that the indexing for characters is different from that for points. Here, the first character's position is 1, not zero.)

```
xpointer(string-range(id('user123'),"username: ",1,8))
```

Note that setting the length (the last argument) to zero would result in a range for a zero-length string. This collapsed range is effectively the same as a single point.

An interesting thing about string-range( ) is that it ignores the boundaries of nodes. It's as if all the content were dumped into a plain text file without XML tags. Effectively, text nodes are concatenated together into one long string of text. So in the following markup:

```
free as in <em>freedom</em>
```

This xpointer would match it whether the <em> tags were there or not:

```
xpointer(string-range(/,"free as in freedom"))
```

### Finding range endpoints

The functions start-range( ) and end-range( ) locate the points at the beginning and end of a range, respectively. Each takes one argument, a location set. If that set is a point, the returned value is the point itself. For nodes, the value would be the start or end point for the covering range of that node. These functions fail, however, for nodes of type attribute and namespace.

### Returning points from documents

If the xpointer is inside an XML document, it can use the function here( ) to represent its location. This would be useful for, say, specifying the origin of a link. If the xpointer occurs inside a text node within an element, the return value is the element. Otherwise, the node that directly contains the xpointer is returned. Because the xpointer can only be at one place at any time, only one item is returned in the location set.

Another function is origin( ). It is only meaningful when used in the context of links, returning the location of the link's origin (where the user or program initiated traversal). This is necessary for complex link types defined in XLink where the link's information does not reside at either of the endpoints.

# Transformation with XSLT

Transformation is one of the most important and useful techniques for working with XML. To *transform* XML is to change its structure, its markup, and perhaps its content into another form. A transformed document may be subtly altered or profoundly changed. The process is carefully shaped with a configuration document variously called a stylesheet or transformation script.

There are many reasons to transform XML. Most often, it is to extend the reach of a document into new areas by converting it into a presentational format. Alternatively, you can use a transformation to alter the content, such as extracting a section, or adding a table of numbers together. It can even be used to filter an XML document to change it in very small ways, such as inserting an attribute into a particular kind of element.

Some uses of transformation are:

- Changing a non-presentational application such as DocBook into HTML for display as web pages.
- Formatting a document to create a high-quality presentational format like PDF, through the XSL-FO path.
- Changing one XML vocabulary to another, for example transforming an organization-specific invoice format into a cross-industry format.
- Extracting specific pieces of information and formatting them in another way, such as constructing a table of contents from section titles.
- Changing an instance of XML into text, such as transforming an XML data file into a comma-delimited file that you can import into Excel as a spreadsheet.
- Reformatting or generating content. For example, numeric values can be massaged to turn integers into floating point numbers or Roman numerals as a way to create your own numbered lists or section heads.
- Polishing a rough document to fix common mistakes or remove unneeded markup, preparing it for later processing.

They may seem like magic, but transformations are a very powerful and not too complicated way to squeeze more use out of your XML.

# History

In the very early days of markup languages, the only way to transform documents was by writing a custom software application to do it. Before SGML and XML, this was excruciating at best. Presentational markup is quite difficult to interpret in any way other than the device-dependent behavior it encodes.

SGML made it much easier for applications to manipulate documents. However, any transformation process was tied to a particular programming platform, making it difficult to share with others. The SGML community really needed a portable language specifically designed to handle SGML transformations, and which supported the nuances of print publishing (the major use of SGML at the time). The first solution to address these needs was the Document Style Semantics and Specification Language (DSSSL).

DSSSL (pronounced "dissel") was completed in 1996 under the auspices of the ISO working group for Document Description and Processing Languages. It laid out the fundamental rules for describing the parts of a formatted document that inspired later efforts including XSL and CSS. Concepts such as bounding boxes and font properties are painstakingly defined here.

If you look at a DSSSL script, you'll see that it is a no-fooling-around programming language. The syntax is Scheme, a dialect of Lisp. You have to be a pretty good programmer to be able to work with it, and the parentheses might drive some to distraction. There is really nothing you can't do with DSSSL, but for most transformations, it may be overly complex. I certainly don't miss it.

As XML gained prominence, the early adopters and developers began to map out a strategy for high-quality formatting. They looked at DSSSL and decided it suffered from the same problems as SGML: too big, too hard to learn, not easy to implement. James Clarke, a pioneer in the text processing frontier who was instrumental in DSSSL development, took what he had learned and began to work on a slimmed-down successor. Thus was born the Extensible Stylesheet Language (XSL).

XSL is really three technologies rolled into one:

- XPath, for finding and handling document components.
- XSL Transformations, for changing any XML document into a presentational XSL Formatting Object tree.
- XSL Formatting Objects, a markup language for high-quality formatted text.

XSL Transformations (XSLT) is the subject of this chapter (we already covered XPath in the last chapter, and visit XSL Formatting Objects in the next). First published as a recommendation by the W3C in 1999, it was originally designed just to transform an XML document into an XSL Formatting Object tree, hence the reason why it retains the "XSL" in its name. So it was surprising to everybody involved when XSLT became the generic transformation language of choice.

In retrospect, it is not so surprising. XSLT is a brilliantly designed language. It is simple enough that its basics can be learned in an hour. The elegance of XPath is very intuitive. The idea of templates is natural and flexible enough to apply to a wide variety of situations. And because XSLT is itself an XML application, all the XML APIs and tools will happily dissect and manipulate XSLT stylesheets.

In this chapter, I will show you not only how to use XSLT to generate formatted (presentational) output, but to use it in a wide variety of problems. Once you have the transformation mindset, you'll find that it's useful in so many ways. Things you used to write programs to do can be done much more succinctly and clearly in an XSLT stylesheet.

## Concepts

Before we jump into specifics, I want to explain some important concepts that will help you understand how XSLT works. An XSLT processor (I'll call it an *XSLT engine*) takes two things as input: an XSLT stylesheet to govern the transformation process and an input document called the *source tree*. The output is called the *result tree*.

The XSLT stylesheet controls the transformation process. While it is usually called a stylesheet, it is not necessarily used to apply style. This is just a term inherited from the original intention of using XSLT to construct XSL-FO trees. Since XSLT is used for many other purposes, it may be better to call it an XSLT script or transformation document, but I will stick with the convention to avoid confusion.

The XSLT processor is a state engine. That is, at any point in time, it has a state, and there are rules to drive processing forward based on the state. The state consists of defined variables plus a set of *context nodes*, the nodes that are next in line for processing. The process is recursive, meaning that for each node processed, there may be children that also need processing. In that case, the current context node set is temporarily shelved until the recursion has completed.

The XSLT engine begins by reading in the XSLT stylesheet and caching it as a lookup table. For each node it processes, it will look in the table for the best matching rule to apply. The rule specifies what to output to build its part of the result tree, and also how to continue processing. Starting from the root node, the XSLT engine finds rules, executes them, and continues until there are no more nodes in its context node set to work with. At that point, processing is complete and the XSLT engine outputs the result document.

Let us now look at an example. Consider the document in Example 7-1.

*Example 7-1. Instruction guide for a model rocket*

```
<manual type="assembly" id="model-rocket">
  <parts-list>
    <part label="A" count="1">fuselage, left half</part>
    <part label="B" count="1">fuselage, right half</part>
    <part label="F" count="4">steering fin</part>
    <part label="N" count="3">rocket nozzle</part>
    <part label="C" count="1">crew capsule</part>
  </parts-list>
  <instructions>
    <step>
Glue <part ref="A"/> and <part ref="B"/> together to form the
fuselage.
    </step>
    <step>
For each <part ref="F"/>, apply glue and insert it into slots in the
fuselage.
    </step>
    <step>
Affix <part ref="N"/> to the fuselage bottom with a small amount of
glue.
    </step>
    <step>
Connect <part ref="C"/> to the top of the fuselage. Do not use
any glue, as it is spring-loaded to detach from the fuselage.
    </step>
  </instructions>
</manual>
```

Suppose you want to format this document in HTML with an XSLT transformation. The following plain English rules describe the process:

1. Starting with the manual element, set up the "shell" of the document, in this case the html element, title, and metadata.

2. For the parts-list element, create a list of items.

3. For each part with a label attribute, create a li element in the parts list.

4. For each part with a ref attribute, output some text only: the label and name of the part.

5. The instructions element is a numbered list, so output the container element for that.

6. For each step element, output an item for the instructions list.

The stylesheet in Example 7-2 follows the same structure as these English rules, with a *template* for each.

*Example 7-2. XSLT stylesheet for the instruction guide*

```
<xsl:stylesheet
    xmlns:xsl="http://www.w3.org/1999/XSL/Transform"
    version="1.0"
>
  <xsl:output method="xml" encoding="ISO-8859-1"/>

  <!-- Handle the document element: set up the HTML page -->
  <xsl:template match="manual">
    <html>
      <head><title>Instructions Guide</title></head>
      <body>
        <h1>Instructions Guide</h1>
        <xsl:apply-templates/>
      </body>
    </html>
  </xsl:template>

  <!-- Create a parts list -->
  <xsl:template match="parts-list">
    <h2>Parts</h2>
    <dl>
      <xsl:apply-templates/>
    </dl>
  </xsl:template>

  <!-- One use of the <part> element: item in a list -->
  <xsl:template match="part[@label]">
    <dt>
      <xsl:value-of select="@label"/>
    </dt>
    <dd>
      <xsl:apply-templates/>
    </dd>
  </xsl:template>

  <!-- another use of the <part> element: generate part name -->
  <xsl:template match="part[@ref]">
    <xsl:variable name="label" select="@ref" />
    <xsl:value-of select="//part[@label = $label]" />
    <xsl:text> (Part </xsl:text>
    <xsl:value-of select="@ref" />
    <xsl:text>)</xsl:text>
  </xsl:template>

  <!-- Set up the instructions list -->
  <xsl:template match="instructions">
    <h2>Steps</h2>
    <ol>
      <xsl:apply-templates/>
    </ol>
  </xsl:template>
```

*Example 7-2. XSLT stylesheet for the instruction guide (continued)*

```
<!-- Handle each item (a <step>) in the instructions list -->
<xsl:template match="step">
  <li>
    <xsl:apply-templates/>
  </li>
</xsl:template>

</xsl:stylesheet>
```

You will notice that each rule in the verbal description has a corresponding `template` element that contains a balanced (well-formed) piece of XML. Namespaces help the processor tell the difference between what is an XSLT instruction and what is markup to output in the result tree. In this case, XSLT instructions are elements that have the namespace prefix `xsl`. The `match` attribute in each `template` element assigns it to a piece of the source tree using an *XSLT pattern*, which is based on XPath.

A *template* is a mixture of markup, text content, and XSLT instructions. The instructions may be conditional statements (if these conditions are true, output this), content formatting functions, or instructions to redirect processing to other nodes. The element `apply-templates`, for example, tells the XSLT engine to move processing to a new set of context nodes, the children of the current node.

The result of running a transformation with the above document and XSLT stylesheet is a formatted HTML page (whitespace may vary):

```
<html>
  <head><title>Instructions Guide</title></head>
  <body>
    <h1>Instructions Guide</h1>
    <h2>Parts</h2>
    <dl>
      <dt>A</dt>
      <dd>fuselage, left half</dd>
      <dt>B</dt>
      <dd>fuselage, right half</dd>
      <dt>F</dt>
      <dd>steering fin</dd>
      <dt>N</dt>
      <dd>rocket nozzle</dd>
      <dt>C</dt>
      <dd>crew capsule</dd>
    </dl>
    <h2>Steps</h2>
    <ol>
      <li>
Glue fuselage, left half (Part A) and fuselage, right half (Part B)
together to form the fuselage.
      </li>
```

```
    <li>
For each steering fin (Part F), apply glue and insert it into slots in
the fuselage.
    </li>
    <li>
Affix rocket nozzle (Part N) to the fuselage bottom with a small
amount of glue.
    </li>
    <li>
Connect crew capsule (Part C) to the top of the fuselage. Do not use
any glue, as it is spring-loaded to detach from the fuselage.
    </li>
   </ol>
  </body>
</html>
```

As you see here, the elements in the source tree have been mapped to different elements in the result tree. We have successfully converted a document in one format to another. That is one example of XSLT in action.

# Running Transformations

There are several strategies to performing a transformation, depending on your needs. If you want a transformed document for your own use, you could run a program such as *Saxon* to transform it on your local system. With web documents, the transformation is performed either on the server side or the client side. Some web servers can detect a stylesheet declaration and transform the document as it's being served out. Another possibility is to send the source document to the client to perform the transformation. Internet Explorer 5.0 was the first browser to implement XSLT,[*] opening the door to this procedure. Which method you choose depends on various factors such as how often the data changes, what kind of load your server can handle, and whether there is some benefit to giving the user your source XML files.

If the transformation will be done by the web server or client, you must include a reference to the stylesheet in the document as a processing instruction, similar to the one used to associate documents with CSS stylesheets. It should look like this:

```
<?xml-stylesheet type="text/xml" href="mytrans.xsl"?>
```

The type attribute is a MIME type.[†] The attribute href points to the location of the stylesheet.

---

[*] Actually, this isn't *strictly* true, as one of my reviewers pointed out. Jeni Tennison writes, "Internet Explorer 5.0 didn't support XSLT unless you installed MSXML3 in replace mode. Otherwise, it supported WD-xsl (Microsoft's version)," which is a bastardized attempt at implementing XSLT. It was still useful, but incompatible with every other XSLT implementation, including later Microsoft work.

[†] There is still some confusion at the moment about which value to use here. Sometimes text/xml is sufficient. Internet Explorer 5 will only recognize text/xsl. Fortunately, XSLT 2.0 will clear up this mess, recommending the MIME type text/xslt+xml.

# The stylesheet Element

As mentioned before, XSLT is an XML application, so stylesheets are XML documents. The document element is stylesheet, although you are also allowed to use transform if the term stylesheet bugs you. This element is where you must declare the XSLT's namespace and version. The namespace identifier is *http://www.w3.org/1999/XSL/Transform/*. Both the namespace and version attributes are required.

XSLT can be extended by the implementer to perform special functions not contained in the specification. For example, you can add a feature to redirect output to multiple files. These extensions are identified by a separate namespace that you must declare if you want to use them. And, just to make things clear for the XSLT engine, you should set the attribute extension-element-prefixes to contain the namespace prefixes of extensions.

As an example, consider the stylesheet element below. It declares namespaces for XSLT control elements (prefix xsl) and implementation-specific elements (prefix ext). Finally, it specifies the version 1.0 of XSLT in the last attribute.

```
<xsl:stylesheet
    xmlns:xsl="http://www.w3.org/1999/XSL/Transform"
    xmlns:ext="http://www.myxslt.org/extentions"
    extension-element-prefixes="ext"
    version="1.0"
>
```

The namespace, represented here as xsl is used by the transformation processor to determine which elements control the process. Any elements or attributes not in that namespace nor the extensions namespace will be interpreted as data to be output in the result tree.

# Templates

XSLT stylesheets are collections of templates. Each template associates a condition (e.g., an element in the source tree with a particular attribute) with a mixture of output data and instructions. These instructions refine and redirect processing, extending the simple matching mechanism to give you full control over the transformation.

A template does three things. First, it *matches* a class of node. The match attribute holds an XSLT pattern which, much like an XPath expression, matches nodes. When an XSLT processor is told to apply templates to a particular node, the processor runs through all the templates in the stylesheet and tests whether the node matches the template's pattern. All the templates that match this node are candidates for processing, and the XSLT processor must select one.

Second, the template contributes a priority value to help the processor decide which among eligible templates is the best to use. The template that matches the current node with the highest import precedence, or highest priority, is the one that will be used to process it. Different factors contribute to this priority. A template with more specific information will overrule one that is more generic. For example, one template may match all elements with the XPath expression *. Another may match a specific element, while a third matches that element and further requires an attribute. Alternatively, a template can simply state its precedence to the processor using a `priority` attribute. This is useful when you want to force a template to be used where otherwise it would be overlooked.

The third role of a template is to specify the structure of the result tree. The template's content actually contains the elements and character data to be output in the result tree. So it is often possible to see, at a glance, how the result tree will look. XSLT elements interspersed throughout this content direct the processing to other templates.

This model for scripting a transformation has strong benefits. Templates are (usually) compact pieces of code that are easy to read and manage, like functions in a programming language. The `match` and `priority` attributes show exactly when each template is to be used. Transformation stylesheets are modular and can be combined with others to enhance or alter the flow of transformation.

## Matching Nodes

The XSLT patterns used inside the `match` attributes of `template` elements are a subset of XPath expressions. The first restriction on XSLT patterns is that only descending axes may be used: `child` and `attribute`. The shorthand `//` can be used but it's not expanded. It simply would not make sense to use other axes in XSLT patterns.

The second difference is that paths are actually evaluated right to left, not the other direction as is usual with XPath. This is a more natural fit for the XSLT style of processing. As the processor moves through the source tree, it keeps a running list of nodes to process next, called the *context node set*. Each node in this set is processed in turn. The processor looks at the set of rules in the stylesheet, finds a few that apply to the node to be processed, and out of this set selects the best matching rule. The right-to-left processing helps the XSLT engine prioritize eligible templates.

Suppose there is a rule with a match pattern `chapter/section/para`. To test this pattern, the XSLT engine first instantiates the node-to-process as the context node. Then it asks these questions in order:

1. Is the context node an element of type `para`?
2. Is the parent of this node an element of type `section`?
3. Is the grandparent of this node an element of type `chapter`?

Logically, this is not so different from traditional XPath processing, which usually starts from some absolute node and works its way into the depths of the document.

You just have to change your notion of where the path is starting from. It might make more sense to rewrite the match pattern like this:

```
abstract-node/child::chapter/child::section/child::para
```

where *abstract-node* is some node such that a location path extending from it matches a set of nodes that includes the node-to-process.

## Resolving Conflicts Among Rules

It is possible for more than one rule to match a node. In this case, the XSLT processor must select exactly one rule from the mix, and that rule should meet our expectations for best match. Here are the rules of precedence among matching patterns:

1. If the pattern contains multiple alternatives separated by vertical bars (|), each alternative is treated with equal importance, as though there were a separate rule for each.

2. A pattern that contains specific hierarchical information has higher priority than a pattern that contains general information. For example, the pattern chapter/section/para is more specific than para, so it takes precedence.

3. A wildcard is more general than a specific element or attribute name and therefore has lower priority. The pattern stuff takes priority over the wildcard pattern *. Note that this is not true when hierarchical information is included. stuff/cruft has exactly the same priority as stuff/* because they both specify hierarchical information about the node.

4. A pattern with a successful test expression in square brackets ([ ]) overrides a pattern with no test expression but that is otherwise identical. So bobo[@role="clown"] has higher priority than bobo. Again, this only works when no hierarchical information is included. circus/bobo and circus/bobo[@role="clown"] have the same priority.

5. Other information, such as position in the stylesheet, may be used to pare down the set if there is still more than one rule remaining.

The basic assumption is that rules that are more specific in their application take precedence over rules that are more general. If this were not the case, it would be impossible to write catch-all rules and default cases. Position and order don't come into play unless all other means of discrimination fail. It's up to the transformation processor to determine how to handle the final tie-breaking.

The xsl:template element has an optional priority attribute that can be set to give it precedence over other rules and override the process of determination. The value must be a real number (i.e., it must have a decimal point unless it is zero) and can be positive, negative, or zero. A larger number overrides a smaller number.

## Default Rules

XSLT defines a set of default rules to make the job of writing stylesheets easier. If no rule from the stylesheet matches, the default rules provide an emergency backup system. Their general behavior is to carry over any text data in elements from the source tree to the result tree, and to assume an implicit `xsl:apply-templates` element to allow recursive processing. Attributes without matching templates are not processed. The following list sums up the default rules for each type of node:

*Root*

Processing starts at the root. To force processing of the entire tree, the default behavior is to apply templates to all the children. The rule looks like this:

```
<xsl:template match="/">
  <xsl:apply-templates/>
</xsl:template>
```

*Element*

We want the processor to touch every element in the tree so it does not miss any branches for which rules are defined. The rule is similar to that for the root node:

```
<xsl:template match="*">
  <xsl:apply-templates/>
</xsl:template>
```

*Attribute*

Attributes without matching templates are simply ignored:

```
<xsl:template match="@*"/>
```

*Text*

It is inconvenient to include the `xsl:value-of` element in every template to output text. Since we almost always want the text data to be output, it is done by default:

```
<xsl:template match="text()">
  <xsl:value-of select="."/>
</xsl:template>
```

*Processing instruction*

By default, these nodes are left out. The rule is this:

```
<xsl:template match="processing-instruction()"/>
```

*Comment*

Comments are also omitted from the result tree by default:

```
<xsl:template match="comment()"/>
```

## Redirecting Processing

The template model of transformation creates islands of markup separate from each other. We need some way of connecting them so that processing continues through the document. According to the default rules, for every element that has no matching template, the XSLT engine should output its text value. This requires processing not only its text nodes, but all the descendants in case they have text values too.

If a template does match an element, it is not required to do anything with the element or its content. In fact, it is often the case that you want certain elements to be ignored. Perhaps they contain metadata that is not to be included with the formatted data. So you are allowed to leave a template empty. Here, the element ignore-me will be passed over by the XSLT processor (unless another rule matches with higher priority):

```
<xsl:template match="ignore-me"/>
```

Unless you explicitly tell the XSLT engine how to proceed with processing in the template, it will go no further. Instead, it will revert to the context node set and evaluate the next node in line. If you do want processing to go on to the children, or you want to insert other nodes to process before the next node in the context set, there are some directives at your disposal.

### The apply-templates instruction

The element apply-templates interrupts the current processing in the template and forces the XSLT engine to move on to the children of the current node. This enables recursive behavior so that processing can descend through the tree of a document. It is called apply-templates because the processor has to find new templates to process the children.

The first template in Example 7-2 contains an apply-templates element:

```
<xsl:template match="manual">
  <html>
    <head><title>Instructions Guide</title></head>
    <body>
      <h1>Instructions Guide</h1>
      <xsl:apply-templates/>
    </body>
  </html>
</xsl:template>
```

When processing this template, the XSLT engine would first output the markup starting from the html start tag all the way to the end tag of the h1 element. When it gets to the xsl:apply-templates element, it jumps to the children of the current (manual) element and processes those with their own templates: the attributes type and id, then the elements parts-list and instructions. After all these have been processed, the XSLT engine returns to its work on the above template and outputs the end tags for body and html.

Suppose that you did not want to handle all the children of a node, but just a few. You can restrict the set of children to process using the attribute select. It takes an

XPath location path as its value, giving you a rich assortment of options. For example, we could rewrite the second template in Example 7-2 like so:

```
<xsl:template match="manual">
  <html>
    <head><title>Parts List</title></head>
    <body>
      <h1>Parts List</h1>
      <xsl:apply-templates select="parts-list"/>
    </body>
  </html>
</xsl:template>
```

Now only the parts-list element will be processed. All other children of manual, including its attributes and the instructions element, would be skipped. Alternatively, you can skip a particular element type like this:

```
<xsl:template match="manual">
  <html>
    <head><title>Assembly Steps</title></head>
    <body>
      <h1>Assembly Steps</h1>
      <xsl:apply-templates select="not(parts-list)"/>
    </body>
  </html>
</xsl:template>
```

And everything but the parts-list element will be handled.

 While it is possible to set the select attribute to point to an ancestor of the current node, be very careful about doing this, as it might set up an infinite loop.

### The for-each instruction

The for-each element creates a template-within-a-template. Instead of relying on the XSLT engine to find matching templates, this directive encloses its own region of markup. Inside that region, the context node set is redefined to a different node set, again determined by a select attribute. Once outside the for-each, the old context node set is reinstantiated.

Consider this template:

```
<xsl:template match="book">
  <xsl:for-each select="chapter">
    <xsl:text>Chapter </xsl:text>
    <xsl:value-of select="position()"/>
    <xsl:text>. </xsl:text>
    <xsl:value-of select="title"/>
    <xsl:text>
    </xsl:text>
  </xsl:for-each>
  <xsl:apply-templates/>
</xsl:template>
```

It creates a table of contents from a DocBook document. The for-each element goes through the book and retrieves every child element of type chapter. This set becomes the new context node set, and within the for-each we know nothing about the old context nodes.

The first value-of element outputs the string value of the XPath expression position( ), which is the position in the set of the chapter being evaluated in this iteration through the loop. The next value-of outputs the title of this chapter. Note that it is a child of chapter, not book.

Since the output of this is plain text, I had to insert the second text element to output a newline character. (We will cover formatting and whitespace issues later in the chapter.) The result of this transformation would be something like this:

```
Chapter 1. Teething on Transistors: My Early Years
Chapter 2. Running With the Geek Gang
Chapter 3. My First White Collar Crime
Chapter 4. Hacking the Pentagon
```

You may wonder what happens when the for-each directive fails to match any nodes. The answer is, nothing. The XSLT processor never enters the region of the element and instead just continues on with the template. There is no "or else" contingency in for-each, but you can get that functionality by using if and choose constructs covered later in the chapter.

## Named Templates

All the template rules we have seen so far are specified by their match patterns. They are accessible only by the XSLT engine's template-matching facility. Sometimes, however, you may find it more convenient to create a *named template* to which you can direct processing manually.

The concept is similar to defining functions in programming. You set aside a block of code and give it a name. Later, you can reference that function and pass it data through arguments. This makes your code simpler and easier to read overall, and functions keep frequently accessed code in one place for easier maintenance. These same benefits are available in your XSLT stylesheet through named templates.

A named template is like any other template except that it has a name attribute. You can use this with a match attribute or in place of one. Its value is a name (a qualified name, to be specific) that uniquely identifies the template.

### The call-template directive

To direct processing to this template, use the directive call-template, identifying it with a name attribute. For example:

```
<xsl:template match="document">
  <!-- regular page markup here -->
  <xsl:call-template name="copyright-info"/>
```

```
    <!-- generate a page number -->
</xsl:template>

<xsl:template name="copyright-info">
  <p>
This is some text the lawyers make us write. It appears at the bottom
of every single document, ad nauseum. Blah blah, all rights reserved,
blah blah blah, under penalty of eating yogurt, blah blah...
  </p>
</xsl:template>
```

The first template calls the second, named template. Processing jumps over to the named template, then returns to where it left off in the first template. The context node set does not change in this jump. So even in the named template, you could check what is the current node with `self::node( )` and it would be exactly the same.

Here is another example. This named template generates a menu of navigation links for an HTML page:

```
<xsl:template name="navbar">
  <div class="navbar">
    <xsl:text>Current document: </xsl:text>
    <xsl:value-of select="title"/>
    <br/>
    <a href="index.htm">Home</a> |
    <a href="help.htm">Help</a> |
    <a href="toc.htm">Contents</a>
  </div>
</xsl:template>
```

Before the links, I placed two lines to print the current document's title demonstrating that the current node is the same as it was in the rule that invoked the named template. Since you can call a named template as many times as you want, let us put the navigation menu at the top and bottom of the page:

```
<xsl:template match="page">
  <body>
    <xsl:call-template name="navbar"/>
    <xsl:apply-templates/>
    <xsl:call-template name="navbar"/>
  </body>
</xsl:template>
```

If you want to change the context node set for a named template, you must enclose the call in a for-each element:

```
<xsl:template match="cross-reference">
  <xsl:variable name="reference" select="@ref"/>
  <xsl:for-each select="//*[@id=$reference]">
    <xsl:call-template name="generate-ref-text"/>
  </xsl:for-each>
</xsl:template>
```

What this template does is handle the occurrence of a cross-reference, which is a link to another element in the same document. For example, an entry in a dictionary might have a "see also" link to another entry. For an element of type cross-reference, this template finds the value of its ref attribute and assigns it to a variable. (As we will see later on when I talk more about variables, this is a useful way of inserting a piece of text into an XPath expression.) The for-each element then locates the element whose ID matches the reference value and sets that to be the context node before passing control over to the template named generate-ref-text. That template will generate some text appropriate for the kind of cross-reference we want.

### Parameters

Like subroutines from programming languages, named templates can accept parameters from the templates that call them. This is a way to pass extra information to the template that it needs for processing.

For example, you may have a template that creates a highlighted node or sidebar in a formatted document. You can use a parameter to add some text to the title to set the tone: tip, caution, warning, information, and so on. Here is how that might look:

```
<programlisting><xsl:template match="warning">
  <xsl:call-template name="generic-note">
    <xsl:with-param name="label">Look out! </xsl:with-param>
  </xsl:call-template>
</xsl:template>

<xsl:template match="tip">
  <xsl:call-template name="generic-note">
    <xsl:with-param name="label">Useful Tip: </xsl:with-param>
  </xsl:call-template>
</xsl:template>

<xsl:template match="note">
  <xsl:call-template name="generic-note"/>
</xsl:template>

<xsl:template name="generic-note">
  <xsl:param name="label">Note: </xsl:param>
  <blockquote class="note">
    <h3>
      <xsl:value-of select="$label"/>
      <xsl:value-of select="title"/>
    </h3>
    <xsl:apply-templates/>
  </blockquote>
</xsl:template>
```

This example creates a named template called generic-note that takes one parameter, named label. Each template calling generic-note may define this parameter with the with-param element as a child of the call-template element. Or it may defer to the default value defined in the param element inside the named template, as is the case with the template matching note.

param declares the parameter in the named template. The name attribute gives it a label that you can refer to later in an attribute with a dollar sign preceding, as in the value-of element above. You may use as many parameters as you wish, but each one has to be declared.

If you use the parameter reference inside a non-XPath attribute, you need to enclose it in curly braces ({ }) to force the XSLT engine to resolve it to its text value:

```
<a href="{$file}">Next Page</a>
```

Optionally, param may assign a default value using its content. The value is a result tree fragment constructed by evaluating the content of the param element. For example, you can set it with:

```
<xsl:param name="label">
  <span class="highlight">Note: </span>
</xsl:param>
```

and the parameter will be set to a result tree fragment containing a span element.

# Formatting

Since XSLT was originally intended for producing human-readable formatted documents, and not just as a general transformation tool, it comes with a decent supply of formatting capabilities.

## Setting the Output Mode

A global setting you may want to include in your stylesheet is the <output> element. It controls how the XSLT engine constructs the result tree by forcing start and end tags, handling whitespace in a certain way, and so on. It is a top-level element that should reside outside of any template.

Three choices are provided: XML, HTML, and text. The default output type, XML, is simple: whitespace and predefined entities are handled exactly the same in the result tree as in the input tree, so there are no surprises when you look at the output. If your result document will be an application of XML, place this directive in your stylesheet:

```
<xsl:output method="xml"/>
```

HTML is a special case necessary for older browsers that do not understand some of the new syntax required by XML. It is unlikely you will need to use this mode instead of XML (for XHTML); nevertheless it is here if you need it. The exact output conforms to HTML version 4.0. Empty elements will not contain a slash at the end and processing instructions will contain only one question mark. So in this mode, the XSLT engine will not generate well-formed XML.

Text mode is useful for generating non-XML output. For example, you may want to dump a document to plain text with all the tags stripped out. Or you may want to output to a format such as troff or T<sub>E</sub>X. In this mode, the XSLT engine is required to resolve all character entities rather than keep them as references. It also handles whitespace differently, preserving all newlines and indentation.

## Outputting Node Values

XPath introduced the notion of a node's string value. All the text in an element is assembled into a string and that is what you get. So in this element:

```
<sentence><subject>The quick, brown
<noun>fox</noun></subject> <action>jumped over</action> <object>the
lazy <noun>dog</noun></object>.</sentence>
```

The text value is "The quick, brown fox jumped over the lazy dog."

In the default rules, all text nodes that are the children of elements are output literally. If you have no explicit template for text nodes, then any apply-templates directive that matches a text node will resort to the default rule and the text will be output normally.

However, there are cases when you can't rely on the default rules. You may want to output the value of an attribute, for example. Or else you might want to get a string without any markup tags in it. When this is the case, you should use value-of.

This element requires an attribute select which takes an XPath expression as its value. value-of simply outputs the string value of that expression.

Recall from Example 7-2 this template:

```
<xsl:template match="part[@label]">
  <dt>
    <xsl:value-of select="@label"/>
  </dt>
  <dd>
    <xsl:apply-templates/>
  </dd>
</xsl:template>
```

It extracts the value of the attribute label and outputs it literally as the content of a dt element.

Besides nodes, value-of can be used to resolve variables, as you will see in the next section.

# Variables

A convenience provided in XSLT is the ability to create placeholders for text called *variables*. Contrary to what the name suggests, it is not actually a variable that can be modified over the course of processing. It's really a constant that is set once and read multiple times. A variable must be defined before it can be used. For that, you can use the variable element.

Here are some examples of declaring variables:

```
<!-- A numeric constant -->
<xsl:variable name="year" select="2001"/>

<!-- A string consisting of two blank lines, useful for making
output XML easier to read -->
<xsl:variable name="double-blank-line">
  <xsl:text>
  </xsl:text>
</xsl:variable>

<!-- A concatenation of two elements' string values -->
<xsl:variable name="author-name">
  <xsl:value-of select="/book/bookinfo/authorgroup/author/firstname"/>
  <xsl:text> </xsl:text>
  <xsl:value-of select="/book/bookinfo/authorgroup/author/surname"/>
</xsl:variable>
```

The first example sets the variable to a string value. The last two examples set the variables to result tree fragments. These are XML node trees that will be copied into the result tree.

Like parameters, a variable reference has a required dollar sign ($) prefix, and when referenced in non-XPath attribute values, it must be enclosed in curly braces ({ }). Variables can be used in other declarations, but be wary of creating looped definitions.

Here is a dangerous, mutually referential set of variable assignments:

```
<!-- ASKING FOR TROUBLE -->
<xsl:variable name="thing1" select="$thing2" />
<xsl:variable name="thing2" select="$thing1" />
```

Variables can be declared outside of templates, where they are visible by all, or inside one, where its scope is limited to that template. The following template creates a bracketed number to mark a footnote, and makes it a link to the footnote text at the end of the page. The number of the footnote is calculated once, but used twice.

```
<xsl:template match="footnote">
  <xsl:variable name="fnum"
      select="count(preceding::footnote[ancestor::chapter//.])+1"/>
  <a>
    <xsl:attribute name="href">
      <xsl:text>#FOOTNOTE-</xsl:text>
      <xsl:number value="$fnum" format="1"/>
```

```
      </xsl:attribute>
      <xsl:text>[</xsl:text>
      <xsl:number value="$fnum"/>
      <xsl:text>]</xsl:text>
    </a>
  </xsl:template>
```

Instead of performing the calculation in the content of the element, I did it inside a select attribute. Using select is generally better because it doesn't incur the cost of creating a result tree fragment, but sometimes you have to use the element content method when more complex calculations such as those involving choices are necessary.

## Creating Nodes

You can create elements and attributes just by typing them out in template rules, as we have seen in previous examples. Although this method is generally preferable for its simplicity, it has its limitations. For example, you may want to create an attribute with a value that must be determined through a complex process:

```
<xsl:template match="a">
  <p>See the
    <a>
      <xsl:attribute
        name="href">http://www.oreilly.com/catalog/<xsl:call-template
        name="prodname"/></xsl:attribute>
        catalog page
    </a> for more information.)
  </p>
</xsl:template>
```

In this template, the element attribute creates a new attribute node named <href>. The value of this attribute is the content of the node-creating element, in this case a URI with some variable text provided by a call-template element. As I have written it here, the variable text is impossible to include inside the a element, so I have broken it out in a separate attribute node creation step.

### Elements

XSLT provides an element for each node type you would want to create. element creates elements. Usually, you don't need this because you can just type in the element tags. In some circumstances, the element name may not be known at the time you write the stylesheet. It has to be generated dynamically. This would be an application of element.

The name attribute sets the element type. For example:

```
<xsl:template match="shape">
  <xsl:element name="{@type}">
    <xsl:value-of select="."/>
  </xsl:element>
</xsl:template>
```

If this template is applied to an element shape with attribute type="circle," it would create an element of type circle.

### Attributes and attribute sets

I have already shown you how to create attributes with attribute. As with element generation, you can derive the attribute name and value on the fly. Note, however, that an attribute directive must come before any other content. It is an error to try to create an attribute after an element or text node.

To apply a single set of attributes to many different elements, you can use attribute-set. First, define the set like this:

```
<xsl:attribute-set name="common-atts">
  <xsl:attribute name="id"/>
    <xsl:value-of select="generate-id()"/>
  </xsl:attribute>
  <xsl:attribute name="class">
    <xsl:text>shape</xsl:text>
  </xsl:attribute>
</xsl:attribute-set>
```

This creates a set of two attributes, id with a unique identifier value and class="shape". The set can be accessed from any element through its name common-atts. Use the attribute use-attribute-sets to refer to the attribute set you defined:

```
<xsl:template match="quote">
  <blockquote xsl:use-attribute-sets="common-atts">
    <xsl:value-of select="."/>
  </blockquote>
</xsl:template>
```

You can include as many attribute sets as you want by including them in a space-separated list.

### Text nodes

Creating a text node is as simple as typing in character data to the template. However, it may not always come out as you expect. For example, whitespace is stripped from certain places in the template before processing. And if you want to output a reserved character such as <, it will be output as the entity reference, not the literal character.

The container element text gives you more control over your character data. It preserves all whitespace literally, and, in my opinion, it makes templates easier to read. The element has an optional attribute disable-output-escaping, which if set to yes, turns off the tendency of the XSLT engine to escape reserved characters in the result tree. The following is an example of this.

```
<xsl:template match="codelisting">
  <xsl:text disable-output-escaping="yes">&lt;hey&gt;</xsl:text>
</xsl:template>
```

This produces the result <hey>.

### Processing instructions and comments

Creating processing instructions and comments is a simple task. The element processing-instruction takes an attribute name and some textual content to create a processing instruction:

```
<xsl:template match="marker">
  <xsl:processing-instruction name="formatter">
    pagenumber=<xsl:value-of select="@page"/>
  </xsl:processing-instruction>
</xsl:template>
```

This rule creates the following output:

```
<?formatter pagenumber=1?>
```

You can create a comment with the element comment, with no attributes:

```
<xsl:template match="comment">
  <xsl:comment>
    <xsl:value-of select="."/>
  </xsl:comment>
</xsl:template>
```

To create the processing instruction or content of a comment, you have to specify either plain text or an element such as value-of that becomes text. Any other kind of specification produces an error.

## Numeric Text

Although value-of can output any numeric value as a string, it does not offer any special formatting for numbers. You are stuck with decimals and that's it. For more options, you should move up to the more flexible number instruction. With this element, you can output numbers as Roman numerals, with zeros prepended, or as letters. It also has a built-in facility for counting nodes.

Returning to the table of contents example, here is how you could create one with number:

```
<xsl:template match="book">
  <xsl:for-each select="chapter">
    <xsl:number value="position()" format="I"/>.
    <xsl:value-of select="title"/>.
  </xsl:for-each>
</xsl:template>
```

You'll get output like this:

```
I. Evil King Oystro Sends Assassins
II. Aquaman is Poisoned by Pufferfish
III. Aqualad Delivers the Antidote
IV. Atlantis Votes Aquaman into Office
```

The attribute value contains the numeric expression or value to be formatted, and the attribute format controls the appearance (in this case, Roman numerals). The default value for format is the same as value-of: plain decimal.

Table 7-1 shows some ways to use the format attribute.

*Table 7-1. Number formats*

| Format string | Numbering scheme |
| --- | --- |
| 1 | 1, 2, 3, 4, ... |
| 0 | 0, 1, 2, 3, ... |
| 01 | 01, 02, 03, ..., 09, 10, 11, ... |
| I | I, II, III, IV, ... |
| i | i, ii, iii, iv, ... |
| A | A, B, C, D, ... |
| a | a, b, c, d, ... |

One stickler is if you wanted an alphabetical list starting with the Roman numeral i. You cannot use format="i" because that indicates lowercase Roman numerals. To resolve the ambiguity, use an additional attribute, letter-value, to force the format type to be alphabetical.

Very large integers often require separator characters to group the digits. For example, in the United States a comma is used (e.g., 1,000,000 for a million). In Germany, the comma means decimal point, so you need to be able to specify which scheme you want. You have two attributes to help you. The first, grouping-separator, sets the character used to delimit groups. The other, grouping-size, determines how many digits to put in a group.

The following would result in the text 1*0000*0000:

```
<xsl:number
  value="100000000"
  grouping-separator="*"
  grouping-size="4"/>
```

An interesting feature of number is its ability to count nodes. The count attribute specifies the kind of node to count. Say you wanted to print the title of a chapter with a preceding number like this:

```
<h1>Chapter 3. Bouncing Kittens</h1>
```

Perhaps you could use this template:

```
<xsl:template match="chapter/title">
  <xsl:text>Chapter </xsl:text>
  <xsl:value-of select="count(../preceding-sibling::chapter)+1"/>
  <xsl:text>. </xsl:text>
  <xsl:value-of select="."/>
</xsl:template>
```

That will work, but it is a little difficult to read. Instead you can write it like this:

```
<xsl:template match="chapter/title">
  <xsl:text>Chapter </xsl:text>
  <xsl:number count="chapter" format "1. ">
  <xsl:value-of select="."/>
</xsl:template>
```

count looks only at nodes that are siblings. If you want to count nodes that may appear at different levels, you need to add more information. The attribute level determines where to look for matching nodes. It has three possible values: single, multiple, and any.

If single is selected (the default), the XSLT engine looks for the most recent ancestor that matches the pattern in the count attribute. Then it counts backward among nodes at the same level. With the value multiple selected, all matching nodes among the ancestors, and their preceding siblings, may be considered. Finally, if you select any, then all previous nodes matching the pattern are counted. These options correspond to decreasing order of efficiency in implementation.

Consider:

```
<xsl:template match="footnote">
  <xsl:text>[<xsl/text>
  <xsl:number count="footnote" from="chapter" level="any"/>
  <xsl:text>]<xsl/text>
</xsl:template>
```

This rule inserts a bracketed number where the footnote appears. The attribute from="chapter" causes the numbering to begin at the last chapter start tag. level="any" ensures that all footnotes are counted, regardless of the level at which they appear.

The purpose of level="multiple" is to create multilevel numbers like 1.B.iii. In this example, we use number to generate a multilevel section label:

```
<xsl:template match="section/head">
  <xsl:number count="section" level="multiple" format="I.A.1."/>
  <xsl:apply-templates/>
</template>
```

Assuming that sections can be nested three levels deep, you will see section labels like IV.C.4. and XX.A.10.

## Sorting

Elements often must be sorted to make them useful. Spreadsheets, catalogs, and surveys are a few examples of documents that require sorting. Imagine a telephone book sorted by three keys: last name, first name, and town. The document looks like this:

```
<telephone-book>
  ...
  <entry id="44456">
    <surname>Mentary</surname>
    <firstname>Rudy</firstname>
    <town>Simpleton</town>
    <street>123 Bushwack Ln</street>
    <phone>555-1234</phone>
  </entry>

  <entry id="44457">
    <surname>Chains</surname>
    <firstname>Allison</firstname>
    <town>Simpleton</town>
    <street>999 Leafy Rd</street>
    <phone>555-4321</phone>
  </entry>
  ...
</telephone-book>
```

By default, the transformation processes each node in the order it appears in the document. So the entry with `id="44456"` is output before `id="44457"`. Obviously, that would not be in alphabetical order, so we need to sort the results somehow. It just so happens that we can do this with an element called sort. Here's how the document element's rule might look:

```
<xsl:template match="telephone-book">
  <xsl:apply-templates>
    <xsl:sort select="town"/>
    <xsl:sort select="surname"/>
    <xsl:sort select="firstname"/>
  </xsl:apply-templates>
</xsl:template>
```

There are three sorting axes here. First, all the results are sorted by town. Next, the entries are sorted by surname. Finally, the entries are sorted by first name.

## Handling Whitespace

Character data from the source tree is not generally normalized. You can force the XSLT engine to strip space of selected elements by adding their names to a list in the stylesheet. The element strip-space contains a list of element names in its elements attribute. This is a top-level element that should be outside of any template.

There is also a list of elements to preserve space called preserve-space. The reason for having both these elements is that you can set up a default behavior and then override it with a more specific case. For example:

```
<xsl:strip-space elements="*"/>
<xsl:preserve-space elements="poem codelisting asciiart"/>
```

Whitespace will be normalized for elements except poem, codelisting, and asciiart.

## Example: A Checkbook

This example demonstrates the concepts discussed so far. First, Example 7-3 is a sample XML document representing a checkbook.

*Example 7-3. Checkbook document*

```
<checkbook>

  <deposit type="direct-deposit">
    <payor>Bob's Bolts</payor>
    <amount>987.32</amount>
    <date>21-6-00</date>
    <description category="income">Paycheck</description>
  </deposit>

  <payment type="check" number="980">
    <payee>Kimora's Sports Equipment</payee>
    <amount>132.77</amount>
    <date>23-6-00</date>
    <description category="entertainment">kendo equipment</description>
  </payment>

  <payment type="atm">
    <amount>40.00</amount>
    <date>24-6-00</date>
    <description category="cash">pocket money</description>
  </payment>

  <payment type="debit">
    <payee>Lone Star Cafe</payee>
    <amount>36.86</amount>
    <date>26-6-00</date>
    <description category="food">lunch with Greg</description>
  </payment>

  <payment type="check" number="981">
    <payee>Wild Oats Market</payee>
    <amount>47.28</amount>
    <date>29-6-00</date>
    <description category="food">groceries</description>
  </payment>

  <payment type="debit">
    <payee>Barnes and Noble</payee>
```

*Example 7-3. Checkbook document (continued)*

```
    <amount>58.79</amount>
    <date>30-6-00</date>
    <description category="work">O'Reilly Books</description>
  </payment>

  <payment type="check" number="982">
    <payee>Old Man Ferguson</payee>
    <amount>800.00</amount>
    <date>31-6-00</date>
    <description category="misc">a 3-legged antique credenza that once
    belonged to Alfred Hitchcock</description>
  </payment>

</checkbook>
```

Now we will write an XSLT stylesheet to change this type of document into a nicely formatted HTML page. As a further benefit, our stylesheet will add up the transactions and print a final balance (assuming that the initial balance is zero). The first template sets up the HTML page's outermost structure:

```
<xsl:template match="checkbook">
  <html>
    <head/>
    <body>
                <!-- page content goes here -->
    </body>
  </html>
</xsl:template>
```

Let us add a section that summarizes income activity. The section header, wrapped inside an h3 element, is generated using new text (with text) not present in the document and the dates from the first and last transactions (using value-of). After the header, all the income transactions are listed, in the order they appear, with apply-templates. The rule now looks like this:

```
<xsl:template match="checkbook">
  <html>
    <head/>
    <body>

      <!-- income information -->
      <h3>
        <xsl:text>Income from </xsl:text>
        <xsl:value-of select="child::*[1]/date"/>
        <xsl:text> until </xsl:text>
        <xsl:value-of select="child::*[last()]/date"/>
        <xsl:text>:</xsl:text>
      </h3>
      <xsl:apply-templates select="deposit"/>

    </body>
  </html>
</xsl:template>
```

After that, we will add a section to describe the deductions from the checking account. It would be nice to sort this list of transactions from highest to lowest, so let's use the sort element. The rule is now:

```
<xsl:template match="checkbook">
  <html>
    <head/>
    <body>

      <!-- income information -->
      <h3>
        <xsl:text>Income from </xsl:text>
        <xsl:value-of select="child::*[1]/date"/>
        <xsl:text> until </xsl:text>
        <xsl:value-of select="child::*[last()]/date"/>
        <xsl:text>:</xsl:text>
      </h3>
      <xsl:apply-templates select="deposit"/>

      <!-- payment information -->
      <h3>
        <xsl:text>Expenditures from </xsl:text>
        <xsl:value-of select="child::*[1]/date"/>
        <xsl:text> until </xsl:text>
        <xsl:value-of select="child::*[last()]/date"/>
        <xsl:text>, ranked from highest to lowest:</xsl:text>
      </h3>
      <xsl:apply-templates select="payment">
        <xsl:sort data-type="number" order="descending"
                  select="amount"/>
      </xsl:apply-templates>

    </body>
  </html>
</xsl:template>
```

And finally, we'll display the account balance. We'll use number to calculate the sum of the transactions. Two sum( ) terms are necessary: one for the payment total and one for the income total. Then we'll subtract the total payment from the total income. To make it clear whether the user is in debt or not, we'll color-code the calculated result and print a warning if it's negative. Here is the template:

```
<xsl:template match="checkbook">
  <html>
    <head/>
    <body>

      <!-- income information -->
      <h3>
        <xsl:text>Income from </xsl:text>
        <xsl:value-of select="child::*[1]/date"/>
        <xsl:text> until </xsl:text>
        <xsl:value-of select="child::*[last()]/date"/>
```

```
      <xsl:text>:</xsl:text>
    </h3>
    <xsl:apply-templates select="deposit"/>

    <!-- payment information -->
    <h3>
      <xsl:text>Expenditures from </xsl:text>
      <xsl:value-of select="child::*[1]/date"/>
      <xsl:text> until </xsl:text>
      <xsl:value-of select="child::*[last()]/date"/>
      <xsl:text>, ranked from highest to lowest:</xsl:text>
    </h3>
    <xsl:apply-templates select="payment">
      <xsl:sort data-type="number" order="descending"
                select="amount"/>
    </xsl:apply-templates>

    <h3>Balance</h3>
    <p>
      <xsl:text>Your balance as of </xsl:text>
      <xsl:value-of select="child::*[last()]/date"/>
      <xsl:text> is </xsl:text>
      <tt><b>
        <xsl:choose>
          <xsl:when test="sum( payment/amount )
                          > sum( deposit/amount )">
            <font color="red">
              <xsl:text>$</xsl:text>
              <xsl:value-of select="sum( deposit/amount )
                                    - sum( payment/amount )"/>
            </font>
          </xsl:when>
          <xsl:otherwise>
            <font color="blue">
              <xsl:text>$</xsl:text>
              <xsl:value-of select="sum( deposit/amount )
                                    - sum( payment/amount )"/>
            </font>
          </xsl:otherwise>
        </xsl:choose>
      </b></tt>
    </p>
    <xsl:if test="sum( payment/amount )> sum( deposit/amount )">
      <p>
        <font color="red">
          <xsl:text>DANGER! Deposit money quick!</xsl:text>
        </font>
      </p>
    </xsl:if>
  </body>
 </html>
</xsl:template>
```

Now we need some rules to handle the payment and deposit elements. The first, shown below, numbers each payment and summarizes it nicely in a sentence:

```
<xsl:template match="payment">
  <p>
    <xsl:value-of select="position()"/>
    <xsl:text>. On </xsl:text>
    <xsl:value-of select="date"/>
    <xsl:text>, you paid </xsl:text>
    <tt><b>
      <xsl:text>$</xsl:text>
      <xsl:value-of select="amount"/>
    </b></tt>
    <xsl:text> to </xsl:text>
    <i>
      <xsl:value-of select="payee"/>
    </i>
    <xsl:text> for </xsl:text>
    <xsl:value-of select="description"/>
    <xsl:text>.</xsl:text>
  </p>
</xsl:template>
```

This works well enough for most payment types, but doesn't quite work when type="atm". Notice in the document instance that the atm payment lacks any description of the payee, since we assume that the checkbook's author is receiving the funds. Let's make a special rule just for this case:

```
<xsl:template match="payment[@type='atm']">
  <p>
    <xsl:value-of select="position()"/>
    <xsl:text>. On </xsl:text>
    <xsl:value-of select="date"/>
    <xsl:text>, you withdrew </xsl:text>
    <tt><b>
      <xsl:text>$</xsl:text>
      <xsl:value-of select="amount"/>
    </b></tt>
    <xsl:text> from an ATM for </xsl:text>
    <xsl:value-of select="description"/>
    <xsl:text>.</xsl:text>
  </p>
</xsl:template>
```

Finally, here's the rule for deposit:

```
<xsl:template match="deposit">
  <p>
    <xsl:value-of select="position()"/>
    <xsl:text>. On </xsl:text>
    <xsl:value-of select="date"/>
    <xsl:text>, </xsl:text>
    <tt><b>
      <xsl:text>$</xsl:text>
```

```
      <xsl:value-of select="amount"/>
    </b></tt>
    <xsl:text> was deposited into your account by </xsl:text>
    <i>
      <xsl:value-of select="payor"/>
    </i>
    <xsl:text>.</xsl:text>
  </p>
</xsl:template>
```

Putting it all together in one stylesheet, we get the listing in Example 7-4.

*Example 7-4. Checkbook transformation stylesheet*

```
<?xml version="1.0"?>

<!--

A simple transformation stylesheet to get information out of
a checkbook.

-->

<xsl:stylesheet xmlns:xsl="http://www.w3.org/1999/XSL/Transform"
                version="1.0">

<xsl:template match="checkbook">
  <html>
    <head/>
    <body>
      <h3>
        <xsl:text>Income from </xsl:text>
        <xsl:value-of select="child::*[1]/date"/>
        <xsl:text> until </xsl:text>
        <xsl:value-of select="child::*[last()]/date"/>
        <xsl:text>:</xsl:text>
      </h3>
      <xsl:apply-templates select="deposit"/>
      <h3>
        <xsl:text>Expenditures from </xsl:text>
        <xsl:value-of select="child::*[1]/date"/>
        <xsl:text> until </xsl:text>
        <xsl:value-of select="child::*[last()]/date"/>
        <xsl:text>, ranked from highest to lowest:</xsl:text>
      </h3>
      <xsl:apply-templates select="payment">
        <xsl:sort data-type="number" order="descending" select="amount"/>
      </xsl:apply-templates>
      <h3>Balance</h3>
      <p>
        <xsl:text>Your balance as of </xsl:text>
        <xsl:value-of select="child::*[last()]/date"/>
        <xsl:text> is </xsl:text>
        <tt><b>
```

*Example 7-4. Checkbook transformation stylesheet (continued)*

```
        <xsl:choose>
          <xsl:when test="sum( payment/amount )> sum( deposit/amount )">
            <font color="red">
              <xsl:text>$</xsl:text>
              <xsl:value-of select="sum( deposit/amount )
                                  - sum( payment/amount )"/>
            </font>
          </xsl:when>
          <xsl:otherwise>
            <font color="blue">
              <xsl:text>$</xsl:text>
              <xsl:value-of select="sum( deposit/amount )
                                  - sum( payment/amount )"/>
            </font>
          </xsl:otherwise>
        </xsl:choose>
      </b></tt>
    </p>
    <xsl:if test="sum( payment/amount )> sum( deposit/amount )">
      <p>
        <font color="red">
          <xsl:text>DANGER! Deposit money quick!</xsl:text>
        </font>
      </p>
    </xsl:if>
  </body>
</html>
</xsl:template>

<xsl:template match="payment[@type='atm']">
  <p>
    <xsl:value-of select="position()"/>
    <xsl:text>. On </xsl:text>
    <xsl:value-of select="date"/>
    <xsl:text>, you withdrew </xsl:text>
    <tt><b>
      <xsl:text>$</xsl:text>
      <xsl:value-of select="amount"/>
    </b></tt>
    <xsl:text> from an ATM for </xsl:text>
    <xsl:value-of select="description"/>
    <xsl:text>.</xsl:text>
  </p>
</xsl:template>

<xsl:template match="payment">
  <p>
    <xsl:value-of select="position()"/>
    <xsl:text>. On </xsl:text>
    <xsl:value-of select="date"/>
    <xsl:text>, you paid </xsl:text>
    <tt><b>
```

*Example 7-4. Checkbook transformation stylesheet (continued)*

```
      <xsl:text>$</xsl:text>
      <xsl:value-of select="amount"/>
    </b></tt>
    <xsl:text> to </xsl:text>
    <i>
      <xsl:value-of select="payee"/>
    </i>
    <xsl:text> for </xsl:text>
    <xsl:value-of select="description"/>
    <xsl:text>.</xsl:text>
  </p>
</xsl:template>

<xsl:template match="deposit">
  <p>
    <xsl:value-of select="position()"/>
    <xsl:text>. On </xsl:text>
    <xsl:value-of select="date"/>
    <xsl:text>, </xsl:text>
    <tt><b>
      <xsl:text>$</xsl:text>
      <xsl:value-of select="amount"/>
    </b></tt>
    <xsl:text> was deposited into your account by </xsl:text>
    <i>
      <xsl:value-of select="payor"/>
    </i>
    <xsl:text>.</xsl:text>
  </p>
</xsl:template>
</xsl:stylesheet>
```

Example 7-5 shows the resulting HTML file. Figure 7-1 shows how it looks in a browser.

*Example 7-5. The result tree*

```
<html>
<body>
<h3>Income from 21-6-00 until 31-6-00:</h3>
<p>1. On 21-6-00, <tt><b>$987.32</b></tt> was deposited into your
account by <i>Bob's Bolts</i>.</p>
<h3>Expenditures from 21-6-00 until 31-6-00, ranked from highest to
lowest:</h3>
<p>1. On 31-6-00, you paid <tt><b>$800.00</b></tt> to <i>Old Man
Ferguson</i> for a 3-legged antique credenza that once belonged to
Alfred Hitchcock.</p>
<p>2. On 23-6-00, you paid <tt><b>$132.77</b></tt> to <i>Kimora's
Sports Equipment</i> for kendo equipment.</p>
<p>3. On 30-6-00, you paid <tt><b>$58.79</b></tt> to <i>Barnes and
Noble</i> for O'Reilly Books.</p>
<p>4. On 29-6-00, you paid <tt><b>$47.28</b></tt> to <i>Wild Oats
```

*Example 7-5. The result tree (continued)*

```
Market</i> for groceries.</p>
<p>5. On 24-6-00, you withdrew <tt><b>$40.00</b></tt> from an ATM for
pocket money.</p>
<p>6. On 26-6-00, you paid <tt><b>$36.86</b></tt> to <i>Lone Star
Cafe</i> for lunch with Greg.</p>
<h3>Balance</h3>
<p>Your balance as of 31-6-00 is <tt><b><font
color="red">$-128.38</font></b></tt>
</p>
<p>
<font color="red">DANGER! Deposit money quick!</font>
</p>
</body>
</html>
```

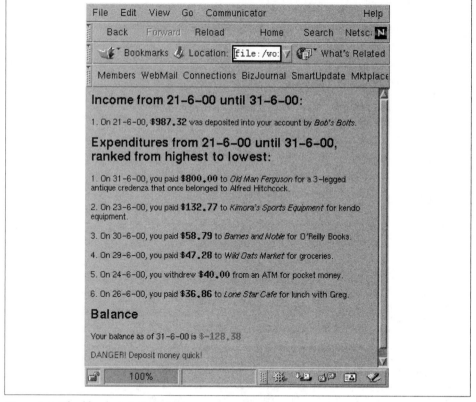

*Figure 7-1. Checkbook statistics in Netscape*

# Combining Stylesheets

There are various reasons to use multiple stylesheets for the same document. For instance, you may be supporting several documents that share most of the same style but have a few local differences between them. Or you might have to combine different namespaces, each with its own style set. You may want to borrow some styles from a library and override the ones you want to customize. XSLT gives you two ways to combine stylesheets: inclusion and importing.

*Including* a stylesheet means inserting its contents directly into the target stylesheet. All the rules and directives will be treated as if they were in your stylesheet all along. The include element has an href attribute, which holds a URI for the stylesheet to include. You can insert this element anywhere in your stylesheet as long as it isn't inside a rule.

The levels of presentness of incoming templates are not the same when they are *imported*. Templates in the original stylesheet always override templates in the imported one, no matter what their priority. The element import also uses an href attribute to specify a stylesheet, but it can be placed only at the very top of the stylesheet, before any other rules or directives.

The advantage of this weaker form of merging is that it can override parts of a more complete set of rules to customize the results. While include pours rules in at the same level of precedence as your own, import gives you more control over the remote set, allowing you to pick and choose among rules.

There may be times when you want to override your own rules in favor of those that are imported for a localized region. The element apply-imports is analogous to apply-templates, except that it considers only imported rules, and ignores those that are physically present. Also, it only operates on the current node whereas apply-templates operates on whatever nodes you select (the child nodes by default).

You can include or import any number of stylesheets, which lets you mix and match different vocabularies for transformation. You may have one set for generic document content, another for handling tables, yet another for handling sidebars, and so on. The order of inclusion is used to break ties between conflicting rules from different sets: earlier imports override later ones. Here's how you can import several stylesheets into your own:

```
<xsl:stylesheet version="1.0"
                xmlns:xsl="http://www.w3.org/1999/XSL/Transform">
  <xsl:import href="basic_style.xsl"/>
  <xsl:import href="table_styles.xsl"/>
  <xsl:import href="chem_formulae.xsl"/>
  ...
```

# Modes

Sometimes you want to treat nodes differently depending on where they are used in the document. For example, you may want footnotes in tables to be alphabetized instead of numbered. XSLT provides special rule modifiers called *modes* to accomplish this.

To set up a mode, simply add a mode attribute set to a particular label to the affected template and template-calling elements. The mode label can be anything you want as long as it's unique among mode labels. The following example shows how to do this:

```
<xsl:template match="footnote">
  <xsl:variable name="fnum"
      select="count(preceding::footnote[ancestor::chapter//.])+1"/>
  <a>
    <xsl:attribute name="href">
      <xsl:text>#FOOTNOTE-</xsl:text>
      <xsl:number value="$fnum" format="1"/>
    </xsl:attribute>
    <xsl:text>[</xsl:text>
    <xsl:number value="$fnum"/>
    <xsl:text>]</xsl:text>
  </a>
</xsl:template>

<xsl:template match="footnote" mode="tabular">
  <xsl:variable name="fnum"
      select="count(preceding::footnote[ancestor::chapter//.])+1"/>
  <a>
    <xsl:attribute name="href">
      <xsl:text>#FOOTNOTE-</xsl:text>
      <xsl:number value="$fnum" format="1"/>
    </xsl:attribute>
    <xsl:text>[</xsl:text>
    <xsl:number value="$fnum" format="a"/>
    <xsl:text>]</xsl:text>
  </a>
</xsl:template>

<xsl:template match="table-entry">
  <xsl:apply-templates mode="tabular"/>
</xsl:template>
```

The first rule defines the default behavior of a footnote, while the second one sets up the special case for footnotes in tabular mode. The behavior differs only in how the footnote number is formatted. The third and last rule is a table-cell rule that turns on the tabular mode.

It's important to remember that rules without the mode specifier are not considered by the processor when it's in a specific mode. Instead, the default rules are used. This means you have to write a new rule for every element that might be chosen.

---

# Presentation Part II: XSL-FO

XSL-FO rounds out the trio of standards that make up XSL. The FO stands for Formatting Objects, which are containers of content that preserve structure and associate presentational information. XSLT prepares a document for formatting using XPath to disassemble it and produce an XSL-FO temporary file to drive a formatter.

Under a W3C charter, the XSL Working Group started to design a high-powered formatting language in 1998. XML was still new, but XSL was understood early on to be a factor in making it useful. The group split its efforts on two related technologies, a language for transformations (XSLT) and another for formatting (XSL-FO). XSLT, the first to become a recommendation in 1999, demonstrated itself to be generally useful even outside of publishing applications. XSL followed as a recommendation in 2001.

Cascading Style Sheets, a jewel in the crown of the W3C, had been around for a few years and was a strong influence on the development of XSL. Its simple but numerous property statements make it easy to learn. You will see that quite a few of these properties have been imported into XSL-FO. The CSS box model, elegant and powerful, is the basis for XSL-FO's area model. Mostly what has been added to XSL-FO are semantics for handling page layout and complex writing systems.

The principal advantages of XSL over CSS are:

- Print-specific semantics such as page breaking. CSS happens to be moving in this direction too, so this distinction is less important.
- Out-of-order processing. With CSS, all the elements in a document are processed in order from start to finish. It provides no means of selecting some sections and rejecting others, of pulling information from various parts of a document, or of processing the same element more than once.
- XML syntax. CSS uses its own syntax, making it harder to process.

XSL is not always preferable to CSS. You would choose CSS when you want to keep formatting simple and fast. Most web browsers have CSS processing built in, but none can do anything with XSL-FO. XSL-FO processing is also very resource intensive. You would probably not want to push the burden of formatting on a fickle and impatient user when it could be done ahead of time on your server.

An important goal of XSL was to make it declarative rather than procedural. A *declarative* language expresses a desired outcome with constraints and high-level concepts that make it easy to read and understand. It also tends to be highly portable since it remains on a conceptual plane. By contrast, a *procedural* language is rife with low-level clutter such as variable assignments, algebra, function calls, and so on. It is typically harder to read and requires someone with erudite skills to work with. For example, PostScript, which is nearly impossible to understand unless you are a hardcore programmer, is procedural.

The XSL Working Group has strived to make XSL as flexible as possible. It is device-agnostic, supporting a variety of media from synthesized speech to on-screen display. It is designed for high typographic quality. It is multilingual, with support for bidirectional and vertical scripts, most modern fonts such as OpenType, and the full set of Unicode characters.

At the time of this writing, I find that XSL is still rather rough around the edges. Early adopters will find a variety of tools available with varying degrees of conformance to the standard, but none offer the kind of control you have with a proprietary publishing system like FrameMaker or Quark. If you want a WYSIWYG environment where you can specify pagebreaks and see the document repaginate before your eyes, you will not get that with XSL.

The choice of whether to use XSL may depend on two things. First, how much control do you need while authoring the document? Graphic designers need a very high level of control with instant feedback as they shape and sculpt a document. XSL implementations out there now do not offer anything like that. Second, how much of your workflow is automated? If you have huge stacks of documents to process, as is the case with legal departments and doctors' offices, XSL can help. It works behind the scenes with no human presence required. Just set up your stylesheet, write a batch processing program and let it go.

## How It Works

Unlike CSS which simply applies styles directly to elements in a single pass through the document, XSL gives you the opportunity to do major reorganization of your document. This capability comes at the cost of simplicity. To ease the burden on developers, the designers of XSL have split the process into two parts: transformation and formatting.

The transformation alters the structure of the input document and adds presentational information in a hybrid format composed of formatting objects. A *formatting object* is a container for content that associates styles and rendering instructions with the content. It is compact and easy for a person to understand. The formatting objects are arranged in a tree that retains structure used in building the final presentation.

The result of this transformation is a temporary file that you feed to an XSL-FO formatter. Through a complex series of steps, the formatter calculates the final geometry and appearance of the presentation and churns out a file suitable for printing or viewing on a screen. When it's finished, the formatting objects are flushed from memory and you can discard the temporary FO file. It is important to understand that you are not meant to write your own XSL-FO markup. Make all of your stylistic corrections in the XSLT stylesheet and let the tools do the rest.

## Formatting

Inside the formatter a complex operation in multiple phases takes place, illustrated in Figure 8-1. We start with a result tree (recall from Chapter 7 that a result tree is the product of an XSLT transformation) in the XSL-FO namespace. In phase one of formatting, the formatter translates this document into an object representation in memory in a process called *objectification*. This structure, a *formatting object tree*, is structurally similar to the result tree, but with some details changed. For example, all the character data will be replaced with fo:character node objects. By making the tree more verbose like this, later processing will run more efficiently.

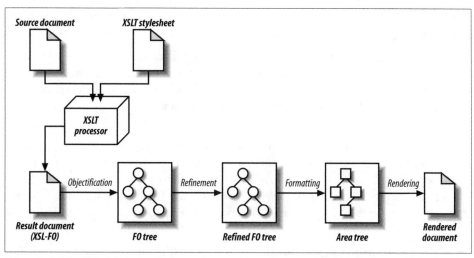

*Figure 8-1. The XSL-FO formatting process*

After objectification comes phase two, *refinement*. The formatter begins to calculate the actual geometry of areas in the presentation, replacing relative values and constraints with concrete numbers. For example, a table cell whose width is specified as a percentage now will show that width as a number of pixels. The percentage value for a relative width in a table will be replaced with a calculated number of pixels. The product of this phase is a *refined formatting object tree*.

Next comes the *formatting* phase, in which formatting object properties are translated into a virtual picture of the document called an *area tree*. This in-memory representation of the output is composed of overlapping and nested canvases called *areas*. Each area is a region of the document with a set of *traits* that describe how its the content should be rendered. An area can be as large as a sidebar or as small as a single glyph.

Finally, the formatter enters its *rendering* phase. The area tree translates directly into some output format such as PDF or troff that exactly conforms to the original specifications. At last, you see something emerge from the black box, a tangible product that hopefully looks the way you wanted it to.

The normal user will not need to know how the phases from objectification to rendering actually work. She has put down her constraints in the XSLT stylesheet and the rest is automatic. The actual work that takes place inside the formatter is more of interest to developers who write and maintain such software.

## Formatting Objects

Formatting objects come in a variety of types representing what you can do typographically in a document. There are FOs for blocks and inlines, section containers and individual character containers, page and style settings. The complete set of formatting objects is the vocabulary for formatting abstractions possible in XSL.

Each FO represents a semantic specification for a particular part of a document. It has default properties that you can override as necessary. These defaults depend on the context, such as whether the current writing mode is horizontal or vertical. An FO can contain other FOs, creating a structure that propagates inheritance of properties.

Some properties have a direct result on the formatting of an FO instance. For example, setting the color will have an immediate and obvious effect on text. Other properties set constraints that may or may not come into play. Widow and orphan settings for paragraphs are only applicable when the paragraph straddles a page-break. In some cases, properties may override other properties when a rule of aesthetics would be violated.

An FO creates or helps to create an abstract positional framework called an area. For every area, an FO specifies its position on the page, how to arrange and display its children, and whether any other decoration, such as a border, is required. For example, a single character will be formatted into an area large enough to hold one glyph.

# Print, Screen, and Beyond

Being device-agnostic means XSL has to support both scrollable online presentation and the printed page. Fortunately, the online and print worlds have much in common. The basic way of fitting content in flows is the same, and both support the notion of floating objects (sidebars and footnotes), marginalia, and headers and footers. But there is much that is different.

Online representations typically involve one long, uninterrupted column of content, whereas pagination produces discrete regions with breaks in content and vertical margins. Pagination has other complexities, such as page layout types and line spacing for vertical justification.

The area model treats visual document structure in a generic way that is compatible with online and print needs. HTML frames can be derived easily from abstract structures, as can page layouts. It can be as complex as you need it to be.

At the top level of the FO tree is a page layout section which declares page layout master templates. These masters can be combined in sequences in a wide variety of ways. Content is stored in page sequence objects. These are the clay from which the document is sculpted.

Many layout settings are available to control page-related formatting. They include hyphenation, widow and orphan control, columnar layout, and so on.

A special concept is the viewport. A *viewport* is the physical region in which you can put content. In a web browser, the dimensions of the window determine the viewport area. Since the window can be resized, the viewport is variable. In print, a piece of paper is the viewport. This geometry does not usually change, except in cases where you rotate the view from portrait to landscape mode.

The XSL recommendation includes a set of aural properties for FOs. This is a radically different medium than print and screen, but an important one nonetheless. Speech synthesis is a maturing technology already in use by visually challenged people. We can expect its use only to increase, so the XSL designers have planned its support from the beginning.

The aural medium has many analogies to typographical styles. Where a visual medium would use space to separate objects, an aural processor would use an interval of silence. Emphasized text could be rendered in higher pitch, different volume, or altered speed. In place of typefaces, you might think of the kind of voice used, such as a child's, older man's, or a robot's.

Though I would love to explore these properties in this book, constraints of scope and the printed medium prevent me from doing an adequate job. So I will leave that for another writer and concentrate on visual formatting instead.

# Formatters

There are a variety of implementations of XSL-FO formatters available, from free and open source to commercial products. At the time of this writing, here is what I found available:

| Name | Maker | Availability |
|------|-------|-------------|
| FOP | Apache.org | Open source Java application |
| XEP | RenderX | Commercial product |
| E3 | Arbortext | Component in commercial XML publishing system |
| PassiveTeX | TEI | Open source |
| Document Server 5.0 | Adobe | Commercial product |
| XSL Formatter | AntennaHouse | Commercial product |

Implementations vary in how well they conform to the XSL specification. The recommendation defines three levels of conformance. It says that the *basic* level "includes the set of formatting objects and properties needed to support a minimum level of pagination or aural rendering." *Extended* adds to that everything else in the standard except *shorthand properties*, which collect a group of properties in one assignment, like border in CSS. *Complete* conformance has all of that plus shorthands.

This division does not frequently work in the real world. As an example, page-oriented formatters usually do not have any support for aural (speech synthesis) formatting, so even the official basic conformance is rare. Most users are probably interested in using XSL for one medium anyway, so it is more useful in my opinion to think of conformance within each medium. For example, does a formatter correctly produce a page layout from the formatting objects in the print medium?

Often developers leave out features that are difficult to implement and that they think will not be in high demand. Bidirectional support needed for scripts such as Hebrew or Chinese is not present in most formatters. Arbortext's formatter does not support mixed language hyphenation. FOP has numerous issues with tables, such as requiring fixed widths of columns. In time, many of these features will be incorporated, but it will depend on demand and developer time.

The XSL-FO recommendation has left out some important features that may be added in future versions. For example, index generation is still rather primitive. In the meantime, vendors are adding their own extensions using XML namespaces. Some examples of this are the fox:outline extensions in FOP to generate PDF bookmarks and rx:page-index in XEP to help create page numbers in indexes.

The formatter I like to use for XSL-FO is the free and open source FOP. It has pretty decent print-oriented support and outputs to PDF, MIF, PostScript, and PCL. The formatter is written in Java and its install package includes Apache's XML parser

Xerces and XSLT engine Xalan, which you can download from *http://xml.apache.org*.[*]
The FOP download includes the parser and XSLT classes in one package. It also contains a shell script, *fop*, that runs Java and supplies the arguments to the formatter.

Below is an example of FOP as invoked from the command line. The argument -xsl db.xsl gives the name of the XSLT stylesheet. The next argument, -xml chap1.xml supplies the source file name. The third, -pdf chap1.pdf, tells which format to output (PDF) and what to call the output file.

```
> fop -xsl db.xsl -xml chap1.xml -pdf chap1.pdf
[INFO] FOP 0.20.4
[INFO] building formatting object tree
[INFO] [1]
[INFO] [2]
[INFO] [3]
...
[INFO] [44]
[INFO] [45]
[INFO] [46]
[INFO] Parsing of document complete, stopping renderer
```

The numbers in brackets represent the number of the page being rendered once the FO tree has been constructed.

If this process doesn't work, there could be several reasons. First, the source document may not be well-formed, and you will see output like this:

```
[INFO] FOP 0.20.4
[ERROR] The markup in the document preceding the root element must be
well-formed.
```

Check the files with a parser to rule out this possibility. Second, the XSLT stylesheet may have an error. It may not be well-formed XML, or it may be invalid XSLT structurally. Here, I misspelled an element name in the XSLT and got a cryptic error message:

```
[INFO] FOP 0.20.4
[ERROR] null
```

Check all the elements in the xsl namespace to make sure it is valid. You might want to test it with an XSLT engine that has verbose output to see where in the file the error occurs. *xsltproc* from *gnome.org* has very good parse error messages.

Third, the formatting object tree may contain invalid markup:

```
[INFO] FOP 0.20.4
[INFO] building formatting object tree
[ERROR] Unknown formatting object http://www.w3.org/1999/XSL/Format^robot
[ERROR] java.lang.NullPointerException
```

---

[*] You do not have to use Xerces and Xalan. You can import XSL-FO documents from any source, even those you create by hand.

This occurred because I changed the name of a formatting object from fo:root to fo:robot. Although FOP's error messages aren't the easiest to read, at least it did manage to tell me that it was a formatting object naming problem.

# A Quick Example

To give you a good overview of the whole process, let us take a look at a short, quick example. This humble XML document will be the source:

```
<mydoc>
  <title>Hello world!</title>
  <message>I am <emphasis>so</emphasis> clever.</message>
</mydoc>
```

The first step in using XSL-FO is to write an XSLT stylesheet that will generate a formatting object tree. Example 8-1 is a very simple (for XSL-FO) stylesheet. There are five templates in all. The first creates a page master, an archetype of real pages that will be created as text is poured in, setting up the geometry of content regions. The second template associates a flow object with the page master. The flow is like a baggage handler, throwing suitcases into a compact space that fits the geometry set up in the page master. The rest of the templates create blocks and inlines to be stacked inside the flow.

*Example 8-1. An XSLT stylesheet to turn mydoc into a formatting object tree*

```
<?xml version="1.0"?>
<xsl:stylesheet xmlns:xsl="http://www.w3.org/1999/XSL/Transform"
                xmlns:fo="http://www.w3.org/1999/XSL/Format"
                version="1.0"
>
<xsl:output method="xml"/>

<!-- The root node, where we set up a page with a single
     region. <layout-master-set> may contain many page masters, but
     here we have defined only one. <simple-page-master> sets up a
     basic page type with width and height dimensions, margins, and a
     name to reference later with a flow.
-->

<xsl:template match="/">
  <fo:root>
    <fo:layout-master-set>
      <fo:simple-page-master
            master-name="the-only-page-type"
            page-height="4in" page-width="4in"
            margin-top="0.5in" margin-bottom="0.5in"
            margin-left="0.5in" margin-right="0.5in">
        <fo:region-body/>
      </fo:simple-page-master>
    </fo:layout-master-set>
    <xsl:apply-templates/>
```

*Example 8-1. An XSLT stylesheet to turn mydoc into a formatting object tree (continued)*

```
    </fo:root>
</xsl:template>

<!-- The first block element, where we insert the document flow.
     <page-sequence> sets up an instance of the page type we defined
     above. <flow> contains all the stackable block objects, shaping
     them so they fit in the page region we defined. The flow contains
     a block that defines font name, size, text alignment, and
     surrounds its content in a 0.25 inch buffer of padding.
-->

<xsl:template match="mydoc">
  <fo:page-sequence master-reference="the-only-page-type">
    <fo:flow flow-name="xsl-region-body">
      <fo:block
        font-family="helvetica, sans-serif"
        font-size="24pt"
        text-align="center"
        padding="0.25in"
      >
        <xsl:apply-templates/>
      </fo:block>
    </fo:flow>
  </fo:page-sequence>
</xsl:template>

<!-- The second block element, a title, is bold, 10 point type, and
     inserts 1 em of space below itself.
-->

<xsl:template match="title">
  <fo:block
    font-weight="bold"
    font-size="10pt"
    space-after="1em"
  >
    <xsl:apply-templates/>
  </fo:block>
</xsl:template>

<!-- The last block element, a message body element. The padding is
     set to 0.25 inches and the border is visible.
-->

<xsl:template match="message">
  <fo:block
    padding="0.25in"
    border="solid 1pt black"
  >
```

```
    <xsl:apply-templates/>
  </fo:block>
</xsl:template>

<!-- The inline emphasis element is set to be italic. -->

<xsl:template match="emphasis">
  <fo:inline
    font-style="italic"
  >
    <xsl:apply-templates/>
  </fo:inline>
</xsl:template>

</xsl:stylesheet>
```

Many of the elements created by this stylesheet have attributes that define properties you may recognize from CSS. Names like font-style and border should be familiar to you already. If you remember the display-type property from CSS, you will understand what the block and inline elements do. They are containers that shape their contents, either to fit a rectangular area in a flow, or to follow the inline progression of lines in a block.

Run the transformation on the source document and you will generate this formatting object tree:

```
<?xml version="1.0"?>
<fo:root xmlns:fo="http://www.w3.org/1999/XSL/Format">
  <fo:layout-master-set>
    <fo:simple-page-master master-name="the-only-page-type"
      page-height="3in" page-width="4in" margin-top="0.5in"
      margin-bottom="0.5in" margin-left="0.5in" margin-right="0.5in">
    <fo:region-body/>
    </fo:simple-page-master>
  </fo:layout-master-set>
  <fo:page-sequence master-reference="the-only-page-type">
    <fo:flow flow-name="xsl-region-body">
      <fo:block font-family="helvetica, sans-serif" font-size="24pt"
        text-align="center" padding="0.25in">
      <fo:block font-weight="bold" font-size="10pt"
        space-after="1em">Hello world!</fo:block>
      <fo:block padding="0.25in" border="solid 1pt black">I am
        <fo:inline font-style="italic">so</fo:inline> clever.</fo:block>
      </fo:block>
    </fo:flow>
  </fo:page-sequence>
</fo:root>
```

Import this into an XSL formatter and it will generate output shown in Figure 8-1.

*Figure 8-2. The message formatted*

# The Area Model

In XSL all the positioning, shaping, and spacing of elements on the page takes place inside of *areas*. An area is an abstract framework used to represent a piece of the formatted document. It contains all the geometric and stylistic information needed to position and render its children correctly. Areas are nested, leading to the concept of an area tree. From the root node, all the way down to the areas containing glyphs and images, a formatted document is completely described by an area tree.

A formatting object tree produces an area tree the way an architectural model leads to a final set of blueprints. Strictly speaking, there is not a one-to-one mapping between formatting objects and areas. An FO can create zero or more areas, and each area is usually produced by a single FO. There are exceptions, however, as in the case of ligatures, which are single glyphs created through the contribution of two or more character objects.

Associated with an area is a collection of details that completely describe its geometry and rendering. These *traits*, as they are called, are derived either directly from formatting object properties or indirectly as a result of calculations involving other traits. These traits are the final, precise data that drive the rendering process in the formatter.

Areas are divided into two types: *block* and *inline*. Blocks and inlines have been described thoroughly in previous chapters and they behave essentially the same here. An area may have block area children or inline area children but never both. One common subtype of block areas is the *line area*, the children of which are all inline areas (for example, a traditional paragraph). A subtype of *inline area* is the *glyph area*, a leaf in the area tree containing a single glyph image as its content.

The area model of XSL is strongly reminiscent of the CSS box model. In fact, areas are a superset of CSS boxes. Areas are somewhat more general, allowing for alternative writing modes that require generic terminology like "start" and "before" instead of "top" and "left." Still, you will find XSL's areas very familiar if you've worked with CSS before. Figure 8-3 shows the area model and its components.

Every area maps out a *content rectangle*, a reference frame against which the formatter positions children and applies space. It separates two buffers of space, a *margin* on the outside, and *padding* on the inside. The visible manifestation of the content

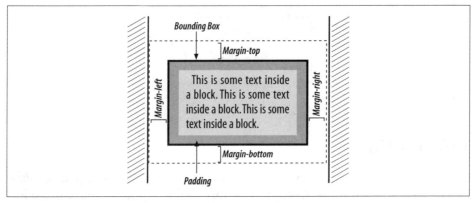

*Figure 8-3. The area model*

rectangle is called the *border*. It is bound on the outside by the *border rectangle* and on the inside by the *padding rectangle*.

## Area Stacking

An area's children reside inside its content rectangle. They may be positioned in explicit terms, but more frequently they're placed, or *stacked*, according to an algorithm. The direction in which this stacking proceeds depends on the writing mode in use for that area. For example, in European writing modes, block areas progress from top to bottom, and the inline areas go from left to right. These are called the *block progression direction* and *inline progression direction* respectively.

XSL is designed to support any writing mode's directionality. XSL supports three basic modes, referred to by their inline and block progression directions:

- Left-to-right, top-to-bottom (lr-tb). European languages are in this category.
- Right-to-left, top-to-bottom (rl-tb). For example, Arabic and Hebrew.
- Top-to-bottom, right-to-left (tb-rl). Chinese and Japanese are examples.

Figure 8-4 is an example of Chinese text. The inline progression is top to bottom and the block progression is right to left.

In contrast, Figure 8-5 shows Italian text, which is left-to-right and top-to-bottom.

You can set the writing mode in any flow block or inline formatting object with the property `writing-mode`. For example, here is how you might write a template for an element `hebrew-phrase`:

```
<xsl:template match="hebrew-phrase">
  <fo:inline writing-mode="rltb">
    <xsl:apply-templates/>
  </fo:inline>
</xsl:template>
```

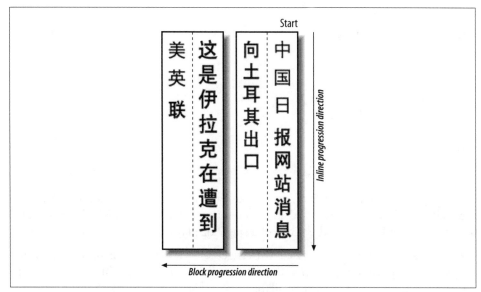

*Figure 8-4. Chinese text, showing block- and inline-progression directions*

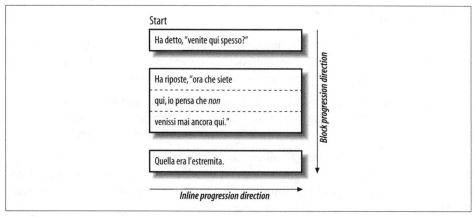

*Figure 8-5. Italian text, showing block- and inline-progression directions*

You can embed this inline in an English paragraph and when rendered, the paragraph will appear lrtb except for the inline which will be rl-tb.

## Dimensions

Since XSL borrows heavily from CSS, it also happens to use the same methods of defining dimensions. You can express them in relative terms, as percentages of the parent FO's dimensions, or in actual units. Points, picas, inches, centimeters, and ems are supported. Combine the value with a unit abbreviation from Table 8-1.

*Table 8-1. Unit abbreviations*

| Unit | Abbreviation |
| --- | --- |
| Centimeter | cm |
| Em | em |
| Inch | in |
| Millimeter | mm |
| Pica (12 pt) | pc |
| Point (1/72 in) | pt |
| Pixel | px |

Ems and pixels are relative units. Their actual length depends on the context. An em is the width of a lowercase letter "m" in the current typeface. A pixel is only meaningful in computer displays, being the width of a single display element on the screen.

Dimensions may also be expressed with algebraic expressions using operators for addition, multiplication, power, and modulus. Functions for absolute value, ceiling, min, max, and rounding are also available.

# Formatting Objects

Formatting objects (FOs) are the building blocks of the transformation result tree that drives the formatter. They are compact containers of content and style with all the information necessary to generate a presentable formatted document.

There are two major kinds of FO. *Flow objects* create areas and appear inside flows. (A *flow* is a continuous stream of text that may be broken across pages.) *Layout objects*, or *auxiliary objects*, help produce areas by contributing parameters.

A block object creates a region of content to be inserted into a flow, so it qualifies as a flow object. In contrast, the initial-page-number FO resets the count of page numbering. Since it only contributes some information to aid in processing, rather than create regions on its own, it is a layout object.

An FO document structure is a tree, like any other XML document. Every element in it is a formatting object, so we call it an FO tree. The root of this tree is a root element. Its children include:

layout-master-set
  This element contains page layout descriptions.

declarations
  Optional, this element contains global settings that will affect overall formatting.

page-sequence
  One or more of these elements contain flow objects that hold the content of the document.

In the coming sections, I will break down this structure further, starting with page layout. From there, we will move to flows, blocks, and finally inlines.

## Page Layout

Contained in the layout-master-set object are specifications for pagination and layout. There are two types. page-masters define properties of a page type: its geometry and how it is subdivided. page-sequence-masters control how page types will appear in sequence.

When the formatter formats pages, it will take the content inside the flow object children of the page-sequence objects and fit it into pages. The shape of the formatted text in a page is determined by the relevent page-master's specifications. Which page-master will be used depends on the page-sequence-master and which pages have come before.

### Page sequence masters

page-sequence-master objects contain pieces of the page sequence, or *sub-sequence specifiers*. The simplest kind is a reference to a single page master, represented as a single-page-master-reference object. For example:

```
<fo:layout-master-set>
  <fo:page-sequence-master>
    <fo:single-page-master-reference master-reference="basic"/>
  </fo:page-sequence-master>
  <fo:simple-page-master master-name="basic">
    <!-- ... -->
  </fo:simple-page-master>
</fo:layout-master-set>
```

This defines a sequence of exactly one page. It is not very useful by itself unless your whole document fits in one page. Often you may want to define a standalone sequence to handle a special kind of page layout, such as a landscape mode table.

Another sub-sequence specifier is repeatable-page-master-reference. It is like single-page-master-reference except that it can repeat by setting the attribute maximum-repeats to a number or no-limit. In this example, the basic page master will be applied to all pages in the document:

```
<fo:layout-master-set>
  <fo:page-sequence-master>
    <fo:repeatable-page-master-reference
      maximum-repeats="no-limit"
      master-reference="basic"/>
  </fo:page-sequence-master>
  <fo:simple-page-master master-name="basic">
    <!-- ... -->
  </fo:simple-page-master>
</fo:layout-master-set>
```

Since this is a common occurrence in simple designs, you can leave out the single-page-master-reference, which will imply the simplest possible sequence, that of using one page master throughout.

The last and most complex type is repeatable-page-master-alternatives. It defines a set of page master references with conditions for use. For example, you might want to have a differentiate between odd-numbered (*recto*) and even-numbered (*verso*) pages. You can accomplish that effect with this page sequence:

```
<fo:layout-master-set>
  <fo:page-sequence-master>
    <fo:repeatable-page-master-alternatives>
      <fo:conditional-page-master-reference
        odd-or-even="even"
        master-reference="verso"/>
      <fo:conditional-page-master-reference
        odd-or-even="odd"
        master-reference="recto"/>
    </fo:repeatable-page-master-alternatives>
  </fo:page-sequence-master>
  <fo:simple-page-master master-name="verso">
    <!-- ... -->
  </fo:simple-page-master>
  <fo:simple-page-master master-name="recto">
    <!-- ... -->
  </fo:simple-page-master>
</fo:layout-master-set>
```

The conditional-page-master-reference object is similar to single-page-master-reference except that it has to fulfill a precondition to be used. The odd-or-even attribute is one such test. Others include blank-or-not-blank and page-position.

### Page masters

A page master defines the content rectangle for a page and how the rectangle is divided into regions. The one page master object in XSL version 1.0 is simple-page-master (its name suggests that other page master types will be added in future versions of XSL). Its master-name attribute is a handle for page sequence masters to reference. Other attributes include space settings for defining the page's content rectangle. For example:

```
<fo:simple-page-master master-name="title-page"
    page-height="11in" page-width="8.5in"
    margin-top="1in" margin-bottom="1in"
    margin-left="1.2in" margin-right="1.2in">
...</fo:simple-page-master>
```

This FO declares a page master type whose name is title-page. Its height and width are 11 inches and 8.5 inches, respectively. The content rectangle is positioned inside that area, one inch from top and bottom, and 1.2 inches from the left and right sides.

After defining the content rectangle, the page master's other task is to outline the regions for content in the page. simple-page-master allows you to divide a page into as many as five different areas, called *body region*, *before region*, *after region*, *start region*, and *end region*. In the European writing mode (lr-tb), these correspond to the page structures typically called body, header, footer, left sidebar, and right sidebar. Figure 8-6 shows how these regions are arranged on a page in lr-tb mode.

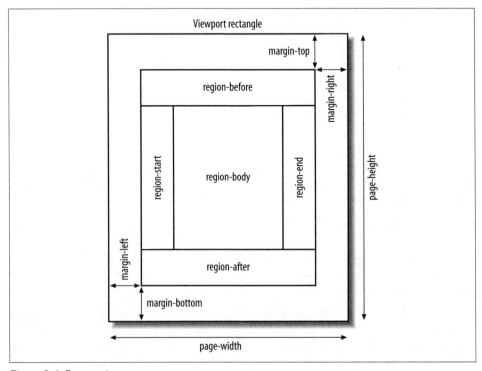

*Figure 8-6. Page regions*

When constructing a page master, you include a formatting object to represent each area. For example, region-body is the FO that sets up the geometry for the body region of a page master. Each region FO may have a region-name attribute that provides a label for flows to attach to it. If you don't define a label, XSL assigns an implicit name with "xsl-" followed by the FO type. For example, the default name for region-body is xsl-region-body.

```
<fo:layout-master-set>
  <fo:simple-page-master master-name="simple"
          page-height="11in" page-width="8.5in"
          margin-top="1in" margin-bottom="1in"
          margin-left="1.2in" margin-right="1.2in">
  >
  <fo:region-body region-name="pamphlet-body"
              margin-top="1in/>
```

```
        <fo:region-before region-name="company-logo"
                         extent="1.1in"
                         display-align="before"/>
        <fo:region-start region-name="navigation-menu"
                         extent="1.1in"/>
    </fo:simple-page-master>
  </fo:layout-master-set>
```

The margin properties for region FOs position them within the content rectangle of the page. In the above example, `margin-top` sets the top of the body region to be one inch below the top of the page's content rectangle. In the peripheral regions, the attribute extent defines the width (if it is on the left or right side) or height (if on the top or bottom). The `display-align` property adjusts where the region sits inside its reference area, such as centered or flush left or right.

## Flows

A *flow* is a stream of formatting objects that is to be inserted into an area. In the FO tree, flows are stored inside `page-sequence` objects. They may span many pages or be restricted to a specific area and repeated on multiple pages. The latter type is called a *static flow* and is typically seen inside a header or footer.

The children of a flow object are block-level flow objects. The sequence of these children determine the order in which they will be stacked when formatted inside an area. The formatter takes these flow objects and places them into pages according to the layout of the appropriate page master. Which page master is used depends on the pages that have come before and the page master sequence in use.

Formatting flows in pages is like pouring liquid into containers. The page master is like a mold for casting containers of different shapes: tall vases or squat trays. The flow objects are a moldable substance that can be poured into these containers. The formatter will create some kind of container depending on which mold it selects. When the container is full, it casts a new container and pours flow objects into it. This process continues until all the objects from all flows have been used up.

How flows are applied to regions is determined by a *flow map*. Each region defined in a page master has a `region-name` property. This is a unique identifier that distinguishes the region in the page master. Every flow must announce where it is to be placed by setting a `flow-name` attribute with one of the declared `region-name`s. The flow map is the implicit connection between flow names and region names. In future versions of XSL, this model is expected to change to make the flow map a separate object.

Regions have default values for region names corresponding to the names of their FOs. For example, the body region is named `xsl-region-body` unless you override that with a name of your own.

# Blocks

Block-level FOs are the objects that fill a flow. Each block has at least one area to control. For example, a paragraph in a document will map to a block object in the FO tree. It will stack inside the flow as a single area with a margin, padding, font, and other properties.

Some properties that are common in all blocks can be categorized in these groups: background, border, fonts, margin, and padding. We will look at these groups now in more detail.

## Spacing properties

CSS gives you two ways to add space to a block. Padding pushes children further inside, and margin pushes the block away from other blocks. In XSL-FO, the padding property is still here, and there are four directional variants of the form:

```
padding-side
```

Where *side* is before, after, start, or end.

Padding properties may be expressed with relative (percentage) or absolute settings (with units). Percentages are calculated in relation to the current block's region.

In XSL-FO, the term *margin* has been renamed *space*, as in space-before. It follows the same scheme as above, with "padding" replaced with "space."

The names of directions have changed from CSS. Instead of "top" and "left" we have the more abstract "before" and "start." This nomenclature is a little confusing, but it is necessary to overcome the bias of Western scripts that go left-to-right and top-to-bottom. In Western-style documents, before, after, start, and end mean top, bottom, left, and right, respectively.

The formatter takes properties like space-after as a rigid constraint. This limits its flexibility and consequently can result in some ugly formatting. For example, two paragraphs in a row will be separated by sum of their space-after and space-before properties. It would be better if you could request an optimal space and also require a minimum and possibly maximum space to give the formatter some room to optimize.

As it happens, each of the space-* properties can specify minimum, optimum, and maximum values. Each is a *compound property*, able to express these different values by extending the attribute name with a dot and a component name. For example:

```
space-before.minimum="2pt"
```

If you use space-before="3pt", forgoing the components, it will be equivalent to this:

```
space-before.minimum="3pt"
space-before.optimum="3pt"
space-before.maximum="3pt"
```

Let's illustrate these spacing techniques in an example. We will use the following source document:

```
<article>
<title>Batten Down the Hatches!</title>
<para>People who download copyrighted materials from the Internet
should have their computers destroyed, said Senator Orrin Hatch
(R-Utah) in a recent statement.</para>
<para>In a sweet twist of irony, Wired News reported that the
Senator's own web site was guilty of using unlicensed software to
generate menus.</para>
</article>
```

Here is an XSLT stylesheet to format this document with space around blocks:

```
<?xml version="1.0"?>
<xsl:stylesheet xmlns:xsl="http://www.w3.org/1999/XSL/Transform"
                xmlns:fo="http://www.w3.org/1999/XSL/Format"
                version="1.0"
>
<xsl:output method="xml"/>

<!-- Set up the master page and apply a flow to it. -->

<xsl:template match="/">
  <fo:root>
    <fo:layout-master-set>
      <fo:simple-page-master
            master-name="the-only-page-type"
            page-height="6in" page-width="3in"
            margin-top="0.5in" margin-bottom="0.5in"
            margin-left="0.5in" margin-right="0.5in">
        <fo:region-body/>
      </fo:simple-page-master>
    </fo:layout-master-set>
    <fo:page-sequence master-reference="the-only-page-type">
      <fo:flow flow-name="xsl-region-body">
        <xsl:apply-templates/>
      </fo:flow>
    </fo:page-sequence>
  </fo:root>
</xsl:template>

<!-- Make the article a box with a quarter inch of padding inside. -->

<xsl:template match="article">
  <fo:block
    font-family="times, serif"
    font-size="12pt"
    padding="0.25in"
    border="solid 1pt black"
  >
    <xsl:apply-templates/>
  </fo:block>
</xsl:template>
```

```
<!-- The title has no spacing properties. -->

<xsl:template match="title">
  <fo:block
    font-weight="bold"
    text-align="center"
  >
    <xsl:apply-templates/>
  </fo:block>
</xsl:template>

<!-- A para has a set of space constraints: minimum of 2 points,
     maximum of 4 points, and ideal of 3 points. I added a silver
     border for reference.
-->

<xsl:template match="para">
  <fo:block
    space-before.minimum="2.0pt"
    space-before.optimum="3.0pt"
    space-before.maximum="4.0pt"
    space-after.minimum="2.0pt"
    space-after.optimum="3.0pt"
    space-after.maximum="4.0pt"
    border="solid 1pt silver"
    text-align="left"
  >
    <xsl:apply-templates/>
  </fo:block>
</xsl:template>

</xsl:stylesheet>
```

Figure 8-7 shows how it looks when formatted.

It is possible to make the current block inherit the aforementioned properties from its parent with the value inherit.

### Background properties

There are many options to alter the background of a block. You can set a color, make the background transparent, or display a graphic. Listed below are the background properties, along with their allowed values (default values in bold).

background-attachment
: Allows the background image to be scrolled along with the foreground of the object. Values: **scroll**, fixed, inherit.

background-color
: Sets the background to some named color or makes it transparent. Values: *color*, **transparent**, inherit.

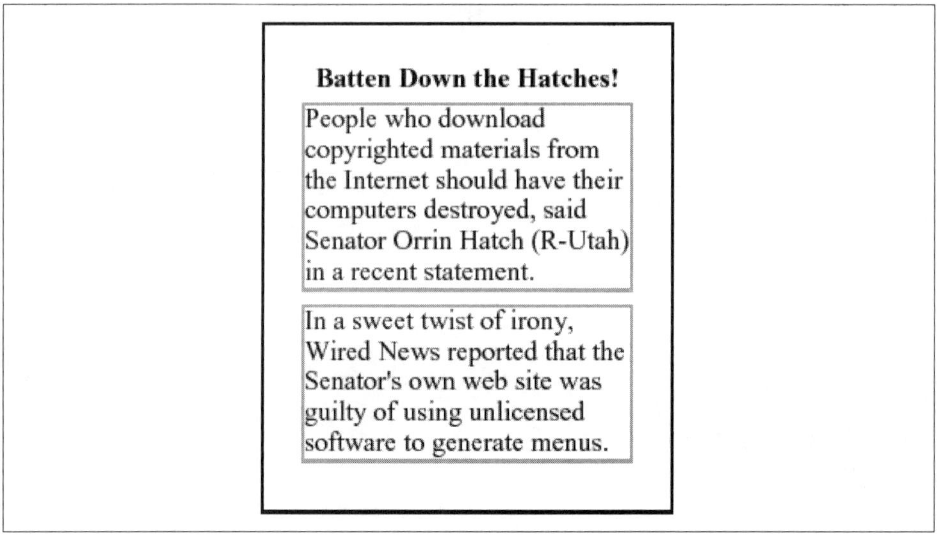

*Figure 8-7. The article formatted*

background-image

Places a graphic in the background. Values: *URI*, **none**, inherit.

background-repeat

Controls how the image is tiled in the background. Values: **repeat** (tile in all directions), repeat-x (tile horizontally only), repeat-y (only tile vertically), no-repeat, inherit.

background-position-horizontal

Specifies where in the background an image is placed horizontally. Percentage and length are with respect to the left edge. Left, center, and right are equivalent to 0%, 50%, and 100% respectively. Values: *percentage*, *length*, left, right, center, inherit. Default: **0%**.

background-position-horizontal

Specifies where in the background an image is placed vertically. Percentage and length are with respect to the top edge. Top, center, and bottom are equivalent to 0%, 50%, and 100% respectively. Values: *percentage*, *length*, top, center, bottom, inherit. Default: **0%**.

## Border properties

The border is an optional visual component located on the block's perimeter. It can be a complete rectangle, or any combination of the individual edges. Each edge can be styled individually for a huge number of combinations. The basic pattern of a border property is:

    border-*side-option*

Where *side* is top, bottom, left, or right and *option* is color, width, or style.

XSL 1.0 offers three different ways of specifying color. The *RGB* (Red, Green, Blue) scheme uses hexadecimal numbers in ranges of 0 to 255 combined in a triple. In RGB, green would be represented as 00ff00 and white would be ffffff. You can derive colors using functions in expressions. Named colors may also be used, if supported by your XSL implementation. Using the value inherit will cause the FO to inherit this property from its parent in the FO tree.

The width parameter can be specified either as a named value (thin, medium, thick), or as an explicit length. The actual thickness of the named values is not specified by XSL 1.0, so it will likely be different depending on the implementation. Width properties may be inherited by setting the value to inherit.

The last component is style. A large set of named styles are available:

none
> No visible border. The width is effectively zero. This is the default value for the style property.

hidden
> Like none, but behaves differently in border conflicts between adjacent blocks.

dotted
> The border appears as a string of dots.

dashed
> The border is broken at intervals.

solid
> A contiguous, single line with no breaks.

double
> Like solid, but with two parallel lines.

groove
> A 3D effect that paints the border to appear recessed, as a trench.

ridge
> The opposite of groove; the border seems to be a raised wall.

inset
> Another 3D effect in which the whole area seems to be recessed like a valley.

outset
> The opposite of inset; the area seems to be raised over surrounding terrain like a plateau.

Style properties can be inherited from parents in the FO tree by setting them to inherit.

### Font properties

Most of the font properties available in CSS are present in FOs. XSL goes a little further in some respects by allowing you to be more precise in specifying fallback fonts. The specification gets very detailed about how font positioning works, but it is out of the scope of this book. So let us move on to the specific properties.

You select a typeface with the `font-family` property as with CSS. The form is a list of names, each of which may be a *family name*, like Verdana or Helvetica, or a *generic name* that allows the formatter to choose one from a category. The generic names include `serif`, `sans-serif`, `cursive`, `fantasy`, and `monospace`.

The formatter will choose a typeface in the order of font names given. If the first cannot be found, does not support the style or weight requested, or does not contain all the glyphs necessary to render the FO properly, it will move to the next font name in the list. Typically, you will put your favorite font family name first, and the most generic one last.

The `font-family` property may also be set to the function `system-font()`, which will discover the current system font and use it. This gives the designer some ability to stick with the local environment. Often user agents like web browsers have preference settings that allow the user to select their favorite font for use in stylesheets.

The properties `color`, `font-size`, `font-size-adjust`, `font-style`, `font-variant`, and `font-weight` are all about the same as they are defined in CSS. `font-style` adds one more style to the CSS set: `backslant`, which is like italic but leans in the other direction.

## Inlines

Many block types, such as paragraphs and titles, contain text. The text stream flows from one edge of the content rectangle to the other, breaks and continues line by line until it runs out or hits the bottom of the block. Embedded in these lines are elements that override the default font styles or get replaced with generated content. This is the realm of inline formatting.

### The inline FO

The `inline` FO is a generic container of text that allows you to override prevailing text properties. It shares all of the font and color properties of blocks, and some spacing properties as well (including `space-before` and `space-after`). In the following example, the XSLT template maps the element `emphasis` to an `inline` element that styles its content green and italic.

```
<xsl:template match="emphasis">
  <fo:inline font-style="italic" color="green">
    <xsl:apply-templates/>
  </fo:inline>
</xsl:template>
```

Here is another example. It formats text in superscript by shrinking text to 60% of the default size in the block and raising it with the top of the line.

```
<xsl:template match="superscript">
  <fo:inline
    font-size="60%"
    vertical-align="super"
  >
    <xsl:apply-templates/>
  </fo:inline>
</xsl:template>
```

### Inline formatting without containment

Using inline requires that you know where the content to be styled begins and ends. There are times, however, when you do not have any way to know in advance the extent of content to be styled. For example, your design may call for the first line of a paragraph to rendered in small caps. Only when the text has been rendered will you know the last word to be styled this way.

XSL provides a different strategy for this case. The formatting object initial-property-set applies properties to the first line of a block only. This example defines a paragraph with an indented first line:

```
<xsl:template match="para[@class='init']">
  <fo:block space-after="1em">
    <fo:initial-property-set space-before="2em"/>
    <xsl:apply-templates/>
  </fo:block>
</xsl:template>
```

### Graphics

XSL allows one to import external resources into a document, and one important kind is a graphic. An external graphic is an inline object in XSL to allow it to flow along with the rest of the text. This would be convenient if you were using a special icon that could not be represented in Unicode.

The external-graphic FO is an empty element that marks the place in text where the formatter will insert a picture. Its src attribute identifies the source of the graphic, typically a filename. For example, this XSL-FO markup contains text with an embedded graphic:

```
<fo:block space-after="2em">The alchemist picked
up a bottle and wrote a strange symbol on
the label. It looked like this:
<fo:external-graphic src="images/blarf.eps"/>.
It made me think of a swarm of snakes.</fo:block>
```

Very often, you will want to insert a graphic into a document but have it format as a block. A figure is a structure that acts as a block, set off from the text with a caption.

This is easy to achieve by encapsulating the external-graphic in a block. The following XSLT template formats a figure element this way:

```
<xsl:template match="figure">
  <fo:block margin="10mm">
    <fo:block margin-bottom="3mm">
      <fo:external-graphic src="{@fileref}" />
    </fo:block>
    <fo:block>
      <xsl:apply-templates match="caption"/>
    </fo:block>
  </fo:block>
</xsl:template>
```

### Generated content

Another class of inline objects stand in for text that has to be generated during the formatting process. For example, a cross-reference that cites a page number should not be hardcoded, but left to the formatter to fill in.

The formatting object page-number will be replaced at formatting time with the number of the page it appears on. This is used often in headers or footers where you want to keep a running page number, as in the following example:

```
<fo:static-content flow-name="header-left">
  <fo:block
      font-size="8pt"
      text-align="left"
  >
    <fo:page-number/>
  </fo:block>
</fo:static-content>
```

A similar need is the cross-reference containing the page number of the object it points to. Suppose in the course of writing a book, you want to make a reference to a table in another chapter, giving the page number on which it appears. page-number-citation is the FO you want to use. The XSLT template below will change an xref element into text that includes this type of citation:

```
<xsl:template match="xref[role='@page-number']">
  <!-- The attribute 'linkend' holds the ID of the element being cited. -->
  <xsl:variable name="idref">
    <xsl:value-of select="@linkend"/>
  </xsl:variable>
  <!-- Go to the element being cited and output some text
       depending on its type. -->
  <xsl:for-each select="//*[@id='$idref']">
    <xsl:choose>
      <xsl:when test="self::sect1">the section</xsl:when>
      <xsl:when test="self::table">the table</xsl:when>
      <xsl:when test="self::fig">the figure</xsl:when>
      <xsl:otherwise>the thing</xsl:otherwise>
    </xsl:choose>
  </xsl:for-each>
```

```
      <!-- Finally, output the page number. -->
      <xsl:text> on page </xsl:text>
      <fo:page-number-citation>
        <xsl:attribute name="ref-id">
          <xsl:value-of select="@linkend"/>
        </xsl:attribute>
      </fo:page-number-citation>
    </xsl:template>
```

# An Example: TEI

Let us take a break now from terminology and see an actual example. The document
to format is a Shakespearean sonnet encoded in TEI-XML, a markup language for
scholarly documents, shown in Example 8-2. It consists of a header section with title
and other metadata, followed by the text itself, which is broken into individual lines
of poetry.

*Example 8-2. A TEI-XML document*

```
<?xml version="1.0"?>
<!DOCTYPE TEI.2 SYSTEM "http://www.uic.edu/orgs/tei/lite/teixlite.dtd">
<TEI.2>
<!-- The metadata. TEI has a rich vocabulary for describing a
     document, which is important for scholarly work.
-->
  <teiHeader>
    <fileDesc>
      <titleStmt><title>Shall I Compare Thee to a Summer's Day?</title>
        <author>William Shakespeare</author>
      </titleStmt>
      <publicationStmt>
        <p>
Electronic version by Erik Ray 2003-03-09. This transcription is in
the public domain.
        </p>
      </publicationStmt>
      <sourceDesc>
        <p>Shakespeare's Sonnets XVIII.</p>
      </sourceDesc>
    </fileDesc>
  </teiHeader>

  <!-- The body of the document, where the sonnet lives. <lg> is a
       group of lines, and <l> is a line of text.
    -->
  <text>
    <body>
      <lg>
<l>Shall I compare thee to a summer's day?</l>
<l>Thou art more lovely and more temperate:</l>
<l>Rough winds do shake the darling buds of May,</l>
<l>And summer's lease hath all too short a date:</l>
```

*Example 8-2. A TEI-XML document (continued)*

```
<l>Sometime too hot the eye of heaven shines,</l>
<l>And often is his gold complexion dimm'd;</l>
<l>And every fair from fair sometime declines,</l>
<l>By chance or nature's changing course untrimm'd;</l>
<l>But thy eternal summer shall not fade</l>
<l>Nor lose possession of that fair thou owest;</l>
<l>Nor shall Death brag thou wander'st in his shade,</l>
<l>When in eternal lines to time thou growest:</l>
<l>So long as men can breathe or eyes can see,</l>
<l>So long lives this and this gives life to thee.</l>
      </lg>
    </body>
  </text>
```

```
</TEI.2>
```

A typical TEI document consists of two parts: a metadata section in a `teiHeader` element and the text body in a text element. Using an XSLT stylesheet, we will transform this into an FO tree, then run the tree through a formatter to generate a formatted page. Actually, I used FOP for this, which combines the XSLT transformation and XSL-FO formatting into one step for me.

---

## TEI

The Text Encoding Initiative (TEI) is an international standard for libraries, museums, and academic institutions to encode scholarly texts for online research and sharing. Founded in 2000 by several collaborating research groups, the TEI Consortium is funded by the National Endowment for the Humanities, the European Union, the Canadian Social Research Council, and private donors. It publishes a DTD for marking up texts and a detailed tutorial.

TEI-XML is a markup language that can be applied to anything from groups of books to plays and poetry. Its hallmarks include a header with a very detailed set of metadata elements, and a text body whose structure is reminiscent of DocBook. Although the DTD is very large, it is modular and can be customized for specific needs.

The effort has been very successful with tens of thousands of books, articles, poems, and plays now encoded in TEI-XML. Huge repositories have made these documents available to the public, such as the Electronic Text Center (*http://etext.lib.virginia.edu/*) at the University of Virginia Library. It holds approximately 70,000 humanities texts in 13 languages.

The TEI Consortium's web site (*http://www.tei-c.org/*) is brimming with helpful documents and pointers to resources. The tutorial, *TEI P4: Guidelines for Electronic Text Encoding and Interchange*, is available online at *http://www.tei-c.org/P4X/SG.html*.

---

In designing the stylesheet, I like to start with the page layout. This is a very small document that can fit entirely on one page, so we only need define one page master. (Later on in this chapter, I'll show you a more complex example that uses a lot of different page masters.) Below, I've created a page master that defines two regions, a header and a body. My style is to define this information in an XSLT template matching the root node.

```
<xsl:template match="/">
  <fo:root>   <!-- The root element contains
                      everything in the FO tree -->

    <fo:layout-master-set>

      <!-- The page master object with settings for
           the page's content rectangle -->

      <fo:simple-page-master
           master-name="the-only-page-type"
           page-height="11in" page-width="8.5in"
           margin-top="1in" margin-bottom="1in"
           margin-left="1.2in" margin-right="1.2in">

        <!-- A body region 20 millimeters below the top
             of the page's content rectangle.  -->

        <fo:region-body margin-top="20mm"/>

        <!-- A header that is 3/10 inch tall -->

        <fo:region-before extent="0.3in"/>

      </fo:simple-page-master>
    </fo:layout-master-set>
    <xsl:apply-templates/>
  </fo:root>
</xsl:template>
```

Note that when you set the margin-top of the region-body to less than the extent of the region-before, there's a risk that the header and the region body will overlap.

Next, we have to define the flows. There is one static flow for the header, and one regular flow for the body. In my stylesheet, I chose to output the page-sequence FO from a template matching the document element. First to be defined is the header flow:

```
<xsl:template match="TEI.2">
  <fo:page-sequence master-reference="the-only-page-type">
    <fo:static-content flow-name="xsl-region-before">
      <fo:block
        font-family="geneva, sans-serif"
        font-size="8pt"
        text-align="left"
```

```
           border-bottom="solid 1pt black"
      >
           <xsl:value-of select="teiHeader//sourceDesc"/>
         </fo:block>
       </fo:static-content>
```

The content of this flow is a single block. It sets a sans serif font of 8 points aligned to the left, and a thin rule underneath. The text to be displayed here is taken from the metadata block, the content of a sourceDesc element (i.e., the source of the document.

This is followed by the body flow object:

```
           <fo:flow flow-name="xsl-region-body">
             font-family="didot, serif"
             font-size="10pt"
      >
             <xsl:apply-templates select="teiHeader//title"/>
             <xsl:apply-templates select="teiHeader//author"/>
             <xsl:apply-templates select="text/body"/>
           </fo:flow>
         </fo:page-sequence>
     </xsl:template>
```

The main flow formats the title, author, and finally the body of the document, with apply-templates statements.

All that remains is to write templates for the other element types we wish to format. These are included in the complete XSLT stylesheet listing in Example 8-3.

*Example 8-3. XSLT stylesheet for the TEI-XML document*

```
<?xml version="1.0"?>
<xsl:stylesheet xmlns:xsl="http://www.w3.org/1999/XSL/Transform"
               xmlns:fo="http://www.w3.org/1999/XSL/Format"
               version="1.0"
>
<xsl:output method="xml"/>

<!-- Start the FO tree and layout the page -->

<xsl:template match="/">
  <fo:root>
    <fo:layout-master-set>
      <fo:simple-page-master
           master-name="the-only-page-type"
           page-height="11in" page-width="8.5in"
           margin-top="1in" margin-bottom="1in"
           margin-left="1.2in" margin-right="1.2in">
        <fo:region-body margin-top="20mm"/>
        <fo:region-before extent="0.3in"/>
      </fo:simple-page-master>
    </fo:layout-master-set>
    <xsl:apply-templates/>
```

*Example 8-3. XSLT stylesheet for the TEI-XML document (continued)*

```
    </fo:root>
</xsl:template>

<!-- Begin the flows -->

<xsl:template match="TEI.2">
  <fo:page-sequence master-reference="the-only-page-type">
    <fo:static-content flow-name="xsl-region-before">
      <fo:block
        font-family="geneva, sans-serif"
        font-size="8pt"
        text-align="left"
        border-bottom="solid 1pt black"
     >
        <xsl:value-of select="teiHeader//sourceDesc"/>
      </fo:block>
    </fo:static-content>
    <fo:flow flow-name="xsl-region-body"
      font-family="didot, serif"
      font-size="10pt"
   >
      <xsl:apply-templates select="teiHeader//title"/>
      <xsl:apply-templates select="teiHeader//author"/>
      <xsl:apply-templates select="text/body"/>
    </fo:flow>
  </fo:page-sequence>
</xsl:template>

<!-- Render the title in bold to stand out from the sonnet. -->

<xsl:template match="teiHeader//title">
  <fo:block
    font-weight="bold"
    space-before="2mm"
    space-after="4mm"
 >
    <xsl:apply-templates/>
  </fo:block>
</xsl:template>

<!-- Format the author's name in italic to set it apart
     from the sonnet itself. Add the word "by" for a
     further decorative touch.
-->

<xsl:template match="teiHeader//author">
  <fo:block
    font-style="italic"
    space-after="4mm"
 >
    <xsl:text>by </xsl:text>
    <xsl:apply-templates/>
```

*Example 8-3. XSLT stylesheet for the TEI-XML document (continued)*

```
    </fo:block>
</xsl:template>

<xsl:template match="text/body">
  <xsl:apply-templates/>
</xsl:template>

<!-- Put the lines in one block to group them together. Later, we
     might want to do something special with this grouping, such
     as to surround it in a border. Hint: we use "select" here so that
     we can use position() later to select lines for indenting.
-->

<xsl:template match="lg">
  <fo:block>
    <xsl:apply-templates select="l"/>
  </fo:block>
</xsl:template>

<!-- As a nice formatting effect, we will indent or space certain
     lines. Every other line will be indented 4mm. Add space after
     every fourth line. The final two lines are traditionally
     indented in sonnets.
-->

  <xsl:template match="l">
    <fo:block>
      <xsl:if test="position() mod 4 = 0">
        <xsl:attribute name="space-after">4mm</xsl:attribute>
      </xsl:if>
      <xsl:if test="position()> 11 or
                    position() mod 2 = 0">
        <xsl:attribute name="start-indent">5mm</xsl:attribute>
      </xsl:if>
      <xsl:apply-templates />
    </fo:block>
  </xsl:template>

</xsl:stylesheet>
```

Now, run the XSLT engine on the document using this stylesheet and you will get
the result file in Example 8-4. (I've added some space in places to make it more
readable).

*Example 8-4. Formatting object tree of the TEI document*

```
<?xml version="1.0"?>
<fo:root xmlns:fo="http://www.w3.org/1999/XSL/Format">
  <fo:layout-master-set>
    <fo:simple-page-master master-name="the-only-page-type"
         page-height="11in" page-width="8.5in" margin-top="1in"
         margin-bottom="1in" margin-left="1.2in" margin-right="1.2in">
```

*Example 8-4. Formatting object tree of the TEI document (continued)*

```
        <fo:region-body margin-top="20mm"/>
        <fo:region-before extent="0.3in"/>
    </fo:simple-page-master>
  </fo:layout-master-set>
  <fo:page-sequence master-reference="the-only-page-type">
  <fo:static-content flow-name="xsl-region-before">
    <fo:block font-family="geneva, sans-serif" font-size="8pt"
        text-align="left" border-bottom="solid 1pt black">
      Shakespeare's Sonnets XVIII.
    </fo:block>
  </fo:static-content>
  <fo:flow flow-name="xsl-region-body"
      font-family="didot, serif" font-size="10pt">
    <fo:block font-weight="bold" space-before="2mm" space-after="4mm">
      Shall I Compare Thee to a Summer's Day?
    </fo:block>
    <fo:block font-style="italic" space-after="4mm">
      by William Shakespeare
    </fo:block>
    <fo:block>
      <fo:block>
Shall I compare thee to a summer's day?
      </fo:block>
      <fo:block start-indent="5mm">
Thou art more lovely and more temperate:
      </fo:block>
      <fo:block>
Rough winds do shake the darling buds of May,
      </fo:block>
      <fo:block space-after="4mm" start-indent="5mm">
And summer's lease hath all too short a date:
      </fo:block>
    <!-- Rest removed because it's more of the same -->
    </fo:flow>
  </fo:page-sequence>
</fo:root>
```

I formatted this with FOP and got a PDF file as output. Figure 8-8 shows how it looks in Acrobat Reader.

# A Bigger Example: DocBook

The last example was relatively simple, lacking complex structures like lists, tables and footnotes. It also was quite short, taking up only one page. Clearly, this lack of a challenge is an insult to any self-respecting XSL formatter. So let us set our sights on something more challenging.

Let us return to our old friend DocBook for inspiration. We will include support for most of the common elements you would find in technical prose, including some

```
Shakespeare's Sonnets XVIII.
```

**Shall I Compare Thee to a Summer's Day?**

*by William Shakespeare*

Shall I compare thee to a summer's day?
    Thou art more lovely and more temperate:
Rough winds do shake the darling buds of May,
    And summer's lease hath all too short a date:

Sometime too hot the eye of heaven shines,
    And often is his gold complexion dimm'd;
And every fair from fair sometime declines,
    By chance or nature's changing course untrimm'd;

But thy eternal summer shall not fade
    Nor lose possession of that fair thou owest;
Nor shall Death brag thou wander'st in his shade,
    When in eternal lines to time thou growest:

        So long as men can breathe or eyes can see,
        So long lives this and this gives life to thee.

*Figure 8-8. The sonnet in PDF*

objects we have not covered yet, such as tables, lists, and footnotes. To flex the muscles of pagination, we will also explore the use of different page masters and conditional master sequences.

To save you from having to look at a huge, monolithic listing, I'll break up the stylesheet into manageable chunks interspersed with friendly narrative.

## Page Masters

We will start by setting up the page masters. This is a very verbose piece of the stylesheet, since we want to create a page master for each type of page. I chose to cover these types:

1. Lefthand (verso) page starting a chapter. It happens to have an even numbered page number, which we will use to identify it in the page sequence master. The layout will include a header that shows the chapter title and number and a body that is pushed down further than a non-starting page.

2. Righthand (recto) page starting a chapter. The main difference is that its page number is odd, and the header is right-justified instead of justified on the left.

3. Verso page that does not start a chapter. It has a plain header and body that reaches up almost to the top.

4. Recto page that does not start a chapter. Again, the distinctive layout involves right-justifying header and footer.

Below is the stylesheet portion containing page master definitions. The template matching the root node in the source document calls a named template that sets up the page masters and also the page sequence masters.

```xml
<?xml version="1.0"?>
<xsl:stylesheet version="1.0"
                xmlns:xsl="http://www.w3.org/1999/XSL/Transform"
                xmlns:fo="http://www.w3.org/1999/XSL/Format">

<!--       ROOT RULE
           Set up page layout and main flow.
-->

<xsl:template match="/">
  <fo:root>
    <fo:layout-master-set>
      <xsl:call-template name="page-masters"/>
      <xsl:call-template name="page-sequence-masters"/>
    </fo:layout-master-set>
    <xsl:apply-templates/>
  </fo:root>
</xsl:template>

<!--       PAGE MASTERS
           Where we define layout and regions for page types.
-->

<xsl:template name="page-masters">

<!--
Even-numbered first page of a chapter.
-->
  <fo:simple-page-master master-name="chapter-first-verso"
    page-height="9in"
    page-width="7in"
    margin-left="1in"
    margin-right="1in"
    margin-top="0.5in"
    margin-bottom="0.4in"
  >

    <!-- body -->
    <fo:region-body
      margin-top="2.5in"
      margin-bottom="0.6in"
    />
```

```
    <!-- header -->
    <fo:region-before region-name="region-first-verso-before"
      extent="1in"
    />

    <!-- footer -->
    <fo:region-after region-name="region-first-verso-after"
      extent="0.5in"
    />
  </fo:simple-page-master>

<!--
Odd-numbered first page of a chapter.
-->
  <fo:simple-page-master master-name="chapter-first-recto"
    page-height="9in"
    page-width="7in"
    margin-left="1in"
    margin-right="1in"
    margin-top="0.5in"
    margin-bottom="0.4in"
  >
    <fo:region-body
      margin-top="2.5in"
      margin-bottom="0.6in"
    />
    <fo:region-before region-name="region-first-recto-before"
      extent="1in"
    />
    <fo:region-after region-name="region-first-recto-after"
      extent="0.5in"
    />
  </fo:simple-page-master>

<!--
Even-numbered page of a chapter not including the first.
-->
  <fo:simple-page-master master-name="chapter-other-verso"
    page-height="9in"
    page-width="7in"
    margin-left="1in"
    margin-right="1in"
    margin-top="0.5in"
    margin-bottom="0.4in"
  >
    <fo:region-body
      margin-bottom="0.6in"
    />
    <fo:region-after region-name="region-other-verso-after"
      extent="0.5in"
    />
  </fo:simple-page-master>
```

```
<!--
Odd-numbered first page of a chapter other than the first.
-->
  <fo:simple-page-master master-name="chapter-other-recto"
    page-height="9in"
    page-width="7in"
    margin-left="1in"
    margin-right="1in"
    margin-top="0.5in"
    margin-bottom="0.4in"
  >
    <fo:region-body
      margin-bottom="0.6in"
    />
    <fo:region-after region-name="region-other-recto-after"
      extent="0.5in"
    />
  </fo:simple-page-master>
```

Notice how I had to choose distinctive names for the page masters as well as the regions inside them, except for the body regions. Why not name the body regions? They get the implicit name xsl-region-body which is good enough because the text will flow inside it the same way no matter what the page type.

## Page Sequence Masters

Now we define the page sequence masters. Well, there is only one sequence. When I first wrote this example, I had two. One was used for chapters, and another for front matter. The front matter includes dedication, preface, foreword, and other junk at the beginning of the book. The distinction was necessary because these pages are typically numbered with Roman numerals, and the page count resets to 1 at the first chapter. However, this example was so large it would have caused many trees to die unnecessarily for the extra pages. I did the right (green) thing and left it out.

The sequence master uses a repeatable-page-master-alternatives FO to hold a reference for each of the possible page types. Remember, there are four of them. The conditional-page-master-reference FO has attributes page-position and odd-or-even to determine which page type to select:

```
<xsl:template name="page-sequence-masters">
  <fo:page-sequence-master master-name="chapter"
    initial-page-number="1"
    format="1"
  >
    <fo:repeatable-page-master-alternatives>
      <fo:conditional-page-master-reference
        master-reference="chapter-other-verso"
        page-position="rest"
        odd-or-even="even"
      />
      <fo:conditional-page-master-reference
```

```
             master-reference="chapter-other-recto"
             page-position="rest"
             odd-or-even="odd"
          />
          <fo:conditional-page-master-reference
             master-reference="chapter-first-verso"
             page-position="first"
             odd-or-even="even"
          />
          <fo:conditional-page-master-reference
             master-reference="chapter-first-recto"
             page-position="first"
             odd-or-even="odd"
          />
        </fo:repeatable-page-master-alternatives>
      </fo:page-sequence-master>
  </xsl:template>
```

## Top-Level Elements and Flows

I like to structure my XSLT stylesheets with the outermost container elements first.
So the next two templates match book and its children which include chapter,
preface, and the like. The second template includes the flow and static-flow FOs.
Recall that static flows are used for small, single-page items like headers and footers.

```
<xsl:template match="book">
  <xsl:apply-templates/>
</xsl:template>

<xsl:template match="chapter | appendix | glossary |
                     bibliography | index | colophon |
                     preface | dedication | foreword | toc">
  <fo:page-sequence
    master-reference="chapter"
    force-page-count="odd"
  >

    <!-- START OF CHAPTER ON ODD PAGE -->

    <fo:static-content flow-name="region-first-verso-before">
      <fo:block
        font-family="myriad, verdana, sans-serif"
        font-weight="bold"
        font-size="12pt"
        space-after="2mm"
      >
      <xsl:choose>
        <xsl:when test="self::chapter">
          <xsl:text>CHAPTER </xsl:text>
          <xsl:call-template name="chapnum"/>
        </xsl:when>
        <xsl:when test="self::appendix">
          <xsl:text>APPENDIX </xsl:text>
```

```
          <xsl:call-template name="chapnum"/>
        </xsl:when>
      </xsl:choose>
  </fo:block>
  <fo:block
    border-top="solid 1pt black"
    padding-before="2mm"
    font-family="myriad, verdana, sans-serif"
    font-weight="bold"
    font-size="18pt"
  >
      <xsl:apply-templates select="title"/>
    </fo:block>
</fo:static-content>

<fo:static-content flow-name="region-first-verso-after">
  <fo:block
    border-top="solid 1pt black"
    padding-before="2mm"
    font-family="myriad, verdana, sans-serif"
    font-weight="bold"
    font-size="8pt"
    text-align="left"
  >
      <fo:page-number/>
    </fo:block>
</fo:static-content>

<!-- START OF CHAPTER ON EVEN PAGE -->

<fo:static-content flow-name="region-first-recto-before">
  <fo:block
    font-family="myriad, verdana, sans-serif"
    font-weight="bold"
    font-size="12pt"
    text-align="right"
    space-after="2mm"
  >
      <xsl:choose>
        <xsl:when test="self::chapter">
          <xsl:text>CHAPTER </xsl:text>
          <xsl:call-template name="chapnum"/>
        </xsl:when>
        <xsl:when test="self::appendix">
          <xsl:text>APPENDIX </xsl:text>
          <xsl:call-template name="chapnum"/>
        </xsl:when>
      </xsl:choose>
  </fo:block>
  <fo:block
    border-top="solid 1pt black"
    padding-before="2mm"
    font-family="myriad, verdana, sans-serif"
    font-weight="bold"
```

```
      font-size="18pt"
      text-align="right"
  >
      <xsl:apply-templates select="title"/>
    </fo:block>
</fo:static-content>

<fo:static-content flow-name="region-first-recto-after">
    <fo:block
      border-top="solid 1pt black"
      padding-before="2mm"
      font-family="myriad, verdana, sans-serif"
      font-weight="bold"
      font-size="8pt"
      text-align="right"
  >
      <fo:page-number/>
    </fo:block>
</fo:static-content>

<!-- REST OF CHAPTER ON ODD PAGE -->

<fo:static-content flow-name="region-other-verso-after">
    <fo:block
      border-top="solid 1pt black"
      padding-before="2mm"
      font-family="myriad, verdana, sans-serif"
      font-weight="bold"
      font-size="8pt"
      text-align="left"
  >
      <fo:page-number/>
      <fo:inline
        font-size="12pt"
    >
        <xsl:text> | </xsl:text>
      </fo:inline>
      <xsl:choose>
        <xsl:when test="self::chapter">
          <xsl:text>Chapter </xsl:text>
          <xsl:call-template name="chapnum"/>
        </xsl:when>
        <xsl:when test="self::appendix">
          <xsl:text>Appendix </xsl:text>
          <xsl:call-template name="chapnum"/>
        </xsl:when>
      </xsl:choose>
      <xsl:text>: </xsl:text>
      <xsl:value-of select="title"/>
    </fo:block>
</fo:static-content>

<!-- REST OF CHAPTER ON EVEN PAGE -->
```

```
    <fo:static-content flow-name="region-other-recto-after">
      <fo:block
        border-top="solid 1pt black"
        padding-before="2mm"
        font-family="myriad, verdana, sans-serif"
        font-weight="bold"
        font-size="8pt"
        text-align="right"
      >
        <fo:page-number/>
      </fo:block>
    </fo:static-content>

    <!-- REGULAR BODY FLOW -->
    <fo:flow flow-name="xsl-region-body">
      <fo:block
        font-size="10pt"
        font-family="garamond, palatino, serif"
        break-before="page"
      >
        <xsl:apply-templates select="*[not(self::title)]"/>
      </fo:block>
    </fo:flow>

  </fo:page-sequence>
</xsl:template>

<xsl:template match="simplesect | partintro | sect1 | sect2 | sect3">
  <xsl:apply-templates/>
</xsl:template>
```

## Simple Blocks

The next crop of templates are for more mundane blocks, namely heads of chapters, tables, figures, and so on. One interestingly named template, called chapnum, determines how to label a chapter-level element. If it is called from the context of a chapter, it will just return a number. But from inside an appendix, the function will return a letter.

```
<xsl:template match="book/title"/>

<xsl:template match="chapter/title | appendix/title | preface/title">
  <xsl:apply-templates/>
</xsl:template>

<xsl:template match="sect1/title">
  <fo:block
    font-family="myriad, verdana, sans-serif"
    font-size="18pt"
    font-weight="bold"
    space-before="8mm"
    space-after="4mm"
  >
```

```
      <xsl:apply-templates/>
    </fo:block>
</xsl:template>

<xsl:template match="sect2/title">
  <fo:block
    font-family="myriad, verdana, sans-serif"
    font-size="16pt"
    font-weight="bold"
    space-before="8mm"
    space-after="4mm"
  >
    <xsl:apply-templates/>
  </fo:block>
</xsl:template>

<xsl:template match="example/title">
  <fo:block
    font-size="8pt"
    font-style="italic"
    space-after="2mm"
    keep-with-next.within-page="always"
  >
    <xsl:text>Example </xsl:text>
    <xsl:call-template name="chapnum"/>
    <xsl:text>-</xsl:text>
    <xsl:number format="1. " count="example"
        from="chapter|appendix" level="any"/>
    <xsl:apply-templates/>
  </fo:block>
</xsl:template>

<!--
Return the chapter number or appendix letter. If the element contains
a label attribute, use that. (Useful if you want to split a document
up into multiple documents.
-->
<xsl:template name="chapnum">
  <xsl:choose>
    <xsl:when test="ancestor-or-self::chapter/@label">
      <xsl:value-of select="ancestor-or-self::chapter/@label"/>
    </xsl:when>
    <xsl:when test="ancestor-or-self::appendix/@label">
      <xsl:value-of select="ancestor-or-self::appendix/@label"/>
    </xsl:when>
    <xsl:when test="ancestor-or-self::chapter">
      <xsl:number format="1" value="count(preceding::chapter)+1"/>
    </xsl:when>
    <xsl:when test="ancestor-or-self::appendix">
      <xsl:number format="A" value="count(preceding::appendix)+1"/>
    </xsl:when>
    <xsl:when test="ancestor-or-self::preface">
      <xsl:text>0</xsl:text>
    </xsl:when>
```

```
      <xsl:otherwise>
        <xsl:text>?</xsl:text>
      </xsl:otherwise>
  </xsl:choose>
</xsl:template>

<xsl:template match="figure/title">
  <fo:block
    font-size="8pt"
    font-style="italic"
    space-after="2mm"
    keep-with-next.within-page="always"
  >
    <xsl:text>Figure </xsl:text>
    <xsl:call-template name="chapnum"/>
    <xsl:text>-</xsl:text>
    <xsl:number format="1" count="figure"
        from="chapter|appendix" level="any"/>
    <xsl:text>. </xsl:text>
    <xsl:apply-templates/>
  </fo:block>
</xsl:template>

<!-- Catch-all: just a small head -->
<xsl:template match="title">
  <fo:block
    font-size="12pt"
    font-weight="bold"
    space-after="4mm"
  >
    <xsl:apply-templates/>
  </fo:block>
</xsl:template>
```

Next follow a bunch of paragraph-level blocks.

```
<xsl:template match="para">
  <fo:block
    space-after="3mm"
    text-align="justify"
  >
    <xsl:apply-templates/>
  </fo:block>
</xsl:template>

<xsl:template match="programlisting | screen">
  <fo:block
    space-after="5mm"
    font-family="monoco, monospace"
    font-size="8pt"
    wrap-option="no-wrap"
  >
    <xsl:apply-templates/>
  </fo:block>
</xsl:template>
```

```
<xsl:template match="remark">
  <fo:block
    margin-left="2em"
    margin-right="2em"
    space-after="1em"
    color="blue"
    font-weight="bold"
  >
    <xsl:apply-templates/>
  </fo:block>
</xsl:template>

<!-- Container of graphic and caption. Normally <fo:external-graphic>
     is treated as an inline, so we have to put it inside a block.
-->
<xsl:template match="figure">
  <fo:block
    text-align="center"
    width="4in"
    height="3in"
    border="solid 1pt black"
    background-color="silver"
  >
    <fo:external-graphic>
      <xsl:attribute name="src">
        <xsl:value-of select="graphic/@fileref"/>
      </xsl:attribute>
    </fo:external-graphic>
  </fo:block>
  <fo:block
    space-before="4mm"
  >
    <xsl:apply-templates select="title"/>
  </fo:block>
</xsl:template>

<xsl:template match="example">
  <xsl:apply-templates/>
</xsl:template>

<xsl:template match="sidebar">
  <fo:block
    background-color="silver"
    padding="1em"
    margin="2em"
  >
    <xsl:apply-templates/>
  </fo:block>
</xsl:template>

<xsl:template match="note | tip | warning">
  <fo:block
    margin-left="20mm"
    margin-right="10mm"
```

```
  >
      <xsl:apply-templates/>
    </fo:block>
  </xsl:template>
```

# Lists

Lists are more complex than your average block. They contain a sequence of *list items*, with an optional *label*.

You can think of a really simple list as a bunch of small paragraphs. However, lists are often more complicated than that. In numbered lists, the item has a number or letter for a label. Bulleted lists use some kind of symbol for a label. A label may even be a piece of text, such as in a term definition list.

XSL uses four FOs to put together a list. The root of the list is list-block, a container of list-item objects. Each list-item has two children, a list-item-label and list-item-body. Figure 8-9 diagrams this list structure.

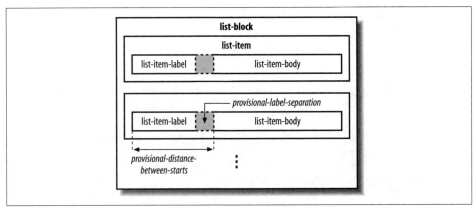

*Figure 8-9. The structure of lists*

list-block has two parameters for fudging the geometry of list-items. provisional-distance-between-starts sets the preferred distance between the start of the label and the item body. The space between the end of the label and the item body is controlled by the property provisional-label-separation.

In list-item-label, you can set the parameter end-indent to label-end(). This function returns the indent of the item body. Similarly, you can set the parameter start-indent in list-item-body to body-start(), a function that returns the indent of the start of the body of the list item. These values are calculated based on the property provisional-distance-between-starts. You don't have to use them, but without them you run the risk of the label overlapping the body or not being able to fit into the space allotted to it.

The following part of the stylesheet creates a numbered list.

```
<xsl:template match="orderedlist">
  <fo:list-block
    margin-left="5mm"
    space-before="5mm"
    space-after="5mm"
    provisional-distance-between-starts="15mm"
    provisional-label-separation="5mm"
  >
    <xsl:apply-templates/>
  </fo:list-block>
</xsl:template>

<xsl:template match="orderedlist/listitem">
  <fo:list-item>
    <fo:list-item-label start-indent="5mm" end-indent="label-end()">
      <fo:block>
        <xsl:number format="1."/>
      </fo:block>
    </fo:list-item-label>
    <fo:list-item-body start-indent="body-start()">
      <fo:block>
        <xsl:apply-templates/>
      </fo:block>
    </fo:list-item-body>
  </fo:list-item>
</xsl:template>
```

To format a bulleted list, simply replace the number with some other character:

```
<xsl:template match="itemizedlist">
  <fo:list-block
    margin-left="5mm"
    space-before="5mm"
    space-after="5mm"
    provisional-distance-between-starts="15mm"
    provisional-label-separation="5mm"
  >
    <xsl:apply-templates/>
  </fo:list-block>
</xsl:template>

<xsl:template match="itemizedlist/listitem">
  <fo:list-item>
    <fo:list-item-label start-indent="5mm" end-indent="label-end()">
      <fo:block>•</fo:block>
    </fo:list-item-label>
    <fo:list-item-body start-indent="body-start()">
      <fo:block>
        <xsl:apply-templates/>
      </fo:block>
    </fo:list-item-body>
  </fo:list-item>
</xsl:template>
```

Following is a term definition list. I wanted the terms and definitions to appear on separate lines, so I decided to forgo the traditional list FOs.

```
<xsl:template match="variablelist">
  <xsl:apply-templates/>
</xsl:template>

<xsl:template match="varlistentry">
  <xsl:apply-templates/>
</xsl:template>

<xsl:template match="varlistentry/term">
  <fo:block
    font-weight="bold"
    space-after="2mm"
    keep-with-next.within-page="2"
  >
      <xsl:apply-templates/>
    </fo:block>
</xsl:template>

<xsl:template match="varlistentry/listitem">
  <fo:block
    margin-left="10mm"
    space-after="2mm"
  >
      <xsl:apply-templates/>
    </fo:block>
</xsl:template>
```

## Footnotes

Footnotes are the strangest objects yet. Even though in the DocBook source the content is embedded in the narrative, in the presentation it pops out of the flow and drops to the bottom of the page. A footnote also leaves behind a referential symbol to bring it to the attention of the reader. Because of this unusual behavior, XSL has devoted an FO specifically to footnotes.

The following template shows how to set up a formatting object for a footnote. The first child of the object is an inline FO describing what to place in the main text as an indication of the footnote's existence (in this case, the number of the footnote in the chapter). The second child contains the footnote body which will be positioned at the bottom of the page. For convenience, I've used some list-related elements to help format the footnote text with a number.

```
<xsl:template match="footnote">
  <fo:footnote>
    <fo:inline
      font-size="70%"
      vertical-align="super"
    >
```

```
        <xsl:number count="footnote" from="chapter" level="any" format="1"/>
      </fo:inline>
      <fo:footnote-body>
        <fo:list-block>
          <fo:list-item
            space-before="5mm"
          >
            <fo:list-item-label end-indent="label-end()">
              <fo:block
                font-size="7pt"
              >
                <xsl:number count="footnote" from="chapter"
                  level="any" format="1"/>
              </fo:block>
            </fo:list-item-label>
            <fo:list-item-body start-indent="body-start()">
              <fo:block
                font-size="7pt"
              >
                <xsl:apply-templates/>
              </fo:block>
            </fo:list-item-body>
          </fo:list-item>
        </fo:list-block>
      </fo:footnote-body>
    </fo:footnote>
  </xsl:template>
```

# Tables

Tables are very intuitive in XSL. Virtually anything you want to do in a table is possible. The following FO types are used to build tables.

table-and-caption
> A block encapsulating a table and its caption.

table-caption
> A block containing text describing the table.

table
> The container of basic table components. Its children include a number of table-column objects, an optional table-header, an optional table-footer, and at least one table-body.

table-column
> An informational element describing details about a column, such as its width. Set the column-number property to a positive integer to refer to a specific column. (A column is a stack of cells perpendicular to the inline propagation direction).

table-body
> A collection of table-row objects. Rows stack in the block progression direction.

table-header
: An optional container of rows or cells that must appear before the body. This is traditionally where column heads reside.

table-footer
: Like `table-header`, except that it must appear after the body. Typically used for things like column totals.

table-row
: A block containing some number of `table-cells`. Usually, the number of cells is constant for all rows in the table, and the formatter will attempt to align them so that their edges parallel to the block progression direction line up. These lined up cells are called columns and a `table-column` object can be used to define group behavior of each column.

table-cell
: The innermost table component. Cells stack along the inline progression direction inside rows. A cell may take up more than one column width or row height by setting the `number-columns-spanned` or `number-rows-spanned` properties to a value greater than 1.

Figure 8-10 outlines the structure of a typical table.

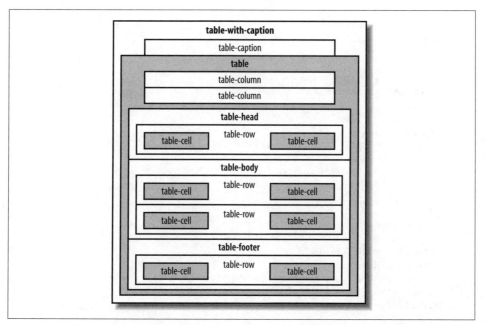

*Figure 8-10. The structure of tables*

Properties common to all the table components include height and width which are useful in tuning the size of the areas they control. Border properties also apply, making it easy to create rules.

The following XSLT templates are my attempt to handle CALS tables (the standard adopted by DocBook). They allow for tables that have captions, but no cell spans are allowed.

```
<xsl:template match="table">
  <fo:table-with-caption>
    <xsl:apply-templates/>
  </fo:table-with-caption>
</xsl:template>

<xsl:template match="table/title">
  <fo:table-caption
    font-size="8pt"
    font-style="italic"
    space-after="2mm"
  >
    <xsl:text>Table </xsl:text>
    <xsl:call-template name="chapnum"/>
    <xsl:text>-</xsl:text>
    <xsl:number format="1" count="table"
        from="chapter|appendix" level="any"/>
    <xsl:text>. </xsl:text>
    <xsl:apply-templates/>
  </fo:table-caption>
</xsl:template>

<xsl:template match="tgroup">
  <fo:table
    table-layout="fixed"
    width="4.7in"
    space-after="4mm"
    margin-left="4mm"
    border-bottom="dotted 1pt gray"
  >
    <xsl:apply-templates/>
  </fo:table>
</xsl:template>

<xsl:template match="colspec">
  <fo:table-column
    column-number="{count(preceding-sibling::colspec) + 1}"
    column-width="{@colwidth}" />
</xsl:template>

<xsl:template match="thead">
  <fo:table-header
      background-color="silver"
      font-weight="bold"
  >
```

```
      <xsl:apply-templates/>
    </fo:table-header>
</xsl:template>

<xsl:template match="tbody">
  <fo:table-body>
    <xsl:apply-templates/>
  </fo:table-body>
</xsl:template>

<xsl:template match="tfoot">
  <fo:table-footer>
    <xsl:apply-templates/>
  </fo:table-footer>
</xsl:template>

<xsl:template match="row">
  <fo:table-row>
    <xsl:apply-templates/>
  </fo:table-row>
</xsl:template>

<xsl:template match="entry">
  <fo:table-cell>
    <fo:block
      font-family="verdana, sans-serif"
      padding-top="1mm"
      padding-bottom="1mm"
      padding-left="3mm"
      padding-right="3mm"
      text-align="left"
    >
      <xsl:apply-templates/>
    </fo:block>
  </fo:table-cell>
</xsl:template>
```

## Inlines

Finally, we can define the templates for inline elements. In this particular stylesheet, they fall into a few categories of presentation: italic, monospace, subscript, super-script, and small caps.

```
<xsl:template match="citetitle | command | emphasis | filename |
                     firstterm | foreignphrase | replaceable">
  <fo:inline font-style="italic">
    <xsl:apply-templates/>
  </fo:inline>
</xsl:template>

<xsl:template match="function | literal | option | parameter |
                     returnvalue | symbol | type">
  <fo:inline font-family="monoco, monospace" font-size="9pt">
```

```
    <xsl:apply-templates/>
  </fo:inline>
</xsl:template>

<!-- Note use of vertical-align property to lower the font baseline.
     Also using relative size to make it smaller. -->
<xsl:template match="subscript">
  <fo:inline
    font-size="60%"
    vertical-align="sub"
  >
    <xsl:apply-templates/>
  </fo:inline>
</xsl:template>

<xsl:template match="superscript">
  <fo:inline
    font-size="60%"
    vertical-align="super"
  >
    <xsl:apply-templates/>
  </fo:inline>
</xsl:template>

<!-- Font-variant property here to set all-caps for acronyms. -->
<xsl:template match="acronym">
  <fo:inline font-variant="small-caps">
    <xsl:apply-templates/>
  </fo:inline>
</xsl:template>

</xsl:stylesheet>
```

## Results

As a source document, I chose to revisit Example 3-6. It's long enough to span several pages and contains some complex objects, such as tables, lists, and footnotes. And as a bonus, it includes chapters and sections with titles that need to be differentiated stylistically.

Figure 8-11 is a screenshot of a page with a variety of block and inline areas. There is a section head on the top left, an inline style on the top right, a program listing on the bottom, and a paragraph in the middle. The paragraph contains a footnote marker.

Figure 8-12 shows the bottom of the same page. At the top of the screenshot is the body of the footnote previously mentioned. It is at the bottom of the body flow. Under it is the static flow area of the footer, which contains a generated page number and the chapter title.

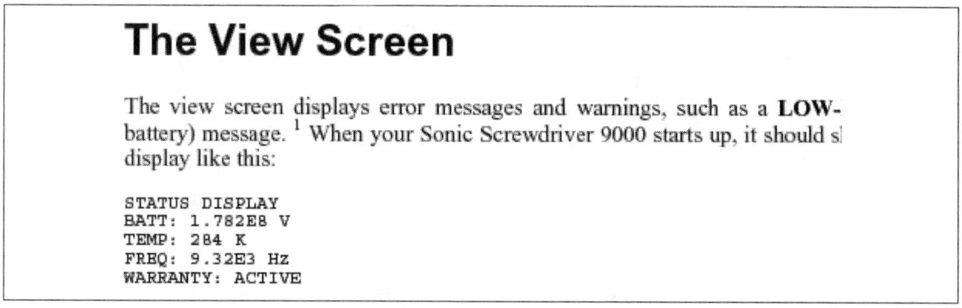

## The View Screen

The view screen displays error messages and warnings, such as a **LOW-battery) message. [1]** When your Sonic Screwdriver 9000 starts up, it should s| display like this:

```
STATUS DISPLAY
BATT: 1.782E8 V
TEMP: 284 K
FREQ: 9.32E3 Hz
WARRANTY: ACTIVE
```

*Figure 8-11. A screenshot of the middle of the page*

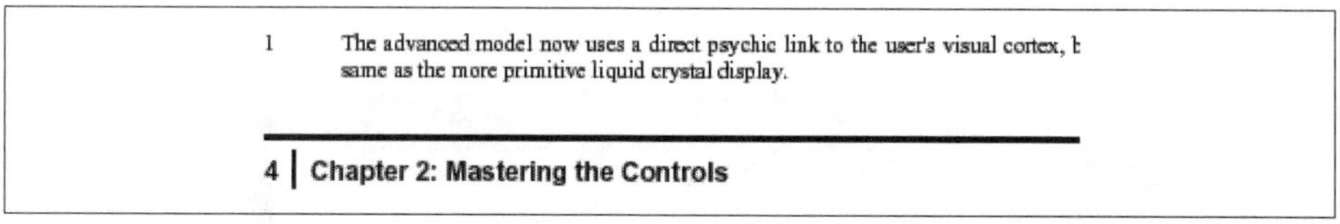

[1]    The advanced model now uses a direct psychic link to the user's visual cortex, b
same as the more primitive liquid crystal display.

**4 | Chapter 2: Mastering the Controls**

*Figure 8-12. A screenshot of a footer*

In Figure 8-13 we see a close-up of a table. The table header area is shaded gray with bold text.

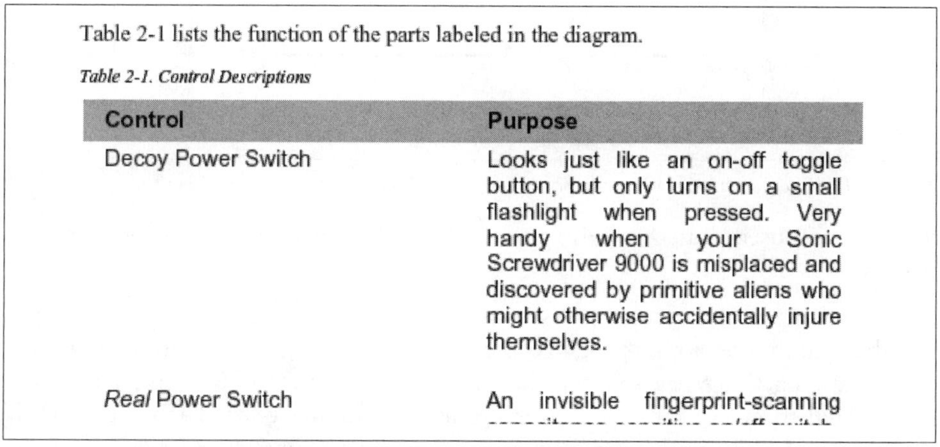

Table 2-1 lists the function of the parts labeled in the diagram.

*Table 2-1. Control Descriptions*

| Control | Purpose |
|---------|---------|
| Decoy Power Switch | Looks just like an on-off toggle button, but only turns on a small flashlight when pressed. Very handy when your Sonic Screwdriver 9000 is misplaced and discovered by primitive aliens who might otherwise accidentally injure themselves. |
| *Real* Power Switch | An invisible fingerprint-scanning |

*Figure 8-13. A screenshot of a table*

Finally, a view of a whole page appears in Figure 8-14. Of note here are the chapter opener header, a bulleted list, and a comment in italic.

Overall, my experience with XSL-FO was very positive. I found it easy to learn and 95% of the things I wanted to do were straightforward. A few irritating wrinkles arose because the formatter I used, FOP, is still a beta version and is missing some functionality. For example, I could not figure out how to get Roman numerals for the page number references in the preface. Tables are limited to fixed-width format in

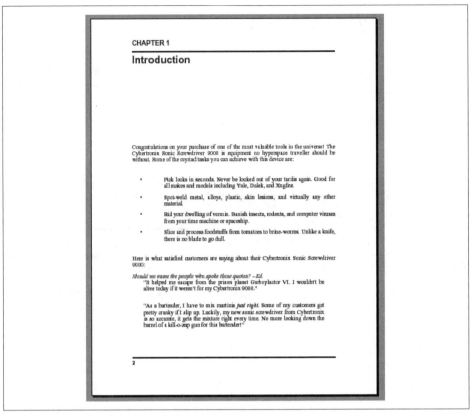

*Figure 8-14. A screenshot of the whole page*

the version I used, but this is documented and I'm prepared to accept it for my purposes.

For a free system, I'm quite impressed with FOP. I cannot recommend it to companies that want professional-quality typesetting yet, but it's good for turning my XML copy into something readable with a reasonably accurate page count. I certainly expect FOP to evolve into a stronger product in coming years. High-end systems have more complete implementation as well as technical support and nice GUI interfaces. Of course, those advantages come at a price.

# Internationalization

XML was built from the ground up to support information in many different languages. While you and your application may not understand markup and content in foreign languages, XML makes certain that XML-compliant tools let more of the world work in and share information created in whatever language they want.

## Character Encodings

Throughout the book, I have treated characters as a sort of commodity, just something used to fill up documents. But understanding characters and how they are represented in documents is of great importance in XML. After all, characters are both the building material for markup and the cargo it was meant to carry.

Every XML document has a character encoding property. I'll give you a quick explanation now and a more complete description later. In a nutshell, it is the way the numerical values in files and streams are transformed into the symbols that you see on the screen. Encodings come in many different kinds, reflecting the cultural diversity of users, the capabilities of systems, and the inevitable cycle of progress and obsolescence.

Character encodings are probably the most confusing topic in the study of XML. Partly, this is because of a glut of acronyms and confusing names: UTF-8, UCS-4, Shift-JIS, and ISO-8859-1-Windows-3.1-Latin-1, to name a few. Also hampering our efforts to understand is the interchangeability of incompatible terms. Sometimes a character encoding is called a set, as in the MIME standard, which is incorrect and misleading.

In this section, I will try to explain the terms and concepts clearly, and describe some of the common character encodings in use by XML authors.

## Specifying an Encoding

If you choose to experiment with the character encoding for your document, you will need to specify it in the XML declaration. For example:

```
<?xml version="1.0" encoding="encoding-name"?>
```

*encoding-name* is a registered string corresponding to a formal character encoding. No distinction is made between uppercase and lowercase letters, but spaces are disallowed (use hyphens instead). Some examples are UTF-16, ISO-8859-1, and Shift_JIS.

A comprehensive list of encoding names is maintained by the Internet Assigned Numbers Authority (IANA), available on the Web at *http://www.iana.org/ assignments/character-sets*. Many of these encoding names have aliases. The aliases for US-ASCII include ASCII, US-ASCII, and ISO646-US.

If you do not explicitly state otherwise, the parser will assume your encoding is UTF-8, unless it can determine the encoding another way. Sometimes a file will contain a *byte order mark* (BOM), a hidden piece of information in the file inserted by software that generated it. The XML processor can use a BOM to determine which character encoding to use, such as UTF-16. Every XML processor is required to support both UTF-8 and UTF-16. Other encodings are optional, so you enter that territory at your own risk.

## Basic Concepts

The atomic unit of information in XML is the character. A character can be a visible symbol, such as the letters on this page, or a formatting code, like the ones that force space between words and separate lines in paragraphs. It may come from a Latin script or Greek, Thai, or Japanese. It may be a dingbat or punctuation mark. Most generally, a character is any symbol, with possibly different representations, whose meaning is understood by a community of people.

Every character belongs to a finite, ordered list called a *character set* (also called a *coded character set*). It is really not a set in the mathematical sense, but more of a sequence or table. Perhaps the best description, according to Dan Connolly in his article "Character Set Considered Harmful,"* is to think of it as "a function whose domain is a subset of the integers, and whose range is a set of characters." In other words, give the function a positive integer, or *code position*, and it will give you back a character from that place in its *character repertoire*.

The earliest character set in common use is the American Standard Code for Information Interchange (US-ASCII), also known as ISO-646. It contains just 128 characters, listed in Figure 9-1.

---

* Read it on the Web at *http://www.w3.org/MarkUp/html-spec/charset-harmful.html*.

---

| 00 NUL 0 | 01 SOH 1 | 02 STX 2 | 03 ETX 3 | 04 EOT 4 | 05 ENQ 5 | 06 ACK 6 | 07 BEL 7 |
|---|---|---|---|---|---|---|---|
| 08 BS 8 | 09 TAB 9 | 0A LF 10 | 0B VTB 11 | 0C FF 12 | 0D CR 13 | 0E SO 14 | 0F SI 15 |
| 10 DLE 16 | 11 DC1 17 | 11 DC2 18 | 13 DC3 19 | 14 DC4 20 | 15 NAK 21 | 16 SYN 22 | 17 ETB 23 |
| 18 CAN 24 | 19 EM 25 | 1A SUB 26 | 1B ESC 27 | 1C IS4 28 | 1D IS3 29 | 1E IS2 30 | 1F IS1 31 |
| 20 SP 32 | 21 ! 33 | 22 " 34 | 23 # 35 | 24 $ 36 | 25 % 37 | 26 & 38 | 27 ' 39 |
| 28 ( 40 | 29 ) 41 | 2A * 42 | 2B + 43 | 2C , 44 | 2D - 45 | 2E . 46 | 2F / 47 |
| 30 0 48 | 31 1 49 | 32 2 50 | 33 3 51 | 34 4 52 | 35 5 53 | 36 6 54 | 37 7 55 |
| 38 8 56 | 39 9 57 | 3A : 58 | 3B ; 59 | 3C < 60 | 3D = 61 | 3E > 62 | 3F ? 63 |
| 40 @ 64 | 41 A 65 | 42 B 66 | 43 C 67 | 44 D 68 | 45 E 69 | 46 F 70 | 47 G 71 |
| 48 H 72 | 49 I 73 | 4A J 74 | 4B K 75 | 4C L 76 | 4D M 77 | 4E N 78 | 4F O 79 |
| 50 P 80 | 51 Q 81 | 52 R 82 | 53 S 83 | 54 T 84 | 55 U 85 | 56 V 86 | 57 W 87 |
| 58 X 88 | 59 Y 89 | 5A Z 90 | 5B [ 91 | 5C \ 92 | 5D ] 93 | 5E ^ 94 | 5F _ 95 |
| 60 ` 96 | 61 a 97 | 62 b 98 | 63 c 99 | 64 d 100 | 65 e 101 | 66 f 102 | 67 g 103 |
| 68 h 104 | 69 i 105 | 6A j 106 | 6B k 107 | 6C l 108 | 6D m 109 | 6E n 110 | 6F o 111 |
| 70 p 112 | 71 q 113 | 72 r 114 | 73 s 115 | 74 t 116 | 75 u 117 | 76 v 118 | 77 w 119 |
| 78 x 120 | 79 y 121 | 7A z 122 | 7B { 123 | 7C \| 124 | 7D } 125 | 7E ~ 126 | 7F DEL 127 |

*Figure 9-1. The US-ASCII character set*

The first 32 codes are for control characters, invoking some action from the device, such as CR (carriage return: originally, it used to make the print head on a teletype return to its leftmost position) and BEL (bell: used to make a "ding" noise in the terminal). Today, many of the meanings behind these codes are somewhat ambiguous, since the devices have changed.

The rest of the characters produce some kind of visible shape called a *glyph*. These include uppercase and lowercase versions of the latin alphabet, plus an assortment of punctuation, digits, and other typographical conveniences.

If you think of US-ASCII as a function, its domain is the set of integers from 0 to 127. Plug in the hexadecimal numbers 48, 65, 6C, 6C, 6F, and 21, and you will get the string "Hello!" back. You might think that this is how all electronic documents are represented. In truth, however, it is usually more complex than that.

The *character encoding* for a document is the scheme by which characters are derived from the numerical values in its underlying form. An encoding scheme is a function that maps sequences of positive integers to a subset of a character set's repertoire. The input sequence may or may not have anything to do with the actual code position. Quite often, an algorithm must be applied to arrive at an actual code position.

The need for encodings becomes clear when you consider the vast gulf between character sets and the requirements of devices and protocols. Character sets range from tiny, 7-bit ASCII to huge, 32-bit Unicode. Devices and protocols may not be flexible enough to handle this wide variation.

Internet protocols historically have been defined in terms of 8-bit characters, or *octets*. ISO-646, which is based on the 7-bit ASCII character code, is designed for 8-bit systems, recommending that the eighth bit be set to zero. This encoding is just a simple way of making 7 bits seem like 8 bits.

Mail transport systems such as the simple mail transfer protocol (SMTP) have a restriction of 7 bits per character. Binary files such as compiled executables have to be encoded such that only the lower 7 bits per byte are used. 8-bit character sets also have to be encoded specially so they don't confuse the email transport agent. The Unix program uuencode, for example, turns any binary file into an ASCII string that looks like gibberish, but can be turned back into the original binary format later.

Large character sets such as Unicode are a sticky problem for legacy programs that were programmed for 8-bit character sets. Some encodings, such as UTF-8, repackage 16-bit and 32-bit characters as strings of octets so that they can be handled safely with older programs. These characters may not be rendered correctly, but at least they will pass through unmolested, and without crashing the software. For example, the text editor I like to use on my documents is Emacs. Emacs does not understand Unicode yet, but it can open and edit UTF-8 encoded files, and treat the unknown high characters in a way that I can see and work around.

## Unicode and UCS

Compared to most other alphabets and scripts around the world, the English alphabet is extremely compact. While it may be suitable for English speakers, it lacks too many pieces for use with other languages. Most languages based on the Latin alphabet use ligatures and accents not found in ASCII. And Latin is just a minority among the many writing systems around the world.

Many attempts to accommodate other alphabets simply packed new characters into the unused 128 characters from the extra bit in 8-bit ASCII. Extensions specializing in everything from Greek to Icelandic appeared. Computer manufacturers also made up their own versions of 8-bit character sets. The result was a huge number of specialty character sets. Many of these have been standardized, such as ISO 8859, which includes character sets like the popular ISO Latin-1, Cyrillic, Arabic, Hebrew, and others.

One critical flaw in using specialty character sets is how to include characters from different sets in the same document. A hackish solution is to use *code switching*, a technique of replacing a byte with a sequence of bytes headed by a special control character. Thus, you could switch between character sets as necessary and still maintain the 8-bit character stream. Although it worked okay, it was not an ideal solution.

By the late 1980s, pressure was building to create a 16-bit character set that included all the writing systems into one superset. In 1991, the Unicode Consortium began work on the ambitious Unicode character set. With 16 bits per code position, it had space for $2^{16} = 65,536$ characters. The first 256 characters were patterned after ISO 8859-1 (ISO Latin-1), of which the first 128 are ASCII. The Unicode Consortium publishes the specification in a weighty tome with pictures of every glyph and extensive annotations.

Whereas Western languages tend to be alphabetic, composing words in sequences of characters, many Eastern languages represent entire words and ideas as single pictures, or *ideographs*. Since there are many more concepts than sounds in a language, the number of ideographs tends to run in the thousands. Three scripts, Chinese, Japanese, and Korean, have some overlapping glyphs. By throwing out the redundancies and combining them in one unified ideographic system (often called CJK for the initials of each language), their number was reduced to the point where it was practical to add them to Unicode.

This is often cited as one of the critical flaws of Unicode. Although it is fairly comprehensive in including the most used glyphs, the way it combines different systems together makes it very inconvenient for constructing a Unicode font, or to divide it into useful contiguous subsets. An ideograph found in both Chinese and Japanese should really be represented as two different characters, each keeping with the styling of the uniquely Chinese or Japanese characters. Furthermore, even though over 20,000 Han ideographs found a place in Unicode, this is still just a fraction of the total. There are still 60,000 that didn't make the cut.

Meanwhile, ISO had also been working to develop a multilingual character set. Called the Universal Multiple-Octet Coded Character Set (UCS), or ISO/IEC 10646-1, it was based on a 31-bit character, providing for over 2 billion characters. That is certainly enough to hold all the glyphs and symbols the human race has developed since a person first got the urge to scribble.

Quickly realizing the redundancy of their projects, the Unicode Consortium and ISO got together to figure out how to pool their work. UCS, being the larger of the two, simply made Unicode a subset. Today, both groups publish independent specifications, but they are totally compatible.

Some terminology helps to divide the vast space of UCS. A *row* is 256 characters. Wherever possible, an 8-bit character set is stuffed into a single row. For example, ISO Latin-1 inhabits the first row (positions 0x0000 to 0x00FF).[*] 256 rows (65,534 characters) is called a *plane*. Most of Unicode lives in the first plane (0x0000 to 0xFFFD), also called the Basic Multilingual Plane (BMP), though recent versions have moved beyond that set.

UCS/Unicode assigns to each character in the BMP a code number, which is the string "U+" and four hexadecimal numbers, and a formal name. The number for "A" is U+0041 and its name is "Latin capital letter A." In ASCII, it would be 0x41, and the same in ISO Latin-1. Converting between these character sets is not difficult once you know the base number in UCS.

In addition to defining the character ordering, the Unicode Standard includes semantics related to issues such as sorting, string comparison, handling leftward and rightward scripts, and mixing together bidirectional scripts. UCS, in contrast, is not much more than a big table. The Unicode Consortium's web page (*http://www.unicode.org/* ) has a wealth of resources including character tables, an FAQ, and descriptions of related technologies.

In the decade it has been around Unicode managed to attract enough favorable attention to become a necessary component in the Internet. Most operating systems ship with some support for Unicode, including extensive font sets and Unicode-cognizant web browsers and editing tools. Most programming languages in use today support Unicode. Java was designed from the start with Unicode support. Others, like Perl, added support later. And, most important for readers of this book, Unicode is the standard character set for XML.

## Common Encodings

When choosing a character encoding for your document, you must consider several things. Do the constraints of your authoring environment require an 8-bit encoding

---

[*] The syntax 0xNNNN is used to represent a hexadecimal number. This is a base-16 system convenient for representing integers in systems based on powers of 2. It's more convenient than decimal because it can be easily divided by powers of 2 merely by shifting the decimal point. Since character encoding domains are frequently based on powers of 2, I will frequently use hexadecimal numbers to describe code positions.

or can you move up to 16-bits or higher? Do you really need the high characters of Unicode or can you live with the limitations of a smaller set like ISO Latin-1? Do you have the fonts to support your encoding's character repertoire? Does it support the byte order of your operating system? In this section, I will present a few of the more common character encodings available and attempt to answer these questions for each.

## ISO 8859

ISO 8859 is a collection of 8-bit character encodings developed in the late 1980s. It includes ISO 8859-1 (Latin 1), the most common character encoding used on Unix systems today. Table 9-1 lists encodings in this specification.

*Table 9-1. ISO character encodings*

| Encoding | Character set |
| --- | --- |
| ISO 8859-2 | Latin 2 (Central European characters) |
| ISO 8859-4 | Latin 4 (Baltic languages) |
| ISO 8859-5 | Cyrillic |
| ISO 8859-6 | Arabic |
| ISO 8859-7 | Greek |
| ISO 8859-8 | Hebrew |
| ISO 8859-9 | Latin 5 |
| ISO 8859-14 | Celtic |

ISO 8859-1 is a popular choice for documents because it is contains most European characters and, because it is a straight 8-bit mapping, it is compatible with a wide range of legacy software. If you suspect that your software is rejecting your document because of the default UTF-8 encoding, try setting the encoding to Latin 1. Then, if you need to use special symbols or high characters, you can insert them with character entity references. IANA-registered encoding names for ISO Latin-1 include ISO-8859-1 (the preferred MIME name), latin1, and l1.

A variant of Latin 1 is ISO-8859-1-Windows-3.1-Latin-1. This is the encoding used by U.S. and Western European versions of Microsoft Windows. It's almost the same as ISO 8859-1, but adds some useful punctuation in an area reserved for control characters in the ISO character sets. This encoding is also known as codepage 1252, but that's not a registered encoding name.

## UCS-2 and UCS-4

A straight mapping of 16-bit Unicode is UCS-2. Every character occupies two bytes in the document. Likewise, 32-bit UCS is represented by the encoding UCS-4 and requires four bytes per character. Since Unicode and UCS are just big code tables assigning integers to characters, it is not difficult to understand these encoding schemes. You can convert a US-ASCII or Latin-1 file into UCS-2 simply by adding a 0x00 byte in front of every ASCII byte. Make that three 0x00 bytes to convert to UCS-4.

UCS-2 and UCS-4 have issues about byte ordering. On some systems, including Intel and VAX architectures, multibyte numbers are stored least significant byte first. The number 0x1234 would be stored as 0x34 followed by 0x12. This is called a *little-endian* architecture. In contrast, many Unix systems such as Solaris put the most significant byte first, which is called *big-endian* architecture.

UCS-2 and UCS-4 generally follow the big-endian convention. As a developer this is very important to know, because software written for a little-endian system will need to transpose adjacent bytes as it reads them into memory. As a user, you only need to know if your software is aware of UCS-2 or UCS-4, and you can trust that it will be handled correctly.

On some systems (namely, Win32), every Unicode file starts with the a special character known as the byte order mark (BOM), with the value U+FEFF. This is the zero-width, no-break space character, which is typically invisible and so will not change the appearance of your document. However, it helps to disambiguate whether the encoding is big-endian or little-endian. Transpose the bytes and you will get U+FFFE, which is not a valid Unicode character. This simple test gives a quick and automatic way to determine the endian-ness of the file.

UCS-2 and UCS-4 (and even UTF-16) have not been that widely deployed because, for Western alphabets, where most characters can be encoded within 8-bits, it effectively doubles the size of every file.

Another, and perhaps more worrisome, reason is that most software was written to handle text with one-byte characters. Running these programs on multibyte characters can have unpredictable, even dangerous, results. Most low-level routines in Unix are written in C and read 8-bit char datatypes. Certain bytes have special meaning, such as / in filenames and \0 as a stream terminator. When the program reads in a wide UCS character as a sequence of bytes, one of those bytes may map to a control character and then who knows what could happen.

A better alternative is an encoding that passes through 8-bit systems unmolested, yet retains the information of Unicode high characters. Both of these requirements are satisfied by UTF-8.

## UTF-8

The UCS Transformation Format for 8-bits (UTF-8) was developed by the X/Open Joint Internationalization Group (XOJIG) in 1992 and later included in both the Unicode and UCS standards. It is particularly important to us because it is the default character encoding for XML documents. If you do not set the character encoding in the XML declaration explicitly, XML parsers are supposed to assume the document is encoded with UTF-8.[*]

The main attraction of UTF-8 is that it allows Unicode characters to be included in documents without posing any danger to legacy text handling software. It was originally called UTF-FSS (UTF File System Safe), because it was designed with the sensitivity of Unix file system utilities in mind. Recall from the last section that wide 2-byte and 4-byte characters from UCS-2 and UCS-4 pose a risk because they may be decomposed into bytes that resemble reserved characters.

UTF-8 encoded text uses variable-length strings of bytes to represent each Unicode/UCS character. The first byte describes the type of byte sequence. If its value is between 0x0000 and 0x007F (0 through 127), then it will be interpreted as an ASCII character. Files and strings containing only 7-bit ASCII characters have the same encoding under US-ASCII and UTF-8.

If the first byte is 0x0080 or greater, a number of bytes following it will be used to determine the Unicode/UCS character. Table 9-2 shows the encoding algorithm for UCS. (The algorithm is the same for Unicode if you substitute 2-byte code positions, but only the first four rows in the table apply.) I use the binary representation of UTF-8 byte strings to show how certain bits are used to pad the bytes. The "xxx" portion is to be filled with bits of the character code number when converted to binary, and the rightmost bit is the least significant.

*Table 9-2. UTF-8 Encoding Algorithm for UCS*

| UCS character number | UTF-8 byte string (in binary) |
| --- | --- |
| U-00000000 – U-0000007F | 0xxxxxxx |
| U-00000080 – U-000007FF | 110xxxxx 10xxxxxx |
| U-00000800 – U-0000FFFF | 1110xxxx 10xxxxxx 10xxxxxx |
| U-00010000 – U-001FFFFF | 11110xxx 10xxxxxx 10xxxxxx 10xxxxxx |
| U-00200000 – U-03FFFFFF | 111110xx 10xxxxxx 10xxxxxx 10xxxxxx 10xxxxxx |
| U-04000000 – U-7FFFFFFF | 1111110x 10xxxxxx 10xxxxxx 10xxxxxx 10xxxxxx 10xxxxxx |

To encode the Unicode character 0+x03C0 (the Greek small letter pi), first compose it in binary: 0011 1100 0000. We select the second row from the table and pack the bits into "x" slots to get, in binary: 11001111 10000000. So the byte sequence in UTF-8 for this character is 0xCF 0x80.

You can see from this algorithm that the only time a byte sequence contains bytes with values between 0x00 and 0x7F is when they are one byte in length and represent the ASCII characters with those code positions. Other byte sequences range

[*] see RFC 2279

from 0xC0 to 0xFD for the first byte, and from 0x80 to 0xBF in following bytes. Keeping the first and following bytes in different ranges makes allows for error detection and easy resynchronization in the event of missing bytes during a transmission.

UTF-8 encoding is optimized for common Western characters. The lower a character's position in the Unicode/UCS pool, the shorter its encoded string of bytes. While UTF-8 characters can theoretically be as long as 6 bytes, those in the BMP portion of UCS will be at most 3 bytes long. Many European scripts will be just 2 bytes in length, and all ASCII characters only 1 byte. If there is any disadvantage to using UTF-8, it is that non-Western scripts are penalized with longer characters and increased document size.

### UTF-16

UTF-16 is closely related to UTF-8, using a similar transformation algorithm to get from Unicode positions to numeric sequences. In this case, the sequences consist of 16-bit integers, not bytes. As with UCS-2 and UCS-4, byte is an issue you have to take into account. Some systems will use a BOM (byte order mark) and be able to detect byte order automatically. You can also explicitly select a byte order by using the more specific encoding name UTF-16LE (low-endian) or UTF-16BE (big-endian).

This encoding is one of the two required encodings all proper XML parsers must support. In reality, a few handle UTF-8 but not UTF-16, as 16-bit support for characters is not yet a universal feature in programming languages. Perl, for example, is moving that way but some legacy parsers still are not there.

This concludes my list of most common encodings used in XML documents. There are literally hundreds more, but they are either beyond the scope of this book or only of esoteric value. In case you are interested in researching this topic more, I will include some resources in Appendix A for you to follow.

## Character References

Although Unicode puts a vast range of characters in one place for authors to use, many XML editing software packages do not offer a convenient way to access those characters. Recognizing that this difficulty could hurt its adoption, the designers of XML have included a convenient mechanism for placing Unicode characters in a document. Character entity references (also called character references) that incorporate the character number in their names stand in for those characters and do not need to be declared beforehand.

There are two forms, based on decimal and hexadecimal representations of the code position. The decimal character reference uses the form &#n;, where n is the decimal position of the character in Unicode. The hexadecimal variation has the form &#xNNNN;, where NNNN is a hexadecimal value for the position of the Unicode character. For example, the Greek small letter pi can be represented in XML as &#960; or as

&#x3C0;. In general, you may find the hexadecimal version to be more useful. Unicode specifications always give character code positions in hexadecimal.

The problem with numerical character references like these is that they are hard to remember. You have to keep looking them up in a table, cluttering your workspace, and generally going mad in the process. A better idea might be to use named entity references, such as those defined in ISO 8879.

This specification defines a few hundred useful entity declarations divided by knowledge area into a handful of files. For each character, there is a declaration for a general entity with an intuitive name. Here are a few of the defined characters:

| Description | Unicode character | Entity name |
| --- | --- | --- |
| Latin small letter "a" with breve accent | U+0103 | abreve |
| Planck constant over two pi | U+210F | planck |
| Yen sign | U+00A5 | yen |

To use named entity references in your document, you need to obtain the entity declarations and either import them through the internal subset of your document, or import them into your DTD. I got a set when I downloaded DocBook-XML from the OASIS web site (thanks to DocBook maintainer Norm Walsh for creating an XML version of ISO 8879).

# MIME and Media Types

The Multipurpose Internet Mail Extensions (MIME) standard is a means of specifying media types such as images, program data, audio files, and text. Described in Internet Engineering Task Force (IETF) Request for Comments (RFC) documents 2045 through 2049, it includes a comprehensive list of known types and has inspired a registry for many more.

MIME was developed originally to extend the paradigm of email from plain text to a rich array of media. Email transport systems, such as the Simple Mail Transfer Protocol (SMTP), can only deal with 7-bit ASCII text. You cannot simply append a binary file to the end of a message and have it bounce happily across the Internet. The data has to be encoded in an ASCII-compatible way. There are other requirements as well, such as a minimum line length and absence of certain control characters. MIME introduces methods to transform data into a safe form. It also describes how to package this data in a recognizable way for mail transfer agents and clients to work with.

One of the ways MIME describes a resource is by assigning it a *media type* (or *content-type*) which names the general category that best describes the data. Each type includes a set of subtypes that exactly identify the resource. The type and subtype are usually written together, joined by a slash character (/). For example, `image/jpeg` denotes a graphical resource in the JPEG format. The major types include:

*text*

> Textual information that can be read in a traditional text editor without any special processing. `text/plain` is as simple as you can get: just ASCII characters without any kind of formatting other than whitespace.

*image*

> Graphical data requiring some display device such as a printer or display terminal. `image/gif` is a popular image subtype on the Web.

*audio*

> Sound data requiring an audio output device such as a speaker to reproduce. `audio/wav` is one common example.

*video*

> Animated graphical data requiring a viewing device, such as the movie format `video/mpeg`.

*application*

> Some undetermined kind of data. It may be a binary format, or else requiring some processing to be useful. A good example is `application/PostScript` which looks like dense program code until sent to a printer. Uninterpreted binary data is labeled `application/octet-stream`, a grab bag for unknown types.

*multipart*

> More of a meta-type, really, it packages up a group of possibly unrelated resources. Subtypes like `multipart/mixed` and `multipart/parallel` describe how to present the resources (e.g., positioned together on a screen).

*message*

> Another meta-type that packages resources. In this case, the resources all pertain to a single message object, presumably adding up to a single communicative package.

You can see that MIME tackles a huge problem in attempting to label every conceivable kind of data that could be transmitted over a network. It works well because of a well-publicized registry of media types maintained by the Internet Assigned Numbers Authority (IANA). You can see the latest list at *http://www.iana.org/assignments/media-types/index.html*.

MIME content types are important in many areas outside of email. General-purpose *MIME dispatchers* analyze a document as it appears and routes it to the correct media handler. For example, web browsers rely on HTTP headers to tell them what kind of data is arriving. The following HTTP content type field tells us that the incoming resource is text and should be handled as HTML:

```
Content-Type: text/html; charset=ISO-8859-1
```

The charset portion is optional and actually means "character encoding" (another case of confusing terms). This is another mechanism, besides XML declarations, for specifying a character encoding.

In XML, too, there are cases in which MIME is useful. For example, in linking with XPointers, it would be helpful to the XML processor to know in advance what resource is being imported. Another example is specifying a stylesheet in a document:

```
<?xml-stylesheet type="text/css" href="ex2_memo.css"?>
```

Here, the type attribute is set to a MIME content type for CSS stylesheets.

As XML rises in prominence as an exchange medium on the Internet, the need for media types that identify XML-related data grows. A recent specification, RFC 3023, adds a few new XML-related media types to the mix and a way to extend other media types to include a "+xml" suffix. For example, you can make the type image/svg more descriptive by adding the tag to make it image/svg+xml. A system that recognizes and treats XML data specially will benefit from that extra information. The new media types are:

text/xml

> This is your basic XML document with no special processing requested. The recipient is expected to know what to do with the data. (Some developers would like to see text/xml deprecated in favor of application/xml, as XML doesn't precisely fit IETF expectations for the text top-level type.)

application/xml

> This is an XML document that requires some preparation before it is useful for viewing. Some indication of what application to use will be included. The recipient might look inside the document for a DOCTYPE declaration, for example.

text/xml-external-parsed-entity, application/xml-external-parsed-entity

> Like the above, but not necessarily a complete document. The recipient will have to assemble the entities into a complete package before parsing the document. (Like text/xml, some developers want text/xml-external-parse-entity deprecated.)

application/xml-dtd

> The item is a document type definition (DTD), and not an actual XML document. In some cases, it may be useful to supply a DTD in addition to the document to help out the XML processor.

# Specifying Human Languages

Specifying a character encoding is crucial for correctly processing and displaying an XML document in a multilingual world. But there is a higher level to address than just the symbols on the page. Different languages may use the same characters. If a document is encoded with UTF-8, how can you know if it is speaking Vietnamese or Italian?

You may wonder why it matters if software should handle all documents the same way no matter what the language. The push for globalization is not a dream shared by everybody. Sure, we all want equal access to resources, but we would also like to keep our uniqueness intact. So many developers would love a way to know in advance what language a reader prefers to use, and have some automatic means to serve that preference.

XML and many related standards have included some devices to allow special handling based on language. You can use labels to create variations on a document and to customize its appearance and behavior. I will describe a few of the important mechanisms in this section.

## The xml:lang Attribute and Language Codes

XML defines the attribute xml:lang as a language label for any element. There is no official action that an XML processor must take when encountering this attribute, but we can imagine some future applications. For example, search engines could be designed to pay attention to the language of a document and use it to categorize its entries. The search interface could then provide a menu for languages to include or exclude in a search. Another use for xml:lang might be to combine several versions of a text in one document, each version labeled with a different language. A web browser could be set to ignore all but a particular language, filtering the document so that it displays only what the reader wants. Or, if you're writing a book that includes text in different languages, you could configure your spellchecker to use a different dictionary for each version.

The attribute's value is a string containing a two-letter language code, like so:

```
xml:lang="en"
```

The code "en" stands for English. The language codes, standardized in ISO-639, are case-insensitive, so there are $26^2 = 676$ possible codes. Three-letter codes are also specified, but XML only recognizes two-letter codes; this could be a problem in a world with thousands of different languages, dialects, and subdialects.

Fortunately, we can also specify a language variant using a *qualifier*, like this:

```
xml:lang="en-US"
```

This refers to the American variant of English. By convention, we usually write the language code in lowercase and the qualifier in uppercase. Now we can separate different kinds of English like so:

```
<para xml:lang="en-US">Please consult the program.</para>
<para xml:lang="en-GB">Please consult the programme.</para>
```

If for some reason you need to define your own language, you can do so by using the language code x. Some examples could include: x-pascal, x-java, x-martian, and x-babytalk.

## Language Support in Stylesheets

CSS and XSLT both have tests that let you specify different behaviors depending on the language of your audience. For example, your document may contain an element that renders as a note with a stylesheet-generated title "CAUTION." In a German translation, you may want it to say "VORSICHT" instead. The following sections describe how this conditional behavior can be implemented.

### CSS and the :lang( ) pseudo-class

Cascading Style Sheets Level 2 includes a pseudo-class for adding language options to a stylesheet. It determines the language from the xml:lang attribute or from the encoding attribute from the XML declaration. For example, the following rule changes the color of French phrase elements to red:

```
phrase:lang(fr) { color: 'red'; }
```

### XSLT and the lang( ) function

XSLT also pays attention to language. In Chapter 7, we discussed Boolean functions and their roles in conditional template rules. One important function is lang( ), whose value is true if the current node's language is the same as that of the argument. Consider the following template:

```
<xsl:template match="para">
  <xsl:choose>
    <xsl:when test="lang('de')">
      <h1>ACHTUNG</h1>
      <xsl:apply-templates/>
    </if>
    <xsl:otherwise>
      <h1>ATTENTION</h1>
      <xsl:apply-templates/>
    </xsl:otherwise>
  </xsl:template>
```

The XSLT template rule outputs the word "ACHTUNG" if the language is de, or "ATTENTION" otherwise. Let's apply this rule to the following input tree:

```
<warning xml:lang="de">
  <para>Bitte, kein rauchen.</para>
</warning>
```

The para inherits its language property from the warning that contains it, and the first choice in the template rule will be used.

# Programming

XML was designed to bridge the gap between humans and computers, making data easily grappled by both. If you aren't able to find an existing application to take care of your XML needs, you may find writing your own a good option.

XML has great possibilities for programmers. It is well suited to being read, written, and altered by software. Its syntax is straightforward and easy to parse. It has rules for being well-formed that reduce the amount of software error checking and exception handling required. It's well documented, and there are many tools and code libraries available for developers in just about every programming language. And as an open standard accepted by financial institutions and open source hackers alike, with support from virtually every popular programming language, XML stands a good chance of becoming the lingua franca for computer communications.

We begin the chapter by examining the issues around working with XML from a developer's point of view. From there, we move to common coding strategies and best practices. The two main methods, event streams and object trees, will be described. And finally, we visit the two reigning standards in XML programming: SAX and DOM. I will include examples in Java and Perl, my two favorite programming environments, both of which have excellent support for XML wrangling.

## Limitations

Like any good technology, XML does not try to be the solution to every problem. There are some things it just cannot do well, and it would be foolish to try to force it to do them. The foremost requirement of XML is that it be universally accessible, a lowest common denominator for applications. This necessarily throws out many optimizations that are necessary in some situations.

Let's review some of these limitations:

- XML is not optimized for access speed. XML documents are meant to be completely loaded, and *then* used as a data source. The parser is required to do a syntax check every time it reads in the markup. In contrast, modern databases are optimized for quick data lookups and updates.

- XML is not compact. There is no official scheme for compressing XML. XML parsers expect uncompressed text. You either have to put up with large text files, or you have to create a complex mechanism for compressing and decompressing on the fly, which will add to your processing overhead. Most proprietary applications, like Microsoft Word and Adobe FrameMaker, save data in a binary format by default, saving disk space and perhaps speeding up file transfers. (HTTP offers compression for transmission, which helps reduce this cost.)

- Many kinds of data are not suited for embedded markup. XML is most useful for text data with a hierarchical structure. It does not offer much for binary data. For example, raster graphic images are long streams of binary data, unreadable to anyone until passed through a graphic viewing program. This binary data may contain dangerous characters that would need to be escaped. Binary data is optimized for size and speed of loading, two qualities that would be hindered by XML.

- XML may raise expectations too high. Quite often, software vendors tout XML support as a great new feature in their product, only to disappoint users with poor implementation. For example, the early version of Adobe FrameMaker's XML export capability was nearly unusable, as much of the data was structured badly, was missing information, changed figure filenames, and so on. Instead of viewing it as a magic bullet, developers should approach XML as a framework in which intelligent design focusing on the quality of markup structures can achieve magnificent results.

# Streams and Events

The stream approach treats XML content as a pipeline. As it rushes past, you have one chance to work with it, no look-ahead or look-behind. It is fast and efficient, allowing you to work with enormous files in a short time, but depends on simple markup that closely follows the order of processing.

In programming jargon, a *stream* is a sequence of data chunks to be processed. A file, for example, is a sequence of characters (one or more bytes each, depending on the encoding). A program using this data can open a filehandle to the file, creating a character stream, and it can choose to read in data in chunks of whatever size it chooses. Streams can be dynamically generated too, whether from another program, received over a network, or typed in by a user. A stream is an abstraction, making the source of the data irrelevant for the purpose of processing.

To summarize, here are a stream's important qualities:

- It consists of a sequence of data fragments.
- The order of fragments transmitted is significant.
- The source of data (e.g., file or program output) is not important.

XML streams are more clumpy than character streams, which are just long sequences of characters. An XML stream emits a series of tokens or *events*, signals that denote changes in markup status. For example, an element has at least three events associated with it: the start tag, the content, and the end tag. The XML stream is constructed as it is read, so events happen in lexical order. The content of an element will always come after the start tag, and the end tag will follow that.

Parsers can assemble this kind of stream very quickly and efficiently thanks to XML's parser-friendly design. Other formats often require some look-ahead or complex lookup tables before processing can begin. For example, SGML does not have a rule requiring nonempty elements to have an end tag. To know when an element ends requires sophisticated reasoning by the parser, making code more complex, slowing down processing speed, and increasing memory usage.

You might wonder why an XML stream does not package up complete elements for processing. The reason is that XML is hierarchical. Elements are nested, so it is not possible to separate them into discrete packages in a stream. In fact, it would resemble the tree method, handing out exactly one element, the root of the document assembled into a single data structure.

The event model of processing is quite simple. There are only a few event types to keep track of, including element tags, character data, comments, processing instructions, and the boundaries of the document itself. Let us look at an example of how a parser might slice up a document into an XML event stream. Consider the data file in Example 10-1.

*Example 10-1. A simple XML document with lots of markup types*

```
<recipe>
  <name>peanut butter and jelly sandwich</name>
  <!-- add picture of sandwich here -->
  <ingredients>
    <ingredient>Gloppy™ brand peanut butter</ingredient>
    <ingredient>bread</ingredient>
    <ingredient>jelly</ingredient>
  </ingredients>
  <instructions>
    <step>Spread peanut butter on one slice of bread.</step>
    <step>Spread jelly on the other slice of bread.</step>
    <step>Put bread slices together, with peanut butter and
jelly touching.</step>
  </instructions>
</recipe>
```

A stream-generating parser would report these events:

1. A document start
2. A start tag for the recipe element
3. A start tag for the name element
4. The piece of text "peanut butter and jelly sandwich"
5. An end tag for the name element
6. A comment with the text "add picture of sandwich here"
7. A start tag for the ingredients element
8. A start tag for the ingredient element
9. The text "Gloppy"
10. A reference to the entity trade
11. The text "brand peanut butter"
12. An end tag for the ingredient element

...and so on, until the final event—the end of the document—is reached.

Somewhere between chopping up a stream into tokens and processing the tokens is a layer one might call an *event dispatcher*. It branches the processing depending on the type of token. The code that deals with a particular token type is called an *event handler*. There could be a handler for start tags, another for character data, and so on. A common technique is to create a function or subroutine for each event type and register it with the parser as a call-back, something that gets called when a given event occurs.

Streams are good for a wide variety of XML processing tasks. Programs that use streams will be fast and able to handle very large documents. The code will be simple and fit the source data like a glove. Where streams fail are situations in which data is so complex that it requires a lot of searching around. For example, XSLT jumps from element to element in an order that may not match the lexical order at all. When that is the case, we prefer to use the tree model.

# Trees and Objects

The tree method is luxurious in comparison to streams. To use an analogy, think of a stream generator as a hose gushing out XML. A tree is that same XML frozen into an ice sculpture. You can peruse it at your leisure, returning to any point in the document when you need it. This structure requires more resources to build and store, so you will only want to use it when the stream method cannot help.

There are many reasons why a tree structure representing a piece of XML is a handy thing to have. Since a tree is acyclic (it has no circular links), you can use simple traversal methods that won't get stuck in infinite loops. Like a filesystem directory tree, you can represent the location of a node easily in simple shorthand. Like real trees, you can break a piece off and treat it like a smaller tree. Most important, you have all the information in one place for as long as you need it.

This persistence is the key reason for using trees. If you can live with the overhead of memory and time to construct the tree, then you will enjoy luxuries like being able to pull data from anywhere in the document at any point of the processing. With streams, you are forced to work with events as they arrive, perhaps storing bits of data for later use.

Tree processing is usually object-oriented. The data structure representing the document is composed of objects whose methods allow you to traverse in different directions, pull out data, or modify values. DOM, as we will see later in the chapter, is a standard that defines the interfaces of objects used to built document trees. Encapsulating XML data in objects is as natural as using markup, with as many benefits.

## Pull Parsing

Tim Bray, lead editor of XML 1.0, calls pull parsing "the way to go in the future." Like event-based parsing, it's fast, memory efficient, streamable, and read-only. The difference is in how the application and parser interact. SAX implements what we call *push parsing*. The parser pushes events at the program, requiring it to react. The parser doesn't store any *state information*, contextual clues that would help in decisions for how to parse, so the application has to store this information itself.

*Pull parsing* is just the opposite. The program takes control and tells the parser when to fetch the next item. Instead of reacting to events, it proactively seeks out events. This allows the developer more freedom in designing data handlers, and greater ability to catch invalid markup. Consider the following example XML:

```
<catalog>
  <product id="ronco-728">
    <name>Widget</name>
    <price>19.99</price>
  </product>
  <product id="acme-229">
    <name>Gizmo</name>
    <price>28.98</price>
  </product>
</catalog>
```

It is easy to write a SAX program to read this XML and build a data structure. The following code assembles an array of products composed of instances of this class:

```
class Product {
    String name;
    String price;
}
```

Here is the code to do it:

```
StringBuffer cdata = new StringBuffer();
Product[] catalog = new Product[10];
String name;
Float price;

public void startDocument () {
  index = 0;
}

public void startElement( String uri, String local,
                          String raw, Attributes attrs )
        throws SAXException {
  cdata.clear();
}

public void characters( char ch[], int start, int length )
        throws SAXException {
  cdata.append( ch, start, length );
}

public void endElement( String uri, String local, String raw )
        throws SAXException {
  if("product".equals(local)) {
    index ++;
  } else if( "name".equals(local) ) {
    catalog[index].name = cdata.toString;
  } else if( "price".equals(local) ) {
    catalog[index].price = cdata.toString;
  } else {
    throw new SAXException( "Unexpected element: " + local );
  }
}
```

The program maintains a little bit of state information in the form of an index variable. As this counter increments, it stores data from the next product in the next slot. Thus it builds a growing list of products in its catalog array.

At first glance, this program seems to be adequate. It will handle a data file that is valid, but if you throw some bad markup at it, it will do strange things. Imagine what would happen if you gave it this data file:

```
<catalog>
  <product id="grigsby-123">
    <name>Woofinator</name>
  </product>
  <price>8.77</price>
</catalog>
```

Oops. The price element is not inside the product like it should be. The program we wrote will not catch the mistake. Instead, it will save the product data for the woofinator, without a price, then increment the index. When the parser finally reaches the price, it will be too late to insert into the product slot. Clearly, this ought to be a validation error, but our program is not smart enough to catch it.

To protect against problems like this, we could add a test for a missing price element, or an extra one outside the product element. But then we would have to insert tests everywhere and the code would get ugly quickly. A better solution is provided by pull parsing.

This example uses the XMLPULL API (see *http://www.xmlpull.org/*) in a *recursive descent* style of processing:

```java
import org.xmlpull.v1.XmlPullParser;
import org.kxml2.io.*;
import org.xmlpull.v1.*;
import java.io.*;
import java.util.Vector;


public class test {


    public static void main(String[] args)
            throws IOException, XmlPullParserException {

    Vector products=new Vector();

        try {
            XmlPullParser parser = new KXmlParser();
            parser.setInput(new FileReader(args[0]));

            parser.nextTag();
            parser.require(XmlPullParser.START_TAG, null, "catalog");

            while (parser.nextTag () != XmlPullParser.END_TAG) {
                Product newProduct=readProduct(parser);
                products.add(newProduct);
            }
            parser.require(XmlPullParser.END_TAG, null, "catalog");
            parser.next();

            parser.require(XmlPullParser.END_DOCUMENT, null, null);
        } catch (Exception e) {
            e.printStackTrace();
        }

        System.out.println("Products:");
        int count=products.size();
        for (int i=0; i<count; i++) {
            Product report=(Product) products.get(i);
        System.out.println("Name: "+report.name );
            System.out.println("Price: "+report.price );
        }
    }
```

```
        static public Product readProduct(XmlPullParser parser)
                        throws IOException, XmlPullParserException {
            Vector products=new Vector();

                parser.require(XmlPullParser.START_TAG, null, "product");

                String productName = null;
                String price = null;

                while (parser.nextTag() != XmlPullParser.END_TAG) {

                        parser.require(XmlPullParser.START_TAG, null, null);
                        String name = parser.getName();

                        String text = parser.nextText();

                        if (name.equals("name"))
                                productName = text;
                        else if (name.equals("price"))
                                price = text;

                        parser.require(XmlPullParser.END_TAG, null, name);
                }
                parser.require(XmlPullParser.END_TAG, null, "product");

        Product newProduct=new Product();
        newProduct.name=productName;
        newProduct.price=price;

        return newProduct;

                }

    }
```

Pull parsing is quickly becoming a favorite of developers. Current implementations include Microsoft's .NET XML libraries, the streamable API for XML (StAX), XMLPULL, and NekoPull. Sun is standardizing a pull API for Java through JSR-172.

# Standard APIs

Nowadays, all programs are written as layered components, where libraries provide functions or objects to take care of routine tasks like parsing and writing XML. An *application programming interface* (API) is a way of delegating routine work to a dedicated component. An automobile's human interface is a good example. It is essentially the same from car to car, with an ignition, steering wheel, gas and brake pedals, and so on. You do not have to know anything about the engine itself, such as how many cylinders are firing and in what order. Just as you never have to fire the spark plugs manually, you should never have to write your own XML parser, unless you want to do something really unusual.

Linking to another developer's parser is a good idea not just because it saves **you** work, but because it turns the parser into a commodity. By that I mean you **can** unplug one parser and plug in another. Or you could unplug a parser and plug **in a** driver from a database or some real-time source. XML does not have to come **from** files, after all. None of this would be possible, however, without the use of stand**ard** APIs.

This chapter will demonstrate a few examples of this. For event streams, the stan**-** dard is SAX. DOM is a standard for object tree interfaces. Most programming lan**-** guages have a few conforming implementations of each. When possible, it is alway**s** a good idea to use SAX or DOM.

# Choosing a Parser

After choosing your programming strategy (SAX, DOM, XMLPULL, etc.), the **next** step in writing an XML application is to select a parser. There is no reason to **write** your own parser when so many excellent ones already exist. Some qualities to **look** for are API support, speed and efficiency, and robustness. Table 10-1 lists some **of** the best, although there are so many out there today that I could not hope to **list** them all.

*Table 10-1. Some popular XML parsers*

| Name | Language | APIs | Web Site |
|------|----------|------|----------|
| Expat | C, Perl (via XML::Parser module), Python (via xml.parsers.expat) | Low-level stream parser | *http://www.jclark.com/xml/expat.html* |
| XP | Java | Low-level stream parser | *http://www.jclark.com/xml/xp/* |
| libxml2 | C++, Perl (via XML::LibXML module) | DTD validation, SAX (minimal), DOM2 (core, need gdome2 library for the API), XPath, Relax NG, XML Schemas (data types) | *http://xmlsoft.org/* |
| Xerces2 | Java | DTD validation, SAX2 (core, extension), DOM2 (core, events, traversal), DOM3 (experimental core), Xerces Native Interface (XNI), XML Schema (structures and data types), Java APIs for XML Parsing (JAXP) | *http://xml.apache.org/* |
| Xerces | Java, C++, Perl (via XML::Xerces module) | DTD validation, SAX2 (core, extension), DOM2 (core, events, traversal), DOM3 (partial core), Xerces Native Interface (XNI), XML Schema (structures and data types) | *http://xml.apache.org/* |

*Table 10-1. Some popular XML parsers (continued)*

| Name | Language | APIs | Web Site |
|------|----------|------|----------|
| Java API for XML Parsing (JAXP) | Java | DTD validation, DOM, SAX, XSLT, XML Schema | *http://java.sun.com/xml/jaxp/* |
| JDOM | Java | XPath, JDOM, an alternative to SAX and DOM | *http://www.jdom.org* |
| Microsoft XML Parser | Java, C++, C# | DTD validation, SAX, DOM, XSLT, XML Schema, XPath, XML Schema definition language (XSD), Schema Object Model (SOM) | *http://msdn.microsoft.com/xml/* |
| PyXML | Python | DTD validation, SAX2, DOM2, PullDOM | *http://pyxml.sourceforge.net/* |
| Xparse | JavaScript | Basic stream parser | *http://www.jeremie.com/Dev/XML/* |

# PYX

PYX is an early XML stream solution that converts XML into character data compatible with text applications like grep, awk, and sed. Its name represents the fact that it was the first XML solution in the programming language Python. XML events are separated by newline characters, fitting nicely into the line-oriented paradigm of many Unix programs. Table 10-2 summarizes the notation of PYX.

*Table 10-2. PYX notation*

| Symbol | Represents |
|--------|------------|
| ( | An element start tag |
| ) | An element end tag |
| - | Character data |
| A | An attribute |
| ? | A processing instruction |

For every event coming through the stream, PYX starts a new line, beginning with one of the five event symbols. This line is followed by the element name or whatever other data is pertinent. Special characters are escaped with a backslash, as you would see in Unix shell or Perl code.

Here's how a parser converting an XML document into PYX notation would look. The following code is XML input by the parser:

```
<shoppinglist>
  <!-- brand is not important -->
  <item>toothpaste</item>
  <item>rocket engine</item>
  <item optional="yes">caviar</item>
</shoppinglist>
```

As PYX, it would look like this:

```
(shoppinglist
-\n
(item
-toothpaste
)item
-\n
(item
-rocket engine
)item
-\n
(item
Aoptional yes
-caviar
)item
-\n
)shoppinglist
```

Notice that the comment didn't come through in the PYX translation. PYX is a little simplistic in some ways, omitting some details in the markup. It will not alert you to CDATA markup sections, although it will let the content pass through. Perhaps the most serious loss is character entity references, which disappear from the stream. You should make sure you don't need that information before working with PYX.

PYX is an interesting alternative to SAX and DOM for quick-and-dirty XML processing. It's useful for simple tasks like element counting, separating content from markup, and reporting simple events. However, it does lack sophistication, making it less attractive for complex processing. Today, I consider it to be more of interest for historical reasons than as a recommendation.

# SAX

The Simple API for XML (SAX) is one of the first and currently the most popular method for working with XML data. It evolved from discussions on the XML-DEV mailing list and, shepherded by David Megginson,* was quickly shaped into a useful specification.

The first incarnation, called SAX Level 1 (or just SAX1), supports elements, attributes, and processing instructions. It doesn't handle some other things like namespaces or CDATA sections, so the second iteration, SAX2, was devised, adding support for just about any event you can imagine in generic XML. Since there's no good reason not to use SAX2, you can assume that SAX2 is what we are talking about when we say "SAX."

---

* David Megginson maintains a web page about SAX at *http://www.saxproject.org*.

SAX was originally developed in Java in a package called `org.xml.sax`. As a consequence, most of the literature about SAX is Java-centric and assumes that is the environment you will be working in. Furthermore, there is no formal specification for SAX in any programming language but Java. Analogs in other languages exist, such as XML::SAX in Perl, but they are not bound by the official SAX description. Really they are just whatever their developer community thinks they should be.

 David Megginson has made SAX public domain and has allowed anyone to use the name. An unfortunate consequence is that many implementations are really just "flavors" of SAX and do not match in every detail. This is especially true for SAX in other programming languages where the notion of strict compliance would not even make sense. This is kind of like the plethora of Unix flavors out today; they seem much alike, but have some big differences under the surface.

## Drivers

SAX describes a universal interface that any SAX-aware program can use, no matter where the data is coming from. Figure 10-1 shows how this works. Your program is at the right. It contacts the ParserFactory object to request a parser that will serve up a stream of SAX events. The factory finds a parser and starts it running, routing the SAX stream to your program through the interface.

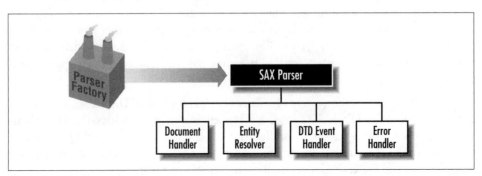

*Figure 10-1. ParserFactory*

The workhorse of SAX is the SAX driver. A *SAX driver* is any program that implements the SAX2 *XMLReader interface*. It may include a parser that reads XML directly, or it may just be a wrapper for another parser to adapt it to the interface. It may even be a converter, transmuting data of one kind (say, SQL queries) into XML. From your program's point of view, the source doesn't matter, because it is all packaged in the same way.

The SAX driver calls subroutines that you supply to handle various events. These *call-backs* fall into four categories, usually grouped into objects:

- Document handler
- Entity resolver
- DTD handler
- Error handler

To use a SAX driver, you need to create some or all of these handler classes and pass them to the driver so it can call their call-back routines. The document handler is the minimal requirement, providing methods that deal with element tags, attributes, processing instructions, and character data. The others override default behavior of the core API. To ensure that your handler classes are written correctly, the Java version of SAX includes *interfaces*, program constructs that describe methods to be implemented in a class.

 The characters method of the content handler may be called multiple times for the same text node, as SAX drivers are allowed to split text into smaller pieces. Your code will need to anticipate this and stitch text together if necessary.

The entity resolver overrides the default method for resolving external entity references. Ordinarily, it is assumed that you just want all external entity references resolved automatically, and the driver tries to comply, but in some cases, entity resolution has to be handled specially. For example, a resource located in a database would require that you write a routine to extract the data, since it is an application-specific process.

The core API doesn't create events for lexical structures like CDATA sections, comments, and DOCTYPE declarations. If your environment provides the DTD handling extension, you can write a handler for that. If not, then you should just assume that the CDATA sections are treated as regular character data, comments are stripped out, and DOCTYPE declarations are out of your reach.

The error handler package gives the programmer a graceful way to deal with those unexpected nasty situations like a badly formed document or an entity that cannot be resolved. Unless you want an angry mob of users breaking down your door, you had better put in some good error checking code.

## A Java Example: Element Counter

In this first example, we will use SAX to create a Java program that counts elements in a document. We start by creating a class that manages the parsing process, shown in Example 10-2.

*Example 10-2. Contents of SAXCounter.java*

```java
import org.xml.sax.XMLReader;
import org.xml.sax.helpers.XMLReaderFactory;
import org.xml.sax.InputSource;
import java.io.FileReader;

public class SAXCounter {

  public SAXCounter () {
  }

  public static void main (String args[]) throws Exception {
    XMLReader xr = XMLReaderFactory.createXMLReader();
    SAXCounterHandler h = new SAXCounterHandler();      // create a handler
    xr.setContentHandler(h);                  // register it with the driver
    FileReader r = new FileReader(args[0]);
    xr.parse(new InputSource(r));
  }
}
```

This class sets up the SAX environment and requests a SAX driver from the parser factory XMLReaderFactory. Then it creates a handler and registers it with the driver via the setContentHandler( ) method. Finally, it reads a file (supplied on the command line) and parses it. Because I am trying to keep this example short, I will not register an error handler, although ordinarily this would be a mistake.

The next step is to write the handler class, shown in Example 10-3.

*Example 10-3. Contents of SAXCounterHandler.java*

```java
import org.xml.sax.helpers.DefaultHandler;
import org.xml.sax.Attributes;

public class SAXCounterHandler extends DefaultHandler {

  private int elements;

  public SAXCounterHandler () {
    super();
  }

  // handle a start-of-document event
  public void startDocument ()
  {
    System.out.println("Starting to parse...");
    elements = 0;
  }

  // handle an end-of-document event
  public void endDocument ()
  {
    System.out.println("All done!");
    System.out.println("There were " + elements + " elements.");
```

*Example 10-3. Contents of SAXCounterHandler.java (continued)*

```
    }

    // handle a start-of-element event
    public void startElement (String uri, String name,
                              String qName, Attributes atts) {
      System.out.println("starting element (" + qName + ")");
      if ("".equals(uri));
      else
        System.out.println("  namespace: " + uri);
      System.out.println("  number of attributes: " + atts.getLength());
    }

    // handle an end-of-element event
    public void endElement (String uri, String name, String qName)
    {
      elements ++;
      System.out.println("ending element (" + qName + ")");
    }

    // handle a characters event
    public void characters (char ch[], int start, int length)
    {
        System.out.println("CDATA: " + length + " characters.");
    }
}
```

This class implements five types of events:

*Start of document*
    Initialize the elements counter and print a message.

*End of document*
    Print the number of elements counted.

*Start of element*
    Output the qualified name of the element, the namespace URI, and the number
    of attributes.

*End of element*
    Increment the element counter and print a message.

Any other events are handled by the superclass DefaultHandler.

We run the program on the data in Example 10-4.

*Example 10-4. Contents of text.xml*

```
<?xml version="1.0"?>
<bcb:breakfast-cereal-box xmlns:bcb="http://www.grubblythings.com/">
  <bcb:name>Sugar Froot Snaps</bcb:name>
  <bcb:graphic file="bcbcover.tif"/>
  <bcb:prize>Decoder ring</bcb:prize>
</bcb:breakfast-cereal-box>
```

The full command is:

```
java -Dorg.xml.sax.driver=org.apache.xerces.parsers.SAXParser
SAXCounter test.xml
```

The -D option sets the property org.xml.sax.driver to the Xerces parser. This is necessary because my Java environment does not have a default SAX driver. Here is the output:

```
Starting to parse...
starting element (bcb:breakfast-cereal-box)
  namespace: http://www.grubblythings.com/
  number of attributes: 0
CDATA: 3 characters.
starting element (bcb:name)
  namespace: http://www.grubblythings.com/
  number of attributes: 0
CDATA: 17 characters.
ending element (bcb:name)
CDATA: 3 characters.
starting element (bcb:graphic)
  namespace: http://www.grubblythings.com/
  number of attributes: 1
ending element (bcb:graphic)
CDATA: 3 characters.
starting element (bcb:prize)
  namespace: http://www.grubblythings.com/
  number of attributes: 0
CDATA: 12 characters.
ending element (bcb:prize)
CDATA: 1 characters.
ending element (bcb:breakfast-cereal-box)
All done!
There were 4 elements.
```

There you have it. Living up to its name, SAX is uncomplicated and wonderfully easy to use. It does not try to do too much, instead offloading the work on your handler program. It works best when the processing of a document follows the order of elements, and only one pass through it is sufficient. One common task by event processors is to assemble tree structures, which brings us to the next topic, the tree processing API known as DOM.

# DOM

DOM is a recommendation by the World Wide Web Consortium (W3C). Designed to be a language-neutral interface to an in-memory representation of an XML document, versions of DOM are available in Java, ECMAscript,[*] Perl, and other languages.

---

[*] A standards-friendly language patterned after JavaScript.

While SAX defines an interface of handler methods, the DOM specification calls for a number of classes, each with an interface of methods that affect a particular type of XML markup. Thus, every object instance manages a portion of the document tree, providing accessor methods to add, remove, or modify nodes and data. These objects are typically created by a factory object, making it a little easier for programmers who only have to initialize the factory object themselves.

In DOM, every piece of XML (the element, text, comment, etc.) is a node represented by a node object. The Node class is extended by more specific classes that represent the types of XML markup, including Element, Attr (attribute), ProcessingInstruction, Comment, EntityReference, Text, CDATASection, and Document. These classes are the building blocks of every XML tree in DOM.

The standard also calls for a couple of classes that serve as containers for nodes, convenient for shuttling XML fragments from place to place. These classes are NodeList, an ordered list of nodes, like all the children of an element; and NamedNodeMap, an unordered set of nodes. These objects are frequently required as arguments or given as return values from methods. Note that these objects are all live, meaning that any changes done to them will immediately affect the nodes in the document itself, rather than a copy.

When naming these classes and their methods, DOM merely specifies the outward appearance of an implementation and leaves the internal specifics up to the developer. Particulars like memory management, data structures, and algorithms are not addressed at all, as those issues may vary among programming languages and the needs of users. This is like describing a key so a locksmith can make a lock that it will fit into; you know the key will unlock the door, but you have no idea how it really works. Specifically, the outward appearance makes it easy to write extensions to legacy modules so they can comply with the standard, but it does not guarantee efficiency or speed.

DOM is a very large standard, and you will find that implementations vary in their level of compliance. To make things worse, the standard has not one, but two (soon to be three) levels. DOM1 has been around since 1998, DOM2 emerged more recently, and they're already working on a third. The main difference between Levels 1 and 2 is that the latter adds support for namespaces. If you aren't concerned about namespaces, then DOM1 should be suitable for your needs.

# Class Interface Reference

In this section, I describe the interfaces specified in DOM.

## Document

The `Document` class controls the overall document, creating new objects when requested and maintaining high-level information such as references to the document type declaration and the root element.

**Properties.**  Following are the properties for the `Document` class.

*doctype*
> Document Type Declaration (DTD).

*documentElement*
> The root element of the document.

**Methods.**  Here are the methods for the `Document` class:

`createElement, createTextNode, createComment, createCDATASection,`
`createProcessingInstruction, createAttribute, createEntityReference`
> Generates a new node object.

`createElementNS, createAttributeNS` *(DOM2 only)*
> Generates a new element or attribute node object with a specified namespace qualifier.

`createDocumentFragment`
> Creates a container object for a document's subtree.

`getElementsByTagName`
> Returns a NodeList of all elements having a given tag name at any level of the document.

`getElementsByTagNameNS` *(DOM2 only)*
> Returns a NodeList of all elements having a given namespace qualifier and local name. The asterisk character (*) matches any element or any namespace, allowing you to find all elements in a given namespace.

`getElementById` *(DOM2 only)*
> Returns a reference to the node that has a specified ID attribute.

`importNode` *(DOM2 only)*
> Creates a new node that is the copy of a node from another document. Acts like a "copy to the clipboard" operation for importing markup.

## DocumentFragment

The DocumentFragment class is used to contain a document fragment. Its children are (zero or more) nodes representing the tops of XML trees. This class contrasts with Document, which has at most one child element, the document root, plus metadata like the document type. In this respect, DocumentFragment's content is not well-formed, though it must obey the XML well-formed rules in all other respects (no illegal characters in text, etc.)

No specific methods or properties are defined; use the generic node methods to access data.

## DocumentType

This class contains all the information contained in the document type declaration at the beginning of the document, except the specifics about an external DTD. Thus, it names the root element and any declared entities or notations in the internal subset.

No specific methods are defined for this class, but the properties are public (but read-only).

**Properties.** Here are the properties for the DocumentType class:

name
  The name of the root element.

entities
  A NamedNodeMap of entity declarations.

notation
  A NamedNodeMap of notation declarations.

internalSubset *(DOM2 only)*
  The internal subset of the DTD represented as a string.

publicId *(DOM2 only)*
  The external subset of the DTD's public identifier.

systemId *(DOM2 only)*
  The external subset of the DTD's system identifier.

## Node

All node types inherit from the class Node. Any properties or methods common to all node types can be accessed through this class. A few properties, such as the value of the node, are undefined for some node types, like Element. The generic methods of this class are useful in some programming contexts, such as when writing code that processes nodes of different types. At other times, you'll know in advance what type you're working with, and you should use the specific class's methods instead.

All properties but nodeValue and prefix are read-only.

**Properties.** Here are the properties for the Node class:

nodeName
> A property that is defined for elements, attributes, and entities. In the context of elements this property would be the tag's name.

nodeValue
> A property defined for attributes, text nodes, CDATA nodes, processing instructions, and comments.

nodeType
> One of the following types of nodes: Element, Attr, Text, CDATASection, EntityReference, Entity, ProcessingInstruction, Comment, Document, DocumentType, DocumentFragment, or Notation.

parentNode
> A reference to the parent of this node.

childNodes
> An ordered list of references to children of this node (if any).

firstChild, lastChild
> References to the first and last of the node's children (if any).

previousSibling, nextSibling
> The node immediately preceding or following this one, respectively.

attributes
> An unordered list (NamedNodeMap) of nodes that are attributes of this one (if any).

ownerDocument
> A reference to the object containing the whole document. It's useful when you need to generate a new node.

namespaceURI *(DOM2 only)*
> A namespace URI if this node has a namespace prefix; otherwise it is null.

prefix *(DOM2 only)*
> The namespace prefix associated with this node.

**Methods.** Here are the methods for the Node class:

insertBefore
> Inserts a node before a reference child element.

replaceChild
> Swaps a child node with a new one you supply, giving you the old one in return.

appendChild
> Adds a new node to the end of this node's list of children.

hasChildNodes
> True if there are children of this node; otherwise, it is false.

cloneNode

Returns a duplicate copy of this node. It provides an alternate way to generate nodes. All properties will be identical except for parentNode, which will be undefined, and childNodes, which will be empty. Cloned elements will all have the same attributes as the original. If the argument deep is set to true, then the node and all its descendants will be copied.

hasAttributes *(DOM2 only)*

Returns true if this node has defined attributes.

isSupported *(DOM2 only)*

Returns true if this implementation supports a specific feature.

## NodeList

This class is a container for an ordered list of nodes. It is "live," meaning that any changes to the nodes it references will appear in the document immediately.

**Properties.**  Here are the properties for the NodeList class:

length

Returns an integer indicating the number of nodes in the list.

**Methods.**  Here are the properties for the NodeList class:

item

Given an integer value *n*, returns a reference to the *n*th node in the list, starting at zero.

## NamedNodeMap

This unordered set of nodes is designed to allow access to nodes by name. An alternate access by index is also provided for enumerations, but no order is implied.

**Properties.**  Here are the properties for the NamedNodeMap class:

length

Returns an integer indicating the number of nodes in the list.

**Methods.**  Here are the properties for the NamedNodeMap class:

getNamedItem, setNamedItem

Retrieves or adds a node using the node's nodeName property as the key.

removeNamedItem

Takes a node with the specified name out of the set and returns it.

item

Given an integer value *n*, returns a reference to the *n*th node in the set. Note that this method does not imply any order and is provided only for unique enumeration.

---

getNamedItemNS *(DOM2 only)*
>   Retrieves a node based on a namespace-qualified name (a namespace prefix and a local name).

removeNamedItemNS *(DOM2 only)*
>   Takes an item out of the list and returns it, based on its namespace-qualified name.

setNamedItemNS *(DOM2 only)*
>   Adds a node to the list using its namespace-qualified name.

## CharacterData

This class extends Node to facilitate access to certain types of nodes that contain character data, such as Text, CDATASection, Comment, and ProcessingInstruction. Specific classes like Text inherit from this class.

**Properties.**  Here are the properties for the CharacterData class:

data
>   The character data itself.

length
>   The number of characters in the data.

**Methods.**  Here are the methods for the CharacterData class:

appendData
>   Appends a string of character data to the end of the data property.

substringData
>   Extracts and returns a segment of the data property from *offset* to *offset + count*.

insertData
>   Inserts a string inside the data property at the location given by *offset*.

deleteData
>   Sets the data property to an empty string.

replaceData
>   Changes the contents of data property with a new string that you provide.

## Element

This is the most common type of node you will encounter. An element can contain other nodes and has attribute nodes.

**Properties.**  Here are the properties for the Element class:

tagname
>   The name of the element.

**Methods.** Here are the methods for the `Element` class:

`getAttribute, getAttributeNode`
> Returns the value of an attribute, or a reference to the attribute node, with a given name.

`setAttribute, setAttributeNode`
> Adds a new attribute to the element's list or replaces an existing attribute of the same name.

`removeAttribute, removeAttributeNode`
> Returns the value of an attribute and removes it from the element's list.

`getElementsByTagName`
> Returns a `NodeList` of descendant elements who match a name.

`normalize`
> Collapses adjacent text nodes. You should use this method whenever you add new text nodes to ensure that the structure of the document remains the same, without erroneous extra children.

`getAttributeNS` *(DOM2 only)*
> Retrieves an attribute value based on its qualified name (the namespace prefix plus the local name).

`getAttributeNodeNS` *(DOM2 only)*
> Gets an attribute's node by using its qualified name.

`getElementsByTagNamesNS` *(DOM2 only)*
> Returns a `NodeList` of elements among this element's descendants that match a qualified name.

`hasAttribute` *(DOM2 only)*
> Returns true if this element has an attribute with a given name.

`hasAttributeNS` *(DOM2 only)*
> Returns true if this element has an attribute with a given qualified name.

`removeAttributeNS` *(DOM2 only)*
> Removes and returns an attribute node from this element's list, based on its namespace-qualified name.

`setAttributeNS` *(DOM2 only)*
> Adds a new attribute to the element's list, given a namespace-qualified name and a value.

`setAttributeNodeNS` *(DOM2 only)*
> Adds a new attribute node to the element's list with a namespace-qualified name.

## Attr

This kind of node represents attributes.

---

**Properties.** Here are the properties for the `Attr` class:

`name`
> The attribute's name.

`specified`
> True if the program or the document explicitly set the attribute. If it was set in the DTD as a default and not reset anywhere else, then it will be false.

`value`
> The attribute's value, represented as a text node.

`ownerElement` *(DOM2 only)*
> The element to which this attribute belongs.

## Text

This type of node represents text.

**Methods.** Here are the methods for the Text class:

`splitText`
> Breaks the text node into two adjacent text nodes, each with part of the original text content. The first node contains text from the beginning of the original node up to, but not including, a character whose position is given by *offset*. The second node has the rest of the original node's content. This method is useful for inserting a new element inside a span of text.

## CDATASection

`CDATASection` is like a text node, but protects its contents from being parsed. It may contain markup characters (<, &) that would be illegal in text nodes. Use generic `Node` methods to access data.

## ProcessingInstruction

This class represents processing instructions.

**Properties.** Here are the properties for the `ProcessingInstruction` class:

`target`
> The target value for the node.

`data`
> The data value for the node.

## Comment

This is a class representing comment nodes. Use the generic `Node` methods to access the data.

### EntityReference

This is a reference to an entity defined by an Entity node. Sometimes the parser will be configured to resolve all entity references into their values for you. If that option is disabled, the parser should create this node. No explicit methods force resolution, but some actions to the node may have that side effect.

### Entity

This class provides access to an entity in the document, based on information in an entity declaration in the DTD.

**Properties.** Here are the properties for the Entity class:

publicId
: A public identifier for the resource (if the entity is external to the document).

systemId
: A system identifier for the resource (if the entity is external to the document).

notationName
: If the entity is unparsed, its notation reference is listed here.

### Notation

Notation represents a notation declaration appearing in the DTD.

**Properties.** Here are the properties for the Notation class:

publicId
: A public identifier for the notation.

systemId
: A system identifier for the notation.

## An Example in Perl

Perl is quite different from Java. It was not designed from the outset to be object oriented. That functionality was added later in kind of an ad hoc manner. Perl is loose with type checking and rather idiomatic. For these reasons, it is not always taken seriously by XML pundits.

Yet Perl is a fixture in the World Wide Web, being the original duct tape that holds web sites together. It has a huge following and excellent support in books and online resources, and it's very easy to get started using it. For small, quick-and-dirty utilities that achieve fast results, it simply cannot be beat. Having cut my teeth in the text processing world of publishing, I found Perl to be a boon.

Including a Perl example to contrast with Java gives us a nice range of programming environments to showcase XML development strategies. If you are developing a large, complex system, you will likely want to consider Java for its robustness and strong object-oriented programming capabilities. If you want a small tool for simple tasks in shaping your XML files, then Perl would be a great candidate.

The example I propose for using DOM is a small application that fixes a simple problem. When I used to prepare DocBook-XML documents for formatting, I found there were a few common structural errors that would cause problems in the formatting software. One of these was the tendency of busy indexing specialists to insert <indexterm> elements inside titles. It is an easy mistake to make, and just as easy to fix.

Now I will show you how to go about solving this problem with Perl. My favorite parser in Perl is Matt Sargent's XML::LibXML. It is an interface to the C library libxml2 which is incredibly fast and reliable. This module also implements most of the DOM2 specification and adds XPath node-fetching capability. In this portion of the script, we set up the parser and use it to assemble DOM trees out of files from the command line:

```
use XML::LibXML;

my $parser = new XML::LibXML;        # a parser object

# This table gives us that ability to test the type of
# most common nodes. It is not a complete list, but these are
# the ones we are most likely to encounter (and care about
# for this example).
my %nodeTypes = (
        element => 1,       attribute => 2,      text => 3,
        cdatasection => 4,  entityref => 5,      entitynode => 6,
        procinstruc => 7,   comment => 8,        document => 9
                 );

# Loop through the arguments on the command line, feeding them to
# the parser as filenames. After testing that parsing was successful,
# apply the map_proc_to_elems subroutine to the document node to
# make the needed fixes. Finally, write the XML back out to the file.
foreach my $fileName ( @ARGV ) {
  my $docRef;
  eval{ $docRef = $parser->parse_file( $fileName ); };
  die( "Parser error: $@" ) if( $@ );
  map_proc_to_elems( \&fix_iterms, $docRef );
  open( OUT, ">$fileName" ) or die( "Can't write $fileName" );
  print OUT $docRef->toString();
  close OUT;
}
```

After instantiating the parser, we created a hash table that maps English words for node types to the numeric codes used in the parser. This will give us the ability to test what kind of node we are looking at when we traverse through the file.

In the loop below that declaration, we take filenames from the command line argument list (@ARGV) and feed them to the parser. The eval{ } statement catches any parse errors, which we detect in the following die( ) statement. The parser puts helpful error messages in $@ to indicate what may have confused the parser. If all goes well, the parser will return a reference to the top of the DOM tree, specifically an XML::LibXML::Document object.

The map_proc_to_elems( ) is a yet-to-be-written subroutine that will apply a procedure (also not yet written) to nodes in the DOM tree. This is where the real work will take place in the program. It makes changes directly to the object tree, so all we have to do is print it out as text with the toString( ) method.

Now let us dig into the map_proc_to_elems( ) routine. The purpose of this function is to map a procedure to every element in the document:

```
sub map_proc_to_elems {
  my( $proc, $nodeRef ) = @_;
  my $nodeType = $nodeRef->nodeType;
  if( $nodeType == $nodeTypes{document} ) {
    map_proc_to_elems( $proc, $nodeRef->getDocumentElement );
  } elsif( $nodeType == $nodeTypes{element} ) {
    &$proc( $nodeRef );
    foreach my $childNodeRef ( $nodeRef->getChildnodes ) {
      map_proc_to_elems( $proc, $childNodeRef );
    }
  }
}
```

You start it with the document node or any element and it will visit every element in that subtree, recursing on the children and their children and so on. Testing the node's type allows us to make sure we don't try to apply the procedure to anything that isn't the document node or an element. The procedure to be applied comes in the form of a subroutine reference, which we dereference to call in two places: when the current node is a document node, and when it is an element. For any other case, the subroutine just returns without doing anything.

Driving this traversal are the methods getDocumentElement( ), which obtains the root element, and getChildnodes( ),* which returns a list of child nodes in the order they appear in the document.

Now we turn our attention to the subroutine that performs the fix on elements. It is called fix_iterms( ) because it moves indexterm elements out of title elements where they would cause trouble. We could just as easily substitute this procedure with another that does something else to elements. That is the beauty of this program: it can be quickly re-engineered to do any task on elements you want. Here it is:

```
sub fix_iterms {
  my $nodeRef = shift;

  # test: is this an indexterm?
  return unless( $nodeRef->nodeName eq 'indexterm' );
```

---

* No, that lowercase "n" is not a typo.

```
    # test: is the parent a title?
    my $parentNodeRef = $nodeRef->parentNode;
    return unless( $parentNodeRef->nodeName eq 'title' );

    # If we get this far, we must be
    # looking at an indexterm inside a title.
    # Therefore, remove this indexterm and
    # stick it just after the parent (title).
    $parentNodeRef->removeChild( $nodeRef );
    my $ancestorNodeRef = $parentNodeRef->parentNode;
    $ancestorNodeRef->insertAfter( $nodeRef, $parentNodeRef );
}
```

At the top of the procedure are lines that select which element to process. Since this procedure is called for every element, we have to weed out the ones we don't want to touch. The first test determines whether the element is an <indexterm> and, if it is not, returns immediately. The next two lines examine the parent of this element, aborting unless it is of type title. If processing gets past these two tests, we know this must be an indexterm inside a title.

The processing that follows removes the offending indexterm element from its parent's list of children and inserts it into the list of its parent's parent's children, just after the parent. So the indexterm goes from being a child of title to being its sibling, positioned immediately after it. This puts the element where it will do no harm to the formatter and will still be seen by an index generator later.

Wasn't that simple? Example 10-5 shows the complete program.

*Example 10-5. A DOM program for moving indexterms out of titles*

```
#!/usr/bin/perl

use XML::LibXML;

my $parser = new XML::LibXML;
my %nodeTypes = (
        element => 1,        attribute => 2,      text => 3,
        cdatasection => 4,   entityref => 5,      entitynode => 6,
        procinstruc => 7,    comment => 8,        document => 9
                  );

foreach my $fileName ( @ARGV ) {
  my $docRef;
  eval{ $docRef = $parser->parse_file( $fileName ); };
  die( "Parser error: $@" ) if( $@ );
  map_proc_to_elems( \&fix_iterms, $docRef );
  open( OUT, ">$fileName" ) or die( "Can't write $fileName" );
  print OUT $docRef->toString();
  close OUT;
}

sub map_proc_to_elems {
  my( $proc, $nodeRef ) = @_;
```

*Example 10-5. A DOM program for moving indexterms out of titles (continued)*

```
  my $nodeType = $nodeRef->nodeType;
  if( $nodeType == $nodeTypes{document} ) {
    map_proc_to_elems( $proc, $nodeRef->getDocumentElement );
  } elsif( $nodeType == $nodeTypes{element} ) {
    &$proc( $nodeRef );
    foreach my $childNodeRef ( $nodeRef->getChildnodes ) {
      map_proc_to_elems( $proc, $childNodeRef );
    }
  }
}

sub fix_iterms {
  my $nodeRef = shift;
  return unless( $nodeRef->nodeName eq 'indexterm' );
  my $parentNodeRef = $nodeRef->parentNode;
  return unless( $parentNodeRef->nodeName eq 'title' );
  $parentNodeRef->removeChild( $nodeRef );
  my $ancestorNodeRef = $parentNodeRef->parentNode;
  $ancestorNodeRef->insertAfter( $nodeRef, $parentNodeRef );
}
```

Now, let's make sure this thing works. Here is a sample data file, before processing:

```
<chapter>
<title><indexterm><primary>wee creatures</primary></indexterm>
Habits of the Wood Sprite
<indexterm><primary>woodland faeries</primary></indexterm></title>
<indexterm>
   <primary>sprites</primary>
   <secondary>woodland</secondary>
</indexterm>
<para>The wood sprite likes to hang around rotting piles of wood and is
easily dazzled by bright lights.</para>
<section>
<title><indexterm><primary>little people</primary></indexterm>
Origins</title>
<para>No one really knows where they came from.</para>
<indexterm><primary>magical folk</primary></indexterm>
</section>
</chapter>
```

I have placed indexterms in various places, both inside and outside titles to see which ones are affected. Here is the result, after running the script on it:

```
<?xml version="1.0"?>
<chapter>
<title>Habits of the Wood Sprite</title><indexterm><primary>woodland faeries</
primary></indexterm>
<indexterm><primary>wee creatures</primary></indexterm>
<indexterm>
   <primary>sprites</primary>
   <secondary>woodland</secondary>
</indexterm>
```

```
<para>The wood sprite likes to hang around rotting piles of wood and is
easily dazzled by bright lights.</para>
<section>
<title>Origins</title><indexterm><primary>little people</primary></indexterm>
<para>No one really knows where they came from.</para>
<indexterm><primary>magical folk</primary></indexterm>
</section>
</chapter>
```

The `indexterms` have been moved out of the `titles` as we expected. Other `indexterms` have not been affected. The other contents in `titles` are still there, unchanged, including some extra space that abutted the `indexterm` elements. In short, it worked!

Perl works well for most of my XML needs. Historically, it has had a few issues with character encodings, but these problems are gradually going away as Perl adopts multibyte characters and adds support for Unicode. Check out *http://www.cpan.org* for a huge list of modules that do everything with XML including XSLT, XPath, DOM, SAX, and more.

You will also want to check out Python, which many people tout as superior in its object-oriented support. It is quickly growing in popularity, though it will be a while before it can match Perl's wealth of libraries.

# Other Options

As XML has spread, more and more people have had creative (and often useful) ideas about how to process it.

## XPath as API

The XPath language provides a convenient method to specify which nodes to return in a tree context. A parser written as a hybrid will only need to return a list of nodes that match an XPath expression. A stream parser efficiently searches through the document to find the nodes, then passes the locations to a tree builder that assembles them into object trees. XPath's advantage is that it is has a very rich language for specifying nodes, giving the developer a lot of control and flexibility. The parsers libxml2 and MSXML are two that come with XPath interfaces.

## JDOM

Despite the name, JDOM is not merely a Java implementation of DOM. Rather, it is an alternative to SAX and DOM that is described by its developers as "lightweight and fast...optimized for the Java programmer." It doesn't actually replace other parsers, but uses them to build object representations of documents with an interface that is easy to manipulate. It is designed to integrate with SAX and DOM, supplying a simple and useful interface layer on top.

The proponents of JDOM say it is needed to reduce the complexity of the factory-based specifications for SAX and DOM. For that reason, the JDOM specification itself is defined with classes and not interfaces. In addition to substituting its own new API, JDOM includes the fabulous XPath API.

## Hybrids

If streams and trees are the two extremes on a spectrum of XML processing techniques, then the middle ground is home to solutions we might call *hybrids*. They combine the best of both worlds, low resource overhead of streams with the convenience of a tree structure, by switching between the two modes as necessary. The idea is, if you are only interested in working with a small slice of a document and can safely ignore the rest, then you only need to work with a subtree. The parser scans through the stream until it sees the part that you want, then switches to tree building mode.

One example is the Perl module XML::Twig by Michel Rodriguez. Before parsing, you tell the parser which *twigs* you want it to find, for example, every section element in a DocBook book. It will return a tree one at a time for processing, nimbly side-stepping the problem of storing the whole book in memory at the same time.

## Data Binding

Some developers don't need direct access to XML document structures—they just want to work with objects or other data structures. Data binding approaches minimize the amount of interaction between the developer and the XML itself. Instead of creating XML directly, an API takes an object and serializes it. Instead of reading an XML document and interpreting its parts, an API takes an XML document and presents it as an object.

Data binding processing tends to focus on schemas, which are used as the foundation for describing the XML representing a particular object. The type and structure information used in the schema provides the data binding processor with information about both the XML documents and the objects, and a simple mapping between them suffices for a large number of cases. Data binding is also at the heart of web services, a set of technologies for using XML to send information over a network between programs.

There are a variety of data binding implementations available, largely for the Java and .NET platforms.

# Resources

The resources listed in this appendix can help you learn even more about XML.

## Online

*XML.com*

The web site *http://www.xml.com* is one of the most complete and timely sources of XML information and news around. It should be on your weekly reading list if you are learning or using XML.

*XML.org*

Sponsored by OASIS, *http://www.xml.org* has XML news and resources, including the XML Catalog, a guide to XML products and services.

*The XML Cover Pages*

Edited by Robin Cover, *http://xml.coverpages.org/* is one of the largest and most up-to-date lists of XML resources.

*Cafe Con Leche*

Elliotte Rusty Harold provides almost daily news, along with a quote of the day, at *http://ibiblio.org/xml*.

*XMLHack*

For programmers itching to work with XML, *http://www.xmlhack.com* is a good place to go for news on the latest developments in specifications and tools.

*DocBook*

OASIS, the maintainers of DocBook, have a web page devoted to the XML application at *http://www.docbook.org/*. You can find the latest version and plenty of documentation here.

*A Tutorial on Character Code Issues*

Jukka Korpela has assembled a huge amount of information related to character sets at *http://www.cs.tut.fi/~jkorpela/chars.html*. The tutorial is well written and very interesting reading.

*XSL mailing list*

Signing up with the XSL mailing list is a great way to keep up with the latest developments in XSL and XSLT tools and techniques. It's also a forum for asking questions and getting advice. The traffic is fairly high, so you should balance your needs with the high volume of messages that will be passing through your mailbox. To sign up, go to *http://www.mulberrytech.com/xsl/* and follow the instructions.

*xml-dev mailing list*

The xml-dev mailing list is an extremely busy forum for discussion of all kinds of XML-related issues and best practices. To sign up, go to *http://lists.xml.org/* and follow the instructions.

*Apache XML Project*

This part of the Apache project focuses on XML technologies and can be found at *http://xml.apache.org*. It develops tools and technologies for using XML with Apache and provides feedback to standards organizations about XML implementations.

*XML Developers Guide*

This guide is the Microsoft Developers Network's online workshop for XML. It contains information about using XML with Microsoft applications and can be found at *http://msdn.microsoft.com/xml/XMLGuide/*.

*Dr. Dobb's Journal*

This journal contains articles, resources, opinions, news, and reviews covering all aspects of programming. Go to *http://www.ddj.com* for online content, and subscribe to the magazine while you're there.

*Perl.com*

Perl is an interpreted programming language for any kind of text processing, including XML. The best place online for information or to download code and modules is *http://www.perl.com*.

*Javasoft*

The best source for Java news and information is *http://www.javasoft.com*. Java is a programming language available for most computers and contains a lot of XML support, including implementations of SAX and DOM, as well as several great parsers.

# Books

*XML in a Nutshell, 2nd Edition, Elliotte Rusty Harold and W. Scott Means (O'Reilly & Associates)*

A comprehensive desktop reference for all things XML.

*The XML Bible, 2nd Edition, Elliotte Rusty Harold (Hungry Minds)*

A solid introduction to XML that provides a comprehensive overview of the XML landscape.

*HTML and XHTML, the Definitive Guide, Chuck Musciano and Bill Kennedy (O'Reilly & Associates)*
 A timely and comprehensive resource for learning about HTML.

*Developing SGML DTDs: From Text to Model to Markup, Eve Maler and Jeanne El Andaloussi (Prentice Hall)*
 A step-by-step tutorial for designing and implementing DTDs. While this book is about SGML, much of its advice is still excellent for XML.

*The SGML Handbook, Charles F. Goldfarb (Oxford University Press)*
 A complete reference for SGML, including an annotated specification. Like its subject, the book is complex and hefty, so beginners may not find it a good introduction.

*Java and XML, 2nd Edition, Brett McLaughlin (O'Reilly & Associates)*
 A guide to combining XML and Java to build real-world applications.

*SAX2, David Brownell (O'Reilly & Associates)*
 A complete guide to using the SAX2 API, in Java.

*Processing XML with Java, Elliotte Rusty Harold (Addison-Wesley)*
 A guide to building programs using a variety of Java techniques for processing XML.

*XML and Java, Hiroshi Murayama et al. (Addison-Wesley)*
 Explores many different aspects and APIs of Java processing with XML.

*Java XML Data Binding, Brett McLaughlin (O'Reilly & Associates)*
 A guide to processing XML with data-binding approaches, covering APIs which insulate developers from the XML.

*Perl and XML, Erik Ray and Jason McIntosh (O'Reilly & Associates)*
 A guide to processing XML with a variety of Perl-based approaches.

*Python and XML, Christopher A. Jones and Frederick Drake (O'Reilly & Associates)*
 A guide to processing XML in Python programs.

*.NET and XML, Niel Bornstein (O'Reilly & Associates)*
 A guide to processing XML using the Microsoft .NET API.

*Building Oracle XML Applications, Steve Muench (O'Reilly & Associates)*
 A detailed look at Oracle tools for XML development, and how to combine the power of XML and XSLT with the functionality of the Oracle database.

*DocBook: the Definitive Guide, Norman Walsh and Leonard Muellner (O'Reilly & Associates)*
 DocBook is a popular and flexible markup language for technical documentation, with versions for SGML and XML. This book has an exhaustive, glossary-style format describing every element in detail. It also has lots of practical information for getting started using XML and stylesheets.

*XML Schema, Eric van der Vlist (O'Reilly & Associates)*
 Explores W3C XML Schema in depth, using many examples to illustrate usage.

*Definitive XML Schema, Patricia Walmsley (Prentice Hall)*
A thorough explanation of the W3C XML Schema specification and usage.

*RELAX NG, Eric van der Vlist (O'Reilly & Associates)*
A thorough explanation of RELAX NG, including both theory and practice.

*Learning XSLT, Mike Fitzgerald (O'Reilly & Associates)*
A carefully paced introduction to XSLT development.

*Beginning XSLT, Jeni Tennison (Wrox Press)*
A tutorial for XSLT, focusing on simple and largely HTML-based examples.

*XSLT, Doug Tidwell (O'Reilly & Associates)*
A guide to XSLT development, from the basics to advanced features.

*XSLT Programmer's Reference, 2nd Edition, Michael Kay (Wrox Press)*
A reference guide for XSLT development, including techniques and best practice.

*Definitive XSLT, G. Ken Holman (Prentice Hall)*
A tutorial and reference for XSLT development.

*XSLT and XPath: On the Edge, Jeni Tennsion (M&T Books)*
An exploration of advanced XSLT and XPath techniques.

*XPath and XPointer, John Simpson (O'Reilly & Associates)*
An introduction to the XPath and XPointer specifications for addressing parts of XML documents.

*XSL-FO, Dave Pawson (O'Reilly & Associates)*
An introduction to XSL Formatting Objects, covering page layout techniques and stylesheet integration.

*Definitive XSL-FO, G. Ken Holman (Prentice Hall)*
Explores many different aspects and APIs of Java processing with XML.

*Understanding XML Web Services, Eric Newcomer (Addison-Wesley)*
An introduction to the world of Web Services.

*Web Services Essentials, Ethan Cerami (O'Reilly & Associates)*
An introduction to the Web Services specifications, including XML-RPC, SOAP 1.1, WSDL, and UDDI.

*Web Services and Perl, Paul Kulchenko and Randy Ray (O'Reilly & Associates)*
A guide to using web services in a Perl environment.

*BEEP: The Definitive Guide, Marshall Rose (O'Reilly & Associates)*
A complete guide to the Blocks Extensible Exchange Protocol, an IETF effort built on XML.

*Programming Jabber, D.J. Adams (O'Reilly & Associates)*
A guide to working with Jabber, an instant messaging program and protocol built on XML.

# Standards Organizations

*ISO*

Visit the International Organization for Standardization, a worldwide federation of national standards organizations, at *http://www.iso.ch*.

*W3C*

The World Wide Web Consortium at *http://www.w3.org* oversees the specifications and guidelines for the technology of the World Wide Web. Check here for information about CSS, DOM, (X)HTML, MathML, XLink, XML, XPath, XPointer, XSL, and other web technologies.

*Unicode Consortium*

The organization responsible for defining the Unicode character set can be visited at *http://www.unicode.org*.

*OASIS*

The Organization for the Advancement of Structured Information Standards is an international consortium that creates interoperable industry specifications based on public standards such as XML and SGML. See the web site at *http://www.oasis-open.org*.

*IETF*

The Internet Engineering Task Force is a less formal organization devoted to the creation of specifications for Internet information exchange. The IETF focuses primarily on protocols, notably HTTP, DNS, and SMTP. It also does some XML work in its MIME type efforts and through its BEEP protocol work. See the web site at *http://www.ietf.org*.

# Tools

*GNU Emacs*

An extraordinarily powerful text editor, and so much more. Learn all about it at *http://www.gnu.org/software/emacs/emacs.html*.

*psgml*

An Emacs major mode for editing XML and SGML documents that is available at *http://www.lysator.liu.se/~lenst/*.

*SAX*

Information on SAX, the Simple API for XML, is available at *http://www.saxproject.org*. Here, you will find the Java source code and some helpful documentation.

*Xalan*

A high-performance XSLT stylesheet processor that fully implements XSLT and XLinks. You can find out more about it at the Apache XML Project web site, *http://xml.apache.org*.

*Xerces*

A fully validating parser that implements XML, DOM levels 1 and 2, and SAX2. Find out more about it at the Apache XML Project, *http://xml.apache.org*.

*XT*

A Java implementation of XSLT, at *http://www.jclark.com/xml/xt.html*.

# Miscellaneous

*User Friendly, Illiad*

Starring the formidably cute dust puppy and a gaggle of computer industry drones, this comic strip will inject much-needed jocularity into your bloodstream after a long day of hacking XML. The whole archive is available online at *http://www.userfriendly.org*, and in two books published by O'Reilly: *User Friendly, the Comic Strip*, and *Evil Geniuses in a Nutshell*.

*The Cathedral and the Bazaar, Eric S. Raymond (O'Reilly & Associates)*

In this philosophical analysis and evangelical sermon about the grassroots open source computer programming movement, Raymond extols the virtues of community, sharing, and that warm feeling you get when you're working for the common good.

# A Taxonomy of Standards

The extensibility of XML is clearly demonstrated when you consider all the standards and specifications that have blossomed from the basic XML idea. This appendix is a handy reference to various XML-related activities.

## Markup and Structure

### XML 1.0

Extensible Markup Language consists of basic rules for markup.

**W3C**

#### Status

XML 1.0 (second edition) became a Recommendation in October 2000. You can read the specification at *http://www.w3.org/TR/REC-xml*.

#### Description

XML is a subset of SGML that is designed to be served, received, and processed on the Web in the way that is now possible with HTML. XML has the advantages of easy implementation and compatibility with both SGML and HTML.

### XML 1.1

Update to XML for changes to Unicode.

**W3C**

#### Status

XML 1.1 became a Candidate Recommendation in October 2002. You can read the specification at *http://www.w3.org/TR/xml11/*.

#### Description

XML updates the character tables and whitespace rules of XML 1.0 to reflect changes to the Unicode specification since XML 1.0 became a Recommendation.

## Namespaces in XML

Namespaces are used to separate elements and attributes into different groups.

**W3C**

### Status

Namespaces became a Recommendation in January 1999, and the specification is published at *http://www.w3.org/TR/REC-xml-names/*.

### Description

XML namespaces provide a simple method for qualifying element and attribute names used in XML documents by associating them with namespaces identified by URI references.

## Namespaces in XML 1.1

Minor update to namespace rules.

**W3C**

### Status

Namespaces in XML 1.1 became a Candidate Recommendation in December 2002, and the specification is published at *http://www.w3.org/TR/xml-names11/*.

### Description

The 1.1 specification cleans up rules for declaring namespaces by making a provision for undeclaring namespaces, making it possible to reduce the number of unused declarations that apply to a given document framework.

## W3C XML Schema

The W3C XML Schema language defines object-like structures for XML documents.

**W3C**

### Status

XML Schema became a W3C Recommendation in May 2001. The recommendation is published in three parts:

*XML Schema Part 0: Primer*
  *http://www.w3.org/TR/xmlschema-0/*

*XML Schema Part 1: Structures*
  *http://www.w3.org/TR/xmlschema-1/*

*XML Schema Part 2: Datatypes*
  *http://www.w3.org/TR/xmlschema-2/*

### Description

The XML Schema language is used to define documents in a way that is beyond the capabilities of DTDs. Schema uses valid XML to declare elements and attributes for structuring a document and also provides extensible facilities for defining datatypes of elements and attributes.

## RELAX NG

A simpler schema language.

OASIS/ISO

### Status

RELAX NG became an OASIS Technical Committee Specification in December 2001. It is published at *http://www.oasis-open.org/committees/tc_home.php?wg_abbrev=relax-ng*. RELAX NG is also part of the ISO Document Structure Description Language (DSDL). Information about that project can be found at *http://www.dsdl.org/*.

### Description

RELAX NG defines a schema language for describing XML document structures. RELAX NG has a mathematical basis similar to regular expressions, making it easy to process, as well as both an XML-based syntax and a human-friendly compact syntax. RELAX NG defines only structural components; for datatyping, RELAX NG schemas typically depend on W3C XML Schema.

## Schematron

An extremely flexible schema language.

ISO

### Status

Schematron is an ongoing community project, and its most recent definition is published at *http://www.ascc.net/xml/resource/schematron/*. Schematron is also part of the ISO Document Structure Description Language (DSDL). Information about that project can be found at *http://www.dsdl.org/*.

### Description

Schematron uses tools from XSLT and XPath to define an extremely flexible set of tests for document structures. Schematron offers precision and customizable error reporting, though that precision can sometimes lead to very verbose schemas. As a result, Schematron is typically used to supplement RELAX NG or W3C XML Schema rather than to replace them.

# Linking

## XLink

XML Linking Language creates links between resources.

W3C

### Status

XLink became a W3C Recommendation in June 2001. The specification is published at *http://www.w3.org/TR/xlink/*.

### Description

XLink allows elements to be inserted into XML documents that create and describe links between resources. It uses XML syntax to create structures to describe links, from the simple unidirectional hyperlinks of today's HTML to more sophisticated links.

## XML Base

XML Base provides a facility for defining base URIs for parts of XML documents.

**W3C**

### Status

XBase became a W3C Recommendation in June 2001. The specification is published at *http://www.w3.org/TR/xmlbase/*.

### Description

XML Base describes a mechanism for providing base URI services to XLink. The specification is modular so that other XML applications can make use of it.

## XInclude

XML Inclusions is a standard for embedding XML documents.

**W3C**

### Status

XInclude became a Candidate Recommendation in September 2002 and is published at *http://www.w3.org/TR/xinclude/*.

### Description

XInclude specifies a processing model and syntax for general-purpose inclusion. Inclusion is accomplished by merging a number of XML infosets into a single composite infoset. Specification of the XML documents (infosets) to be merged and control over the merging process is expressed in XML-friendly syntax (elements, attributes, and URI references).

# Addressing and Querying

## XPath

XML Path Language is used for locating XML objects.

**W3C**

### Status

XPath became a W3C Recommendation in November 1999. The specification is published at *http://www.w3.org/TR/xpath/*. XPath 2.0 Working Drafts include the XQuery 1.0 and XPath 2.0 Data Model at *http://www.w3.org/TR/xpath-datamodel/*, XQuery 1.0 and XPath 2.0 Functions and Operators at *http://www.w3.org/TR/xpath-datamodel/*, XQuery 1.0 and

XPath 2.0 Formal Semantics at *http://www.w3.org/TR/xquery-semantics/*, and XML Path Language (XPath) 2.0 at *http://www.w3.org/TR/xpath20*.

## Description

XPath is a language for addressing parts of an XML document, designed to be used by both XSLT and XPointer. XPath 2.0 was expanded considerably to add support for W3C XML Schema information and XQuery.

---

# XPointer

XML Pointer Language is a standard for specifying paths in URIs.

W3C

## Status

Most of XPointer became a W3C Recommendation in March 2003. The specification is published in four parts. The XPointer Framework can be found at *http://www.w3.org/TR/xptr-framework/*. The XPointer xmlns Scheme can be found at *http://www.w3.org/TR/xptr-xmlns/*, and the XPointer element( ) Scheme can be found at *http://www.w3.org/TR/xptr-element/*. The XPointer xpointer( ) Scheme remains a Working Draft, and can be found at *http://www.w3.org/TR/xptr-xpointer/*.

## Description

XPointer is designed to be used as the basis for a fragment identifier for any URI reference that locates a resource of Internet media type text/xml or application/xml. Based on the XML Path Language (XPath), XPointer supports addressing into the internal structures of XML documents. It allows for examination of a hierarchical document structure and choice of its internal parts based on properties such as element types, attribute values, character content, and relative position.

---

# XQuery

XML Query Language provides database-like query facilities for accessing web documents.

W3C

## Status

XQuery is under development at the W3C. The most recent Working Drafts were published in May 2003. They include the XQuery 1.0 and XPath 2.0 Data Model at *http://www.w3.org/TR/xpath-datamodel/*, XQuery 1.0 and XPath 2.0 Functions and Operators at *http://www.w3.org/TR/xpath-functions/*, XQuery 1.0 and XPath 2.0 Formal Semantics at *http://www.w3.org/TR/xquery-semantics/*, XSLT 2.0 and XQuery 1.0 Serialization at *http://www.w3.org/TR/xslt-xquery-serialization/*, XQuery Use Cases at *http://www.w3.org/TR/xquery-use-cases/*, and XQuery 1.0: An XML Query Language at *http://www.w3.org/TR/xquery/*.

## Description

XQuery is a query language that uses XML as a data model and is bound with XPath. XQuery expressions look more like traditional query and data processing environments than XSLT and XPath, and they can be used in a variety of software environments.

# Style and Transformation

---

**CSS**    The Cascading Style Sheets specification provides a language for assigning formats to document elements.

**W3C**

## Status

CSS Level 2 became a W3C recommendation in May 1998, and it is published at *http:// www.w3.org/TR/REC-CSS2/*. CSS Level 1 became a W3C recommendation in 1996, with a revision in January 1999. It is published at *http://www.w3.org/TR/REC-CSS1*. Work on CSS Level 3 is ongoing, and links to specifications may be found at *http://www.w3.org/Style/ CSS/current-work*.

## Description

CSS is a stylesheet language that allows authors and users to attach styles (e.g., fonts, spacing, and sounds) to structured documents such as HTML documents and XML applications. By separating the presentation style from the content of a document, CSS simplifies web authoring and site maintenance.

CSS2 builds on CSS1, and with few exceptions, all stylesheets valid in CSS1 are also valid in CSS2. CSS2 supports media-specific stylesheets, so authors can tailor the presentation of their documents to visual browsers, aural devices, printers, Braille devices, hand-held devices, etc. This specification also supports content positioning, downloadable fonts, table layout, internationalization features, automatic counters and numbering, and some user interface properties.

---

**XSL**    Extensible Stylesheet Language is a stylesheet language for XML.

**W3C**

## Status

XSL became a W3C Recommendation in October 2001. The specification is published at *http://www.w3.org/TR/xsl/*.

## Description

XSL is a language for formatting XML documents. It consists of an XML vocabulary of formatting objects (XSL-FO) and a language for transforming XML documents into those formatting semantics (XSLT). An XSL stylesheet specifies the presentation of a class of XML documents by describing how an instance of the class is transformed into an XML document that uses the formatting vocabulary.

---

## XSLT

### Status

XSLT became a W3C Recommendation in November 1999. The specification is published at *http://www.w3.org/TR/xslt/*. A working draft of XSLT 2.0 may be found at *http://www.w3.org/TR/xslt20*.

### Description

XSLT is a language for transforming XML documents into other XML documents. It is designed for use as part of XSL, which is a stylesheet language for XML. XSL also includes an XML vocabulary for specifying formatting, and uses XSLT to describe how the document is transformed into another XML document that uses the formatting vocabulary.

# Programming

## DOM

### Status

DOM Level 2 became a W3C Recommendation in November 2000, and is composed of five specifications:

*DOM2 Core Specification*
    *http://www.w3.org/TR/DOM-Level-2-Core/*

*DOM2 Views Specification*
    *http://www.w3.org/TR/DOM-Level-2-Views/*

*DOM2 Events Specification*
    *http://www.w3.org/TR/DOM-Level-2-Events/*

*DOM2 Style Specification*
    *http://www.w3.org/TR/DOM-Level-2-Style/*

*DOM2 Traversal and Range Specification*
    *http://www.w3.org/TR/DOM-Level-2-Traversal-Range/*

Work on DOM Level 3 is in progress. More information on DOM Level 3 (which notably adds XPath and Load and Save support) is available at *http://www.w3.org/DOM/*.

### Description

DOM Level 2 is a platform and language-neutral interface that allows programs and scripts to dynamically access and update the content and structure of documents. The DOM Level 2 Core builds on the DOM Level 1 Core, and consists of a set of core interfaces that create and manipulate the structure and contents of a document. The Core also contains specialized interfaces dedicated to XML.

## SAX

The Simple API for XML is a free API for event-based XML parsing.

**saxproject.org**

### Status

SAX was collaboratively developed by the XML-DEV mailing list (hosted by OASIS). The current release is SAX 2.0, dated May 2000. SAX is maintained by David Brownell at *http://www.saxproject.org/*.

### Description

SAX2 is an event-based API. SAX2 introduces configurable features and properties and adds support for XML Namespaces. It also includes adapters that allow it to interoperate with SAX1 parsers and applications.

## Canonical XML

A standard representation of XML documents for signatures.

**W3C/IETC**

### Status

Canonical XML was collaboratively developed by the W3C and IETF. There are two current Recommendations: the March 2001 Canonical XML 1.0, at *http://www.w3.org/TR/xml-c14n*, and the July 2002 Exclusive XML Canonicalization Version 1.0, at *http://www.w3.org/TR/xml-exc-c14n*.

### Description

Canonical XML is designed to remove all the syntactical variations of XML documents and produce a single representation which can be used reliably for tasks like checksums and signatures.

## XML Signature

A standard representation of XML documents for signatures.

**W3C/IETC**

### Status

XML Signature was collaboratively developed by the W3C and IETF. The February 2002 XML-Signature Syntax and Processing is published at *http://www.w3.org/TR/xmldsig-core/*.

### Description

XML Signature is designed to provide unique identifiers for XML documents which can then be used in other XML-based projects, notably security projects.

# Publishing

## DocBook

DocBook is a DTD for technical publications and software documentation.

**OASIS**

### Status

The latest SGML version of DocBook is 4.2; the latest XML version of DocBook is 4.3b2. DocBook is officially maintained by the DocBook Technical Committee of OASIS, and you can find the official home page at *http://www.oasis-open.org/docbook/index.html*.

### Description

DocBook is a large and robust DTD designed for technical publications, such as documents related to computer hardware and software.

# Hypertext

## XHTML

The Extensible Hypertext Markup Language is a reformulation of HTML in XML.

**W3C**

### Status

XHTML 1.0 became a W3C Recommendation in January 2000, with a Second Edition in August 2002. The specification is published at *http://www.w3.org/TR/xhtml1/*. Modularization of XHTML, which became a Recommendation in April 2001, is published at *http://www.w3.org/TR/xhtml-modularization/*. XHTML 1.1, module-based XHTML, which became a Recommendation in May 2001, is published at *http://www.w3.org/TR/xhtml11/*. A subset of XHTML 1.1, XHTML Basic, became a W3C Recommendation in December 2000, and is published at *http://www.w3.org/TR/xhtml-basic*. Finally, work on XHTML 2.0 has started, and working drafts are available at

### Description

XHTML 1.0 is a reformulation of HTML 4 as an XML 1.0 application. The specification defines three DTDs corresponding to the ones defined by HTML 4. The semantics of the elements and their attributes are defined in the W3C Recommendation for HTML 4, and provide the foundation for future extensibility of XHTML. Compatibility with existing HTML user agents is possible by following a small set of guidelines. XHTML 1.1 reformulates HTML as a set of modules, and XHTML Basic creates a subset of XHTML for use on smaller devices. XHTML 2.0 is now under development, and represents the first major changes to the HTML vocabulary since HTML 4.0.

## HTML
Hypertext Markup Language is the markup language for World Wide Web documents.

**W3C**

### Status

HTML 4.01 is the latest version of the W3C Recommendation, dated December 1999. The specification is published at *http://www.w3.org/TR/html401/*.

### Description

In addition to the text, multimedia, and hyperlink features of previous versions, HTML 4 supports more multimedia options, scripting languages, and stylesheets, as well as better printing facilities and documents that are more accessible to users with disabilities. HTML 4 also takes great strides towards the internationalization of documents.

# Descriptive/Procedural

## SOAP
SOAP is a protocol for exchanging information.

**W3C**

### Status

The SOAP 1.2 specification (formerly the Simple Object Access Protocol) became a W3C Recommendation in June 2003. SOAP 1.2 Part 0: Primer is published at *http://www.w3.org/TR/soap12-part0/*, SOAP 1.2 Part 1: Messaging Framework is published at *http://www.w3.org/TR/soap12-part1/*, and SOAP 1.2 Part 2: Adjuncts is published at *http://www.w3.org/TR/soap12-part2/*. SOAP Version 1.2 Specification Assertions and Test Collection, also a Recommendation, is published at *http://www.w3.org/TR/soap12-testcollection*.

### Description

SOAP is an XML-based protocol for exchanging information in a decentralized, distributed environment. It consists of three parts: an envelope that defines a framework for describing what is in a message and how to process it, a set of encoding rules for expressing instances of application-defined data types, and a convention for representing remote procedure calls and responses.

## RDF
The Resource Description Framework provides a standard way of representing metadata.

**W3C**

### Status

The RDF Model and Syntax Specification became a W3C Recommendation in February 1999, and it is published at *http://www.w3.org/TR/REC-rdf-syntax/*. The RDF Schema Specification became a W3C Candidate Recommendation in March 2000, and it is published at *http://www.w3.org/TR/rdf-schema/*.

More recently, a number of RDF Working Drafts revising those specs have been published. Resource Description Framework (RDF): Concepts and Abstract Syntax is published at *http://www.w3.org/TR/rdf-concepts/*. RDF Semantics is published at *http://www.w3.org/TR/rdf-mt/*. An RDF Primer is published at *http://www.w3.org/TR/rdf-primer/*. RDF Vocabulary Description Language 1.0: RDF Schema is published at *http://www.w3.org/TR/rdf-schema*. RDF/XML Syntax Specification (Revised) is published at *http://www.w3.org/TR/rdf-syntax-grammar*.

## Description

RDF is a foundation for using XML to process metadata. It provides interoperability between applications that exchange machine-understandable information on the Web. RDF emphasizes facilities that enable automated processing of web resources.

# Multimedia

## SVG

Scalable Vector Graphics is a language describing 2D vector graphics.

W3C

### Status

The SVG 1.0 specification became a W3C Recommendation in September 2001. The specification is published at *http://www.w3.org/TR/SVG/*. SVG 1.1, like XHTML 1.1, modularized SVG, and the January 2003 Recommendation is at *http://www.w3.org/TR/SVG11/*. That modularization was used to produce the SVG Mobile Profiles: SVG Tiny and SVG Basic, also published in January 2003 at *http://www.w3.org/TR/SVGMobile/*. Work on SVG 1.2 is ongoing, and the latest drafts can be found at *http://www.w3.org/TR/SVG12*.

### Description

SVG is a language for describing two-dimensional vector and mixed vector/raster graphics in XML.

## SMIL

The Synchronized Multimedia Integration Language is an HTML-like language for creating multimedia presentations.

W3C

### Status

The SMIL 1.0 specification became a W3C Recommendation in June 1998. It is published at *http://www.w3.org/TR/REC-smil/*.

### Description

SMIL allows a set of independent multimedia objects to be integrated into a synchronized multimedia presentation. While SMIL itself hasn't caught on, some important pieces of SMIL are now in SVG.

# Science

---

**MathML**  The Mathematical Markup Language for XML describes mathematical notation.

**W3C**

## Status

MathML 2.0 became a W3C Recommendation in February 2001. The specification is published at *http://www.w3.org/TR/MathML2/*.

## Description

MathML is an XML application for describing mathematical notation and capturing its structure and content. The goal of MathML is to enable mathematics to be served, received, and processed on the Web, just as HTML has done for text.

# Glossary

**absolute location term**

A term that completely identifies the location of a resource via XPointer. A unique ID attribute assigned to an element can be used as an absolute location term. See also **relative location term, XPath, XPointer**.

**activity**

The work being done to produce a standard in some area of interest. See also **standards body**.

**actuation**

How a link in a document is triggered. For example, a link to an imported graphic automatically includes a graphic in the document, and a link to a URL resource requires a signal from a human.

**application**

This word has different meanings in different contexts. In the context of XML, an application is usually a specific markup language based on XML rules. DocBook is one example of an XML application.

In the more general context of computer software, an application is a high-level program for users, such as a web browser, word processor, or spreadsheet manipulator. In other words, it's an application of the computer system.

**arc**

An abstract term for the relationship between a link in a document and its target. See also **resource, simple link**.

**ASCII (American standard code for information interchange)**

Pronounced ASK-ee, this venerable standard describes a set of 128 characters used to display text. When early computer development was taking place in the United States, this was sufficient for all textual needs. However, larger character sets, such as Unicode (which contain letters, symbols, and ideographs for virtually all of the world's languages) are now more common. Still, ASCII will be around for a long time. UTF-8 is a new character set based on ASCII that includes methods for referencing any Unicode character. See also **character encoding, character set**.

**attribute**

A variable or term that defines a specific setting or provides additional information to an element. Attributes appear as name-value pairs contained in an element's start tag. See also **element, markup**.

**block element**

A block of text or content, such as a paragraph, title, or section, that is separated from other text by whitespace. See also **inline element**.

**box model**

A CSS (stylesheet) concept used for formatting block elements. The box model forms a boundary around an element that contains definable properties such as padding and margin widths. See also **presentation, stylesheet**.

**candidate recommendation**

In the standards process, a candidate recommendation is a specification that has achieved enough consensus by its working group to be released for public review. See also **recommendation, standards body**.

## catalog

A specially formatted text file (usually local) whose information is used to resolve public identifiers into system identifiers. The catalog file format was formally specified by OASIS Technical Resolution 9401:1997. See also **formal public identifier, URI**.

## CDATA (character data)

CDATA is an entity data type consisting of nonparsed characters. Entity references included in this data will not be resolved. A CDATA marked section looks like this:

```
<![CDATA unparsed content]]>
```

See also **PCDATA**.

## character encoding

The representation of characters as unique numbers in a character set. See also **character set**.

## character entity

A notation for any character or symbol that uses its character set number or abbreviation. The common syntax for character encoding is an ampersand (&), followed by the name or a #-sign and number, terminated with a semicolon. For example, the copyright symbol © can be output in a document by using either &#169; or &copy;.

## character set

A collection of letters, numbers, and symbols representing a language or set of languages, mapped to specified numbers that can be understood by computer programs. See also **character encoding**.

## comment

Specially marked text in the document source that is not interpreted by the parser. XML comments are surrounded by <!-- and --> delimiters. Everything inside a comment is ignored by the parser, including tagged elements. Comments can provide additional information about a document's markup and content and are a useful way to remove content from a document's output without fully deleting it. See also **markup**.

## container element

An element that contains character data or other elements is called a container. It is a root to its own subtree in the document. See also **content, content model, element**.

## content

Anything in a document that is not markup. Take away the tags, comments, and processing instructions, and what's left is content or character data. Markup allows content to be repurposed many ways. See also **container element, content model**.

## content model

The technical specification of a DTD that describes an element's contents. The content model specifies which kinds of elements and data can occur within an element, how many can occur, and how they are ordered. See also **element, content**.

## CSS (Cascading Style Sheets)

This specification provides a standard way of specifying the presentation of a document by applying formatting rules to elements. Cascading refers to how an element is formatted when several rules overlap, such as a locally applied rule and a global rule. See also **presentation, stylesheet**.

## current node

The node in which an expression is being evaluated. See also **current node set, node, XSLT**.

## current node set

The set of selected nodes that provide the immediate context for an expression. See also **current node, node, XSLT**.

## declaration

A special object that configures the environment of the document. It may introduce a new element, create an entity, or name the type of document. Declarations use a special delimiter to keep them apart from elements, adding an exclamation mark to the opening angle bracket:

```
<!name statement>
```

where *name* is the type of declaration, and *statement* contains the rest of the required information to make a declaration. See also **markup**.

### delimiter

Any character or group of characters that separates data or markup. The angle brackets in XML tags (<>) are delimiters. CDATA sections have three delimiters: <![, [, and ]]>. See also **markup**.

### document

In XML, a document is a complete root element, after all external entity references have been resolved. At most, it has one optional XML declaration and one document type definition. The document may be distributed across many files, perhaps on different systems. See also **document element, root element**.

### document element

Also called the root element, the document element is the outermost element in a document. It contains everything except the document prolog and any comments or processing instructions outside of it. See also **document, root element**.

### document instance

An actual document that conforms to a general document model. See also **document, DTD**.

### document model

A template for a document that defines elements and their content models. A DTD or a schema is a document model. See also **DTD, schema**.

### DOM (document object model)

A specification that defines the structure of a document as a collection of objects and how the document can be accessed and manipulated. A document object model is an API (application programming interface), which describes how programs actually interpret the structure and contents of a document.

### document prolog

A section at the beginning of a document that declares the document to be XML, and specifies the version of XML it conforms to (for example, <?xml version="1.0"?>). Additional information about the document can be declared, including the document type declaration.

The document prolog precedes the document element or root element, which contains all the content of the document. See also **document, document type declaration, XML declaration**.

### document tree

Every XML document can be represented in a special structural form called a tree. It's tree-like because it originates from one point (the root) and branches out into leaves. Each point in the tree where a branching occurs is called a node. A tree consists of a root node, many branch nodes, and a smattering of leaf nodes. Strangely, most document trees are drawn upside-down, with the root on top.

Document trees can be divided into smaller trees, in that any node can be considered the root of its own subtree. This fact is important in understanding XML transformations using XSLT, which effectively chops a tree into smaller and smaller subtrees, then assembles a result tree in reverse fashion. See also **document, node tree**.

### document type declaration

The DOCTYPE section of the document prolog. This section declares the structure to which the document must conform. It can be used to specify a DTD by providing its public identifier and location by URI. It can also specify an internal subset of entity declarations used in the document. See also **document, DTD**.

### DOM (Document Object Model)

A tree-based interface for accessing and manipulating the contents of XML documents.

### DTD (document type definition)

A set of declarations that defines the names of the elements and their attributes and specifies rules for their combination and sequence. See also **document, document type declaration**.

### editor

A software program that packages your keystrokes into files to author text on a computer, one must use an editor. Some editors are fancier than others. The simplest is *vi*, an old but still kicking Unix editor. Emacs is a nice editor with lots of configuration potential, but a somewhat steep learning curve and no style presentation. Both of these editors display the text and markup together, which can make authoring difficult for those who aren't used to seeing all the tags in the content. See also **document, markup**.

element
A defined piece of an XML document. XML elements are denoted by start and end tags, and can contain data and other elements in a specified hierarchy. See also **attribute, content, markup**.

empty element
An element that is comprised of a single tag and contains no content data. An empty element begins with an opening angle bracket (<), followed by the element name, any attributes and their values, and closed with a slash and closing angle bracket (/>). See also **attribute, content, element**.

entity
A name assigned by means of declaration to some chunk of data. Some entities have been predefined for special characters such as <, >, and & that cannot be used directly in the content of an XML document because they would conflict with the markup. See also **entity reference, markup**.

entity reference
A special string that refers to an entity, indicated by a starting & and an ending semicolon. Entity references occur in text and are parsed by the XML processor. See also **entity**.

external entity
An entity that refers to another document. See also **entity, file, URL**.

external subset
A group of declarations, comprising all or part of a document type definition, that is stored in an external entity and referenced from a document's DTD using a public or system identifier. See also **document, DTD**.

FPI (formal public identifier)
A public identifier that conforms to the specification of public identifiers in ISO 8879. An FPI contains information such as the class of the resource (i.e., a DTD), its author, and language. See also **catalog, external entity**.

fragment identifier
An extension of a URL that identifies a location inside an HTML document by a named element. See also **URL**.

HTML (Hypertext Markup Language)
The markup language used to create documents for the World Wide Web. See also **hypertext, markup, XHTML**.

hypertext
A way of linking text or objects in documents that permits nonlinear access to the content. See also **HTML, markup, XHTML**.

inheritance
The method by which an object retains a setting that was instantiated on its parent object. See also **CSS, rule**.

inline element
An element that occurs within the text content of another element, for example, an emphasized term inside a paragraph. See also **block element**.

internal subset
Elements, attributes, and other declarations that compose at least part of a DTD, and are contained within the document type declaration. See. See also **document type declaration, external subset**.

ISO (International Organization for Standardization)
An organization founded in 1947 to create open technical specifications. See also **open standard, recommendation, standards body**.

local resource
A resource that contains a link. See also **remote resource, resource, simple link**.

logical structure
The nodal or hierarchical layout of elements and content in a document, as opposed to the physical location of elements and data. See also **document, physical structure**.

**markup**

A collection of characters that group, organize, and label the pieces of content in a document. Markup tags are interspersed within the content as instructions to the parser, which removes them as it builds a document data structure in memory. Markup includes start and end tags for elements, entity references, declarations, comments, processing instructions, and marked sections. See also **element, tag**.

**markup language**

A set of formal rules for representing data and encoding structures that surround the data. A document that obeys the rules of the markup language is said to be well-formed. A markup language provides ways to label parts using elements, to enforce structure using a DTD, and to import data with entity references. XML is not itself a markup language, but a set of rules for creating markup languages. See also **application, DTD, markup**.

**metadata**

Descriptive data that is not directly included in the content of a document. For example, a document's creation date or author is metadata. See also **document, markup**.

**mixed content**

A mixture of elements and character data that can be specified as valid content for an element via its content model. See also **CDATA, content, content model, element**.

**modular DTD**

A DTD that is divided into logical pieces, allowing for easy maintenance and selection of only the modules required in a document. The modules of a modular DTD are often kept in external files and declared as external entities. See also **DTD**.

**name**

Any object in XML has a type specifier called a name. For example, an element that describes the title of a book might be given the name booktitle. The representa-

tion of the element must include the name in both its start and end tags, like this:

`<booktitle>Wart Removal</booktitle>`

Names in XML must obey rules about character composition. For example, element names must start with either an underscore or a letter. See also **attribute, element, markup**.

**namespace**

Any of a group of specified elements and attributes that can be used in a document by prefixing a namespace identifier to an element name, e.g., `<namespace:element/>`. Namespaces must be declared using the `xmlns` declaration. The following syntax is used for a namespace declaration:

`<xmlns:name=uri>`

The name of the namespace is given by *name*, and the location of the namespace maintainer or version is given by *uri* (though parsers usually don't do anything with this information). Namespaces allow you to mix different sets of element definitions in a single document, for example, using mathematical equations in an HTML document. See also **element, qualified element name**.

**namespace prefix**

The identifier preceding an element's name that indicates the namespace it belongs to, e.g., `<namespace:element/>`. See also **element, qualified element name, namespace**.

**node**

This term comes from the realm of computer science, where it's used to describe a point in an abstract network of connected items. In XML, it refers to either a branching point in a document tree or a leaf of the tree. The nodes recognized by XPath include elements, attributes, processing instructions, comments, contiguous pieces of character data (text), namespace declarations, and the root node. See also **node tree**.

**node tree**

The hierarchical view of the nodes in a document. Starting at the root node, the node tree shows which nodes contain other nodes. See also **document tree, node**.

### notation

Data that should not be parsed or that has special processing needs is labeled as a notation type with an attribute or external entity. A notation declaration in a DTD defines notation types used by the XML processor in order to route the data to a special handler.

### open standard

A technical specification released to the public for unrestricted use.

### PCDATA

An element content type consisting of parsed characters (i.e., entity references) but no elements. Entity references included in this data will be resolved. See also **CDATA, parsed-character data**.

### parsed-character data

Any character data that should be checked by the XML processor for entity references. These references are resolved and their replacement text parsed recursively to replace all entity references. See also **PCDATA**.

### parser

A software program that reads XML, validates it, and passes it on for further processing. If a document is not well-formed (i.e., there's an error in the markup), the parser catches it and reports the problem. See also **markup, XML processor**.

### physical structure

The physical organization of data in a file, as opposed to its document or logical structure. An object-oriented database, for example, is a physical structure that doesn't align with its logical structure. See also **document, logical structure**.

### presentation

The appearance of a document that has been formatted for human consumption. See also **stylesheet**.

### processing instruction

A markup object that conveys information to a specific XML processor. It has the form:

```
<?target data?>
```

where *target* is a keyword to alert a particular processor, and *data* is a text string containing the special information. Any processor that doesn't recognize the processing instruction ignores it.

### properties declaration

The part of a stylesheet rule that sets the formatting for the selected element. See also **CSS, rule, stylesheet**.

### proposed recommendation

A specification that has been evaluated by the public and is deemed by a standards body to warrant a full recommendation.

### pseudo-class

A CSS selector that specifies a certain instance of an element instead of all occurrences of the element. For example, the first paragraph of each section can be grouped as a pseudo-class. See also **CSS, rule, selector**.

### PUBLIC identifier

The identifier in the document prolog that gives the name of a DTD or external entity.

### qualified element name

An element identified in a specific namespace. A qualified element name uses a namespace prefix in the tag name. See also **element, namespace, namespace prefix**.

### recommendation

In the standards process, a recommendation is a specification that has achieved majority approval of its working group and its host organization and is released for outside evaluation.

### reference

To refer to or reference something is to indicate a relationship between the current context and an outside resource. Usually, the intent is to import a value into a collection of data. For example, an entity reference is a fragment of text telling an XML parser to insert the value of an entity that is defined in a DTD and stored in memory. An ID reference is a notation that indicates a relationship with an element possessing a unique ID that resides somewhere else in the document. The term *reference* is used to distinguish between an object or value and the thing that wants to use it. See also **entity, entity reference**.

### relative location term

An XPointer location that is identified in reference to another location such as an absolute location term or the current node. See also **absolute location term, XPath, XPointer**.

### relative URL

A URL that expresses a partial location. This location is understood to be relative to the current location of the reference, called the base URL.

### remote resource

A resource that a simple link points to. See also **local resource, resource, simple,link**.

### resource

A source of information. In XML, a resource is something that can be linked to, such as an XML document, a graphic file, or a program.

### root element

The base-level element of a document, containing all the other elements in the document. (Same as document element.) See also **document, document element, element**.

### root node

The base-level node of a document, containing all the nodes that comprise the document. See also **node**.

### rule

The primary building block of a stylesheet, specifying which element or elements to set a style for (the selector), and the style to be applied (the properties declaration). See also **stylesheet**.

### SAX (Simple API for XML)

An event-driven application programming interface for manipulating XML documents with Java. The API describes a flat document model (no object hierarchy or inheritance) that then allows for quick document processing.

### scheme

A prefix to a URL that establishes the address pattern and protocol to be used.

For example, the prefix `http` specifies that the hypertext transfer protocol is to be used, as in the following URL:

```
http://www.oreilly.com/
```
See also **URL**.

### selector

The part of a CSS stylesheet rule that determines the elements to which the style is applied. See also **CSS, rule, stylesheet**.

### SGML (Standard Generalized Markup Language)

An international standard (ISO 8879) that specifies rules for the creation of platform-independent markup languages for electronic texts.

### simple link

The simplest form of a link, consisting of an element in a document (the local resource) that specifies a target or the location of the remote resource. See also **local resource, remote resource**.

### standards body

An organization that works to produce industry-wide technical standards.

### stylesheet

A set of formatting instructions, either in a separate file or grouped within a document, that specifies the appearance of a document. There are several standards for stylesheets, including CSS, XSLT, and XSL-FO.

### SYSTEM identifier

A local, system-dependent identifier for a document, DTD, or external entity. In XML, a system identifier must be a URI.

### tag

An element name enclosed in angle brackets, used to mark up the semantics or structure of a document.

### Unicode

A character set standard that attempts to encompass characters from all the world's major scripts.

### URI (uniform resource identifier)

The W3C's codification of the name and address syntax of present and future objects on the Internet. In its basic form, a URI consists of a scheme name (such as `http`, `ftp`, `mailto`, etc.) followed by a colon, and then the path as defined by the scheme that precedes it. URI is an umbrella term encompassing URLs and all other uniform resource identifiers.

## URL (uniform resource locator)

The name and address of an existing object accessible over the Internet.

## UTF-8

The UCS Transformation Format for 8-bit platforms. UTF-8 is a transformation encoding that converts Unicode character encodings so they can be used on 8-bit-based systems.

## well-formed

A term describing a document that conforms to the syntax rules of XML. For example, in a well-formed document, tags have proper delimiters, an end tag follows a start tag, and elements do not overlap.

## working draft

An in-progress version of a specification produced by a standards body working group. A working draft often changes substantially before the recommendation phase.

## XHTML (Exntensible Hyptertext Markup Language)

XHTML is a reformulation of HTML 4 as an XML application. The XHTML DTDs define elements and attributes as they are in HTML 4.01. XHTML Basic is a smaller subset of XHTML, but otherwise the XHTML 1.x specifications made no changes to the actual vocabulary. XHTML 2.0 adds new features to the XHTML vocabulary. See also **HTML, hypertext, markup.**

## XML declaration

The first element of a document prolog, declaring that the document is an XML document and the XML version it conforms to. Most documents will have this XML declaration as their first line:

```
<?xml version="1.0"?>
```

## XLink (XML Linking Language)

Specifies elements that can be used in XML documents to create and describe links between resources. XLink provides for more robust linking relationships than do the simple hyperlinks in HTML.

## XML processor

A generic term for any program that takes an XML document as input and does something with it. A program that reads an XML document, parses it, and produces formatted output is an XML processor. See also **parser.**

## XML Schema

An alternative to DTDs for document modeling, schemas are written as **XML,** and like DTDs, define the elements, entities, and content model of documents. Schemas have many additional capabilities such as data type control and content restrictions.

## XPath (XML Path Language)

A language used to address parts of an XML document. XPath locator syntax uses core functions based on the node hierarchy of a document, and evaluates expressions to determine a location object. XPath locations are used by **XSLT** and XPointer.

## XPointer (XML Pointer Language)

A special scheme, based on XPath, that identifies locations using special extensions to URIs. XPointer locations support the use of ID attributes for absolute location references in an XML document, and can step through the node hierarchy to find specific elements.

## XSL (Extensible Stylesheet Language)

A specification for converting XML documents to formatted results. Extensible Stylesheet Language includes two subspecifications, XSL-FO and XSLT. See also **XSLT** and See also **XSL-FO.**

## XSL-FO

A vocabulary for describing formatted documents, typically for print media.

## XSLT (Extensible Stylesheet Language Transformations)

A transformation functions similarly to a stylesheet, except that instead of simply applying formatting rules to elements, it can alter the structure of a document to produce a document with a new structure.

# Index

## About the Author

**Erik T. Ray** works at the Harvard-MIT Data Center as a Unix Systems Programmer. He lives with his wife Jeannine and 5 parrots in Saugus, Massachusetts. When not writing, he collects old books, plays strategy games, practices kendo, and follows events in space exploration.

## Colophon

Our look is the result of reader comments, our own experimentation, and feedback from distribution channels. Distinctive covers complement our distinctive approach to technical topics, breathing personality and life into potentially dry subjects.

The animal on the cover of *Learning XML*, Second Edition is a hatching chick. Chickens have been around for at least 3,000 years. A hen typically lays one egg at a time and will sit on the egg, keeping it warm, until it hatches. The incubation period for a chicken egg is approximately 21 days from fertilization to hatching. Before hatching, the chick absorbs the egg yolk, which can sustain it for the first three days of its life. The most popular laying chicken in North America is the leghorn, which can produce eggs from five months of age until about a year and a half.

Philip Dangler was the production editor and proofreader for *Learning XML*, Second Edition. Melanie Wang was the copyeditor. Mary Brady and Darren Kelly provided quality control. James Quill provided production assistance. Octal Publishing wrote the index.

Ellie Volckhausen designed the cover of this book, based on a series design by Edie Freedman. The cover image is a 19th-century engraving from the Dover Pictorial Archive. Emma Colby produced the cover layout with QuarkXPress 4.1 using Adobe's ITC Garamond font.

David Futato designed the interior layout. This book was converted by Andrew Savikas to FrameMaker 5.5.6 with a format conversion tool created by Erik T. Ray, Jason McIntosh, Neil Walls, and Mike Sierra that uses Perl and XML technologies. The text font is Linotype Birka; the heading font is Adobe Myriad Condensed; and the code font is LucasFont's TheSans Mono Condensed. The illustrations that appear in the book were produced by Robert Romano and Jessamyn Read using Macromedia FreeHand 9 and Adobe Photoshop 6. The tip and warning icons were drawn by Christopher Bing. This colophon was written by Nicole Arigo.